Macmillan Building and Surveying Series

Macmillan Building and Surveying Series
Series Standing Order
ISBN 0–333–71692–2 hardcover
ISBN 0–333–69333–7 paperback
(*outside North America only*)

You can receive future titles in this series as they are published by placing a
standing order. Please contact your bookseller or, in the case of difficulty, write
to us at the address below with your name and address, the title of the series and
one or both of the ISBNs quoted above.

Customer Services Department, Macmillan Distribution Ltd
Houndmills, Basingstoke, Hampshire RG21 6XS, England

Housing Associations
The Policy and Practice of Registered Social Landlords

Second Edition

Helen Cope
BA(Hons), FCIH, CertHFE

© Helen Cope 1990, 1999

First edition 1990
Reprinted 1992, 1994
Second edition 1999

Published by
MACMILLAN PRESS LTD
Houndmills, Basingstoke, Hampshire RG21 6XS and London
Companies and representatives throughout the world

ISBN 0–333–73199–9

A catalogue record for this book is available
from the British Library.

This book is printed on paper suitable for recycling and made from fully managed and sustained forest sources.

10   9   8   7   6   5   4   3   2   1
08   07   06   05   04   03   02   01   00   99

Printed in Great Britain by
Creative Print and Design (Wales),
Ebbw Vale.

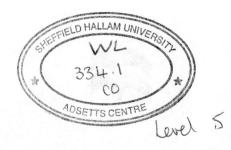

To my beloved William
and in memory of my parents
Irene Cope (1920–98) and
Sydney Cope FRCP (1920–90)
with love and thanks

Contents

List of Tables and Figures

Tables

Figures

Preface to the First Edition

I was stuck in a traffic jam in London when the cab driver, having already elicited my life story asked, 'Well then, what are these housing associations? I've seen their signboards about the place. What makes them different from any other private landlords?'

Although huge sums of public money are invested in associations each year, little is known by the public (even those with 'the knowledge') about the nature and activities of these diverse organisations. Such ignorance must cause concern, given the Government's intention that housing associations should become the major providers of rented housing as part of the process of de-municipalisation, which since 1980 has seen local authority house building virtually cease and one million public sector rented homes sold off through the right to buy. If housing associations are to embrace this wider role then their nature and their work should be widely publicised and subjected to scrutiny. I hope that this book will contribute to that process.

It is aimed at anyone with an interest in the housing association movement – tenants, councillors, committee members, officers and students. Its purpose is to examine the activities of housing associations and the range of needs that they meet. It explores policy issues and attempts to evaluate the movement's performance in the light of best practice.

The Housing Act 1988, which advanced the process of privatisation through tenants' choice and other provisions, also established a new tenancy regime and financial framework for housing associations. The latter incorporated a more limited system of subsidy which will inevitably lead to higher rents. Although the capital programme of new development is to expand, whether the rents produced by the financial framework will enable associations to continue to house their traditional client groups, those on low incomes and in housing need, remains to be seen. The book examines, in detail, the impact of the Housing Act 1988 upon the work of housing associations and explores the challenges which face the movement in the 1990s. It also considers the extent to which housing associations are accountable for their actions and for the public funds that they receive. In 1989/90 alone, over £1000 million was invested in associations yet their committees of management remain self-selecting. It could be argued that this situation is no longer tenable; the record of associations in terms of accountability to their tenants, to the communities in which they are active and to the public at large, is a further theme of the book.

The text commences with an examination of the context in which housing associations operate, their structures and activities and the agencies with which they work. The main disciplines of finance, development and management are then explored. Specialist activities are considered, in particular, the movement's role in meeting the housing needs of older people and in providing shared housing and hostel accommodation for those individuals with special requirements. The development of housing for sale is also considered. It concludes by examining the shape and composition of the housing association movement in the 1990s and assesses the tensions imposed by the increasingly commercial climate which now prevails.

The voluntary housing movement embraces a variety of organisations and activities. The constraints of space make it impossible to cover every aspect of the movement in the desired depth. The book concentrates on the mainstream providers of housing to rent and refers only in the broadest terms to other arms of the movement, such as almshouses and co-operative housing associations which deserve texts in their own right. It also concentrates on the work of housing associations in England, although some reference is made to both Scotland and Wales.

Wider aspects of housing policy, law, finance and management are dealt with in other books. This examination is therefore limited to those aspects of policy and practice which are of particular relevance to housing associations.

I would like to thank the many people who have assisted in the preparation of this text. Officers of the Housing Corporation and the National Federation of Housing Associations: Steve Ongere, David Salathiel, Alan Lewis and Bill Randolph who supplied statistical information. The material provided by numerous housing associations including Anchor, Hanover, Merseyside Improved Houses, North, Orbit and Rodinglea is also appreciated. Special thanks to Laura Donnelly, Grahame Hindes, Ruth Hole, Mike Langstaff, David Murdoch and Pat Rushton who painstakingly read various parts of the text. Any errors which remain are of course mine, and mine alone. To Belinda Dyson and Marie Holly who typed and retyped the constantly changing text and finally to Pete, for an endless supply of food, drink and patient encouragement without which the book would not have been completed.

1990   HELEN COPE

Preface to the Second Edition

Almost a decade on from the first edition of this book, housing associations and their work are perhaps a little better known to the public at large. At least they now feature from time to time in television soap operas or crime series although perhaps that is of dubious benefit!

The sector has grown enormously during this period. Some 2000 housing associations now own over one million social homes and have assets worth over £36 billion. Some £700 million of government capital grants are invested each year in the sector matched by the equivalent in private finance. Private loans presently exceed £14 billion. Housing associations now employ over 60 000 staff involved in the delivery of housing and care services in some of the nation's most deprived areas. Each year over 50 000 new households become residents of housing associations. Since 1989, several local authorities have also transferred their housing stock into large, locally sponsored housing associations. The sector is now of national significance, and the aim of this book continues to be an attempt to inform the wider public, councillors, students and anyone with an interest, about the work of the independent housing sector.

Housing associations are now the most common form of *registered social landlord* (RSL), a term introduced by the Housing Act 1996. Registered social landlords may also include local housing companies and other bodies registered with the Housing Corporation (a government agency which funds and regulates the sector). Throughout this book, the term RSL is used interchangeably with housing association, although this may not be strictly accurate. Presently, as most RSLs are in fact also housing associations, and given that the term housing association still appears in most current texts, is still used in Scotland and is more pleasing on the ear, it is hoped that this slight technical inaccuracy in the use of terminology will be forgiven!

As before, the book commences with a review of the context in which housing associations work and then the key operational areas of finance, development and regeneration, housing management, care and low-cost home-ownership are examined. This edition includes a new Chapter 4, which concentrates on the governance and management of RSLs.

Chapter 8, on supported housing and care, has also been considerably expanded to incorporate an examination of housing associations and community care. The final chapter, as last time, offers some remarks about future prospects as we enter a new millennium. No one can truly see into the future, but crystal ball gazing is enjoyable. Much of the final chapter of the last edition which was offered as a future scenario, has in fact turned up again in Chapter 1 of this edition (as fact, or history)!

The book goes to press less than two years into a new Labour Government and given our very fast-changing environment it has been a challenge to incorporate all the latest developments. These are detailed in the relevant chapters but chapter 11 also functions as a 'stop press' for the most recent announcements by Government.

I hope that you enjoy this book and find it of use and interest. As always I owe a great deal to many people, although I take full responsibility for any mistakes, as these are mine and mine alone. Thank you to my friends and family, especially to my sister, Laura Cope, for endless hours of devotedly reading and re-reading the text and who with William, ensured that this endless project did in fact finally reach its conclusion. Also to Jim Coulter, Chief Executive of the National Housing Federation for his ideas and encouragement and to his staff for assistance, to my personal assistant Christine Forbes for her support throughout and typing of tables, and to the former Chair of East Thames Housing Group, Nicolas Stacey and the Board of Management for their belief that this was a worthwhile project for their Chief Executive. I have since left East Thames and consequently also resigned as chair of the National Housing Federation and would like to take this opportunity to thank all my colleagues at East Thames, the Housing Corporation, the National Housing Federation and across the sector and housing field for their friendship and support throughout my long association with them.

January 1999   HELEN COPE

1

Historical Development to the Present Day

1.1 What are registered social landlords?

Registered social landlords (RSLs) are diverse, independent, not for profit organisations. The term registered social landlord was introduced in 1996. Originally called 'registered housing associations' (ie registered under section 5 of the Housing Associations Act 1985), all registered housing associations automatically became registered social landlords under section 1 of the Housing Act 1996. Thus at the time of writing, the most common type of RSL is a housing association, and many bodies retain the term housing association in their name. This term is also used from time to time in this book, especially when discussing policy prior to 1997. While much of the policy and practice examined in the following chapters applies to all registered social landlords, the work of traditional housing associations and trusts is explored in particular, as at the time of writing few other forms of RSL have yet been established.

As one of two major providers of social housing, the other being local housing authorities, the common aim of the independent sector is to provide affordable housing and related services for people on low incomes and in housing need. RSLs are also voluntary in nature as the housing they provide is not as a result of statutory duty but is the result of the energy and commitment of lay volunteers who have combined to form an organisation to meet perceived housing needs. The volunteers, or members of the RSL and their elected board or committee of management receive no remuneration for their work (although as we shall see, this may change in future). In addition, the smallest RSLs employ no paid staff, with members undertaking the management of the houses that they have provided on a voluntary basis. Larger organisations employ professional officers who execute the objectives and policies of the landlord as determined by the board of management. The committee of management, or board, is legally responsible for the work of the organisation and formulates the policies and strategies to be followed.

Registered social landlords are expected to implement 'fair housing policies': that is, they should not discriminate against minority groups in

1

either their housing or employment practices. They must also meet
certain governance and operational performance standards set by their
regulator and key funder, the Housing Corporation, which are applicable
to all registered social landlords.

RSLs have a rich history with many traditonal trusts and associations
established as long ago as the nineteenth century or before, but following
a period of major expansion in the mid-1970s and increases in public
investment in the period 1987–92, combined with the corresponding
decline in local authority housing investment, by 1996 the independent
sector had become virtually the sole provider of new social housing.
Indeed, several local authorities also elected to transfer their stock into
specially established housing associations. Despite a change of government in 1997, transfer policy remains on the agenda of several councils
that are considering whether to transfer part or all of their stock into new,
independent organisations. The most common form is the local housing
company, a further type of registered social landlord. At the time of
writing few had yet been established, but their potential is explored in the
next chapter.

RSLs do not trade for profit and so they are distinguished from the
private sector. This distinction has led to much debate concerning their
exact status: are they public or private providers of housing? Until 1988
the majority of funding came from central and local government, placing
them squarely in the public sector. Their voluntary nature, however,
clearly distinguishes them from local authority housing providers. At law,
elements of both public and private or contract law apply, adding to the
debate. This lack of clarity has not hindered the sector in any way; indeed
what was known as the housing association movement has always valued
(and argued for) its independent status. After 1988, however, the debate
gathered greater momentum as the regime for housing introduced by the
Housing Act of that year clearly sought to place associations in the private
sector. Since 1988 RSLs have combined public grants with over
£14 billion of private sector loans further clouding this issue. The
Housing Act 1996 introduced a public register of social landlords and has
more clearly defined the concept of independent registered social landlords as neither 'public' nor 'private' housing providers.

RSLs are characterised by their diversity. They differ in their aims,
philosophies, functions, size and organisational structures. The sector
incorporates almshouses, Abbeyfield Societies and co-operative housing
associations, in addition to 'mainstream' traditional housing associations
which provide housing to rent for a range of housing needs. The largest
RSLs own over 40 000 homes, the smallest fewer than 50. Since 1988 new
organisations have also been formed to receive large-scale and partial
transfers of stock from local authorities. RSLs undertake a variety of functions. They may acquire land or existing property to provide housing

through new building, rehabilitation or conversion of existing stock. They may develop family housing or cater for special needs such as the elderly, people with disabilities, or single person households.

They provide both permanent and temporary accommodation, including hostels and the complete range of tenures from rented housing to that for outright sale. Landlords may cater for specific needs or cover the whole range, varying according to their own objectives. Some landlords have concentrated on special needs provision, others perhaps undertaking only new building rather than acquiring and refurbishing older stock. A few such as secondary housing co-operatives (see Chapter 2), provide no housing at all in their own right but concentrate on the provision of advice or related services.

Since 1989, RSLs have been encouraged to expand and to take on new functions such as the management of local authority stock. Others have also entered the field of community care, delivering care services direct to their own and other landlords' residents. Many now manage private sector homes through the Temporary Market Rented Housing initiative (formerly known as Housing Associations as Managing Agents, or HAMA). RSLs are also encouraged to provide 'more than housing' by embracing a wider role in the community using their purchasing power to secure employment and training opportunities and community development initiatives. These activities, known collectively as *'housing plus'*, are explored further in later chapters. Many are now active in the field of urban regeneration working closely with local authorities and other partners. Indeed, partnership is a recurring theme of this book and a major feature of the work of RSLs.

1.2   Meeting housing needs

In 1997 there were 2150 Registered Social Landlords providing housing and related services in England.[1] Of these, some 500 have received significant public funding; and the majority of the development programme since the mid-1970s has been undertaken by 300 or so RSLs. The register is maintained by the Housing Corporation which is a central government agency established in 1964 to fund, supervise and regulate the work of RSLs. Some 30 000 volunteers serve on the boards or committees of management of RSLs and they employ over 60 000 paid staff.[2]

As at March 1997 RSLs in England owned over 989 300 self-contained homes, of which over half have been provided since 1974. A further 115 600 were managed for other landlords.[3] Independent sector stock accounts for some 4 per cent of the total housing stock (see Table 1.1), thus, in terms of the total stock of homes in England housing associations could not be considered particularly significant. The picture, however, is quite different in terms of development activity. From 1980 to 1988,

Table 1.1   Housing stock in Great Britain by tenure, March 1996

	%
Owner-occupied	67
Local authority rented	19
Private rented	10
Housing Association rented	4

Source: Derived from *Housing and Construction Statistics* (Department of the Environment).

following the cutbacks in local authority house building, developments by RSLs accounted for almost the half of new public sector housing starts. Since 1988 they have accounted for the majority of new social housing provision. In terms of their capacity to develop and as clients of the building industry, RSLs are significant. In addition to the one million self-contained homes, RSLs also own some 91 600 bedspaces in hostels and shared housing, and manage a further 17 400 on behalf of others.[4] The particular emphasis on housing with care and support differentiates the independent sector in this country from its much larger counterpart in Europe, where the emphasis has often been on general family provision alone.

Over 230 000 homes have been added to the sector through the voluntary transfer of local authority stock into new or existing bodies; RSLs established by stock transfers are examined in the next chapter.

The greatest concentration of independent sector homes is in London and the South East: some 39 per cent are concentrated in this region. The North-East, including Yorkshire and Humberside accounts for 11.5 per cent and the North-West and Merseyside 15.5 per cent. The other English regions West Midlands, the East and the South-West have similar stock holdings of between 8 and 10 per cent.

Of the one million self-contained homes 40 per cent have one bedroom or less, 32 per cent two bedrooms, 26 per cent three bedrooms and a further 26 per cent have four bedrooms or more. Some 17 per cent are specifically designed to meet the housing needs of elderly people.

Since 1980, RSLs have also been able to develop homes for part sale and tenants of non-charitable RSLs have had the 'right to buy' their homes on the same basis as secure tenants of council housing. The Housing Act 1996 extended this right to all tenants of homes built after 1 April 1997 by charitable RSLs through what is known as the 'right to acquire'. Housing for sale activities are explored in Chapter 10.

The National Housing Federation, the sector's representative body, has undertaken censi of new lettings by RSLs and developed a continuous recording system of lettings known as CORE. Figure 1.1 shows that in

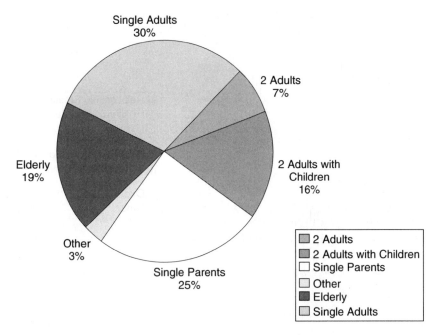

Single Adults
30%

2 Adults
7%

Elderly
19%

2 Adults with
Children
16%

Other
3%

Single Parents
25%

☐ 2 Adults
☐ 2 Adults with Children
☐ Single Parents
☐ Other
☐ Elderly
☐ Single Adults

Figure 1.1   Profile of lettings by household type

1997, the largest group of lettings was to the elderly, which is not surprising given the nature of the stock which, as stated, includes a significant
proportion specifically designed for this group. RSLs have also been
active in regenerating older areas of the inner city (areas which have a
high proportion of elderly people), adding to the concentration of older
people in this sector. The work of RSLs with older people is explored in
Chapter 9.

Single adults also represent a high proportion of lettings, having
increased from 16 per cent in 1978 to 30 per cent in 1997. Figure 1.2 illustrates the reasons why tenants sought rehousing in the sector, and highlights the role of RSLs as providers of homes for those in need. The duties
of RSLs, with respect to homeless families and their lettings and allocation policies generally, are investigated further in Chapter 7.

In 1997 some 19 per cent of household heads newly housed were
retired and 29 per cent unemployed (Figure 1.3). Most tenants were on
low incomes. The average net weekly household income of new tenants
in 1997 was £122, and just £96 for non-workers.[5] Over 70 per cent of new
tenants are reliant upon one or more state benefits for their weekly
income. This is a particularly significant factor for both housing management and future development, brought about in part by the changes in

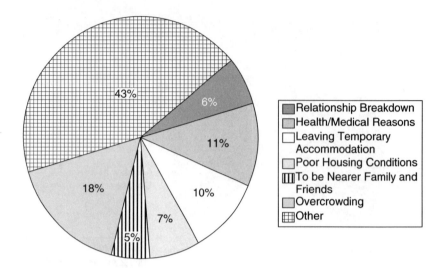

Figure 1.2   Reasons for seeking rehousing

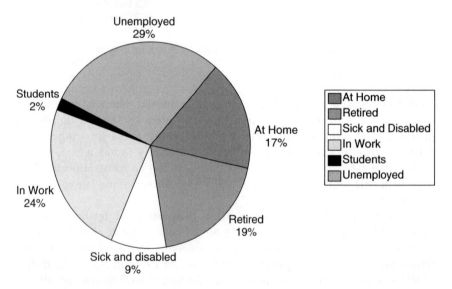

Figure 1.3   Economic status of household head

the financial regime introduced by the Housing Act 1988, which led to increases in rent levels.

The bulk of the development programme to provide homes for these groups has been financed through grants from the Housing Corporation. Local authority funding of associations was greatly reduced as a result of the constraints placed by central government upon their capital expenditure programmes. The position has improved with the release of capital receipts announced in 1997.

Table 1.2 shows the level of Corporation funding of registered social landlords from 1996 to 2000 through its annual cash limit or 'Approved Development Programme' (ADP). The programme which peaked at almost £2 billion in 1994 has been steadily reducing since; by the year 2000 it will stand at half the 1996 level. New completions have consequently fallen too, from 48 000 in 1996/97 to forecast of a 23–28 000 by the year 2000.[6] The reasons behind these cuts and the implications for RSLs are considered in later chapters.

Table 1.2   Housing corporation ADP 1996–2000 (£m)

	1996/97	1997/98 (Forecast Outturn)	1998/99 (Plans)	1999/2000 (Plans)
Housing for rent	794.1	505.2	452.4	411.8
Housing for sale	232.7	156.7	153.0	150.0
Other expenditure	26.0	18.0	19.0	19.0
Gross ADP	1052.8	679.9	624.4	580.8

Source: Derived from Housing Corporation *ADP Bulletin* (1997–98).

1.3   Historical development

Almshouses

Much of the diversity of the sector may be attributed to its historical development. The movement can trace its roots back to the almshouses of the twelfth century. These were founded by individual benefactors or guilds concerned with the charitable provision of accommodation as part of their Christian duty, at a time when individuals could depend less than today upon the state for their welfare. Almshouses also provided health care and other supportive services. Many early almshouse developments still remain clearly identifiable owing to their distinctive architecture, the most common form being one or two-storey terraced cottages built around a quadrangle. Eventually, the almshouses concentrated on meeting the particular housing needs of the elderly as predecessors to the current providers of sheltered housing. In 1946, almshouses which had developed all over the country voted to join forces to form a single representative body to promote their work: the National Association of Almshouses. The movement consists of over 1700 members providing 26 000 homes. This great arm of the voluntary housing movement has clearly stood the test of time and although they are legally and administratively distinct from other RSLs, almshouses continue to grow in their own right, using both public and charitable funding.

The nineteenth century

The more recent origins of the independent housing sector lie in the mid-nineteenth century and in particular, in the reaction of reformers and philanthropists to the intolerable housing conditions which were prevalent throughout our cities as a result of the Industrial Revolution. The great movements in population from the countryside to the towns, often in search of work, led to intense overcrowding, disease and squalor. Conditions deteriorated as slums were demolished to make way for expansion of the railways, forcing homeless people to crowd together in even greater density. Reaction to these appalling conditions created in some a fervour for reform. For example, Edwin Chadwick and Octavia Hill (in their respective spheres of public health and housing management) laid the foundations for our modern environmental health and housing services.

Many of the largest philanthropic trusts were founded through endowments during this period. The Peabody Trust founded from a gift of £150 000 in 1862 by George Peabody now owns over 13 500 homes. In 1890 Edward Cecil Guinness established the Guinness Trust with an endowment of £200 000. Today the Trust operates across the country, owning some 15 000 homes.[7] Most trusts concentrated on the provision of housing in London, although the Sutton Housing Trust formed in 1900 operated in other parts of the country too. In 1906 the Samuel Lewis Trust (now part of the Southern Housing Group) was founded, based in London. The trusts developed mansion or tenement style blocks; solidly built, the majority still survive today. Many are undergoing programmes of refurbishment and will continue to provide much needed housing in the years to come. The work of the philanthropic trusts set an example of what could be achieved in terms of the improvement of living conditions for the 'labouring classes' at a time when state action on welfare was still anathema to political leaders and the philosophy of *laissez-faire* prevailed. Although the concept of 'the deserving and undeserving poor' was at its height during the mid- to late nineteenth century, and homeless people faced the principle of 'less eligibility' and the 'Workhouse Test', many new societies and trusts were formed to alleviate these hardships, in particular through the concept of 5 per cent philanthropy. Public spirited people lent money to these bodies on the basis of a limited financial return, 5 per cent or less. Such investments therefore afforded the opportunity to committed individuals to invest safely at low rates of return whilst also meeting their philanthropic ideals. The Octavia Hill & Rowe, and Birmingham Copec Trusts (the latter now being part of the merged Focus Housing Group), started in this way at the turn of the century, and many others continued to be formed throughout the early decades of the twentieth century.

The inter-war period

The end of the First World War, and the sense of euphoria that accompanied it, heralded a new era for British housing policy. Returning war heroes could not be allowed to face the slum conditions that they had left in order to serve their country. Such feelings were channelled into the campaign, led by Lloyd George, for 'Homes fit for Heroes'. This culminated in the Housing and Town Planning Act 1919 which firmly placed the responsibility for the provision of 'working class' housing with local authorities. For the first time local authorities could develop housing for rent, and own and retain it, directly subsidising the costs of provision from the local rates (now Council Tax). Local authorities were to become the major providers of rented housing, with a concomitant growth in owner-occupation, particularly following the Second World War. The legislation that underpinned the growth of council housing resulted in Britain developing the largest public rented sector in the western world; the voluntary sector has never equalled that of other countries, such as Sweden, as a major provider of housing. Nevertheless, the independent sector continued to grow steadily with some further periods of significant expansion.

The 1960s

During the 1960s there were several factors which brought about further growth: firstly, the response to the Housing Act 1957. The deregulation of rents in the private rented sector introduced by the Conservative Government created an unprecedented period of harassment of tenants by landlords wishing to obtain vacant possession of their properties. Such behaviour, known as 'Rachmanism' after one particularly notorious landlord, led to a strengthening of public opinion that wanted to see improved housing conditions and increased security of tenure. New housing societies were formed during this period in response. A second factor was the growing dissatisfaction with the wholesale slum clearance policies practised by some local authorities which led indirectly to the formation of other local, community-based associations to acquire and rehabilitate homes in inner-city areas that were threatened with demolition. Many were set up with the assistance of Shelter (the campaign for the homeless, itself established in 1966). There was a growing awareness of the increasing levels of homelessness, highlighted by the famous BBC documentary 'Cathy Come Home', which fuelled public opinion in favour of increased public sector house-building. Many young people at that time were inspired by these issues to enter the housing profession including the independent sector.

Furthermore, in 1964 the Housing Corporation was established with powers to provide loans to housing societies for cost-rent and co-ownership schemes. High interest rates and rising land prices soon led to the demise of cost-rent schemes, as these received no public subsidy. An interesting point is that in encouraging such voluntary societies to promote cost-rent schemes, the government was in effect using the voluntary housing movement as a model, which they hoped would be imitated by the private sector. This was an early attempt to regenerate private renting, a cause to which the Conservative Party remained espoused throughout its 1979 to 1997 administration. Co-ownership schemes were entirely new; often set up by property 'professionals', they offered co-owners a share in the increase of the market value of their home on leaving. They offered a 'premium payment' paid for by the higher monthly payments of incoming co-owners. This scheme was also discontinued when the high costs of premium payments became unsustainable as market values rocketed in the 1970s.

The Housing Act 1974

Although, as we have seen, the sector has a long history, one of the most intensive periods of expansion and development took place as a direct result of the Housing Act 1974.

The Act introduced new grants and subsidies for housing associations which remained in place until 1989. A new subsidy for capital works, the Housing Association Grant (HAG), combined with public sector loan finance provided by the Housing Corporation or local authorities, encouraged the rapid expansion of associations providing low-cost rented housing. The Act also introduced a revenue subsidy (Revenue Deficit Grant). The powers of the Housing Corporation were extended, making it responsible for sponsoring, promoting, funding and supervising the work of housing associations. The Corporation set up a public register of associations and only those registered with it could take advantage of the new loans and grants. Many new associations were formed during this period responding to the housing needs of their area. Once registered and eligible for loans and grants they were able to provide homes at 'fair rents' set by the independent Rent Officer Service. The work of the Housing Corporation and the details of the current financial framework are fully explored in later chapters.

The introduction of large-scale public subsidy compromised to some extent the independence of the movement, as inevitably bureaucratic controls were imposed as a quid pro quo for the receipt of public funds. The year 1974 was not only one which brought expansion, but it also marked the end of an era of reliance upon largely voluntary effort and charitable donations. Limited public loans had been available since the nineteenth century and there had been some subsidy since the First World War but the scale of support following the 1974 Act was unprecedented.

It was during this period that the sector developed its expertise in meeting the needs of single people and couples, the elderly and those with disabilities. Supported housing projects and initiatives to provide hostels giving extra care for vulnerable people also expanded. Despite the broad support for the legislation some local authorities were unhappy with its provisions, seeing it as a direct vote of no confidence in the authorities' own roles. The subsidy systems offered were also more generous than those available to local authorities at that time. Labour-controlled authorities, in particular, were concerned that large sums of public money should be made available to organisations with no electoral accountability.

Accountability is an issue which is raised throughout this book, but it is sufficient to note here that much of the work of the Housing Corporation is aimed at improving the accountability of registered social landlords to the public, including tenants, and that most landlords have taken this issue seriously and have attempted to improve their record on account-ability. For example, in 1994 an independent inquiry into the governance of associations was established which proposed a code of governance to enhance accountability. Although confidence has developed in the sector over the years and most local authorities now work closely with RSLs operating in their areas, rapid growth during the early 1990s (combined with increases in rents and concern over development standards) led to some criticism of them which the inquiry adressed. The inquiry panel's findings are considered further in Chapter 4.

Most of the provisions of the Housing Act 1974 relating to housing asso-ciations were re-enacted in the consolidating legislation of 1985. This simplified the legislative framework under which associations operated.

Six Acts are of current significance and their provisions are outlined at relevant points throughout the text. They are: the Housing Associations Act 1985, the Housing Act 1985, the Housing and Planning Act 1986, The Local Government and Housing Act 1989, and the Housing Acts of 1988 and 1996.

The 1980s

In 1980 the Conservative Government implemented a series of cutbacks to public expenditure. Housing association funding through the Housing Corporation and local authorities in particular was, as a direct result, dramatically cut.

A new system of cash-limited capital expenditure was introduced, which restricted housing association development to a level lower than its true capacity. Associations nevertheless fared better than local authority housing departments over this decade in terms of permitted programmes of capital expenditure. Local authority Housing Investment Programmes (HIPs) continued to fall and so did their ability to fund the work of housing associations. The reduction in the housing association programme reflected the Conservative view that associations had strayed too far into the public sector.

The Housing Act 1980 introduced the right to buy for tenants of non-charitable housing associations and the Housing and Building Control Act 1984 created a new discretionary scheme of home ownership discounts for tenants of charitable housing associations (HOTCHA) which was replaced by the Tenants' Incentive Scheme (TIS) in 1989 (see Chapter 10). In addition, a greater proportion of the Approved Development Programme (ADP) of the Housing Corporation became devoted to low-cost home-ownership schemes such as shared ownership and improvement for sale, reflecting Conservative housing policy which sought to privatise housing through the twin approach of reduced public sector housing investment and the pursuit of mass home ownership.

The Housing Act 1980 also introduced a new form of tenancy for public sector tenants including those of housing associations: the secure tenancy. In addition to the right to buy, embodied within the Act were additional rights to information, consultation, to sub-let and others known as the 'tenants' charter'. All the provisions of the 1980 Act were re-enacted in the consolidating legislation of 1985. Those who were tenants of housing associations as at 15 January 1989 continue to enjoy those rights and the right to an independently set 'fair rent'. Tenancies after that date are assured tenancies and are subject to the provisions of the Housing Acts 1988 and 1996.

1.4   The Housing Act 1988: an overview

The Housing Act 1988 had an even more radical impact upon the nature and work of the independent social housing sector than the 1974 legislation. Its detailed provisions, where still current, are discussed in the relevant chapters but at this point it may be appropriate to take a brief overview of the Act and the philosophy underlying it.

The White Paper *Housing: the Government's Proposals* issued in 1987, outlined four major policy objectives which the then government hoped to achieve through the provisions of future legislation. The decline of the private rented sector was to be stemmed through the deregulation of rents and reductions in security of tenure. The Housing Act 1988 introduced assured tenancies with deregulated rents for both private sector tenants and new tenants of housing associations. Through these provisions the Government sought to encourage what it termed the 'independent rented sector'.

Tenants' choice

The second objective was to give tenants of local authorities the right to transfer to other landlords. This initiative did not progress on the scale expected however. Tenants may have been discouraged by the loss of security and likely increase in rent levels that a transfer to a different landlord would bring. Only two notable tenant choice transfers happened; in particular the Walterton and Elgin Community Housing Association which was established in the London Borough of Westminster. The provisions were therefore repealed by the Housing Act 1996. The policy reflected the Government's desire to break up large council estates rather than to bring about the extension of choice and the period also heralded the demise of local authorities as direct housing providers. The White Paper stated: 'Local authorities should increasingly see themselves as enablers who ensure that everyone in their area is adequately housed; but not by them.' Since 1989 local housing authorities have embraced this enabling role with varying degrees of enthusiasm as outlined in Chapter 3. The Labour administration elected in 1997 shows little intention of departing from this philosophy, however.

Housing Action Trusts

A further objective of the legislation was to 'target' money on estates with the most acute problems. The Act introduced the concept of Housing Action Trusts, or HATs. HATs have been established in areas designated by the Secretary of State, following consultation with the tenants, and funds channelled through them to regenerate some of the worst estates. HATs also remove these estates from the ownership of the local authority, although they may have the opportunity to reacquire them once works are completed. HATS, like Urban Development Corporations, can be seen as a further mechanism to by-pass local authorities which were viewed as too bureaucratic and cumbersome to undertake the vital work of regenerating run-down estates. Critics viewed this as yet another example of local democracy under threat, arguing that if funding was to be made available then it should be channelled through locally elected and politically accountable bodies.

Since 1989 six HATs have been established throughout England and work is on-going, although several are now beginning to wind down. Housing associations have had a role in their development often providing new infill accommodation where tower blocks have been demolished. As some HATs are as yet uncompleted the intentions of some tenants remain unclear; they may vote to return as tenants of their respective local authorities or may pursue other options, such as forming their own housing association or local housing company to either stand alone or be a subsidiary of an existing registered social landlord.

The final objective of the Housing Act 1988 was to continue to encourage the growth of home ownership. The Government successfully pursued this policy partly through the right to buy initiative introduced in 1980 but also as a result of economic policy and the boom years of the mid 1980s. Home ownership increased from 55 per cent of all tenures in 1979 to 67 per cent in 1996. This is a radical shift achieved by a housing policy which some would argue ignored deteriorating house conditions and increases in homelessness in order to pursue relentlessly this particular goal. One of the greatest criticisms of the 1988 legislation made at the time, was that it made no mention of the growing army of homeless households. Homelessness increased from 11 000 known households in 1979 to 110 660 by 1988. Nothing in the 1988 Act would, according to critics, make an impact upon the misery signified by these statistics.

The impact upon housing associations

The White Paper stated:

> the Government believes that housing associations have a vitally important part to play in the revival of the independent rented sector. During recent years they have been almost alone in the independent sector in investing in rented housing, and have played a key part in developing new styles of management and new forms of low cost home ownership. It will be important to build on this success and develop it further.

The Housing Act 1988 introduced a new form of tenancy, the freedom for associations to set their own rents, an expanded role for the Housing Corporation and a new financial framework. The regime built upon earlier experiments to mix public sector grants with private sector loans raised from financial institutions; the new form of finance was therefore termed 'mixed funding'.

Since 1974 the housing assocation movement had relied almost entirely upon public sector funding for its work. In the late 1980s however, several associations began to experiment with schemes utilising mixed funding. These schemes provided homes let on assured tenancies introduced by the Housing Act 1980. The intention was to make public funding go further, and to produce more homes for every pound of public money spent. The Treasury broke with an old and illogical convention, thereby allowing the mixture of public and private funding to proceed with only the public sector grant counting as public expenditure. Prior to this *private* loans raised by a housing association counted as *public* expenditure in Treasury accounting terms. The abandonment of this principle allowed mixed funded schemes to proceed.

As outlined earlier, the previous system of finance allowed for the payment of grant on the completion of a scheme once all the final costs were known. Fair rents were set by the Rent Officer service independently of the association. Grant met the difference between capital expenditure and the size of a public sector loan provided by the Housing Corporation (at fixed interest rates), or local authorities, that rental income net of management and maintenance costs could support. Grant levels averaged between 80 and 90 per cent, rising to 100 per cent for special needs schemes in many cases. Furthermore, revenue deficits were met by a Revenue Deficit Grant, provided that those deficits could be accounted for according to strict rules of eligibility. The new framework introduced in 1989 fixed levels of grant, set according to scheme location and type. The grant became predetermined – that is, set at the outset – placing the onus upon associations to prevent cost increases or cost overruns during the development period. Grant rates were cut. In 1989/90 the average grant rate for schemes across the country was 75 per cent. By 1997/98 this had reduced to 54 per cent. The reductions in grant have largely been met by higher rents. Loans are now raised from the private sector and interest rates clearly affect rents. RSLs were expected to set up provisions for future major repairs to their properties, previously eligible for 100 per cent capital grant, which also impacted upon rent levels. Government policy for the next decade was to switch subsidy to personal subsidies rather than bricks and mortar. Thus Housing Benefit had to take the strain of rising rents. By 1997 the incoming Labour Government inherited a housing benefit bill (for all sectors), which had increased to £11 billion per annum.

In an additional White Paper, *Finance for Housing Associations* (1987), the Government set out the philosophy underlying the new regime. It wished to encourage development by associations and argued that mixed funding would produce more homes for a given level of public funding, as private loans would not score against public expenditure. It also argued that the proposals 'will create new incentives to associations to deliver their services in the most cost-effective manner, bringing to bear the disciplines of the private sector and strengthening the machinery of public support'.[8] The regime attempted to place associations squarely in the private sector, transferring the development risk to them. *Finance for Housing Associations* also stated: 'The injection of market disciplines will itself lead to greater efficiency and make associations more independent and more responsible for the quality and effectiveness of their investment decisions and the competence of their management.'[9]

The Act had far-reaching effects upon the sector. A research report published by the National Housing Federation,[10] examined the impact of the

Act upon housing association development, housing management and affordability. It also considered the effect of the introduction of private finance into the sector. In the first two years immediately following the passage of the Act, the impact on the development programme in particular was dramatic.

Commercialism and development drift

The increasingly commercial climate in which associations now operate and the new emphases on cost-effectiveness and value for money (which are explored in later chapters) led initially to a dramatic decline in rehabilitation activity, from 50 per cent of the programme in 1989/90 to 20 per cent by 1991. Consequently, there was also a shift of emphasis in the early years from work in inner city areas to development of green field sites in suburban and out of town sites. By 1998, however, the balance had virtually been restored and most RSLs are now actively involved in urban regeneration schemes, with 65 per cent of the Housing Corporation programme invested on 'brown land' sites.

In order to attempt to keep rents affordable many schemes (up to 30 per cent) were supported by internal funds, a practice which increased further in the mid-1990s as competition for development grant increased. Standards in some schemes also fell in the early years, the average floor space falling by up to 10 per cent. The early 1990s were marked by a period of expansion facilitated by the doubling of the Approved Development Programme and the introduction of private finance. The use of internal funding support (explored further in Chapters 5 and 6), stemmed also from desires to survive in the 'new era' and were fuelled in some by expansionist goals too. Between 1990 and 1996 a number of associations doubled their stock through new development, although growth was also facilitated by some stock transfers and mergers. The emphasis on larger schemes and the need to keep costs down led many associations into closer partnership with private developers. Whilst this brought advantages in some instances, the innovative design and high standards of space and amenity associated with the movement's development activity was at times compromised. As links with private developers grew there was mounting pressure to make grant available to them.

Indeed as noted later, the 1995 White Paper envisaged a development grant regime that would be open to profit-making bodies too, although by 1996 these proposals had been shelved as the 1997 general election approached. The willingness of RSLs to subsidise development costs internally using income from the rents of older properties, to help keep rents on new homes lower or indeed to accept lower grants in order to win competitions against other associations, compromised any attempts by the sector to lobby for grant rates that produced affordable rents; hence the successive reduction in grant levels. Each year the Housing Corporation received bids at four or five times the level of the available programme and, as explored in Chapter 6, it was clear to Treasury officials that the development programme was sustainable even with cuts in grant despite arguments to the contrary. The policy was clearly to let rents take the strain and one of the most disturbing outcomes of the period to 1996 was the huge increase in rent levels. As early as 1991 the National Housing Federation study found that rents on new but as yet uncompleted homes were consistently above the average 'reasonable market' rents set by the Rent Officers for private sector homes in the same areas and had risen at three times the rate of household incomes.[11] This in turn led some to question the purpose of subsidising new homes with capital grants at all. Throughout the 1990s rents have taken the strain of an inadequate Grant regime. Consequently the Housing Benefit bill has risen to unsustainable levels. In response, in 1996 some control on housing association rents was introduced for the first time through the capital grant bidding process. Many tenants have, however, already become caught in a deepening poverty trap. The steep withdrawal of housing benefit as income rises, which taxes tenants at a marginal rate of 96 per cent, contributes to this process but it is exacerbated by the rent levels charged by some associations, which are unaffordable by those in low paid employment. From 1998, the Government insisted that all rent rises in the sector be constrained to within Retail Price Index (RPI) plus 1%.

The introduction of private finance *per se* has, however, been a spectacular success. As stated, by 1999 over £14 billion had been raised by the sector. RSLs have had to develop new skills such as treasury management, and to learn to manage the risks that are attendant upon large loan portfolios which are sensitive to movements in interest rates.

Internal control and the management of change

In coming to terms with the 1988 Act all RSLs have had to adjust to change. Those which have adapted to the more commercial climate most effectively are those which are most responsive to change. Each RSL has had to adopt new practices and review its organisation in terms of its strengths and capacity to develop and with a view to overcoming areas of weakness. There is now a greater emphasis on self-monitoring, the management of risk and internal control.

The board or committee of management, together with officers of the RSL, must ensure that there are proper systems of delegated authority, clear lines of accountability and adequate reporting systems in order that they can effectively control and manage the organisation. Performance indicators with measurable targets have become standard management tools. Indeed the publication of housing management indicators against targets has been a requirement since 1991. The spotlight placed on the sector by enhanced support led to a number of studies (see Chapter 7) which test the managerial efficiency of housing associations, in the manner that local authorities have faced for some years.

Accountability

As the sector expanded questions began to be raised regarding its account-ability to both tenants and the local community. Some commentators still argue that housing associations have some way to go to improve their record on accountability, equal opportunities and tenant participation. The demands currently being made upon staff to adapt to change and to improve services and accountability to tenants, whilst holding down costs, represent one of the greatest challenges. Staff have been asked to maximise income against a background of increasing poverty and reduc-tions in housing benefit. It is hoped that the Green Paper announced at the time of the 1999 Budget will begin to address these issues.

1.5   1989 to the present

The period since the 1988 Act has been marked by fundamental change in the nature and increasing diversity of the activities of the most active RSLs. As highlighted above, competition, value for money, accountability, performance standards and the need for reinvestment in their stock are now familiar issues in their work as is the need to work in partnership. In addition to the 1988 Act itself a number of other issues have impacted on their work and shaped the environment in which they operate. As the effect of the Act became clearer the spotlight fell on the sector's activities and support from both major political parties began to wane. From 1993 onwards a series of reports raised questions about the sector's develop-ment activities; in particular,the work of Page[12] and Karn[13] which are considered further in Chapters 6 and 7.

In December 1992 the Select Committee on the Environment estab-lished an Inquiry into the Housing Corporation, and soon expanded the nature of the Inquiry to cover a whole range of issues impacting on the work of associations. Reporting in July 1993,[14] its main findings were to endorse a strong campaign waged by the movement against cuts in the grant rate confirming the need to protect rent levels and to maintain the diversity of associations which was by then coming under increasing threat as grant rates were successively cut year on year, making it harder for smaller associations to participate. It also recommended that rehabili-tation programmmes should be increased. In relation to the Corporation itself (see Chapter 3), it called for greater accountability by the introduction of tenants and members with local authority and housing management experience at board level, and suggested that the Corporation be restructured to match Department of the Environment (DOE) regional boundaries. It also recommended that a tenants' ombudsman be established.

The committee report raised the profile of housing associations and was swiftly followed by a report from the National Audit Office into the Housing Corporation's financial management of housing associations.[15] Critical of associations' financial managment systems, the report led to greater financial and audit control of associations' work by the Corporation and associations themselves (as detailed in Chapters 3 and 4). The accountability and control of associations was clearly becoming a major issue. In 1995, an independent Inquiry into the governance of associations was sponsored by the National Housing Federation and in 1996 the Nolan Committee on Standards in Public Life also reported on housing association activity. Both reports are fully explored in Chapter 4.

Housing Market Package

The Environment Select Committee and National Audit Office reports followed in the wake of the Housing Market Package announced in the autumn of 1992 as a measure to rescue the collapsed property market. Associations acquired 18 430 new homes with £591 million that had to be spent by 31 March 1993 in just 93 working days.[16] Only 27 housing associations were selected to be involved in the initiative and many acquired new unsold homes from builders and developers. Although the initiative was a great success and showed how swiftly and flexibly associations and the Housing Corporation could respond to such a challenge, it also brought much criticism: firstly, that a super league of developing associations was emerging or indeed was soon to be established which would again impact upon the diversity of the movement; secondly, social rented homes were being provided in some areas for the first time, alongside owner-occupied houses, leading to a new form of 'nimbyism' and complaints from residents (and, indeed, from some Members of Parliament) regarding neighbour disputes. Some commentators trace the fall in popularity of the sector generally and with some Members of Parliament, in particular, to the Housing Market Package.

Sustainable communities

It was in 1993 that the Joseph Rowntree Foundation published *Building Communities: A Study of New Housing Association Estates*. Written by David Page, the seminal study is now often referred to as the Page Report. The study highlighted the increasing concentration of tenants dependent upon benefit in new estates. This had arisen partly as a result of wider socio-economic trends but specifically as a result of housing associations becoming virtually the sole providers of new social housing after 1988.

Nominations from local authority lists, particularly of homeless households, also contributed to the changing profile of housing association tenants and, as nominations increased to 75 per cent of new homes, so the effect intensified. The report emphasised the problems associated with the development of larger estates in that ghettos of deprivation were being created. The report, which is considered in greater detail in Chapter 6, argued for smaller developments and for the need to create balanced communities comprising economically active households too, which would integrate better with existing communities. This report recommended the development of community and other related facilities on larger estates and led indirectly to the objective of the sector delivering 'more than housing' as a result of capital investment in an area.

Although the political climate was becoming tougher, many organisations continued to expand and develop throughout the early to mid 1990s. In 1991 the City Challenge programme was announced: this aimed at regenerating concentrated geographical areas over a five-year period. Many associations have had an active role in these programmes working in partnership with others and the Housing Corporation earmarked funding for them. In addition, in 1994 the Government announced the new Single Regeneration Budget (SRB) bringing together in one programme the budgets from a number of departments. Part of the Housing Corporation programme was also available for this activity and so by 1996 the pendulum had once again begun to swing back towards regeneration and away from new building. Regeneration activities are considered further in Chapter 6.

Finally, in addition to responding to the community care legislation (see Chapter 8) associations have delivered a range of other initiatives. These include DIYSO (Do It Yourself Shared Ownership) re-launched in 1992, Living Over Shops initiative (LOTS) and Temporary Market Rented Housing amongst others. As discussed in later chapters, although these activities are relatively marginal, this has led to further criticism that associations are overdiversifying and losing sight of their original objectives. The combined effect of these new activities with the explosive growth outlined earlier and the receipt of stock from partial local authority transfers, confirmed the view of critics that some associations had become overextended and unaccountable. Support began to fall away. The annual Approved Development Programme which peaked at over £2 billion in 1994, was cut each year from 1994 onwards so that by 1997/98 (as we have seen) the programme was running at only £680 million.

Some began to question the exclusivity of capital grants to to the sector. Should these grants not now become available to other landlords within prescribed criteria, private companies perhaps, given the entrepreneurial spirit which now characterises so much of the sector's work? In one sense associations appeared to have become victims of their own success and it seemed that, having squeezed as much efficiency and innovation from them as possible, the Conservative Government was intent upon whole-sale competition for funding as outlined in its 1995 White Paper. It is to this and to the Housing Act 1996 that we now turn.

The 1995 Housing White Paper

In June 1995 the Conservative Administration published a White Paper on housing entitled *Our Future Homes: Opportunity, Choice and Responsibility – the Government's Housing Policies for England and Wales.* A number of consultation documents also accompanied the White Paper. The White Paper emphasised the then government's continuing commitment to sustainable home ownership, emphasising the require-ment to meet inner-city needs through regeneration. It also proposed a new grant to enable tenants of charitable housing associations to buy their homes (Voluntary Purchase Grant, or VPG). In relation to the social rented sector, the proposals included encouragement to local authorities to trans-fer their stock, particularly to local housing companies. Commercial organisations were to be permitted to compete for what was then still known as Housing Association Grant (HAG), which is now Social Housing Grant (SHG). This proposal was eventually shelved as the 1997 general election approached, however. The Housing Corporation would have extended powers to license social landlords and to supervise their activities. The White Paper also proposed radical changes to the home-lessness legislation, removing the right of homeless persons to have prior-ity access to permanent social housing ahead of other applicants on council waiting lists. Common housing registers between all social land-lords were to be established and central guidance given on allocation policies. Various measures were proposed in relation to housing manage-ment practice, especially to deal, with anti-social tenants. The Housing Association Tenants Ombudsman Service (HATOS) was also to be placed on a statutory footing.

More choice in the social rented sector

The consultation paper entitled *More Choice in the Social Rented Sector,* which accompanied the White Paper along with other consulta-tion papers on VPG and the private rented sector, spelt out the Government's plans further. In particular, the consultation paper empha-sised the desire to widen the range of landlords who would develop and manage social housing and so compete for capital grants. The original concept was of licensed landlords, who could also be profit-making.

This was eventually shelved in favour of the concept of the independent social landlords to be known as registered social landlords (RSLs). This, more than any other feature of the legislation, could herald a new era of tougher competition for limited resources within the sector, an issue we return to in the final chapter. The White Paper spelt out the nature of the competition: local housing companies would compete with housing associations for funds to provide housing including supported housing, and this would enable greater choice of landlord to be extended to tenants. The impact of all costs of housing provision would be taken into account in this competition: that is, not only capital costs, but also the revenue costs to the Exchequer in the form of housing benefit expenditure. The Housing Corporation was to be given wider powers to regulate social landlords, including the ability to limit rent charges and the surpluses made. This latter proposal was dropped, although the perceived level of housing association reserves remains a controversial issue, as outlined in Chapter 5.

Private developers were also to be encouraged to bid for 'develop only grants' whereby a partner housing association or RSL would acquire the properties on completion. This proposal was also eventually shelved.

All types of organisation were to be eligible for registration provided that they could demonstrate that they met the defined tests and requirements of the Housing Corporation (see Chapter 2) and could also demonstrate independence from the local authority. A genuine private sector identity, with no single group dominating the membership, must also be shown to prevail.

All RSLs would have to be capable of delivering the housing and related services according to agreed standards. Originally mooted as the 'social housing product', this concept became the 'Social Housing Standard' and is now implemented through the Housing Corporation's *Performance Standards*, which are referred to throughout this book. As stated, a rent formula was also introduced to ensure that rent increases could be pegged and thus the housing benefit bill controlled. The resultant formula, RPI plus 1% is discussed further in Chapter 5.

1.6 The Housing Act 1996

By the time the legislation was enacted in July 1996 many of the more radical proposals embodied in the White Paper and the Housing Bill had been shelved as the general election approached. The National Housing Federation had also lobbied effectively on a number of issues including its insistence upon a 'level playing field' between the social and commercial 'licensed' landlords. While reference is made throughout the book to the relevant sections of the Act, some of the key points are summarised next.

The Act comprises eight parts:

I. Social Rented Sector
II. Houses in Multiple Occupation
III. Landlord and tenant
IV. Housing Benefit and related matters
V. Conduct of Tenants
VI. Allocation of housing accommodation
VII. Homelessness
VIII. Miscellaneous and general provisions

Non-profit companies may register with the Housing Corporation as registered social landlords, providing they meet certain criteria. All registered housing associations were automatically transferred on to the Register as stated at the outset of this chapter. The Housing Corporation was given powers to set standards and to monitor the performance of RSLs. Housing Association Grant was replaced by Social Housing Grant, and tenants of property developed after 1 April 1997 have the right to acquire their homes.

Houses in multiple occupation can be more tightly regulated and leaseholders have additional powers to challenge the cost and appropriateness of service charges. A local authority's duty to homeless households was diluted, and waiting lists and allocation policies were subjected to statutory control for the first time.

The Housing Act 1996 may prove to be as radical as the Housing Act 1988 despite the exclusion of the more controversial proposals. It will create a new operating climate for RSLs. In addition to increased competition, there will be a greater emphasis on and scrutiny of performance; associations will be expected to produce more for less without any diminution of quality. Expectations of both tenants and other external partners are high, and only those adept at change will survive; these are issues to which we return in Chapter 11.

The Labour Government's policy towards RSLs and early policy decisions indicate a plurality of approach, with increased expectations in relation to tenant participation and accountability to local communities. Although now perceived by some as part of the problem of social exclusion, through the creation of 'welfare ghettos' and high rents, the sector actually has much to contribute to the Government's agenda for alleviating social exclusion, particularly the 'The New Deal'. The announcement of a new area renewal strategy in 1998 (New Deal for Communities) will also place the sector at the heart of government policy. RSLs will also continue actively to engage with a whole range of bodies which impact upon their work including health and social services, probation services, the police and employment and training agencies. Partnership with such bodies is explored throughout the following chapters. We commence however with a further look at the organisation and diversity of registered social landlords, to which we now turn.

References

1 *Registered Social Landlords in 1997 – General Report* (The Housing Corporation 1998).
2 Ibid.
3 Ibid.
4 Ibid.
5 *CORE Lettings Bulletin* (NHF 1997).
6 *ADP 1997/98* (The Housing Corporation 1997).
7 *Registered Social Landlords in 1997 – Performance Indicators Table 10* (The Housing Corporation 1998).
8 Finance for Housing Associations: the Government's Proposals (DOE 1987), p. 1 para. 2.
9 Ibid, p. 2 para. 6.
10 B. Randolph (ed.) *Housing Associations after the Act, Research Report 16* (NFHA 1992).
11 Ibid.
12 D. Page *Building for Communities: A Study of New Housing Association Estates* (Joseph Rowntree Foundation 1994)
13 V. Karn and L. Sheridan, *New Homes in the 1990s: A Study of Design, Space and Amenities in Housing Association and Private Sector Housing* (Joseph Rowntree Foundation 1994).
14 *The Environment Committee second report: The Housing Corporation*, House of Commons Paper 46/1 (HMSO 1993).
15 *Housing Corporation: Financial Management of Housing Associations*, House of Commons Paper 204 (HMSO 1994).
16 *The Housing Corporation's implementation of the Housing Market Package Source Insight* (The Housing Corporation February 1995).

2

Diverse Organisations

The diversity of registered social landlords can in part be attributed to their historical development. Size, structure, function and aims, in addition to legal status, also add to this diversity. Furthermore, since 1988 new organisations have been established, to receive the transfer of local authority stock, originally known as voluntary transfer housing associations. In addition, the Housing Act 1996 established a register of registered social landlords (RSLs), of which the traditional housing association is just one type. Following this Act a further common form of RSL will be the local housing company, although (at the time of writing) whilst many were under active consideration, few had actually been registered. It should be noted at the the outset that the recent trend for transfers and local housing companies largely derives from local authority attempts to circumvent resource restrictions, rather than a desire to divest stock *per se*.

This chapter commences with the legal definition of what constitutes a housing association and registered social landlord. It then examines the process of registration with the Housing Corporation as introduced by the Housing Act 1996. The activities and structures that registered social landlords may undertake and adopt are also considered. The chapter reviews the issues facing particular types of RSL including: small associations, black and minority ethnic RSLs, co-operative housing associations, and voluntary transfer organisations. The chapter concludes with an overview of the role and development of local housing companies, which could represent one of the most significant developments for this sector.

2.1   Definitions

The independent social housing sector comprises a formidable array of organisations including housing trusts, charities, societies,companies, almshouses, co-operatives and self-build groups. In particular the

Housing Associations Act 1985 (section 1) defines a housing association as a

> society, body of trustees or company a) which is established for the purpose of, or amongst whose objects or powers are included those of, providing, constructing, improving or managing, or facilitating or encouraging the construction or improvement of, housing accommodation and, b) which does not trade for profit or whose constitution or rules prohibit the issue of capital with interest or dividend exceeding such rate as may be determined by the Treasury, whether with or without distinction between share and loan capital.

The definition of a housing association remains unchanged by the Housing Act 1996. In order, therefore, to qualify as a housing association, the body must be a society, a body of trustees or a company. A society may be unincorporated, a mere contractual arrangement between individuals,[1] but in the housing association context 'society' usually refers to an Industrial and Provident Society, registered under the Industrial and Provident Societies Act 1965. Some three-quarters of housing associations are in fact so registered and were often referred to as I and P Act Societies or 1965 Act Societies. The work of Registrar of Friendly Societies in relation to RSLs is however, to be absorbed by an enlarged Financial Services Authority with effect from 1999. At the time of writing the Industrial and Provident Societies Act was also under review.

A housing trust is an organisation, established by trust deed, which is required by its constitution to use most or all of its funds and surpluses to provide housing accommodation. A 'company' means a company limited by guarantee incorporated with a memorandum and articles of association and governed by the provisions of the Companies Acts. The definition states that associations must not trade for profit. This does not mean that a housing association cannot make a profit, but rather that the pursuit of profit cannot be the main aim of the organisation. Profits or surpluses must be ploughed back for housing purposes and not distributed to members of the association.

The definition does not limit the term 'housing association' to those bodies which actually provide housing. So long as one of the purposes of the organisation falls within the above definition the body may be defined as a housing association. Thus those organisations that sponsor or promote housing provision by other groups would be included. Such bodies are known as 'secondary housing associations'. There is no legal restriction, however, on an organisation calling itself a housing association, although it may have no connection with the sector.

Charitable status

Some associations may be 'registered charities'. This is a body registered under the Charities Act 1960. Many associations also have the status of 'exempt charity'. This is a body registered under the I and P Act 1965 which has charitable status but is not directly controlled by the Charity Commissioners.

Charitable status confers privileges, not least tax advantages, but it may also constrain the activities of an association as it may only undertake those activities which are in accordance with its objects. Typical objects might read thus (in the rather archaic language of the charitable tradition):

> The objects of the association shall be to carry on for the benefit of the community the business of
> (a) providing housing and associated amenities for persons in neces-sitous circumstances upon terms appropriate to their means;
> (b) providing for aged persons in need, housing and any associated amenities specially designed or adapted to meet the disabilities or requirements of such persons.

Thus the objects are limited to providing housing for the poor and the aged and, furthermore, may only be altered with the permission of the Charity Commissioners. This area is complex and governed by case law. In general terms, however, it is accepted that persons who cannot secure appropriate social rented housing or afford to purchase a home owing to the high cost of housing in that area would count as being in housing need and be relevant to the objects of a charity.

Charitable status does restrict what an association can achieve although it is perceived as valuable in establishing credibility (for example, in fund raising). Several associations converted to charitable status as a means of avoiding the right to buy provisions of the 1980 Housing Act. More asso-ciations may yet seek this status to avoid Corporation Tax, relief from which was withdrawn from non-charitable associations following the 1997 Autumn Budget.

The limitations imposed by charitable status are of particular relevance if a charity wishes to purchase tenanted accommodation, for example. There has been a lack of clarity as to whether this activity is properly within the objects of a charity. In the case of the acquisition of portfolios of housing from the private sector this has usually been regarded as acceptable as it is in the interests of the community that the houses be purchased and improved by a charitable housing association.

A further limitation recently reviewed, was that charitable associations could not build for sale and were therefore precluded from undertaking shared ownership or outright sale activities. An association wishing to undertake such activities had to form a non-charitable subsidiary. Since

1994, however, on the advice of the Charities Commission and the Department of the Environment, in certain circumstances charitable associations can undertake new build shared ownership and Do It Yourself Shared Ownership (DIYSO) schemes. Details of the advice are set out in Corporation circular 29/94, *Charitable Housing Associations and Shared Ownership.* There are three sets of circumstances where this is permissible: first, direct provision where the recipient is in housing need owing to poverty or in 'necessitous circumstances' owing to age or infirmity. Associations must ensure that recipients are proper beneficiaries, however. The second set of circumstances relate to indirect provision: for example, where shared ownership is provided to a tenant whose means have improved in order to create a vacancy for a person who would be considered as a charitable beneficiary.

The third circumstance is incidental development. In this case shared ownership dwellings may be provided as part of a rented development to achieve financial viability of the development as a whole. Charitable associations wishing to undertake shared ownership should therefore ensure that the activity remains a relatively small part of the total operation in order to comply with charity law.

The law surrounding charitable objects is complex and readers wishing to study the matter in greater detail are referred to Alder and Handy (1991, 2nd edn).

Housing associations may provide housing for others or for members, the latter are known as co-operative housing associations. These are fully mutual housing associations usually registered under the I and P Act 1965. 'Fully mutual' means that, in accordance with its rules, all members must be tenants or prospective tenants and all tenants must be members. Conversely, non-mutual associations provide housing for others. A form of housing co-operative is the self-build society, which has the object of providing housing for occupation by its members built by the members themselves using their own labour.

Finally, a 'registered housing association' is one that was registered with the Housing Corporation under section 5 of the Housing Associations Act 1985 prior to the implementation the registration system introduced by the Housing Act 1996.

2.2   Registration with the Housing Corporation

Section 1 of the Housing Act 1996 charges the Housing Corporation with the responsibility for establishing a register of social landlords which must be open to public inspection. As registration confers privileges, not least access to public funding, the criteria for registration are clearly laid down. As one would expect, the criteria mirror to a large extent the definitions of a housing association. The criteria apply to all registered social landlords, (RSLs) and not just traditional housing associations, however.

Eligibility for registration

There are three types of bodies eligible for registration: a registered charity that is also an housing association, an industrial and provident society and a company. The conditions require that, (section 2.(2)):

> the body is non-profit making and is established for the purpose of, or has among its objects or powers, the provision, construction, improvement or management of –

(a) houses to be kept available for letting, or
(b) houses for occupation by members of the body, where the rules of the body restrict membership to persons entitled or prospectively entitled (as tenants or otherwise) to occupy a house provided or managed by the body,or
(c) hostels.

These are known as main purposes. The body may also have as permissible, additional purposes or objects as specified in section 2 (subsection 4), one or more of the following:

(a) providing land, amenities or services, or providing, constructing or repairing or improving buildings, for its residents, either exclusively or together with other persons;
(b) acquiring, or repairing and improving, or creating by the conversion of houses or other property, houses to be disposed of on sale, on lease or on shared ownership terms;
(c) constructing houses to be disposed of on shared ownership terms;
(d) managing houses which are held on leases or other lettings (not being houses within subsection (2)(a) or (b)) or blocks of flats);
(e) providing services of any description for owners or occupiers of houses in arranging or carrying out works of maintenance, repair or improvement, or encouraging or facilitating the carrying out of such works;
(f) encouraging and giving advice on the forming of housing associations or providing services for, and giving advice on the running of, such associations and other voluntary organisations concerned with housing, or matters connected with housing.

It should be noted that the additional purposes of RSLs include the power to provide services of any description for owners and occupiers of properties where they are undertaking maintenance or improvement works. These services may not be purely housing services. This power is particularly valuable for bodies undertaking 'care and repair' schemes for elderly occupiers who wish to stay in their own homes (see Chapter 9). They may also give advice to any voluntary organisation on housing and related matters. RSLs may also acquire and convert commercial premises that form an incidental part of a main development project and for a limited period of time may even continue to run the business that they have acquired. The Secretary of State has the power to add to these purposes by order. In 1999 the permissable purposes were extended to enable RSLs to provide services and amenities to people who are not resident in their property (so long as some of their residents benefit), and to engage in certain regeneration activities. This extension will enable RSLs to fully engage in activities such as the New Deal for Communities.

In order to be eligible for registration a body must include the fundamental housing purposes in its rules. If an existing association wishes to undertake any of the additional activities for the first time it must change its rules to permit it. Registered social landlords may also set up subsidiary bodies to undertake these additional objects.

The Housing Corporation must publish and consult on the registration criteria. The Corporation may register any eligible body, and may also remove landlords from the register. Appeals against involuntary de-registration lie with the High Court. Prior to registration the Corporation will examine the governing instrument or rules of the proposed RSL, and its business plan forecasting the outturn for the next five years; management and staffing details and the skills and qualifications of the board, including other directorships are also important. The criteria also require the body to demonstrate that it is adequately controlled by its governing body, usually known as the committee of management or board. The board must be able to demonstrate independence from other organisations (this is particularly relevant to voluntary transfer bodies). The Housing Corporation insist on no more than 20 per cent local authority representation on the boards of these organisations. The criteria also require it to be demonstrated that there is no duality or conflict of interest between board members and the RSL. This issue relates to the accountability of the RSL generally and is discussed further in Chapter 4. The criteria also govern financial requirements including the requirement to submit to the Corporation audited annual accounts and the need to demonstrate financial viability through the business plan. The Corporation will consider the likely managerial efficiency of the association and its future role. The Corporation is unlikely to register an RSL which will duplicate the work of one already registered. The criteria also take into account the priority given by the RSL to equal opportunities in its policies and practices.

Once registered, the RSL may bid for capital grants from the Housing Corporation and for revenue funding on a competitive basis. However, on registration, an RSL loses some of its independence in return for public funding. The Corporation's powers to deal with registered social land-lords are very wide and increased following the Housing Act 1996. These regulatory powers and duties are discussed in detail in Chapter 3 and are set out in schedule 1 of the 1996 Housing Act. The Corporation approves disposals by registered social landlords and must approve any merger, transfer of engagements or winding-down of an RSL. The Corporation can also bring about the demise of an RSL under statutory powers of inquiry if it has cause to believe that it would be in the public interest to do so. Such controls are the price paid for public funding and to ensure as great a degree of public accountability as possible, in the operation and practices of registered social landlords. The presence of a statutory regula-tor also provides reassurance to the private funders.

Registered Social Landlords are subject to the provisions of the Performance Standards and Residents' Charters established by the Housing Corporation which safeguard the rights of tenants and give guid-ance to tenants on expectations of how RSLs should deliver services.

Readers should note that there are separate registration criteria for RSLs formed as a result of housing stock transfers from local authorities.

De-registration

The Housing Act 1996 section 4(4) also permits registered social landlords to seek de-registration in certain circumstances. Under section 5(2), the Housing Corporation has published *'de-registration criteria for registered social landlords'* (circular R4 38/96) which sets out the circumstances under which this would be considered. The criteria are based on the twin princi-ples of safeguarding public assets and protecting the interests of residents. De-registration is only available to small organisations which have under 50 homes or bedspaces in management or which have received no more than £1 million of capital public subsidy. The Corporation will consult with other stakeholders before making its final decision. The de-registration process was introduced to assist small almshouses and Abbeyfield Societies in particular, which are neither expanding nor developing, in order to relieve them (and the Housing Corporation) from the bureaucracy attendant upon registered social landlord status. It remains to be seen how many smaller bodies will take up this opportunity to de-register.

2.3   Structures and activities

Table 2.1 shows the relative size of RSLs. It should be noted that few are of the size approaching a small local authority housing department (10 000+) with by far the largest group comprising the 'smalls' with fewer than 100 homes in ownership. Since the mid-1980s the Housing

Table 2.1   *Registered Social Landlord size as at March 1997 (England)*
(self-contained stock)

10 000 homes	1001–10 000	101–1000	0–100	Total
15	200	238	1697	2150

Source: *RSLs in 1997 – General Report* (The Housing Corporation 1998).

Corporation has registered about 80 new bodies per annum. These were largely new co-operatives, almshouses, Abbeyfield Societies and voluntary transfer associations. This figure looks set to increase as other bodies (especially local housing companies) are formed to receive the transfer of local authority stock.

Since 1980 the range and type of RSL activity has grown. In particular, many organisations have set up subsidiary bodies to undertake activities that the rules of the parent body may not permit. The objects of a charitable association outlined earlier may preclude it from undertaking any activity that does not meet the narrow objects of housing the aged, relief of poverty, or housing those in necessitous circumstances. Some have registered companies to build houses for sale with the profits covenanted to the parent body.

Some of these subsidiaries undertake to provide community services and non-housing activities. In 1987 the National Federation of Housing Associations (NFHA) published the first directory of such initiatives. The survey found that the schemes fitted broadly into five main categories: (a) general community services which cover an enormous range from child care and home insulation projects to care and repair schemes and housing advice centres, (b) Employment and Training Schemes assisting young people, often from ethnic minorities; (c) separate bodies for mixed use and commercial development schemes; (d) property maintenance and building services; (e) some associations have separate bodies providing financial services. By 1998 such activities had become more prevalent with the growing role of RSLs in partnerships to bring about urban regeneration and as a result of their assuming the major role as providers of new social rented housing. In developing larger-scale estates, and through transfers of local authority stock, they have become often the only new providers of housing in an area and, as major investors with many assets, not just their stock but in terms of skills, purchasing power and community links, many have been well placed to develop this wider role. Initiatives that provide more than housing have been collectively termed 'housing plus'. These activities are examined in more detail in Chapter 7.

In addition, since 1990 more landlords have become actively involved in the provision of community care services. Several have established subsidiaries to deliver these services. The partial or full transfer of stock from local authorities and Housing Action Trusts to existing RSLs, and the trend towards the restructuring of the sector through merger, have also led to developments in the structures of RSLs.

Group structures

Some RSLs are actively forming a group structure comprising one or more subsidiaries of a parent body. The subsidiaries may be an RSL or an un-registered body. The development of such susidiaries has in turn led to revised (and at times contradictory) guidance from the Housing Corporation which has become concerned that the activities of subsidiaries, especially unregistered ones over which it has no regulatory control, could adversely affect the financial position of the 'parent', exposing it, the Corporation's investment and the tenants to undue risk. Guidance has been revised regularly in this somewhat complex and vexed area. The complexity derives from the need to ensure that a number of potentially conflicting interests are reconciled, and these are highlighted below.

Subsidiaries are defined by sections 60 and 61 of the Housing Act 1996. Broadly, a subsidiary exists where there is a company or industrial and provident society where the RSL is a member and controls the composition of the board or holds more than half the nominal value of the company's equity share capital or if it is a subsidiary of another company which is a subsidiary of the RSL.

A corporation circular was issued in 1994[2] revising guidance issued in 1988, which in turn was revised in 1997[3] pending the outcome of a further policy review. In summary, the policy which had prevented an RSL from establishing a subsidiary to undertake any activity unless it was legally able to support this activity itself was overturned. Parent RSLs are no longer legally required to be (legally) capable of supporting their registered subsidiaries although they are expected to if legally capable of doing so. Thus a charitable parent can establish a non-charitable subsidiary.

The principles of group structures are based upon the following objectives:

(a)   investment in the social housing sector must be protected;
(b)   tenants' interests must be protected;
(c)   the reputation of the sector must be protected in order to secure private finance;
(d)   the main focus of RSLs both individually and within the Group must be the provision of social housing;
(e)   RSLs must be allowed to structure their operations in an efficient and businesslike way.

The Corporation's requirements for RSLs within a group are that its vertical and horizontal relationships with all RSLs and unregistered organisations within the group should be made explicit within all annual returns and accounts. These should make clear the status of each entity and its relationship with the parent. Each RSL within a group is expected to be financially viable and able to stand alone.

Conflicts of interest of Board members must be recognised and dealt with and parent bodies should at all times be satisfied that they are in control of their subsidiaries. In the case of non-registered subsidiaries these must be:

(a)   separate legal entities;
(b)   at arms length in respect of all financial and contractual arrangements;
(c)   on a commercial and secure low risk basis;
(d)   established only after professional advice.

The assets of the parent RSL must not be allowed to leak into the subsidiary to ensure that public funded assets and tenants' interests are not put at risk. In effect, registered social landlords should not stand behind any non-registered subsidiaries that run into difficulty.

Several new group structures have been formed in recent years. They are also a potential route for smaller associations to share services in a group with others, or with a larger parent body while still maintaining some autonomy and independent identity. Group structures offer varying degrees of control between the parent and the subsidiary. In a wholly controlled subsidiary the parent has the right to appoint the whole of the management board. The board of the parent, which may be merely a holding company providing financial and development services across the Group, will decide overall policy and strategy and agree the budget and financial plans. The subsidiaries may then have devolved powers with regard to the delivery of housing management and maintenance services. The parent body will also monitor the activities of the Group through reports and formal agreements between it and the subsidiaries. Careful attention must be paid to the servicing arrangements between member organisations: for example, staff may be shared but only within well-defined limitations.

There is no doubt that group structures will represent an important feature of the sector in the coming years as, in addition to the circumstances outlined above, the group structure also offers a natural home for the development of local housing companies in the years ahead. Furthermore, massing into larger groups should lead to economies of scale and consequent savings in operational costs and overheads. This is now an important issue to many RSLs which are examining ways of cutting costs to keep rents down and to enable greater reinvestment in their stock.

If associations wish to share services or co-operate in other ways without the formal linkage of a group structure, then federal structures are also permitted, allowing each association to remain entirely independent.

Regulating Diversity

In 1999 the Housing Corporation published a consultation document *Regulating Diversity*. The paper is concerned with regulating the risks faced by RSLs when they diversify into new areas of activity, often through the group structure route. The paper introduces the concept of 'core activities', essentially the provision of grant aided social housing, and suggests that limits should be set on the extent to which RSLs should diversify, for example, into care activities or market rented accommodation. The Corporation will, in future, seek a balance of 2:1 in favour of social housing and require RSLs to notify them of any project that might disturb this balance, prior to proceeding with it. Those with a high-level of non-core activities are recommended to pursue them through non-registered subsidiaries to protect their social housing assets.

2.4   Small registered social landlords

It is appropriate to consider at this point the structure, activities and concerns of the so-called 'smalls' or (as many prefer to be thought of, 'the not-so-big' RSLs). The small RSLs represent over 80 per cent of the sector. A small association is officially defined as having fewer than 250 units in management, or no more than one scheme in development. In 1995 42 per cent of registered housing associations had no full-time paid staff and a further 32 per cent had between one and five staff members.

The majority of problems faced by small RSLs emanate from their size, yet this is also a source of their quality. It has been said that small RSLs harness the latent resources of thousands of lay volunteers. They may also be particularly responsive to the needs of tenants. In addition, as board members carry out many of the functions themselves, they may also achieve a greater degree of accountability to tenants and possibly the community that they serve. They can be responsive to a very particular local need and have been responsible for much of the sector's pioneering work. It is important to remember that all established RSLs were small once, and it is to be hoped that the diverse qualities they offer will still be valued in future years, despite current trends.

Small landlords face a number of difficulties. In particular, they do not always have access to the staff and skills resources of the larger organisations, and must rely on board members, one or two generic staff members and consultancy services, often from larger RSLs, to undertake financial and, in particular, development activities. The National Housing

Federation has always valued the contribution of the small associations which represent nearly half its membership. A standing group of the NHF represents and lobbies in the interests of the small associations and the NHF produces publications and runs seminars to assist in their development. The funding regime has included some concessions to small associations in the past.

When the Housing Act 1988 was first enacted there was a great deal of concern that smaller housing associations would be unable to compete and have a sufficient asset base to continue to develop under the new regime. Wide-scale mergers were predicted which have not materialised to date. On the contrary, although some associations did expand dramatically in the early 1990s with some very large development allocations, the small associations continued to develop and often provided good value for money on their schemes. Nevertheless the ability to compete is going to be even more difficult in the future, given that competition for funds may intensify following the Housing Act 1996. Value for money criteria now include rent levels which have tended to be higher in small associations which do not have the ability to rent pool. These RSLs will inevitably find it harder to raise finance against limited assets in future too.

Whether mergers or federations will increasingly happen remains to be seen. Apart from intense lobbying by the RSLs themselves, part of their success to date can be attributed to the consensus that the diversity that they bring to the sector is valuable. This was confirmed by the Housing Corporation in their joint publication with the National Housing Federation, *Role and Diversity of Housing Associations*.[4] The document set out a range of strategies to ensure that organisations of a range of sizes and function could continue to contribute whilst at the same time meeting performance and accountability criteria. Although not all strategies were eventually realised, the Corporation continued to monitor the proportion of the annual Approved Development Programme allocated to small housing associations. It encouraged larger RSLs to ensure that smaller ones were involved in larger developments through the consortium route. This in itself has caused some difficulties for the management of the resulting multi-landlord estates, which are explored further in Chapter 7.

The Corporation has also encouraged lenders to support small RSLs and has endorsed development agency arrangements with larger partners. In 1996/97 over 500 associations received Housing Corporation funding, representing a reduction from 620 in 1991/92, which is an indication of the gradually declining role of the smaller RSL in new development. The future for the smaller landlord may then lie in co-operation with others, especially for new development and more particularly in concentrating aspirations on the management of homes owned and developed by larger partners on their behalf, rather than the pursuit of ownership *per se*. This could be of benefit to the tenants if they then enjoy lower rents through this model whilst still having access to the local management and particular skills prevalent in many smaller organisations.

2.5 Black and minority ethnic associations

In recognising the housing needs of the black and ethnic minority communities, the Housing Corporation has sought to develop provision for these groups through small specialist RSLs. In addition, as set out in Chapter 3, the Housing Corporation also has a duty to ensure that equal opportunities strategies are implemented in RSLs. It has had two five-year programmes since 1986. The first, 'The Five Year Programme', was established with the aim of registering 25 new black-led associations with a programme that would provide 150 dwellings for each association by 1991. The second strategy, from 1991 to 1996, aimed to build on this start, helping those associations to achieve viability.

The aims of the programmes have been two-fold: first, to increase the provision of housing for black and minority ethnic communities and, second, to increase the participation of people from these groups in the housing association sector. These organisations were to be led and controlled by the communities themselves.

The strategy has been successful. By March 1996 the number of these bodies registered with the Housing Corporation had risen from 18 in 1991 to 60; two RSLs established before the strategy was introduced – ASRA catering for the needs of Asian people and Ujima, a black-led association – have been especially successful and have grown enormously. Ujima now owns over 3000 homes. Black and minority ethnic RSLs now manage over 17 000 homes, over half of which are in London, and have received over £660million in capital grants from the Housing Corporation.

Revenue grants have amounted to £3.5 million. In addition, stock transfers from other larger RSLs to these fledgling bodies have amounted to some 2800 homes. Forty RSLs are now viable as opposed to only four in 1991.[5] The strategy was also concerned with the housing of people from the black and ethnic minority communities. Approximately 13 per cent of new RSL lettings go to households from these communities. Landlords are also employing more black and ethnic minority staff who now comprise 10 per cent of all staff. The initiative has been successful across the country but the role of these associations (especially in London) has been highlighted in an NHF report.[6] This report recognised the achievements to date and put the case for continuing training, stock transfer and funding initiatives to further build on these.

As smaller RSLs, black and minority ethnic organisations have faced the same difficulties as all small RSLs in the light of the prevailing competitive climate and the constraints imposed by the financial regime.

Several have been successful at raising private finance and have developed new housing both in their own right and as partners of larger landlords or in consortia as highlighted in the section above. The Corporation introduced a further black and minority ethnic Housing Needs and Enabling Framework document in 1996 and another, policy document in 1998.[7] The enabling framework and the 1998 policy document emphasise the support for consumers rather than the promotion of RSLs as providers of social housing for these groups. It covers commitments to empowering black and minority ethnic communities through improvements in representation on the governing bodies of all RSLs and improved recruitment levels of staff from these communities into the sector. The policy reaffirms support for specialist associations and promises a major re-evaluation of the policy in 2002/03.

2.6   Housing co-operatives

Co-operatives are also small associations but are different in that they concentrate on housing for members. No study of the housing association sector would be complete without some comment on their nature and their work. Co-operative housing has enjoyed a period of expansion since 1975, and represents an innovative and radical alternative to the traditional tenures of owner-occupation and renting from a social or private landlord. Housing co-operatives take many different forms, reflecting the nature and extent of ownership of the dwellings by the co-op members and have been defined as 'associations by which dwellers control their own housing, even if they do not own it'.[8]

Thus, control over the process of housing by the dweller is the central concept of the co-operative housing movement. In Britain, the most common form is the 'par value' (or non-equity) rented co-operative where each member holds a nominal £1 share. Ownership of this nature is referred to as common ownership. In addition, there are shared ownership co-operatives where members have a stake in the equity which they can sell on. These co-ops have been established to encourage low-cost home ownership rather than to develop the co-operative ideal. co-ownership societies, mentioned in Chapter 1, are a further form of co-operative but again the object of membership is to obtain a share in the increasing value of the equity with the aim of moving on possibly into owner-occupation using the premium payment as a deposit.

Self-build societies

A further form of co-operative is the self-build society. Self-build societies co-operate to undertake the actual process of building their own homes, traditionally for owner-occupation but more recently for rent. In the case of self-build for sale or rent, the 'sweat equity' created by the labour of members of the group reduces the cost of producing the homes. Some 2000 new homes per annum are currently being built by these societies, and in 1989 a new agency 'The Community Self-Build Agency', was founded to promote the self-build concept.

The NHF has published guides to encourage young homeless people and unemployed people to become involved, and a manual for self-build associations in association with the Housing Corporation.

Tenant management co-operatives

Housing co-operatives may not involve ownership at all, as is the case when groups of tenants take over the management and maintenance of their own homes with the existing landlord retaining ownership. Known as tenant management co-operatives, these organisations represent a more sophisticated level of tenant participation and are considered further in Chapter 7.

Par value co-operatives

Co-ops may be companies limited by guarantee but if they wish to take advantage of Housing Corporation funding, they must register with the Corporation itself. Co-operative housing associations are eligible for grant which assists them in providing housing for members at affordable rent levels, through the acquisition and rehabilitation of old properties or new building.

Par value co-operative housing associations are usually 'fully mutual' defined in the Housing Associations Act 1985 as bodies where all tenants are members and all members are either tenants or prospective tenants. Fully mutual co-operatives may grant and assign tenancies to members only. Registration as an Industrial and Provident Society can be important as it confers advantages upon the co-op. Such bodies do not pay tax on rental income and may also claim mortgage interest tax relief on loans raised to provide the dwellings.

Secondary co-operatives

The organisations which own dwellings are known as primary co-operatives. Secondary co-operatives own no properties but exist to provide development advice and other services to the primaries and are funded through a variety of grants. Secondary co-operatives act as catalysts and provide each fledgling primary with the resources and skills to guide the members through the formation and registration process. Once a primary is registered, the secondary will usually act as development agent, procuring the site and undertaking the administration to secure loans and grants from the funding authority. The secondary will oversee the consultation process and also advise on the future management of the completed dwellings. The secondaries are vital to the growth and expansion of the co-operative housing movement. They argued for and achieved the introduction of a co-operative promotion allowance to assist in covering the cost of development work. Nevertheless, secondaries still have to struggle to survive. Part of the role of secondaries is to provide education. Without this process co-operatives cannot expand. They will only grow in proportion to the time and effort that can be devoted to the educational process.

2.7   Voluntary transfer associations

An important development in the shape and composition of the sector has been the establishment of many new registered social landlords as a result of large-scale or partial voluntary transfers of local authority stock. Transfers have been to new local authority sponsored associations or (in fewer cases) partial transfers and single estates have been transferred to existing RSLs. Local authorities have the power to dispose of their stock to autonomous, independent bodies subject to the consent of the Secretary of State under sections 32–43 of the Housing Act 1985 as amended by the Housing and Planning Act 1986. Under section 10 of the Housing and Planning Act 1986 local authorities may also transfer their management functions to housing associations or other bodies. In both cases, the local authority has a duty to consult with its tenants on the proposals under section 6 of the Housing Act 1986. In 1988 the Department of the Environment issued guidance on the large scale voluntary transfer of local authority housing to private bodies. The guidance set out the criteria that the Secretary of State would consider when giving consent to such stock transfers and emphasised the need for the independence of the new landlord from the local authority.

By September 1997, since the completion of the first stock transfer by Chiltern District Council to Chiltern Hundreds Housing Association, some 50 authorities had achieved a transfer. Over 250 000 homes (or 5 per cent of public sector stock) had been transferred, supported by private finance amounting to over £3 billion. The reasons behind stock transfers are varied. From the authorities' point of view however, the financial regime introduced by the Local Government and Housing Act of 1989 placed new constraints upon them.

Local Government and Housing Act 1989

The benefits of the maturing assets of council housing have long been recognised. Government has attempted over the last 20 years or so to have the benefits of these assets transferred to the Exchequer rather than enjoyed by the local authorities. The 1989 Act finally succeeded in this through the control of spending of capital receipts requiring 75 per cent to be set aside for debt redemption and allowing only 25 per cent to be reinvested. In addition, the ring-fencing of Housing Revenue Account surpluses, so that they could not contribute to the general fund of local authorities and, importantly, using those surpluses to offset the costs of housing benefit subsidy, added to this effect. As Wilcox *et al.* stated in a Joseph Rowntree Research report: 'in effect the 1989 Act "nationalised" both the capital and revenue benefits from the maturing asset of council housing for the Treasury by imposing new financial controls'.[9]

Wilcox also noted that it was during this time that housing associations were enjoying the benefits of large-scale investment having moved centre-stage in the provision of social housing. Freed from public expenditure contraints, with only the subsidy counting against the PSBR (Public Sector Borrowing Requirement), their programmes as we have seen were expanding rapidly. This was purely as a result of political dogma as no evidence at the time suggested that associations were more effective managers of housing than councils.

Large scale voluntary transfers were therefore seen by some local authorities as a way forward that would secure housing assets for the benefit of the local community.

Faced with virtually no ability to provide new housing, but having to cope with the increasing demands of homelessness and (in some cases) major disrepair of the stock, transfer was seen as a favourable route forward. Transfers have succeeded mainly in the shire districts where the value of the stock has enabled substantial receipts to be generated which have then been partly available for investment in social housing. It does not provide a solution for those many more authorities, particularly in urban areas, whose debts exceed the value of the homes. It is the position of these authorities combined with a number of other motivating factors that has led to the development of the local housing company concept, which is explored further later. The concept of transfer, therefore, emanated more from the need to circumvent resource restrictions rather than from a desire to transfer stock for political or operational advantage.

The transfer of the stock reduces an authority's housing debt and allows it to invest 25 per cent of its net receipts in local authority development grant. The creation of a locally sponsored housing association also enables the transferor authority to keep much of its stock together and to have some influence on the board of management. The favoured route for transfer has been the creation of an industrial and provident society, which is also registered with the Housing Corporation. Although some local authority staff, especially housing staff, have transferred with the stock, finance, administration and development functions have usually been newly created.

In 1992 the Department of the Environment published a consultation paper on voluntary transfers.[10] The scale of transfers at that time had impacted on public sector finances. While the benefits from receipts in terms of social investment had been substantial, the cost to the Exchequer had also been high as it was faced with meeting the costs of the housing benefit subsidy bill for the newly transferred tenants. In just one case the cost to the Treasury of forgone rent surpluses contributing to the cost of housing benefit subsidy amounted to some £7 million.

Clearly the Conservative Government could not allow transfers to continue on this scale without ensuring that there were real financial as well as political benefits from the programme. The consultation paper addressed these issues by proposing a limit to the size of transfers to a single landlord which was eventually set at 5000 homes. In addition it introduced a 'levy' to be paid to central government from receipts after repayment of housing debt, to offset the cost to the Treasury of the transfer. A limit was to be placed on the total number of transfers to be granted consent each year based on the resources available.

Following consultation the proposals were incorporated into the current guidelines.[11] All transfers over 500 homes are subject to these rules which set out the stages through which the transfer should progress to enable formal consent to be granted. In the autumn of each year the Secretary of State invites local authorities to put forward bids for transfer. Since 1993 the programme has had a guide limit of 25 000 homes per annum although this has often been exceeded. Costs to the Treasury, the impact on the PSBR and general government expenditure, in addition to other housing and related outputs, are taken into account in assessing which bids will be approved. The Department undertakes a rigorous financial appraisal of all bids in accordance with further financial guidelines which were published in 1995.[12] These guidelines set out the financial appraisal of both large-scale (whole) and partial transfers of stock. In the case of partial transfers pursued for regeneration purposes, for example, the evaluation takes into account the value for money achieved by any new development envisaged following transfer. It takes as its benchmark the grant that would be available for a similar new development undertaken by a housing association funded through the Housing Corporation's new development programme. Once an authority has secured a place on the programme it is expected to complete the transfer before the end of that programme year. It must also be able to demonstrate that the transfer has tenants' support through a ballot showing a simple majority in favour.

Consultation with tenants

The position of tenants after the transfer is paramount. A ballot of those tenants affected is expected. It is also, of course, good practice to ensure that tenants are fully aware of the impact on their homes of future rent levels and rights and services in order that they can take an informed view of what the proposals offer. Consultation proceeds in two stages. First, informal consultation on general proposals takes place once the potential transferee is established. Formal consultation is required through section 106A and schedule 3A of the Housing Act 1985 (as inserted by section 6 and schedule 1 to the Housing and Planning Act 1986). This requires that all secure tenants be consulted regarding transfer of their homes. Informal consultation will make use of a variety of methods including pamphlets, newsletters, meetings, telephone hot-lines and advertisements. Formal consultation commences following the valuation of the stock to ensure that reliable information can be given about future rent levels and repairs. Formal consultation is also in two stages. Stage one involves a formal notice to tenants which will set out the details of the proposal and the identity of the prospective new landlord, the likely consequences of disposal for the tenant and their position regarding the right to buy. The consequences that must be explained include rent levels and future mechanisms for increase; repairs and capital improvement programmes; security of tenure and grounds for possession, tenancy rights including those of succession and the right to buy. Tenants transferring to a new landlord become assured tenants but have a 'preserved right to buy'. The consultation document should also set out details of the mandate required by the local authority, details of funding, the purchaser's policies on rent arrears, allocations and tenant participation. The purchaser's view regarding any existing or proposed Tenant Management Organisations under the right to manage framework is also important. The notice should also invite representations within a reasonable period. The second stage notice sets out any significant changes to the proposals; it also gives 28 days notice of objections to be made to the Secretary of State noting that the Secretary of State may not approve the transfer if it appears that the majority of tenants object to it. A ballot usually takes place immediately after the second stage notice has been served and is overseen by an independent body. It is essential that the consultation process is meaningful and effective, and to assist this an adviser to the tenants is appointed, known as a 'tenants' friend'. Consultative fora should also be established.

In appraising the stock transfer option the authority will usually appoint an external consultant. The stock must be valued and a long-term 30-year business plan drawn up. This will need to take into account the costs of private finance, the need to undertake a programme of repairs,

rent increases required, right to buy receipts and how these are apportioned to the transferor authority. There will also be collateral agreements
with the transferor regarding homelessness obligations and nominations
to the stock. The business plan is essential in that it will inform the
Department as to the costs and viability of the transfer, and it will also be
required by the private funder and the Housing Corporation. Given that
the preferred vehicle is likely to be a registered socal landlord, the
Housing Corporation is usually quite closely involved from the outset in
any proposed transfer. The valuation of the stock is preceded by a stock
condition survey. The valuation method is carried out according to 'tenanted market value' based upon a contractual commitment to retain the
housing for social letting.

Once established, the funding and regulation of LSVT associations is
as for all registered social landlords. Although many concentrate on the
delivery of services, several are now in a position to undertake new
development and they must bid for Corporation funding as set out in
Chapter 6. Some are funded by their sponsoring authority to provide new
homes although they may still have to compete for this with other
housing associations. Their financial position is different in that some
remain heavily encumbered by the loans they had to raise to fund the
purchase, and any programme of capital improvements. Their business
plans often forecast deficits which will not reduce until the medium
term. This position will alter over time and many LSVTs will eventually
start to accrue surpluses after which time they will have the ability to
develop new homes on a greater scale. Some have already been able to
re-finance their activities and are indeed already producing surpluses,
while others now operate in several local authority districts. While seen
by many as a symbol of successful transfer, the sponsoring authority has
in some cases felt that this gives cause for concern; the association is
now no longer sufficiently focused on its original community and local
area.

Partial transfers

Partial transfers, often to existing RSLs are becoming more common. They
represent a major opportunity for partnership and growth for existing
associations. Individual estates such as the Partington area in Manchester
(which transferred just over 1400 homes to the Manchester and District
Housing Group) is an example. The 1995 financial guidelines set out how
these transfers are appraised. Partial transfers of stock have also occurred
where ballots for large scale transfer have failed. Proposals for minority
transfers at Cherwell and and Thanet District Councils, for example, succeeded where large-scale proposals had failed. The 5000 maximum limit
has also led to partial transfers. They are useful as part of a regeneration

initiative as in the London Borough of Hackney. Partial transfers are flexible and can be pursued for a variety of different purposes, helping to meet the aspirations of both councils and tenants. In some cases local authorities are also transferring homes by trickle-transfer. This involves the transfer of vacant homes usually to existing associations. The partial transfer sets the scene for transfer in future to local housing companies and it is to these that we now turn.

2.8   Local housing companies

Local housing companies are defined as:

> An organisation:
> - constituted independently of the public sector;
> - structured to be formally accountable to the local authority, tenants and others;
> - in which the local authority interest is in a minority and the company is not under the effective control of the authority; and
> - which improves, develops and manages housing, usually transferred from the public sector.

This is the definition given at the start of the *Good Practice Guide on Local Housing Companies* published in 1995 by the Chartered Institute of Housing which has championed their development.[13]

Local housing companies may become one of the most common forms of registered social landlord under the provisions of the Housing Act 1996. It is therefore important to understand their nature and how they relate to traditional housing associations. Local authorities had the power to establish local housing companies prior to the passage of the 1996 Act but the recent legislation provides a coherent regulatory framework for these potential landlords.

The search for an alternative

As stated, voluntary transfer to a housing association at tenanted market value only benefited those districts where value of the stock exceeded the housing debt, although this looked set to change at the time of writing. Dowries were not payable either (prior to the introduction of Estate Renewal Challenge Funding), excluding most urban authorities from the transfer process even if the political will was there. The housing association route is also perceived as insufficiently accountable to the local authority or community, particularly by some Labour controlled authorities. Another model was required to achieve a number of aims. Firstly, the need to increase investment in social housing to enable new provision to take place, and even more importantly to fund the massive backlog of repair and improvement to local authority stock, especially in urban areas. This needed to be achieved without major requirements for public sector investment and its consequent effects on the PSBR. Secondly, a model needed to be found that would permit local authorities to compete on a level playing field with housing associations where only public subsidy and not private funding counts as public expenditure. Third, a model that was more accountable to the local community, in which the local authority had a greater role than the voluntary transfer association, was considered desirable. At the outset the need to limit the amounts of private finance required, given the demands on these funds from the housing association development programme and voluntary transfers, was also considered important. Initial research also suggested that companies could be more cost-effective in terms of costs or savings to the Treasury than voluntary transfers.

Wilcox *et al.*[14] noted that the development of thinking regarding local housing companies stems from the the Second Inquiry into British Housing in 1991 which originally suggested a 'transfer of engagements' of all the assets and liabilities relating to council's housing stock to financially independent bodies. The concept of arm's-length companies had also been promoted by Nick Raynsford, MP. This approach would have removed the need to raise large sums of private finance as the receiving company takes over the loan debts of the stock, raising only what was required for further renovation and development. This had its attractions and would have marked the end of the spectacle of huge sums of private finance chasing the transfer of existing homes without a jot more new housing being created.

The Joseph Rowntree Foundation commissioned research based on these ideas from the University of Wales College of Cardiff, which placed local housing companies firmly on the housing policy agenda. The report prepared by Wilcox *et al.* set out the rationale for local housing companies as highlighted above and evaluated them using financial case studies of ten English and three Scottish authorities against a range of models. The report noted that legislation was not required to establish local housing companies but that local authorities already had the powers to establish companies under the revised framework established by the 1989 Act.

This legislation would allow a minority interest in them up to 49 per cent despite the 20 per cent interest restriction operating in the case of LSVTs. The latter are restricted not by legislation but by the Housing Corporation's registration criteria which impose effective independence from local authority control. In 1997 however, the Corporation indicated to the Anglia Group that up to 51 per cent council representation might be permissible for registration purposes. The rules surrounding local authority controlled, arm's-length and influenced companies are quite complex and are set out in Part V of the 1989 Act as amended by statutory instrument No. 849 1995.

The Rowntree research also highlighted the flexibility of the company model and its enhanced accountability when compared with either local council housing or housing associations. The model would allow much greater representation by tenants on the controlling Board. They could take up to two thirds of the places and in effect become majority shareholders. The report argued that the national potential for companies was huge. It concluded by stating:

> They offer the prospect of, not of the end of council housing, but of a fitting and beneficial evolution ... Social policy choices that offer the prospects of 'all win' outcomes for all parties are all too rare. Local housing companies should be given the opportunity to offer a new future for council tenants and their homes.

Interest in local housing companies developed following this seminal report. They were championed by the Chartered Institute of Housing as stated, not as a means of privatising council stock but as the only realistic means of obtaining adequate resources to deal with public sector housing disrepair.

Two factors have since combined to ensure momentum behind the development of local housing companies, particularly in urban areas: first, the 1996 Act permits the registration of companies as registered social landlords with access to funding and second, the introduction of the Estate Renewal Challenge Fund. In the 1995 Autumn budget statement the then Conservative Government announced an Estates Renewal Challenge Fund of £314 million designed to aid the transfer of estates in need of refurbishment to new landlords. The fund is intended to assist the process of transfer where the estate has a negative value because of poor stock condition or low values. With £40 million in 1996/97, £110 million in 1997/98 and £164 million in 1998/99 the fund will in effect provide a dowry to pay for setting-up costs or repairs prior to transfer.

The new landlord, be it a subsidiary of an existing association or a stand alone housing company, would then be able to lever in private finance.

Models for housing companies

The model put forward by Jeff Zitron for the Chartered Institute of Housing suggests that companies would have to raise private finance on the basis of tenanted market value for the transfer either paying a price for the stock or receiving a dowry. The Guide suggests a number of overall constitutional options, including:

(a)   an Industrial and Provident Society
(b)   a company limited by guarantee
(c)   a company limited by share capital.

The Industrial and Provident Society is the form of incorporation most commonly adopted by traditional housing associations, and the model rules are considered further in Chapter 4. However, all shares carry one vote and no one member may own more than one share. Companies are more flexible. A company limited by guarantee as noted above is one registered under the Companies Acts which may take a variety of membership forms. Members can be divided into voting classes with defined voting rights at the Annual General Meeting (AGM). This could enable open membership for tenants to be offered, enhancing the accountability of the company. A company limited by share capital has shareholders who invest money in it and who then own shares in proportion to their investment.

Local housing companies will be not-for-profit bodies with boards elected by members (and possibly non-members), again through a variety of different models. For example, election could be on a constituency basis with representatives from tenants, community organisations and the local authority. The board may devolve decision-making to local areas in the case of a larger company through a group structure similar to that explored above. This is a means of increasing local control over services and activities although, to have teeth, some financial decision-making and budgets would have to be devolved too. The acountability of local housing companies is viewed as one of their advantages over existing housing associations. One of the attractions of the company model is the opportunity for increased tenant involvement and control of the services they receive. The Tenant Participation Advisory Service has already developed guidelines for tenant involvement in companies. Local housing companies have already been established in Scotland which also has a tradition of transferring stock to tenant-led organisations. Companies may choose charitable or non-charitable staus. Several are now opting for charitable status given the relatively tight definition of the permissible activities of non-charitable registered social landlords highlighted at the beginning of this chapter. Many companies may wish to embark on regeneration activities beyond those limited to housing. It is impossible to predict at this stage how they will develop over the next five years, but clearly the company model provides immense possibilities in the area of urban regeneration.

Not all commentators have welcomed the concept by any means. The Association of Metropolitan Authorities (now part of the Local Government Association) views them as back door privatisation. It is opposed to the principle of transfer itself, favouring the benefits which could be obtained by relaxation of controls of public borrowing. Nevertheless, both major political parties have adopted them in principle. The incoming Labour Government signified increased support for the provision of new social housing by announcing in 1997 the phased release of £5 billion of capital receipts. At the time of writing it had just announced approval of the biggest transfer programme ever (130,000 homes in 20 councils), and was about to pave the way for more by enabling transfers to proceed even where the receipt would not cover all the local authority debt attaching to those homes.

Housing associations and local housing companies

Traditional housing associations have much to gain from involvement in local housing companies and transfers, although they could also be viewed as a threat. There is the possibility of genuine partnership through a share in the company or a place on the board and the provision of services to it. Some RSLs (especially those that are unlikely to develop further on a large scale) may even opt for local housing company status. Others may receive stock into a group structure by creating a local housing company as a subsidiary of the parent company, borrowing funds on its behalf. If transfers through this route do expand we shall witness the fragmentation of social housing into smaller, discrete organisations which has benefits in terms of accountability to tenants and the community. The strength of these organisations as social investment businesses, unless part of a formal group structure, will be inevitably weakened by their smaller scale. Local housing companies and transfers generally do, however, have the potential to radically alter the structure and nature of the social housing sector.

References

1 J. Alder and C. Handy, *Housing Association Law* (Sweet & Maxwell 1987) p. 11.
2 *Circular HC 28/94 Group Structures* (The Housing Corporation).
3 *Circular R4 06/97 Group Structures* (The Housing Corporation).
4 *Role and Diversity of Housing Associations*, Corporation News Supplement (The Housing Corporation 1992).
5 *Black and Minority Ethnic Housing Needs: An Enabling Framework Source* (The Housing Corporation Housing Management and Research Division 1996).
6 *Communities within Communities: The Role of Black Housing Associations in London* (London Federation of Housing Associations/NFHA 1995).

7   *Black and Minority Ethnic Housing Policy* (The Housing Corporation 1998).
8   J. Birchall, *Building Communities: The Co-operative Way* (Routledge & Kegan Paul 1988), p. 23
9   S. Wilcox *et al.*, *Local Housing Companies New Opportunities for Council Housing* (Joseph Rowntree Foundation/Chartered Institute of Housing 1993).
10 *Local Authority Housing in England: Voluntary Transfers* (Department of the Environment 1992).
11 *Large Scale Voluntary Transfer Guidelines* (DOE 1993).
12 *Housing Stock Transfer A Guidance paper on the Financial Impact on the Public Sector* (Department of the Environment, Housing and Urban Economics Division 1995).
13 J. Zitron, *Local Housing Companies: A Good Practice Guide* (Chartered Institute of Housing 1995).
14 Op. cit., 9.

3

Partnership with the Housing Corporation and Other Agencies

In the course of their diverse activities housing associations work in partnership with a large number and variety of organisations, local and national, voluntary and statutory. In this chapter we concentrate on a limited number of agencies, those with which associations have the most contact. In particular the chapter explores further the functions and powers of the Housing Corporation and the nature of the regulatory regime. It also examines The National Housing Federation (formerly the National Federation of Housing Associations) and the relationship between housing associations and local authorities. We commence, however, with relationships with central government.

3.1 The Department of the Environment, Transport and the Regions

With the advent of private finance and community care, other government departments such as the Treasury have become increasingly involved in the affairs of registered social landlords. The Departments of Health and Social Security also impinge upon their work. The most important department in England, however, is the Department of the Environment, Transport and the Regions (DETR) and was, until now, the Scottish and Welsh Offices in Scotland and Wales respectively. This has changed with the advent of the Welsh assembly and Scottish Parliament. The DETR retains the overriding responsibility for accounting for the actions and activities of the independent social housing sector to Parliament, and initiates most changes in policy to meet the Government's objectives which affect the work of the sector. Any decisions outside the limits of the Housing Corporation's delegated powers will be referred to the DETR.

The DETR leads the tripartite consultations on new policies and procedures that take place between it, the Housing Corporation and the National Housing Federation. The assistance of DETR officials is essential in negotiations which require ministerial support. It is the DETR which sets the cost limits within which RSLs develop and which, following consultation, negotiates the size of the annual Approved Development Programme (the cash limit) with the Treasury. At national level, relationships with the DETR are as vital as ever, but at regional and local level the Housing Corporation is the main agency with which RSLs work. More recently however, many RSLs have become actively involved in urban regeneration programmes through City Challenge and the Single Regeneration Budget and its successors (see Chapter 6). Funding for these programmes is controlled and awarded through competitive processes by the DETR although they are also supported through the Corporation's programme too. This has brought associations into closer contact with the regional offices of the Department.

Government regional offices

From April 1994 the regional offices of the Departments of Environment and Transport, Trade and Industry and Employment (as they were then) were brought together into integrated regional offices which aimed to provide more comprehensive and accessible services. There are now nine such government offices, including one specifically for London, each headed by a Regional Director. As stated, the government offices administer the Single Regeneration Budget amongst other programmes, which also brought together 20 existing programmes for regeneration and economic development. Several of the existing housing budgets such as Estates Action programmes and funding of Housing Action Trusts were brought into this integrated Budget. A ministerial committee, accountable to Parliament, was also established to oversee the expenditure.

At the time of writing both regional development agencies and an authority for London were being established. It remains to be seen how these agencies will impact upon the the work of RSLs and, indeed, the role of the Housing Corporation.

English Partnerships

'English Partnerships', was also established in 1994, with responsibility for promoting the development of derelict and contaminated sites. Several existing grants, including Derelict Land Grant, City Grant and the work of the former agency ('English Estates') came under its aegis. The reorganisation of the government offices, and the establishment of English Partnerships, have enabled local authorities working with Training and Enterprise councils (TECs), RSLs and other community partners to bid for funding for comprehensive programmes of regeneration which aim to ensure the sustainable revitalisation of an area. There are now a number of capital programmes that contribute to area regeneration which once again may be brought together as a single capital programme, as outlined in Chapter 6.

Housing management training grants

Section 16 of the Housing and Planning Act 1986 empowers the Secretary of State for the Environment, Transport and the Regions to make housing management training grants. Grants (or loans and guarantees) can be given to support training and development costs for new initiatives, often tenant-led, which may provide alternatives to the traditional forms of tenure. Housing associations and other voluntary organisations, particularly secondary housing co-operatives, are given preference for these grants. The training of staff to assist in the formation of tenant management co-operatives or the training of ethnic minority staff are two common areas where grants have been forthcoming. The grant lasts for up to three years and is reviewed annually, however, it covers only half the costs required and thus organisations receiving it must find the remaining funds from other sources.

Section 180 of the Housing Act 1996 also enables the DETR to make special grants to voluntary sector bodies and is used to support more innovative projects including those developed by RSLs.

3.2 The Housing Corporation

Created by the Housing Act 1964, until 1996 the Housing Corporation registered, funded, promoted and supervised the work of registered housing associations only. Following the passage of the Housing Act 1996, however, the Housing Corporation has a wider remit, being responsible for the funding and regulation of all registered social landlords. Clearly, as regulator of all social landlords, including local housing companies and other not-for-profit landlords, the promotional role which the Corporation has played in relation to housing associations has ceased as it is no longer a statutory function of the Corporation. Indeed, the special relationship between associations and the Corporation which developed during their 30-year partnership will inevitably alter, although at the time of writing the extent of this had yet to be seen.

The role and structure of the Housing Corporation

The Corporation plans and manages the annual programme of capital and revenue grants to registered social landlords. Its grant funding powers, the allocation of the capital programme and procedural arrangements are examined in detail in Chapters 5 and 6 respectively. The Corporation also super-

vises and regulates the performance and activities of registered social landlords and safeguards the interests of tenants. Each of these functions and
the Corporation's statutory powers are considered in Section 3.3 below.

The Housing Corporation is an executive non-departmental public body
which depends upon Parliament for its existence. The Corporation comprises a board of up to 15 members who in turn are appointed by the
Secretary of State for the Environment, Transport and the Regions. The
Chairman and Deputy are also appointed by the Secretary of State. Until
1989 the responsibilities of the Housing Corporation included Scotland
and Wales in addition to England. From 1 April 1989 however, the
funding and promotion of housing associations in Scotland was transferred to Scottish Homes, an agency created through the amalgamation of
the Scottish Special Housing Association and the Housing Corporation in
Scotland. The parallel agency in Wales until January 1999 was 'Housing
for Wales' or Tai Cymru.

The Housing Corporation in England is divided into seven regions reor-
ganised in 1994 to largely match the Government regional offices (which
then changed again!). These cover London, the South-East, the South-
West, the West Midlands, East, the North-East, and the North-West and
Merseyside, the latter two having been combined in 1996. The Head
Office is based in London with two main central divisions: Investment,
and Regulation and Supervision. It also has support functions of finance
and personnel, together with central services such as corporate planning,
public relations and legal services.

3.3   The evolution of the Housing Corporation, 1964–98

Since its creation in 1964 the Housing Corporation in England has
expanded from a programme of £50 million per annum to one which
peaked at over £2 billion in 1993/94. Its growth has been dependent upon
shifts in emphasis in government policy since 1964 and mirrors the
expansion of the housing association sector as outlined in Chapter 1.
The original purpose of the Corporation was to promote and supervise the
expansion of cost-rent and co-ownership housing societies.

The work of the Corporation developed further following the Housing
Act 1974 and the introduction of Housing Association Grant and other
subsidies which provided the financial framework for the provision of
subsidised rented homes through housing associations. Since April 1981
its annual programme of funding has become known as the Approved
Development Programme.

As a non-departmental public body with one of the largest capital
budgets the Housing Corporation is subject to regular reviews and
scrutiny. The more recent are considered below.

Environment Select Committee

In December 1992 the House of Commons Select Committee on the Environment resolved to inquire into the Housing Corporation. It was to examine its structure, role and effectiveness, its management and the way in which appointments were made to it. Its regulatory function and tenants' rights and participation were also to be examined. Although initially a narrow remit was set, the final report published in 1993 examined many aspects of the sector as a whole including the scale of the programme and the issue of affordability.[1] The main findings included a statement that grant rates should not be cut further in order to prevent even more people being caught in the poverty trap. It also supported the diversity of the sector and called for an increased share of the programme for rehabilitation of older property. In relation to the Corporation in particular, it recommended that its board should be broadened to include representation by tenants, local authorities and those with housing management experience. It argued that the Ombudsman service for tenants(see below) should be independent and that the Corporation should do more to boost the availablility of private finance. Finally, it argued that the Housing Corporation regions should be altered to coincide with those of the DoE. It recommended that the Housing Corporation should retain its funding and regulatory roles rather than have these split into two separate bodies, but that this issue should be examined again following widespread consultation to determine the best option. In the event this Inquiry though wide-ranging, recommended little that was controversial in relation to the Corporation. Since then the board has been strengthened and the regions restructured as outlined earlier. The issue of the dual function of funding and regulation continued to run, however.

'Financial Management of Housing Associations'

In 1994 the Public Accounts Committee (PAC) considered a 1993 report by the National Audit Office based upon a 1991/92 survey, entitled *Housing Corporation: Financial Management of Housing Associations*. The PAC paper,[2] stated that the Housing Corporation should be prepared to withhold funds from housing associations which perform poorly. The previous report by the National Audit Office had expressed concern that a number of associations were performing unsatisfactorily: for example, in the five-year period to 1992, as many as half of all associations failed to submit their annual accounts within the six-month deadline. The PAC report criticised the Corporation for falling behind in planned inspection visits and suggested that the Corporation reconsider the frequency of visits, placing particular emphasis on the possibility of fraud or irregularity. The report was published in the wake of a fraud perpetrated at Circle 33 Housing Trust in London, which had gone undetected for over seven years and which cost the association over £600 000. The PAC expressed concern at the lack of internal audit within housing associations and recommended that firm guidelines be implemented for the operation of internal audit and that these be monitored closely. The Report also noted the need for improved representation on housing association boards by people with financial and management skills. It also called for increased progress in relation to the development of indicators to measure associations' performance. All these issues are discussed further in the next chapter. The PAC concluded by stating that 'great importance is attached to the safeguards the Corporation's regulatory framework provides for the proper conduct of business within associations and ensuring value for money'. The PAC 'look to the Department to ensure that the Corporation's statutory powers are developed and strenghtened where necessary'.[3] Written in strong, even dramatic language, the report led to some changes in the regulatory function and to the system of internal audit now required of associations (and discussed further in Chapter 4). The Corporation's response to both reports was set out in its Corporate Plans 1995–98, and more recently in its report *Future Directions*.[4] First, the Audit Commission was given a new role as the Corporation's agent to undertake value for money studies of housing association management functions (see Chapter 7). In addition, although regional committees have not been established, regional consultative meetings have been ongoing for some years, chaired by board members. Regulation has been strengthed through requirements relating to internal audit procedures with a code of audit practice. New requirements relating to treasury management (see Chapter 5) were also issued. In April 1994 a new system of regulation 'performance review' was introduced with clearly defined performance standards, and performance indicators were published for the first time in 1995, with associations listed individually in 1996. The Housing Association Tenants' Ombudsman Service was also established. In 1998 the Housing Corporation published a revised set of performance standards pursuant to its regulatory powers under the Housing Act 1996.

A further question that also recurs regularly is whether the Corporation's regulatory role should be split from its funding powers. The concept of two separate bodies has been around for many years and was raised again as a possibility by the National Housing Federation in its publication 'Towards 2000' in 1990 and again in 1995 in its submission to the Prior Options Study.[5] The study, as detailed below rejected this option and the Housing Act 1996 firmly places both functions within the remit of the Housing Corporation, at least for the time being!

Prior Options Study

As stated, the Housing Corporation is an executive non-departmental public body and government policy is that all such bodies should be subject to a five-yearly finance policy and management review (FPMR). FPMRs are conducted in two stages. First, a Prior Options Study which examines the justifications for the organisation on policy grounds and considers the options for transferring, privatising or contracting-out some of the organisation's functions. The second stage examines the financial and management matters in detail. The last Prior Options Study of the Housing Corporation was conducted in 1995.[6] The Study concentrated on whether the Housing Corporation was the right body to undertake the two functions of allocating public subsidies, and regulating subsidy expenditure and the provision of the dwellings it produces. In other words, should the two functions of funding and regulation be collocated within the same organisation? The Study took into account the reports discussed above and also considered the relationship between the Housing Corporation and the (then) Department of the Environment and between their respective regional offices. It also examined the role of local authorities in allocating resources to housing associations and considered the location of the Housing Association Tenants' Ombudsman Sevice. The Study concluded once again that there would be little to be gained and much to be lost if funding and regulation were to be performed by two separate bodies. Although there is a tension inherent in the dual role of regulator and funder, a regulator without funding powers has no teeth and the threat of withdrawal of funding support is a powerful tool. The Study did, however, recommend that the second stage review should look carefully at the strategic and operational relationship between funding and regulation, and that a different regulatory system should be considered for small and non-developing associations. This has been completed and is discussed further in the section on regulatory powers below. The Study went as far as stating that the Housing Corporation should become the sole funder and regulator of any future recipients of grant, and these recommendations were built into the Housing Act 1996. In most other areas maintaining the status quo was recommended, although it was suggested that the Ombudsman Service become statutorily independent. This was also enacted in 1996, as discussed in Section 3.8. Finally, as stated at the outset of this chapter, the Corporation's promotional role was to be reviewed given its remit to fund and regulate all independent social landlords.

The Housing Corporation's functions and powers

The Corporation exercises its powers and fulfils its functions in a variety of ways. In particular, in common with government departments, it manages by circular. It issues circulars on every aspect of its activities which may provide guidance, information or lay down requirements and regulations. In addition, it publishes several procedural guides which it updates regularly as necessary. The Corporation also produces reports and promotional pamphlets updating associations on its work and to inform the public. There are regular meetings between the officers of the Corporation and RSL staff to discuss the progress of the development programme. The close relationship between regional officers and their colleagues in associations has been vital to the successful partnership between the Corporation and the sector.

The Housing Corporation is not a Crown servant or agent which means that ministers are not directly responsible for its activities. It is, however, subject to scrutiny by Parliament in that its annual report and accounts must be laid before Parliament by the Secretary of State. The powers and duties of the Housing Corporation are wide, provoking criticism. As we have seen above, some commentators argue that the principle of separation of powers, in the interests of public accountability, is contradicted. The Corporation's role has been described as 'promoter, banker, policeman, judge and executioner rolled into one'.[7] This view is reinforced by the fact that, with one or two exceptions the Corporation's decisions are not subject to any form of appeal. Most of its powers are discretionary and where and when they are exercised is decided by the Corporation itself.

The powers and functions of the Corporation derive largely from the Housing Associations Act 1985 as extended by the Housing Act 1988 and importantly the Housing Act 1996. They include:

(a) the maintenance of a register of social landlords as outlined in Chapter 2;
(b) the supervision and control of registered social landlords;
(c) duties under section 71 of the Race Relations Act 1976;
(d) guidance on the management of accommodation provided by registered social landlords,
(e) funding and scrutiny of projects

Financial functions

The Corporation's financial powers will be explored further in Chapter 5. In outline they include borrowing powers and the power to make grants. The Housing Act 1996 introduced a new financial regime for registered social landlords. Under section 18 of the 1996 Act, the Housing Corporation is empowered to pay Social Housing Grant to registered social landlords to assist with expenditure on eligible activities. Under section 53 the Housing Corporation must consult with others before the grant determination is issued. The Corporation may also make grants where tenants are exercising their right to acquire under section 16 of the

1996 Act. Grants may also be made in relation to the voluntary purchase grant scheme. The Corporation may also make determinations in relation to the recovery of grant.

3.4 Housing Corporation regulatory powers

As stated, the powers of the Housing Corporation to regulate registered social landlords were extended by the Housing Act 1996. These are set out in schedule 1 to the Act which is in four parts:

Part 1: Control of Payments to Members
Part 2: Constitution, change of rules amalgamation and dissolution
Part 3: Accounts and Audit
Part 4: Inquiry into the affairs of registered social landlords.

Each part is considered in turn.

Control of payments to members

Part I schedule 1 replaces sections 13–15 of the Housing Associations Act 1985 and is considered in detail in Chapter 4.

Constitution, change of rules amalgamation and dissolution

Part II of the schedule replaces sections 16–24 of the Housing Associations Act 1985. The Corporation has the power, on 14 days notice, to insist on the removal of directors (or trustees or committee members) if they have been made bankrupt, are incapable of acting due to mental disorder, or through actions or acts of omission are impeding the management of the RSL. The Corporation may appoint new directors to replace any it has removed or if it believes that the RSL would benefit from additional members.

Rule changes by an industrial and provident society and changes to the memorandum or articles of association of a company require the consent of the Corporation. For example, an association may wish to change its rules to extend its borrowing powers. However, a registered charity cannot alter its objects without the consent of the Charity Commissioners. They, in turn, must consult with the Corporation before such a consent is given. A 1965 Act association (see Chapter 2) must obtain Housing Corporation consent under seal to alter its rules and must also notify the Corporation of any change of name or registered office address.

Mergers and winding up

Sometimes two associations may consider it advantageous to merge their interests, or a smaller association may wish to transfer its assets and engagements to another organisation. A small association which is unable to obtain development funding may find this option attractive. Para. 12 of schedule I requires the Housing Corporation to oversee the merger or winding-up of an association (whether an industrial and provident society or a company). If an association wishes to amalgamate or transfer its engagements to another it must obtain Corporation consent, again under seal. Such consent is needed before the Registrar of Friendly Societies may give his or her consent to the amalgamation or transfer. The Corporation must consent to the winding-up of an association. It may also present a petition for the winding-up of an association itself if it can show that an RSL is failing to meet its objects under the Companies or Industrial and Provident Societies Acts. If this occurs the Corporation may transfer the assets of the RSL to itself or to another registered social landlord. Such a petition would usually follow an inquiry as detailed below. The Corporation has issued guidance on the principles governing the transfer of land in such circumstances.[8]

During the passage of the Housing Bill in 1996 the Corporation sought additional powers to appoint an administrator to deal with the assets of an RSL which had got into financial difficulty. Clauses 41–48 of the Bill allowed the Corporation to intervene ahead of the private lender to transfer assets. This created a furore amongst the lending community and threatened the whole future market for housing association fundings. The clauses were hastily withdrawn and have been replaced by a more limited power. If an RSL is seeking to wind itself up in the case of insolvency there will be a moratorium on the disposal of land for 28 days. The Housing Corporation has this period to establish a solution to try to keep the assets of the RSL for use as social housing. These powers are set out in section 41–50. If the creditors agree the proposals they become binding on all parties. If not they can proceed as they intended prior to the imposition of the moratorium. Under section 46 the Corporation may also appoint a manager to implement its proposals, working to its direction.

Accounts and audit

The Corporation receives both the annual accounts of an RSL and an annual return, called form RSR. This is used to update the statutory register of social landlords which the Corporation is required to maintain and keep available for public inspection. It provides information on each RSL and its subsidiaries, biographical details of directors and trustees, breakdown of the RSL's stock, staffing levels and information on lettings. It also includes information on property sales and vacant units, in addition to information on performance against prescribed standards, and is the basis of the first stage of the performance review process which is conducted as a desk top exercise.

The accounting requirements are laid down in part III of schedule 1 of the Housing Act and replace sections 24–27 of the Housing Associations Act 1985. Section 30 of the 1996 Act also strengthens the Corporation's powers to obtain information relevant to its role as regulator. An RSL is required to submit a copy of its annual accounts and auditor's report to the Corporation within six months of the end of the accounting year. In addition, developing RSLs must also submit quarterly financial returns based on their own quarterly management accounts to the Corporation and a three-year financial projection if bidding for funding. These enable the Corporation to assess the financial robustness of an association at any given point in time. Further details of financial controls are given in Chapter 5.

The Housing Act 1996 also transferred the power to determine accounting standards to the Housing Corporation from the Secretary of State. Generally accounting and audit requirements are more clearly defined in the 1996 Act than in the Housing Associations Act 1985.

Inquiries

If performance review reveals serious problems or if these are brought to the Corporation's attention in some other way it is empowered under part IV of schedule 1 which replaces sections 28–32 of the Housing Associations Act 1985, to appoint an independent agent (i.e., someone who has not been an employee of the Corporation within the last five years) to undertake an inquiry into the affairs of the RSL. That person may require the RSL, its members or any agent of the landlord to produce books of account, files and records including the minutes of the board of management and any other information necessary for the inquiry. Failure to comply with this request can lead to a fine of up to £1000. It may take action against the RSL without waiting for an interim report as it had to before the 1996 Act powers. The Corporation may also insist upon a special audit of the accounts of the landlord by a specified auditor. As a result of these inquiries the Corporation may enforce a number of sanctions derived from the Act. Under para 23 of schedule 1 it may remove any committee member, officer, agent or employee of the landlord who has been responsible for or privy to the mismanagement or misconduct; such persons may be suspended for up to six months. It may 'freeze' the activities of the landlord by ordering any bank or individual who holds money or securities on behalf of the landlord not to part with them without its approval. It may also restrict the transactions of the landlord by allowing only certain payments to be made, with their prior approval. Contravention of these orders can lead to a fine of up to £1000 or up to three months imprisonment. Appeals against the removal of persons mentioned are to the High Court.

The powers of inquiry are obviously extensive. Fortunately the Corporation is only called upon to undertake one or two each year. In most cases the transfer of the association's interests has not been necessary and it has continued to operate.

Land disposal

Section 9 of the 1996 Housing Act requires a landlord to seek Housing Corporation consent prior to the disposal of land or interest in land. There are certain exemptions; non-registered housing associations need only seek consent to dispose of grant-aided land which has received public loans or grants. The consent process is integral to the supervisory and regulatory process discussed below. The Corporation must ensure that a landlord is not placing itself at risk or acting in a way that is 'incompatible with its status'. Publicly funded assets should only be properly disposed of. The granting of consent is at the Housing Corporation's discretion. The regulations are set out in Housing Corporation Circular R2 32/96.[9] A disposition is defined in the Act as a 'sale, lease, mortgage, charge, or any other disposal'.

An association must obtain consent from the Regulation Division for the following categories of disposal:

(a) a voluntary sale to a tenant;
(b) the grant of a lease for either residential or commercial purposes;
(c) the outright sale of vacant property or parcels of land;
(d) the transfer of a property from one registered social landlord to another, although consent to the amalgamation would be required;
(e) the grant of a mortgage or legal charge on a property to a private lender (e.g., bank, building society, etc.) or to a public authority;
(f) the grant of a floating charge over the assets of an association (which will include the land owned by the association: see Chapter 5);
(g) a grant of an easement, or of a restrictive covenant on land.

There are two different types of consent: the general consent and the individual consent. The general consent can be obtained through a streamlined set of procedures and applies to routine disposals. The consent is given by letter rather than under seal and is therefore relatively quick to obtain. The details are given in the guidance attached to the circular. All other disposals are either considered individually by the Corporation according to the circumstances of each case or do not require consent. Consent is normally granted except in the case of sale of tenanted property (unless to another registered social landlord) or if sales are at less than market value. In the latter case this does not, however, prevent disposal of properties at a discount to tenants under the right to buy provisions. Consent will also be withheld if it contravenes a landlord's objects and/or its permissible activities, as discussed in Chapter 2.

3.5 Housing Corporation regulatory processes

The Housing Corporation supervises and controls registered social land-lords through a system of desk top performance review backed up by peri-odic performance review visits. The Corporation also has specific statutory powers which assist it, where necessary, in exercising this func-tion which as we have seen, have been strengthened through the Housing Act 1996. This activity is vital if the Corporation is to act as a 'watchdog' for taxpayers' money; the process is an essential component of the pursuit of public accountability.

The system of regulation has evolved over time and new methods of assessment have been introduced. The approach has also altered. Currently all larger and developing associations are reviewed on an annual basis. An arm's-length approach is adopted based on existing information gleaned from several different returns.

Performance review system

The current system of regulation, known as performance review, was introduced in April 1994 and revised in 1998. There are six key elements:

(a)   performance standards;
(b)   annual regulatory and statistical returns;
(c)   desktop review;
(d)   investigation;
(e)   performance review visits;
(f)   performance review reports to RSLs.

Performance standards

Performance review is based on clear and succinct standards, with a dis-tinction between standards and means of achieving them. The current system therefore concentrates on outputs rather than processes. The system relies on a self-certification approach against these clearly defined standards which are published by the Corporation.[10]

Two key standards are set by the Housing Corporation: first, Governance and Finance Standards. These are concerned with the prudent management of the overall business, and cover constitution and organisation, operation, financial management and prudence. The second set, or Social Housing Standards, are concerned with the housing and related services provided by RSLs to their residents and communities. A further six areas are covered, including:

(a)   rents and service charges;
(b)   development;
(c)   lettings;

(d)   residents' rights;
(e)   housing management services;
(f)   repairs, long-term maintenance and improvements.

Performance Assessment and Investment Summary

The result of the performance review process feed into the Corporation's investment decisions. The review outcome, the assessment of financial viability and the landlord's effectiveness in programme delivery and the result of scheme audit are combined to provide a Performance Assessment and Investment Summary (PAIS). This enables the Corporation to place conditions upon the RSL to improve some aspect of their performance or otherwise withhold potential development allocations.

Schemework audit

The Association Schemework Profile (ASP) is drawn up following a schemework audit visit. Schemework audit takes place every two years and again consists of a visit to the association's offices, but in this instance by schemework and technical officers from the regional office of the Corporation. The officers may undertake site visits, but the process usually involves close inspection of scheme files with particular regard being paid to the extent to which the association has adhered to Housing Corporation procedures and requirements.

The Housing Corporation remains concerned that regulation keeps pace with the changing operating environment. It has issued guidance on risk assessment for RSLs (this will be discussed in the following chapter).

Race Relations Act 1976

Section 56 of the Housing Act 1988 applies the duties under section 71 of the Race Relations Act 1976 (which already encompassed local authorities) to the Housing Corporation. Section 71 states that: 'It shall be the duty of every local authority to make appropriate arrangements with a view to securing that their various functions are carried out with due regard to the need:

a)   to eliminate unlawful racial discrimination; and
b)   to promote equality of opportunity, and good relations, between persons of different racial groups.'

The performance expectations (which preceded performance standards) were the first attempt to set standards in this area on which the Corporation could monitor associations since it issued Circular 22/85, *Race and Housing*. In 1990 a further circular (02/90) *Promotion of Racial Equality*, was added.

The Residents'and Applicants' Charters

Section 36 of the Housing Act 1996 gives the Corporation powers to issue guidance on the matters of housing management after consultation. This section specifies the areas in which guidance should be given, although this does not preclude the Corporation from issuing guidance beyond them. The specified areas are:

(a) housing demand for which provision should be made;
(b) the allocation of housing;
(c) the terms of tenancies and the principles upon which rent levels should be based;
(d) standards of maintenance and repair and how these should be met;
(e) services to be provided to tenants;
(f) procedures to be adopted for dealing with complaints by tenants against a landlord;
(g) consultation and communication with tenants;
(h) the devolution to tenants of decisions concerning the management of housing accommodation.

The Corporation oginally covered many of these areas through what was known as the Tenants' Guarantee. The Guarantee was introduced to compensate for the limited statutory rights enjoyed by assured tenants in comparison with secure tenants who benefit from those rights enshrined by the Housing Act 1985.

In pursuit of these powers, in 1998 the Housing Corporation issued seven charters for the following groups:

(a) assured periodic tenants;
(b) assured shorthold tenants;
(c) secure tenants;
(d) licensees;
(e) leasehold and shared owners;
(f) members of fully mutual co-operatives;
(g) applicants for RSL homes.

All RSLs are required to give residents a copy of the relevant charter which sets out what each group can reasonably expect from the landlord. The charters also set out what residents and applicants should do if dissatisfied with service standards.

Rent influencing

From April 1998 the Performance Standards have included direction as to the level of overall rent increases that may be implemented by an RSL. For 1998/99 this has been set at Retail Price Index (RPI) plus 1 per cent. This is in line with government policy to keep rents down to enhance affordability and importantly to assist in reducing the cost of Housing Benefit to the Exchequer. Rent influencing is fully explored in Chapter 5.

Regulation Arrangements for Smaller Associations

The Housing Corporation has been mindful of the need to rationalise its own regulatory role given its increasing responsibilities following the Housing Act 1996 and its desire to reduce the regulatory burden on smaller RSLs. In its submission to the Nolan Committee, the Corporation noted its desire to move to a more focused and streamlined regime: Regulation Arrangements for Smaller Associations (RASA). RASA involves reducing the number of standards against which an association is assessed and potentially de-registering small associations and almshouses. Introduced in 1996, it applies to associations which manage less than 250 homes.

3.6   Future directions in regulation

Day, Henderson and Klein concluded their 1993 study into the regulation of social housing[11] by stating, 'the story of housing regulation is one of evolution in response to a changing environment. In designing regulatory systems it is therefore essential to avoid setting them in concrete and to ensure that they have the capacity to learn and adapt.' The study compares regulation in the local authority sector with housing association regulation and also considers the Scottish experience. It notes that the Corporation has responded to changes in the external environment by amending the regulatory regime accordingly. In the 1970s monitoring, as it was then known, was a new activity and had to respond to 'revelations of incompetence (or worse)'. In the 1980s the system improved in response to demands for greater efficiency in the process. By the late 1980s the Corporation had developed a 'full blown performance audit system'. This system has altered throughout the 1990s perhaps partly in recognition of the issues raised by Day, Henderson and Klein. The regulatory dilemmas include how to balance the public accountability function, so that resources are effectively used by associations, with the good stewardship function, which needs to ensure that service provision is effective. In addition Day, Henderson and Klein note that the regulatory body must endeavour to ascertain that associations are carrying out national social policy objectives. The study highlighted four issues to be resolved within any regulatory process: selectivity versus comprehensiveness; process versus outcomes; policing versus consultancy; accountability versus autonomy.

The Corporation has responded to some of these issues. For example, it has become more selective in its approach, concentrating on developing landlords. It has also introduced a degree of self-monitoring and certification combined with the collection of information and performance indicators which has enabled visits to be reduced. The Corporation, as we have seen, now concentrates far more on outputs than processes. Nevertheless, the use of performance indicators is not without its difficulties, as discussed in the next chapter. The Corporation having completed an inspection visit, usually avoids a consultancy role but insists that any recommendations be implemented. It will monitor the outcome of those recommendations. Klein also highlighted the dilemma that regulation in the pursuit of accountability may so reduce autonomy that 'whereas in the past the regulatory system was itself shaped by its constituency, it is now increasingly shaping the housing association movement'. A question perhaps of the tail wagging the dog, but one which will continue to tax the Corporation as it assumes its even broader role of regulating all registered social landlords. In a further discussion paper for the National Housing Federation, Klein and Day return again to the issue of regulation for the future.[12] Highlighting the tensions present throughout the regulatory system, they call for greater transparency within it. The report also calls for the publication of stewardship reports without commercially sensitive financial information.

The Klein reports have suggested a greater convergence between the regulation of local authorities and housing associations. We have already touched upon the possibility of a separate body to undertake regulation. It is unlikely in the near future as both major political parties have pledged to support the current dual role of the Corporation. The Corporation is using the skills of the Audit Commission, however, to evaluate the efficiency of housing associations and to compare them with other sectors. This will eventually bring about a greater convergence between the regimes. Furthermore, the Housing Act 1996 has placed the performance indicator system (developed by the Housing Corporation) and the role of the Audit Commission to undertake studies on behalf of the Corporation into the sector's performance on to a statutory footing. The best value system (see Chapters 4 and 7) may also result in a change to the Corporation's regulatory role. In 1998 a new Housing Inspectorate was established as part of the Audit Commission, to monitor best value in local authorities and to evaluate housing's wider role in the community. The relationship between this body and the Corporation has yet to emerge but, as always, the nature of regulation continues to evolve and change as enhanced performance and accountability are sought.

3.7   Innovation and Good Practice Grants

In addition to its regulatory role the Corporation has a promotional role. This role has three main strands: publication of information and performance indicators; commissioning research and value for money studies to promote good practice; and Innovation and Good Practice Grants which have replaced Promotional and Advisory Grants. The Corporation has the power to provide special grants under section 87 of the Housing Associations Act 1985 as amended by schedule 3 para. 5 of the Housing Act 1996. Section 87 grants were traditionally made to registered housing associations or voluntary organisations to assist in the costs of advising on or encouraging the formation of new housing associations and for providing services and giving advice on the running of a registered housing association. In the late 1980s the Corporation also used these grants to support and promote the training of ethnic minority staff and to encourage the development of black and ethnic minority housing associations. A major review of these grants by the Housing Corporation was undertaken in 1995. The outcome was a new system for 1996/97 which would focus on innovation through the introduction new priorities, categories for support and themes. These include best practice in housing management, housing plus and community care links, tenant participation, black and ethnic minority needs, private rented sector relations and organisational development initiatives. Each project is intended to be innovative in the sense of a new initiative, a catalyst for change or to promote best practice. Outputs must be demonstrable, with well defined milestones throughout the life of the project. Guidance on Innovation and Good Practice Grants is given in the 1996 General Determination on this subject and in an advice booklet.[13]

3.8   The position in Wales

From January 1999, housing in Wales has been led by a new Department for housing which combines its predecessor, Tai Cymru, and the Welsh Office Housing Division. Responsibility transfers to the new Welsh Assembly from May 1999. Housing For Wales (Tai Cymru) was established by the Housing Act 1988. Operational from 1 April 1989, it assumed the responsibilities of the Housing Corporation in Wales. Housing associations in Wales were at the forefront of the development of mixed funding, having pioneered the St Mellons scheme in Cardiff. It was this scheme that encouraged the Treasury to abandon previous conventions and agree to the mixing of public and private monies with only the former counting against public expenditure. The Housing Act 1988 extended powers similar to those of the Housing Corporation in England to Tai Cymru; and until 1999 it acted as the parallel body in Wales. The housing association programme in Wales runs at about £93–£98 million per annum. Wales experienced massive cuts in 1995/96 when the programme fell from £112 million to just £93 milion. Tai Cymru was innovative and introduced a number of new and controversial approaches, including standardising contracting procedures and house types. It developed a 'pattern book' of housing design and, although there was some flexibility, associations were expected to conform to them. In addition it set tough bench marks for rent levels in the bid rounds after 1997 and did not fund associations that were unable to match these. The new Department may continue these policy approaches but, at the time of writing, the shape of the future Department was not yet clear.

3.9 Scottish Homes

Created by the amalgamation of Scottish Special Housing Association (SSHA) and the Housing Corporation in Scotland, Scottish Homes is a unified housing agency for Scotland which in addition to funding and supervising the work of housing associations, also has economic and environmental improvement powers. SSHA was a government sponsored association set up in 1937. In 1989 Scottish Homes became responsible for the 74 000 homes inherited from SSHA and for the mainly community based and tenant controlled housing association movement which at that time included some 210 housing associations with some 45 000 homes in management largely funded by the Housing Corporation. However, only three associations had more than 2000 homes in management, with the majority managing between 500 and 1000 homes. The objectives of Scottish Homes were different from both Tai Cymru and the Housing Corporation. Its Chief Executive had a wider brief and he emphasised that the increase in home ownership (which was lower in Scotland, at only 44 per cent) was the first objective. Some believed that this would undermine or dilute the commitment to the development of housing associations which was the driving force of the Housing Corporation in Scotland.

Since 1989 Scottish Homes has indeed managed to increase home ownership. By 1994 it had reached over 54 per cent. In addition, some 20 000 homes had been transferred to smaller community housing associations and other bodies. It plans to continue to transfer its homes until it is no longer a landlord and to achieve this by the year 2000. In addition to its role as landlord it funds new homes to rent and pioneered the payment of grants to private developers known as 'Gro Grants' (a policy intended to be applied in England under the original 1995 White Paper proposals). Housing associations in Scotland have not been funded to expand to the extent experienced in England; however, they have enjoyed substantial growth. There are over 260 registered housing associations and co-operatives in Scotland which by 1995 managed over 70 000 homes. The programme is funded on average at around £275–£300 million per annum. More voluntary transfers will lead to a major boost in these numbers. In addition to Scottish Homes transfers, five New Towns will also have transferred a further 30 000 homes by the end of the century and it is estimated that between 1995 and 1998, around 80–117 000 homes will have transfered from the public sector in total. This may be affected by the reorganisation of local government in Scotland which created 29 new unitary authorities and which may change the relationship between these authorities and Scottish Homes. The impact of the Scottish Parliament must also be taken into account.

3.10   The Independent Housing Ombudsman

In its first annual report on the Citizen's Charter, the Conservative Government undertook to establish an Ombudsman for housing association tenants in England (there is also a separate ombudsman for Scotland). This proposal was incorporated into its 1992 election manifesto. The Housing Corporation was charged with establishing such a body. At that time, complaints against housing associations to the Corporation had increased to around 1000 each year. The service was launched in December 1993 with the following objectives:

(a)   an accessible, fair and effective means of resolving complaints rightfully made to the Ombudsman against registered housing associations by people receiving a direct service from them;
(b)   to seek redress for complaints, where justified;
(c)   to identify deficiencies in service delivery and help improve the quality of service provided by registered housing associations.

The original ombudsman was known as the Housing Associations Tenants' Ombudsman (HATOS) and he examined complaints in cases where the associations' own internal complaints procedures appeared to have been fully exhausted in relation to both tenants and unsuccessful applicants for housing. He also provided arbitration and mediation services.

When first established in 1993, HATOS had much more limited powers than the local authority ombudsman. He was replaced by the Independent Housing Ombudsman in 1996. HATOS was essentially a voluntary scheme, with no statutory powers, with a board appointed and serviced by the Housing Corporation although assisted by an independent Advisory Panel. Despite being welcomed, the proposals were criticised initially for the lack of independence HATOS would enjoy. In fact the Corporation has ensured that associations have taken HATOS seriously. The Tenants' Guarantee was amended to require associations to inform tenants of the existence of the Ombudsman, and in addition they are now expected to publish details of accepted cases within their annual reports. These figures are also published by the Corporation within the annual performance indicator report.

In his first year of operation the Ombudsman received 957 complaints from housing association tenants and other service users. Of these 62 per cent were returned to the associations to complete their own complaints procedures. Six per cent were resolved by alternative methods, 18 per cent were rejected or no maladministration found and 11 per cent remained outstanding.[14]

The Housing Act 1996 has considerably strengthened the powers of the Ombudsman service. The Independent Housing Ombudsman (IHO) who replaced HATOS from 1 April 1997 covers all registered social landlords. He has placed the service on to an independent and statutory footing (which had been consistently advocated by critics of HATOS).

It is now funded by contributions from its users rather than the Housing Corporation. All registered social landlords are required to join the service through section 51 and schedule 2 of the Housing Act 1996. As a condition of membership all landlords will have to agree to comply with recommendations of the Ombudsman and to report on compliance. Ombudsman recommendations, however, remain unenforceable in law. The scheme is also open to non-registered social landlords.

The IHO is a company limited by guarantee with operational matters delegated to an Advisory Council. Further details are given in Housing Corporation Circular R5 03/97.

3.11　The National Housing Federation

The National Housing Federation (fomerly the National Federation of Housing Associations (NFHA)) was established in 1935 for the purpose of promoting the formation and extension of housing associations in England and to give them advice and assistance. Essentially a trade body, it is a wholly independent organisation which actively promotes and represents the interests of its members, which included by 1995 some 1500 societies, trusts and associations. It also seeks to spread ideas and best practices amongst them. Since 1996 membership of the Federation has been extended to all registered social landlords who conform to section 1 of the Housing Act 1996. It is governed by a National Council elected by all members of the Federation, and provides a range of services to its members.

In addition to representing the sector in discussions with the Department of the Environment and the Housing Corporation on all aspects of policy which affect housing associations and (more recently) other social landlords, the National Housing Federation disseminates information through its conferences, seminars and magazine. It also has a continuing and extensive list of publications providing advice, guidance and information to associations on a range of issues.

Further services to members include training and research. In this latter area the Federation has been the main source of data on the nature of housing association tenants through the extensive surveys and censi that it has undertaken. It developed the continuous monitoring system (CORE) for new lettings which provides up-to-date and immediate information on the source of housing association tenants, their income levels and other circumstances. This system has been adopted by the Housing Corporation and all RSLs must now subscribe to it.

The Federation has for many years disseminated best practice. In particular it has developed a Code of Conduct for registered housing associations to which its members must adhere, which was revised and updated in 1996. Since 1982 it has advocated a 'fair housing policy' which promotes equal opportunity in employment, access to housing and the delivery of housing services.

Despite widening its membership following the Housing Act 1996 the Federation still adheres to its core values. These are independence, voluntarism, equality, focusing on need, commitment to local communities, excellence in performance and accountability.

The Federation in England operates with a regional structure for both officers and members. There are nine regional offices plus an office for London. There are separate bodies for Wales, Scotland and Northern Ireland. The English regions are led by Regional Councils made up of elected representatives from local members. The regional offices offer a service to members in their area.

The Federation's National Council – its Board of Directors – currently comprises 38 members. These are all corporate representatives, representing different constituencies. This includes thirteen regional representatives (one from each region and four for London), six representatives who must be voluntary board members and two tenant voluntary board members. The other places are filled by representatives of associations of different sizes and specialisms. The Council executes its functions through a series of subcommittees and adopted a new structure in 1996. A number of advisory panels and standing groups also advise Federation officers. The Federation meets regularly with the Housing Corporation to ensure effective liaison; the Corporation Board and the National Council meet formally each year at an annual joint seminar.

3.13   Relationships with local authorities

There is a long history of housing associations and local authorities working together to meet the needs of their local area. For example, through section 58 of the Housing Act 1985 (replacing section 119 of the

Housing Act 1957) local authorities are empowered to make loans to housing associations.

Following the Housing Act 1974 and the introduction of Housing Action Areas, associations worked with local authorities to upgrade whole areas of run down inner-city housing. By the early 1980s rehabilitation of houses in such areas accounted for some 50 per cent of the Housing Corporation's Approved Development Programme. Some local authorities (such as Hammersmith and Fulham) virtually delegated their role of refurbishing older houses to local housing associations in recognition of the sensitive approach that associations could bring to such work. Since 1988 associations have become the main providers of new homes, and they work in partnership with local authorities in relation to the nature and location of development in their area.

The importance of effective liaison and co-operation between associations and local authorities was first emphasised in the Housing Services Advisory Group report, *Housing Associations and their Part in Current Housing Strategies* published in 1978. A later publication, *Housing Associations and Local Authorities*,[15] published jointly by the National Housing Federation, the Association of Metropolitan Authorities (AMA) and the Association of District Councils (ADC) emphasised certain areas of co-operation including the housing association contribution to the formulation of the local housing strategy where an association has had a long-standing presence in the area.

A further area for co-operation has included nominations to housing association stock by the local authority from its waiting list; these arrangements have become vital in the period since 1988 and nomination rights represent the major route to newly developed stock for applicants on local authority lists. Association performance in this area, and the concept of joint waiting lists introduced by the Housing Act 1996, are both discussed further in Chapter 7.

Most local authorities have some sort of regular liaison meetings attended by their own officers and by the associations which provide a forum at which areas of co-operation and any problems may be discussed.

In 1985 the Chartered Institute of Housing published the report 'Working Together'[16] which once again emphasised the importance of liaison and partnership. The report made over 30 recommendations, which included the importance of establishing the sort of forum mentioned above and ensuring that associations contributed to the formulation of local strategy, regular exchange of information on lettings and nominations, early warnings to the local authority if an association is considering eviction, special arrangements for liaison over housing benefits, the possibility of joint training schemes and secondments and, finally, the monitoring of the performance by the local authority of those associations operating in its area. A second section of the report sub-titled 'A Tri-partite Approach', emphasised the importance of liaison with the Housing Corporation too, and recommended that the Corporation's programme should be discussed at the local forum or liaison meeting. Since the early 1990s liaison between the Housing Corporation and local authorities has improved. Consideration by the Department of the Environment, Transport and the Regions of the Housing Investment Programme of the local authority and the Approved Development Programme of the Corporation have been aligned, which has helped to ensure that local needs (as identified by the local authority) receive Corporation priority. The relationship between the Corporation and local authorities has not been without its difficulties, however; the Corporation has on occasion penalised those authorities that have not fully utilised their enabling powers, while some authorities resented the power over investment decisions held by the Corporation in their area. In addition, authorities have had to implement their strategies through housing associations, bodies over which they have little direct control.

The inability until 1997 of local authorities to fund associations directly, on any significant scale, encouraged the development of partnership arrangements whereby an authority can provide support and resources through other means. Such initiatives include the provision of land (often at discounted value) in return for nomination rights. The Local Government Act 1988, however, restricted these disposals as authorities must seek consent from the Secretary of State to dispose of land at less than market value.

The planning framework has also been used to facilitate partnership for the provision of affordable housing (see Chapter 6). In addition, authorities have also provided revenue support for schemes. This has particularly been true in the case of schemes providing additional care and support and has led to close co-operation not only with local authority housing and planning departments but, more recently, with social services departments too.

Leasing, on a short-term basis from private landlords with revenue subsidies from the authority, in order to provide temporary accommodation for homeless families, has also formed the basis for new partnerships between councils and some housing associations, especially in London. Regeneration of council estates, often involving some partial stock transfer has also led to fruitful partnerships. The voluntary transfer of local authority stock to existing or locally sponsored housing associations, and the impact of the proposed local housing companies upon relationships, was explored in the previous chapter.

In 1997 the National Housing Federation, the Local Government Association and the Chartered Institute of Housing published a report which further explores how partnership between councils and RSLs can be assisted to achieve more, entitled *Making Partnership Work*.

Local authority housing strategies

The importance of a healthy and positive relationship with the local authorities in whose areas an RSL works cannot be overstated. To facilitate this process some authorities have entered into 'social housing agreements' with associations operating in their area. These agreements were devised by the Federation, the Association of District Councils and the Association of Metropolitan Authorities which worked together to devise an agreement that would set out the reciprocal arrangements between the parties.[17] Such agreements set out the expectations of the local authority as enabler. They cover areas such as assessment of need and devising the strategy. Land assembly, planning powers, stock transfer, and provision of efficient housing benefit services may all be included. In relation to the housing associations' role, such agreements will normally cover contributions through new development, assistance through nominations, acquisition and rehabilitation, provision of agency services, accountabiility in terms of provision of information and performance on issues such as equality of opportunity and the affordability of rents. Targets are set for a number of these issues. Although not legally binding, the agreement can help to develop the partnership.

A report by Sue Goss for the National Housing Federation and the Local Government Association, *Local Housing Strategies*,[18] explores the way that the roles and relationships between local authorities, RSLs and the Housing Corporation have changed over the last decade. The report examines how these can be developed and improved for the future. The report was timely, with the return of a Labour Government with a landslide majority in 1997. This will lead to significant changes in these relationships. The release of capital receipts in 1997, some of which is being used to fund development by RSLs, means that local authorities are once again significant funders of the sector.

Joint commissioning

In addition, the Housing Corporation is piloting a process of 'joint commissioning' whereby the new development activity in an area will be jointly commissioned by the Housing Corporation and the local authority. Joint commissioning, which was being piloted at the time of writing, fits squarely within the Government's desire to see an enhanced approach to local housing strategies. A programme of longer-term priorities, at least three years, will be based on the local housing strategy and priorities agreed between the Corporation and the council.

Further aspects of the relationship between RSLs and local authorities are explored in greater detail throughout the remaining chapters.

References

1   *The Environment Committee second report: The Housing Corporation* House of Commons Paper 46/1 (HMSO 1993).
2   *Housing Corporation: Financial Management of Housing Associations.* House of Commons Paper 204 (HMSO 1994).
3   Ibid.
4   *Future Directions, The Housing Corporation's Strategy Statement 1997 to 2000* (The Housing Corporation 1997).
5   *Continuity and Change: The Future of the Housing Corporation* (NFHA 1995).
6   *Housing Corporation Prior Options Study* (The Department of the Environment 1995).
7   J. Alder and C. Handy *Housing Assocation Law*, 1st edn (London: Sweet & Maxwell 1987), p. 151.
8   Circular R1 39/96, *The principles governing the terms of a transfer of land following an inquiry into the affairs of a registered social landlord General Determination 1996* (The Housing Corporation 1996).
9   Circular R2 32/96, *The General Consent 1996* (The Housing Corporation 1996).
10 *Performance Standards and Regulatory Guidance for Registered Social Landlords* (The Housing Corporation December 1997).
11 P. Day, D. Henderson and R. Klein, *Home Rules: Regulation and Accountability in Social Housing* (Joseph Rowntree Foundation 1993).
12 P. Day and R. Klein, *The Regulation of Social Housing* (NFHA 1996).
13 *Innovation and Good Practice Grants* (The Housing Corporation 1996).
14 *Annual Report 1993/4* Housing Association Tenants Ombudsman Service.
15 *Housing Associations and Local Authorities* (AMA, ADC and NFHA 1984).
16 'Working Together' Professional Practice Series Number One (Institute of Housing 1985).
17 *Social Housing Agreements* (ADC, AMA, NFHA 1993).
18 Sue Goss, *Local Housing Strategies* (NHF 1997).

4

Issues of Governance and Management

All registered social landlords are established to meet particular objectives. Once these are agreed, the objects and powers of the organisation are determined by the constitutional route it adopts. The constitution will determine the ownership or shareholding membership of the organisation and composition of its board. Such issues are dealt with in the rules of industrial and provident societies or governing instrument or, in the case of a company its articles or memorandum of association. In the case of housing associations and other registered social landlords issues of governance and accountability (and also, as we have seen in the preceding chapter, regulation) impact upon the nature of the organisation and how it is run. Governance is an important issue of the day not only for this sector but as a result of the reports of the Committee on Standards in Public Life (Nolan Committee) for the public sector generally. Furthermore, the current Labour Government places great store on the local accountability of public bodies in particular and on the concept of citizenship and the rights and responsibilities of all in society.

Some issues of the governance and management of registered social landlords are explored in this chapter starting with an examination of the rules of the most common form of RSL, the Industrial and Provident Society. The role of the board of management (or governing body) is then considered. The accountability and governance of the sector, including the deliberations of the National Housing Federation sponsored Inquiry into the governance of housing associations and the Nolan Committee are also examined. The Governance Inquiry recommended that the term 'board' rather than committee of management be used in relation to the governing body of RSLs and this has now been adopted through the majority of the sector. The chapter also considers the strategic management of an RSL including long-term planning, internal control and the management of risk, concluding with a brief review of performance management approaches, which are referred to throughout this book.

These are all strategic and corporate issues dealt with at board level, hence it would seem appropriate to deal with the governance, strategic planning of the organisiation and the performance management of it within a single chapter. In reality all three issues are linked and will comprise much of the work of the board on a day-to-day basis. Governance and performance management are both substantial topics in their own right and the nature of this book precludes their detailed examination. Inevitably the the need to condense detracts from the coverage of these areas but readers wishing to pursue either topic further may find the references at the end of the chapter useful as sources for further study.

4.1   Rules and constitution

Whatever its objectives each landlord will be governed by a set of rules. As most RSLs are traditional housing associations and of these, 75 per cent are also industrial and provident societies these rules of incorporation are examined as an example of a governing instrument typical of the sector. It should be noted, however, that only a broad outline is given and that the rules of associations will vary according to the detail of their specific governing instrument.

Model rules are formulated by the National Housing Federation with versions for co-operatives and associations with charitable and non-charitable status. Under these rules a society has corporate status, a common seal, and limited liability like a company.

The rules set out the objects and powers of the organisation including its borrowing powers, accounting requirements and permissible activities. To be eligible for registration under the Industrial and Provident Societies Act, rather than the Companies Act 1985 the society must intend to conduct its business either for the benefit of the community or for the benefit of members. Which object applies depends upon whether the society is non-mutual or mutual.

New model rules were issued in 1997 incorporating changes that flowed from the recommendations of the Inquiry into the governance of housing associations and the passage of the Housing Act 1996 and to make them more relevant to the present day.[1] There were some new key features. In particular the rules incorporate a statement of shareholders' duties, clarification of how the board is elected and a statement of the roles of the board, the chair and the duties of the chief executive. The rules also incorporate a requirement for certain policies to be published. The 1997 rules widen the objects of the organisation to include work which is 'for the benefit of the community' thus clarifying RSLs powers to undertake *housing plus* and other community-based activities. The revised rules also permit the chief executive (and potentially other senior officers, such as the finance director) to be co-opted on to the board. This increases the liability of the executive directors as legal liability for the affairs of the RSL rests with the board. Apart from these amendments, the model rules have not changed significantly for many years.

Industrial and provident societies must have a minimum membership of seven but no maximum is prescribed. On joining, each prospective member pays a nominal price of £1 for a share, in the organisation. Details are held in the shareholders register. Membership entitles each shareholder to attend the Annual General Meeting (AGM), to vote at that meeting and to receive the Annual Report. The AGM must be held within six months of the financial year end and notice required for the meeting is set down in the rules. The time and place of the meeting and a general indication of the nature of the business to be discussed must be included in the notice. The AGM elects board members, receives the annual audited accounts and balance sheet of the association, which must be returned to the Registrar of Friendly Societies (which is to become part of the Financial Services Authority) within three months of the financial year end, and appoint the auditors for the coming year. The Annual Report of the organisation is also presented to the AGM.

If an extraordinary matter arises during the year, a Special General Meeting (SGM) can be convened by following procedures similar to those outlined above. The SGM will be quorate if a minimum of one-tenth of the membership is present. An SGM will be called to agree the rescinding or amendment of the rules, or to consider amalgamation or transfer of engagements to another body. In the case of amalgamation, a new legal entity is formed. If the engagements of one RSL are transferred to another, the transferring RSL will lose its identity and be subsumed by the receiving organisation. Although such decisions are taken by the membership, as registered social landlords, Housing Corporation approval is needed to effect such decisions (see Chapter 3).

All RSLs have a governing body, the board. The model rules prescribe that the board is elected from the membership at the AGM and that the board of management may comprise seven to fifteen members. On registration, the founder members of an association become the board and they will retire at the first AGM. From the second AGM onwards one-third of the longest serving members must retire each year but are eligible for re-election. If other members are nominated and those standing for election exceed the number of vacancies, then a ballot is held.

If the nominations equal or are fewer than available vacancies the chair may consider those standing as elected, without the need for a ballot. Casual vacancies that arise during the year can be filled without an election but those committee members must retire at the AGM. The rules permit the addition of five co-opted members; however, co-optees are not permitted to vote on issues affecting membership or officers of the RSL. Co-opted members have a particular value as they may be brought on to the board to provide specific skills or representation.

These electoral regulations allow the same members to be elected year after year. This is particularly true where the pool of members is limited and not very active. This has led to criticism of housing associations as being 'self-perpetuating oligarchies'. The lack of truly democratic representation in comparison with, say, local councils is often cited as one of the greatest weaknesses of the sector. To overcome this, associations have had to adopt measures to achieve improved accountability, in relation to both shareholding membership and board representation (an issue to which we return later).

In addition to the main board, it is common for most RSLs to have sub-committees to share the workload that the board is responsible for. Sub-committees may reflect the organisational structure or geographical spread (or both). An example of geographical representation is the regional or area committee. Alternatively, committees may be structured according to function. Common types of subcommittee include those covering the finance, development or housing management disciplines. Since 1995 larger RSLs have had to establish an audit committee in the wake of the Cadbury Committee Report to monitor the status of internal controls, as discussed further below. All subcommittees must consist of at least one member or co-optee of the main board. The minutes of sub-committees are submitted to the main board and they are subject to the same standing orders as the board. Subcommittees are useful as they can, by concentrating on a certain service or discipline, spend more time on particular issues considering items in detail. Particular expertise can be developed through co-opted members, and subcommittee members generally develop expertise in those areas which usually reflect their particular skills or interests. The use of area or regional committees with local representation may assist in improving the accountability of the landlord to the local community too.

The board must meet at least three times a year. The rules prescribe the notice required and what constitutes a quorum. Minutes of all meetings must be taken and these form part of the official records of the organisation. All decisions should be made on the basis that they are proposed, seconded and put to the vote. The chair of the board has the casting vote.

The model rules demand that an RSL has particular officers elected at the AGM. These include the Chair and the Treasurer. The role of the Chair is crucial in terms of the direction and ethos of the organisation, as is the partnership that should exist between the chief executive and Chair of the RSL. The management of this relationship in some bodies has, at times, given cause for concern and was examined by the Governance Inquiry. So too was the fact that the chief executive could not be a board member under the previous rules.

The RSL must appoint a Company Secretary whose role includes keeping the seal and official records and registers of the organisation, supplying annual returns and convening meetings, and who may be responsible for assembling board papers and taking the minutes. The Secretary may be a staff member and in some organisations the post of director or chief executive and Secretary may be combined, although this is now discouraged by the Housing Corporation in an attempt to enhance accountability through the separation of powers. The Treasurer has a particular responsibility to monitor the budget and finances of the landlord and for financial management.

4.2   The board

The principle of voluntarism

Board members contribute on an entirely voluntary basis although reasonable expenses may be met. The payment of board members has become more of an issue since the introduction of private finance and the consequent increase in both the responsibilities and liabilities of board members. The larger RSLs now have loan debts comparable with those of the largest businesses. The need to attract people of calibre with particular skills to serve as board members was also put to the Governance Inquiry as a further reason to consider some payment for this contribution. The Inquiry, as we shall see, rejected this argument and currently associations are only permitted to pay members up to £50 a year. At the time of writing, jury level loss of earnings was also under consideration by the Housing Corporation, which determines the appropriate level of payment. The voluntary members themselves have been the most vociferous opponents of any dilution of the voluntary principle. Whether this will change over time given the complexities of these businesses remains to be seen. Voluntarism and independence are two of the most important and valued features of the sector that are considered fundamental to its governance, and that differentiate this sector from both the public and private sectors; as such it is likely that they will be vigorously defended in many quarters.

Who sits on the board?

Over 30 000 people sit on the boards of traditional housing associations. Research undertaken in 1994 by Ade Kearns at Glasgow University in relation to the Inquiry into the Governance of Housing Associations, examined the membership of some 300 developing associations to create a picture of a typical board.[2] Men still accounted for two-thirds of board membership and were in a majority in 80 per cent of cases. Two-thirds of board members were in employment and just over one-quarter were retired. The backgrounds of members were little altered, since an earlier study undetaken by the National Housing Federation in 1985. In 1994 over half worked in the private sector, one quarter in the public sector and one fifth in the voluntary sector. Over 60 per cent had work experience in a relevant field. Twenty per cent had a housing background, 12 per cent had a finance background and 10 percent had development and technical experience. One-third of members were professional and nearly half had managerial level responsibilities. The research found that manual social groups were largely absent. Thirty-nine per cent of members had higher educational qualifications. The report concludes that associations are well served by skilled and qualified members. The reasons for the insignificant change in board membership over the 10 year period may simply be that the nature of RSL activity demands representation of these skills on their boards. The question of length of service is not addressed, so whether the lack of change is a result of the notion of a self-perpetuating oligarchy or simply because skills have been replicated as members have been changed is not clear.

What the report does note however, is that the preferred selection route of 40 per cent of the associations surveyed is selection by the chair, chief executive or board, ratified by shareholders. Twenty-two per cent favoured advertisement and recruitment by an appointment panel. Only 38 per cent favoured recruitment by shareholding members.

The report found that neither shareholding membership nor elections were considered important in the search for accountability. It states: 'there is no pretence towards the representative democracy model on which local government is founded'.[3]

The preference for recruitment rather than electoral representation emanates from the desire to attract people with particular skills and values on to the board. This is now viewed as more important than ever as the work becomes increasingly technical and complex. This argument is sometimes put forward for limiting the representation of tenants on the board. Tenant representation is often either absent or token in its nature. Their involvement in management of estates rather than the board having improved means of consultation and information is seen by many as a more appropriate approach than democratic representation. It is this lack of commitment to a representative membership that is seen by some as the Achilles' heel of the sector's accountability and which will have to be addressed if the so-called 'democratic deficit' is to be reversed. This will be important in the future in the light of the potentially more representative and accountable models likely to be adopted by local housing companies, with local councillor and tenant representatives, as discussed in Chapter 2. We return to these issues of governance later.

4.3   Management control

As stated, the governance and strategic management of all RSLs is the
domain of the board which is legally responsible for the activities of the
organisation. It is therefore essential that it exerts full control. The role of
the board is vital in ensuring that the landlord is both effective and yet
accountable to tenants, the local community and for the public funding it
receives. The registration requirements described in Chapter 2 set the
parameters, and the regulatory process examined in Chapter 3 enables the
Housing Corporation to assess whether control and accountability are in
fact being exercised by the board and the RSL in general. In its own submission to the Nolan Committee (see below) the Housing Corporation
stated that board accountability is central to its approach to regulation.
Increasingly letters, reports and circulars are addressed to the Chair in
recognition of this.

As we have seen, performance standards have been set by the Housing
Corporation in the area of governance and finance. All RSLs are expected
to have a properly consituted membership and a suitably competent and
representative board and committee structure, which controls, plans and
oversees all aspects of the RSL's work in an effective and accountable
way.

The board must ensure that the RSL conducts its affairs to the highest
standards of probity and that it complies with the dualities of interest
regime which is explored in section 4.4. The association's affairs should
be conducted in an open and accountable way and its independence safe-
guarded. The board must ensure that the RSL has (and operates within)
equal opportunities policies in accordance with the law and best practice
and that these are regularly reviewed. An organisational and staffing
structure must be adopted which allows the association to carry out its
business effectively and efficiently.

Independence and accountability

The Performance Standards emphasise the importance of the independence and accountability of RSLs. The Standards expect that RSLs should
be independent organisations, free from undue influence. The governing
body should be consituted so as to ensure that no single interest group
may exert undue influence. Tenant majorities on the board are now permitted, but at least one-third of the membership must be drawn from
independent constituencies. Local authority representation is also
limited. In relation to accountability, the Performance Standards state that
RSLs should have in place arrangements which enable them to demonstrate appropriate levels of accountability to those to whom they have
contractual obligations and to those to whom they have responsibility to

account for their actions. The development of the accountability debate is explored further, later in this chapter.

Financial control

The board is also required to 'manage prudently the financial affairs of and risks faced by their organisations, ensuring adequate and appropriate sytems of financial control, and exercising their proper stewardship of public funds'.[4] Some of the strategic issues that flow from these responsibilities, such as risk management and internal control are considered later in this chapter, and financial management is also examined in Chapter 5. There are, as we have seen, performance standards relating to the operational activities of RSLs. These are all explored further in later chapters.

As the ultimate decision-maker the board defines policy, sets objectives and monitors performance against them. The board undertakes several roles. Each board member acts as policy-maker, custodian of funds, employer, landlord and ambassador. Such a wide range of tasks and functions may be daunting for all but the most experienced of members and the board will often rely upon officers for information and advice in decision making. The role of the director or chief executive is essential in ensuring that the committee is given sufficient support whilst taking care that real control remains with them and that they do not become merely a 'rubber stamping' authority, franking decisions that in reality have already been taken by officers.

The increased risks brought about by the post-1988 Act regime, the raising of private finance to fund development and its effects upon the financial viability of the RSL are key issues that members must now tackle. In addition, as landlord, the board determines the rent setting policy. As custodians of the organisation's funds, members must approve annual budgets and ensure that audited accounts are returned annually to the relevant agencies. The board should also ensure that there is adequate investment of RSL funds, sufficient insurance cover for all operations and that taxation matters are dealt with. As employers, the board may agree pay and conditions of service, standards of office accommodation and staff appointments at senior level. As ambassadors, members are expected to represent the RSL to the media, to the local community and other agencies with which the orgnisation works.

The board must ensure that all these requirements are met by establishing the policy and strategy of the RSL in each of these areas and then delegating the detailed scrutiny to subcommittees if they are established, and operational and day-to-day decisions to the paid officers. The distinction between the duties of the board, in effect the non-executive directors of the RSL and those of executive officers accountable to the board is important in that it is only with proper systems of checks and balances throughout the organisation that the board can be assured that business is conducted to the highest standards of probity and efficiency.

There are a number of factors which will improve the effectiveness of the board (they are not exclusive to this sector, of course). The board and each subcommittee should have clear terms of reference and guidelines regarding delegated powers and lines of reporting. A balance needs to be struck in the case of subcommittees, ensuring that they have sufficient authority to encourage a sense of real contribution and control by members whilst ensuring that the main board retains control over the affairs of the organisation. The role of the chair is vital. Officers may also assist committees to be more effective by preparing succint and concise reports with clear options and recommendations. Many RSLs provide seminars and training days to assist members to get to grips with the jargon and bureaucracy of the sector.

4.4 Governance and accountability

Reference has already been made to the importance of the accountability of RSLs. They must be accountable for their actions and policies both to the community in which they operate and for the substantial public funds they receive. This is not a new issue, but one that was first addressed by both the Housing Corporation and the National Housing Federation in the late 1970s following the period of rapid expansion. In 1978 the Corporation published a circular entitled 'In the Public Eye'. Still current, the circular emphasises this issue, noting that although associations are voluntary and independent bodies, certain standards of accountability are required.

The Corporation itself, through its regulatory powers, is part of the process of securing public and financial accountability. The duality of interest regime has been of particular importance in the attempt to ensure probity in particular.

In 1979 the National Housing Federation published the first Code of Conduct for housing associations which included recommendations on committee structures, the conduct of members, and staff, in addition to development and housing management practices. All its members are expected to follow the current Code of Conduct, adopted in 1996. One area of great importance first raised in the original Code is the prevention of the duality of interest of staff and committee members, particularly in relation to possible material or financial gain. The position was formalised by the Housing Act 1980, re-enacted in sections 13 and 15 of the Housing Associations Act 1985 and enacted again virtually unaltered in schedule 1 of the Housing Act 1996. It should be noted, however, that (as discussed earlier) members are now permitted modest payments although no contract of employment exists, provided that such payment is permitted by the body's rules or governing instrument.

Control of payments to members

Schedule 1 para. 1 prevents an association or any registered social land-lord from making any gift or payment of bonus or dividend to anyone who is or has been a member of the association, or members of their family or to any company of which any of these people is a director. This does not apply, however, to interest paid on shares or capital lent to the association in accordance with the rules of the association, or to payments due to former members of fully mutual co-operatives or to fees and expenses subject to any maximum set by the Housing Corporation.

Schedule 1 para. 2 prohibits payment or the grant of any benefit by an RSL to current members, officers or employees or anyone who has been a member, officer or employee within the last 12 months, or is a close rela-tive of one of the above, or to companies trading for profit if a committee member, former member (etc.) is a principal proprietor or concerned with its management. Expenses, payments or benefits under contracts of employment are excluded, as are payments of proper interest or grants or renewals of tenancy to members of fully mutual co-operatives. Schedule 6 of the Housing Act 1988 permitted the granting of tenancies and employ-ment of relatives in certain circumstances. The details of permitted pay-ments and benefits are set out in a Corporation guidance note.[5] Schedule 1 para 3 sets out the Housing Corporation's powers to set the maximum level of fees and allowances to board members.

The Corporation monitors the conduct of RSLs closely with regard to Schedule 1 and must be informed of any contravention. The Schedule has a significant impact upon RSLs in terms of the contractors and consul-tants to whom they may offer work and ensures that neither members or staff may use or abuse their position for reasons of self-interest or personal gain.

The operation of the original duality of interest regime has in recent years been questioned and criticised as overly cumbersome and restrictive at a time when RSLs are expected to take greater risks. Several commenta-tors have argued for a simple declaration of interests regime instead as applies to local authorities. This option was examined by the Inquiry into Governance which favoured a tougher regime based on a public register of such interests. The Housing Corporation itself favoured the retention of the regime even though it is expensive in terms of the resources available for supervision. As can be seen, that was in fact the outcome.

The accountability debate

Accountability is, of course, a much more complex issue than that relat-ing to public or financial accountability or duality of interest. It is an issue that has tested the minds of practitioners and academics alike, and more recently has been placed at the top of the public policy agenda following the deliberations of the Cadbury and Nolan Committees. In the case of housing associations it was a central theme of the Inquiry into Housing Association Governance established in 1994.

The background

The history of the governance of associations goes back to their original roots in the twelfth-century almshouses and nineteenth-century housing trusts. Principles such as philanthropy, voluntarism and charity were what guided the original founders although as one commentator has noted, 'altruism, religion, civic duty and an eye for posterity (not to mention guilt)[6] may also have played a part. In those days independence and freedom from interference by government were considered paramount and this was not inappropriate given that the housing trusts of those times were not in receipt of public funds, and neither was it surprising. In that period, the notion of accountability to the community or to the tenant was also somewhat alien given the prevailing ethos of *laissez-faire* government and the concept of the deserving and undeserving poor. The extent to which the governors of those bodies were either competent or accountable was considered a matter for them alone.

In addition to the great charitable trusts we have noted that the most common form of governance for housing associations is that flowing from the status of industrial and provident society which, as Tickell[7] notes, are inspired by 'the self-help tradition' and with membership structures 'designed to hold the committee accountable to a wider membership'. As housing association activity expanded in the mid-1970s, in return for increased funding new regulatory regimes and expectations were introduced to increase accountability. These were overlaid, however, on to a system governed by instruments or rules adopted for another age and purpose.

Following the Housing Act 1988 which placed associations at the centre of social housing provision, the calls for enhanced accountability and greater openness in their dealings became more intense. This has mirrored a wider public concern over these issues. There is a greater public expectation of more choice and consultation over decisions affecting peoples' lives, coupled with the growth in consumer power. This, in turn, contrasts with the weakening of local democracy experienced over the last two decades, and the growth in government by quango. In addition, concern has grown over increasing examples of the lack of probity in corporate affairs. In 1992 the Cadbury Report into the 'Financial Aspects of Corporate Governance' called for tighter boardroom control over the affairs of commercial companies in the wake of the Maxwell scandal and other events. By 1994 housing associations had become virtually the sole providers of new social housing and had grown enormously in terms of their influence in the communities in which they operated. The scale of the movement, swollen by the transfer of local authority stock, added to this concern.

Members of Parliament, and local authority associations began to call for greater openness and improved accountability. In addition, the nature of associations had changed as they raised huge sums of private finance and became accountable to private lenders and, in effect, major social investment businesses. Thus at a time when the call for greater accountability was particularly intense, the need for competence was equally great. Although still working, it became clear that outmoded rules and (in some cases) governance structures were in need of reform, both to ensure that housing associations could undertake their activities effectively and efficiently at a time when they were expected to take substantial risks and to meet growing criticism of their mode of operation. Effective governance structures would have to strike a balance between these two sets of requirements.

The issue of governance and accountability cannot be separated from that of regulation. Throughout the last 20 years the Housing Corporation has revised its systems of regulation in an attempt to keep pace with the changing role of housing associations and with the scale of their activities. In 1994, as outlined in the preceding chapter, the Corporation responded to pressures from the Public Accounts Committee, the National Audit Office and the Environment Select Committee to widen its regulatory scope by introducing an extensive check list of expectations or standards combined with with a fair degree of self-monitoring. Clearly, any system of governance and regulation should take into account the diversity of RSLs in terms of their size, geographical spread and activities, and a balance also needs to be struck between competence and accountability. In 1994, in recognition of the need to resolve these contradictory pressures before they were forced upon the sector by external forces, the National Housing Federation established an independent Inquiry into Housing Association Governance chaired by Sir David Hancock.[8]

The Inquiry report notes that:

> Governance in any sector is about the exercise of power within a framework. It involves structures, roles and responsibilities as well as checks and balances. An effective system of governance will enhance the control and direction of an organisation in a rapidly changing environment as well as achieve effective accountability for all of its actions. There is a tension between the demands of accountability and those of business efficiency.[9]

The Inquiry sought to reconcile these tensions in particular.

4.5   The Inquiry into housing association governance

Accountability is an ill-defined concept. It is widely talked about but little understood. Terms such as 'accountability' and 'responsibility' are different. The Inquiry dealt with this issue by stating that accountability exists where those to whom account is given can exercise direct sanctions. The term responsibilty is preferred otherwise. However, what is clear is that associations are answerable to a number of interests or 'stakeholders' in relation to the policies that they pursue and the actions that they take. They are accountable through the regulatory system to the wider public or taxpayer for the public funds that they receive. They are also accountable to their members, and must be responsive to their tenants and the local communities in which they operate in a variety of ways. They are responsible to a wide range of bodies such as the Data Protection Registrar and the Office of Fair Trading; they must ensure that they comply with legislation. They have a responsibility to private funders to ensure that they can meet the terms of loans raised. They have a responsibility to prospective tenants too. As their role has grown, so demands for greater accountability have increased. Questions have been raised as to what structures of governance are appropriate. Should the shareholding members have a greater say in the running of the association? Should shareholding membership be increased to better represent the stakeholders and, if so, in what proportions should they be represented? Should all tenants become shareholding members and if so, how is it possible to ensure that other interests are adequately represented on the board or within the membership as a whole? How should the board and the chief officers conduct themselves? How should board members be selected and appointed?.

Written submissions to the Inquiry were made by over 179 organisations, together with six public hearings which heard oral evidence given by 23 organisations and individuals. The National Voluntary Committee Members Forum conducted a survey of board members and made separate representations, assisted by the University of Glasgow. In addition, a submission was made by 14 of the largest associations entitled 'Building On Success'[10]. The Inquiry report was launched in March 1995. Its recommendations were wide. The key sections covered the need to improve the internal and external frameworks, especially the operation and effectiveness of the board. They also covered accountability, responsibility and stewardship, equality of opportunity, audit, conduct and probity.

Findings and recommendations

In the foreword to the report, Sir David Hancock set out the principles that guided the Inquiry Panel. These were that housing associations should be 'accountable, independent and diverse'. He stated, 'Subject to the obligations of competence and accountability, housing associations should in our view be independent. Independent of party politics and pressure groups. Independent of Ministers, government departments and local authorities. Answerable principally to their own values and objectives. They should be no-one's agent or subordinate.'[11] In relation to diversity he stated:

> The housing association movement should continue to be diverse. Different types of association serve different needs and have different strengths. Small associations are able to foster small communities. Specialist associations respond to special needs of people such as those who are elderly, or disabled, or homeless in the short term or members of ethnic minority communities. But there is also a value in large associations to provide and manage homes on a large scale.[12]

The recommendations designed to improve competence and accountability included a Code of Governance,[13] which has since been adopted by many associations, with several of its clauses now incorporated into the Performance Standards of the Housing Corporation. The Report was considered by some to be an excellent attempt to produce a framework for governance that could serve the sector well for the future and which reconciled the diverse range of interests and opinions that inevitably arise in a movement which is itself diverse. The Report included a detailed and comprehensive list of measures designed to improve governance based on best practice in other sectors. The key recommendations included the use of the term 'board' for the governing body, as stated at the outset of this chapter, in order to distinguish the role of the board from the duty of the paid officers to manage. Clear statements of the role of the chair, the board and chief executive were recommended, in addition to formal published and open selection procedures for board members. The report recommended the recruitment of at least one new board member per year to prevent the development of self-perpetuating oligarchies. It suggested compensation for board members to allow for jury level loss of earnings and that the Corporation amend registration criteria to permit representation on the board of senior executives, if the board so wished. This latter issue, and also the question of the payment of board members threatened to overshadow other issues with which the Inquiry was concerned at one point in the proceedings. Strong views were expressed by some associations that without payment of members it would prove difficult to recruit new members of the right calibre and skills.

The recommendation was therefore somewhat of a compromise in recognition of the value placed, not least by the members themselves, on the voluntary ethos of associations. On the matter of the board membership of the chief executive and other senior officers, the Inquiry favoured the separation of powers between board and executive officers. There are some associations, however, which believe that the chief executive at least should be on the board in order to share more fully in decision-making and to take fuller legal responsibility for decisions made. As we have seen, this is now possible as this issue and several of the other recommendations are incorporated into the new model rules.

The Report proved less radical than expected in some quarters in relation to accountability through shareholding membership. Its recommendations refer to shareholding options that contribute to constitutional stability but which 'do not pretend to be more significant than they are'. As shareholding members are appointed by the board, this is seen by some as a major weakness in accountability and governance. Open membership has been suggested as a more accountable and democratic route. The Inquiry recommended against this, stating that different interests need to be balanced and that 'a large individual membership is no more certain to achieve such a balance than a small one even though it may give a greater appearance of accountability'.[14] A number of options for shareholding membership were considered, including a constituency model which attempts to achieve a constitutional balance with a defined range of stakeholders. The Panel expressed concern, however that the board should not become fragmented by representation on it of particular interest groups, or indeed lack competence owing to gaps in certain skills.

In this respect the Inquiry may have been persuaded by the arguments put forward by the larger associations in their submission 'Building on Success'. This emphasised the principle that 'The composition of governing boards should be suitable for the direction of associations' activities, with the emphasis on the selection of competent people who support the association's ethos rather than the representation of interests through elections'.[15] This report argued that accountability to tenants, local authority partners and regulatory bodies could be best achieved through the principles of openness, accessible information and consultation rather than involvement by these groups in governance structures. It emphasised the need for tenant involvement at area or regional level and in design and management of estates, but rejected the notion of representation on the board itself through election via the shareholding membership.

In 1997 the National Housing Federation produced a guide entitled *Action for Accountability* which examines aspects of accountability towards various stakeholders including tenants, local authorities and local communities, and considers mechanisms that can be adopted by RSLs to improve their performance in this area. The report has a foreword by Hilary Armstrong, Minister for Local Government and Housing, highlighting the importance placed by Government on this issue.[16] In the future therefore, as more local housing companies are formed with tenants' interests represented on the board, governance and local accountability will remain high on the policy agenda.

4.6   The Committee on Standards in Public Life (Nolan Committee)

On matters of governance, following swiftly on the heels of the independent Inquiry came the deliberations of the Nolan Committee. Established in October 1994 as a standing committee, the Committee on Standards in Public Life chaired by Lord Nolan turned to local public spending bodies, having considered members of parliament and the Executive. This examination included further and higher education bodies, grant-maintained schools, Training and Enterprise Councils (TECs) and housing associations. The definition of local public spending bodies included 'not for profit bodies which are neither fully elected nor appointed by Ministers, but which provide public services often delivered at local level, which are largely publicly funded'.[17] The issues examined included accountability and openness and the leadership role of the boards and executives. These would be considered in the context of the principles established by the Committee of selflessness, objectivity, integrity and honesty. The Committee indicated three broad themes that would form the basis of its study: the appointment and accountability of board members, the role of boards in relation to the officers and staff and safeguards in respect of conflicts of interest. In their responses to the Nolan Committee both the National Housing Federation and the Housing Corporation[18] referred to the report of the Governance Inquiry discussed above. The Corporation requested the Committee's views on three of the issues raised above: the payment of board members, whether the chief executive should sit on the board and on the duality of interest regime which it had decided to retain following its own review of the regulatory function.

The recommendations of the Nolan Committee

The Report stated that 'housing associations are well-regulated and generally well run'.[19] The work of voluntary board members was recognised and commended but the need to improve accountability was highlighted. The Report suggested that tenant involvement could be improved by widening shareholding membership (a suggestion unlikely to find favour with many of the larger associations). As stated above, a submission to the Governance Inquiry by a group of large asssociations specifically highlighted the view that tenant involvement and increased accountability should be achieved by other means. The Committee made a number of recommendations specific to housing associations:

1   Housing associations receiving public funds should be expected to secure involvement in housing management, and external restrictions on the composition of boards should be avoided wherever possible.

2　Housing associations should be encouraged to develop membership schemes as a means of increasing accountability.

3　The housing regulators should continue to be concerned as much with proper conduct as with financial probity, and should not hesitate to intervene to secure this.

4　No general change in the practice that chief executives of housing associations are not board members is necessary; but regulators should be prepared to approve rule changes which permit this in individual cases.

5　Section 15 of the Housing Associations Act 1985 should be retained, but responsibility for granting exemptions should be fully devolved to the regulators.

6　Safeguards designed to prevent conflicts of interest when staff leave should be introduced not only by the Housing Corporation, but by all executive and other non-departmental public bodies which are regulatory or funding bodies. It should be clearly understood that such rules are not designed to prevent movement between bodies.

7　The Housing Corporation, Scottish Homes and Tai Cymru should publish more information on their regulatory activities, and in particular they should publish reports on regulatory interventions in individual cases where serious mismanagement or fraud has occurred.

8　The housing regulators should pay especially close attention to the stewardship of LSVT housing associations, and of others which are monopolistic suppliers in specific localities.

Of particular importance was the Committee's recommendation that the duality of interest regime should be retained and not replaced by a declaration of interest regime as discussed above. The recommendation that the Housing Corporation should publish regulatory reports was also significant. A number of themes emerged that were common to all local spending bodies. In particular, standard terms of office for board members were proposed. The external adjudication of complaints and access to impartial assistance to help in resolving disputes, especially in relation to customer complaints, were also recommended. The Committee favoured the retention of the voluntary principle and recommended against the payment of board members for other than out of pocket expenses. The Report was, on the whole, well received, with many associations already meeting the suggested requirements. The Committee expressed an intention to return to housing associations and to review progress; there is no doubt that governance and accountability will remain a crucial issue for all registered social landlords and those with a stake in them. Those readers that are interested in pursuing this topic further are referred to Malpass (ed.), *Ownership, Control and Accountability: The New Governance of Housing*, published by the Chartered Institute of Housing.

This concludes our review of governance and issues of accountability, although both topics are referred to throughout this book. The chapter now considers strategic planning, an area in which both the board and senior executive officers work closely together. Good governance should provide a sound foundation for effective strategic planning and efficient management of the organisation. Strategic plans should flow from the principles of governance adopted by the organisation and which will in turn determine its priorities and ethos. It is to these that we now turn.

4.7   Strategic planning and managing the organisation

The chief executive and senior officers are responsible for implementing and advising the board on the policy and strategy that will assist the RSL to meet its aims and objectives, including its commitment to sound governance and accountability. Given the increasingly complex nature of the operations and activities of some housing associations, sound systems for strategic and financial planning are prerequisites for an effective organisation. Most have now adopted planning processes that are prevalent in other sectors. A useful guide to the business planning process and its relevance for social housing organisations has been published by the Chartered Institute of Housing.[20]

Strategic planning

All developing landlords must formulate business plans which will enable the corporate purpose and objectives to be delivered. Most RSLs have an overriding purpose set out in a mission statement. These are usually similar in vein and will make reference to the provision of 'affordable homes' or 'urban regeneration' and 'quality services for tenants and residents'. Long-term aims and objectives are established for each of the operational areas, and an action plan for the short and medium term with measurable targets is developed. Once the strategy has been adopted by the board, the financial implications are set out in the strategic financial or business plans. It is important that strategic plans are owned by everyone in the organisation and to achieve this a consultation process and planning cycle may be adopted. The process may commence with a board away day or weekend to review the past year and consider future opportunities and tasks. Senior management will then consult in their own departments to incorporate the views of as many staff as possible. The corporate plan is then revised and eventually adopted by the board.

Business units of the organisation or each department may develop separate business plans which in turn flow from, and are directed by, the corporate plan. Effective plans must be implemented. This is best achieved by the performance review process. There is a hierarchy of objectives; each objective must be owned and corporate objectives broken down into objectives for each director, department and section concluding with targets for each member of staff. The supervision and appraisal process should monitor the progress against these objectives and targets for the individual, the team, the department and for the organisation as a whole.

The business plan will mirror the main financial statements of the RSL (see Chapter 5). These will include the balance sheet, the income and expenditure account and possibly a cash flow forecast. The financial projections are essential not only to illustrate what can be achieved but to demonstrate to the regulator, lenders and to other partners the future viability of the association and its ability to meet its aims and commitments.

The success or otherwise of implementing the plan will in part be measurable through a series of performance targets and indicators. Performance indicators are increasingly a part of the process of monitoring and regulating the sector, and are considered further below.

The management of risk

Good planning can help to minimise risk. Throughout this book reference is made to the increasingly tough climate in which housing associations now operate and the increase in risk prevalent in their work, much of which arises from the need to raise (and repay) considerable sums of private finance. By adopting a planning process the board can be presented with a series of options and scenarios which highlight sensitivity to various factors. For example, sensitivity analysis can demonstrate the effects of a rise in interest rates, of rent rises below RPI or cuts in the level of grant. This can help the organisation to plan ahead and to prepare contingency plans that will protect it from the worst effects of these changes. There are, however, some general techniques for managing risks in addition to planning and sensitivity analysis, including insurance and the spreading of risks. An introductory booklet published by the National Housing Federation sets out how risk can best be managed.[21] It highlights the ingredients of effective risk management, these being: a strong committee and relevant committee structure, as highlighted above; well conducted meetings; the right calibre of staff with clear performance targets which are monitored; and an effective staff structure. Of equal importance are clear plans and objectives implemented through consistent policies and procedures with responsibility for this clearly delegated to officers. Clearly new development is one of the most risky areas. Poor design, or initial appraisal assumptions leading to cost overruns, and contract delays are all areas that can present problems, and these issues are explored further in Chapter 6. Risks have financial consequences and the raising of large sums of private finance in itself presents risk to an association; some aspects of internal control are considered in the next section, and financial management is explored in greater detail in Chapter 5.

Other operational areas, such as housing management and maintenance, can also present risk. More recently, the move into community care made by some RSLs will increasingly expose them to greater risk. They have become responsible for some of the most vulnerable and on occasion the most challenging members of society and must have in place systems and procedures to prevent abuse of residents or residents' abuse of others, for example. They may also become vulnerable to changes in the revenue position of health authorities and other care funders. Indeed, the whole funding regime for this area is one which presents risk, and this is explored further in Chapter 8.

In 1997 the Housing Corporation published its own guidance on the assessment and management of risk by registered social landlords.[22] Although the guidance is not a regulatory requirement, the best practice it illustrates is recommended for adoption by all RSLs. The Corporation affirms that it 'wants Boards of RSLs to be in control, so they can meet their business objectives without jeopardising:

- their asset base;
- the flow of public and private sector financing;
- the provision of high quality housing and management to tenants;
- the reputation of the sector.'[23]

As expected of the Regulator, these are the priorities to protect and echo those principles upon which regulation itself is based.

In its 1999 Consultation paper *Regulating Diversity* the Housing Corporation proposed a framework for assessing and managing the risks attendant upon diversification. In addition to redefining core and non-core activities (see Chapter 2), a number of tests were suggested for evaluating the financial impact of non-core activities, for example on the future income stream of the RSL. It seems likely that through its regulatory processes that the Housing Corporation will monitor closely such developments in an attempt to protect its past investments and to prevent a major fiasco from occurring.

4.8   Audit and internal control

In response to this increasingly complex and risky environment, and in order to be more accountable, a greater awareness has developed of the importance of internal control within RSLs. Two guides have been published to assist organisations to develop the correct control 'ethos' and 'environment' by the National Housing Federation[24] and the Chartered Institute of Public Finance and Accountancy (CIPFA) with the Federation.[25]

The important concept is that of the hierarchy of control emanating from the Board which itself will operate according to clear standing orders and terms of reference. Each RSL should have a clearly defined set of delegated authorities which sets out what has been delegated by the board to subcommittees, senior officers and staff. The levels of delegation should be clearly stated in relation to levels of authority to commit and approve expenditure to purchase land or enter into contractual commitments. In addition, there will be a set of financial regulations which set out high-level standing orders in terms of how the financial affairs of the organisation should be run, the main books of account and controls that will be established and maintained. All staff need to be fully aware of the importance of internal control and the various mechanisms which together assist in the achievement of an effective control environment. The board, the executive directors and managers, in addition to the regulator, the internal and external auditors, all have a role to play in achieving this. Some regulatory requirements in relation to aspects of internal control and audit are considered next.

Audit practice

As highlighted in the previous chapter, in order to protect the public purse it is a condition of registration with the Housing Corporation that all registered social landlords submit annual financial accounts which have been certified by the RSL's auditors and which are intended to show a true and fair view of the association's financial position. The Housing Corporation expects all RSLs with more than 250 dwellings in management to adopt the 'Code of Housing Association Audit Practice' which sets out best professional practice for, and advises on the appointment of and working relationship with, their auditors. The Code of Practice was revised by the Housing Corporation in 1995. The revision reflected the changing operating environment of associations and followed in the wake of the Cadbury Committee report, *The Financial Aspects of Corporate Governance*. Cadbury recommended that directors of companies should report annually and publicly on the effectiveness of the status of the company's system of internal control, and the implications for RSLs are discussed later.

The responsibilities of an external auditor are to carry out an audit competently and according to recognised professional standards. They must report any weaknesses discovered in accounting or internal control systems and this is done by issuing a management letter to the chair of the RSL, following the annual inspection of the books of account and internal controls and procedures. This will set out any areas of concern or necessary improvements. It must be responded to in writing and must be acted upon by the landlord. The management letter will also consider any areas of non-compliance with statutory or accounting standard requirements. A copy must be forwarded to the Housing Corporation.

Only persons eligible for appointment as auditors under the Companies Act 1989, and which are registered with a supervisory body recognised by this Act, may be appointed as auditors. In respect of a new appointment an RSL is expected to invite firms with experience in this particular field to tender for the audit. The appointment of the auditors should be confirmed at the Annual General Meeting of the landlord, and the Housing Corporation recommends that the audit should be re-tendered regularly. The scope of the audit, the quality of advice and the scale of the fee (which can be substantial) should be reviewed every three years.

It is recommended that larger RSLs (with over 2000 homes) establish an independent audit committee which will examine all control issues in greater detail and advise the main board. If there is no separate committee then responsibility for internal control and audit issues should rest with a specific board member. The Audit Committee should be given maximum discretion to examine internal control issues and should be largely separate from that committee which handles the financial affairs of the organisation.

The requirements of audit under the Industrial and Provident Societies Act 1968 are less stringent, as are those of the Charities Commission. In addition, those RSLs registered under the Companies Acts or which are governed by special trust deeds may have to meet separate audit requirements.

Internal control and regulatory requirements

Each RSL must also have satisfactory procedures and processes to ensure effective systems of internal control, this may be assisted by establishing an internal audit function. The requirements of the Housing Corporation are set out in circular 11/94 'Internal Controls in Registered Housing Associations' and in the *Code of Audit Practice 1995*. Controls should include adherence to policies and procedures laid down by the board, systems to safeguard the assets of the RSL and to prevent fraud and compliance with all statutory and regulatory requirements. Audit should also ensure the integrity of financial information and reporting and the efficient, effective and economic use of resources.

Examples of the issues which internal control should cover include all high-risk areas such as, financial accounts and updates on performance against budget projections and against financial targets or key indicators. An area of particular importance in the internal control of an RSL is rental income. The association must ensure that fair rents are re-registered on time and that rent reviews on assured tenancies are implemented annually. Rent accounting systems must be accurate with proper procedures for monitoring and controlling rent losses arising through arrears, voids and bad debts. Gross rents must be reconciled with cash collected. Expenditure on repairs and maintenance is another vital area. There must be adequate supervision and monitoring of day-to-day repair expenditure, cyclical programmes and any planned maintenance programmes. Budgets should be established and reviewed on a monthly basis.

Systems are also required to record and monitor capital expenditure. This also includes the calculation and submission of grant claims and a means of managing private loans. The finance department must monitor the cash flow position of the association and will also be charged with investing surpluses and making the best use of short-term deposits. Capital expenditure involves large sums of money, so the RSL must have proper procedures for tendering and awarding contracts and authorisation procedures which allow only specified officers to authorise and commit the organisation to expenditure. These regulations will, as stated above, form part of a full set of 'financial regulations' which all RSLs should have in place to ensure the proper stewardship of their finances.

Fraud
To conform with the requirements of circular 11/94, an RSL must also ensure that, where it receives agency services, these are also subject to scrutiny in terms of effective internal control procedures. In addition the circular requires each RSL to establish a register recording any incidents of actual or alleged fraud. All frauds in excess of £1000, or any corrupt act perpetrated by a senior officer of the organisation, must be reported immediately to the Housing Corporation.

Internal audit
Most RSLs have developed some sort of internal audit function as the regime has become more complex and entails greater risk. Internal audit may be provided by employing an internal auditor directly as part of the in-house staff. Some have formed consortia to jointly share the costs and services of an internal auditor. Others tender for the service on contract from an external firm. Advice on audit processes and objectives is set out in the National Housing Federation Audit Manual (1996).

Statements on internal financial controls
Internal audit is a relatively new area for most RSLs. Given the competitive framework in which they now operate and the need for tighter regulation, however, the Housing Corporation is expecting Cadbury-style reports on financial controls to be made. With effect from April 1997, the annual accounts must include a public statement by the board on the

status of internal financial controls.[26] This will involve reporting on the system of internal controls established to safeguard the assets of the association and to confirm the existence of financial accounting records and systems to ensure that the published information provided is reliable and accurate. Boards are expected to receive a report each year from the Audit Committee to enable that statement to be made. In turn the Audit Committee would receive a report from the internal audit service based possibly on a system of self-certification prepared by senior officers.

In practice internal control systems can only offer a reasonable assurance that procedures are in place to prevent loss or fraud. Internal auditors are able to monitor the quality of internal control and adherence to delegated authorities and agreed procedures and thereby assist in the control ethos. Internal audit is, however, only an addition to this process; an internal checking facility and effective internal control is by no means the domain of the internal audit service alone but stems from awareness of this issue throughout the organisation and a determination to ensure that effective control is maintained, driven through from the top down.

Whistle blowing

In order to encourage an ethos of responsibility and high standards of probity, and to provide protection for staff in the case of abuse of procedures, malpractice or bullying, the National Housing Federation has endorsed a whistle-blowing procedure for adoption by its members. The procedure was compiled with the charity Public Concern at Work and the Housing Corporation, and will eventually be adopted and implemented by more progressive bodies.

4.9   Managing staff

Staffing structures

Much of the success and effectiveness of any organisation, depends upon the quality and expertise of its staff. However committed and effective the staff are, an appropriate staffing structure is also required. This should be clear and accountable, cost-effective and meet business needs, amongst other criteria. As noted in Chapter 2, however, given the diversity of the sector it is not appropriate to generalise on many issues. Staffing structures is such an issue but it may be helpful at this point to consider a possible structure for a medium-sized developing RSL. Any RSL, undertaking all housing and related functions, is likely to have several departments, each undertaking one of the main processes. These include innovation and new business; procurement of new housing and maintenance of existing homes; customer services, including housing management, supported

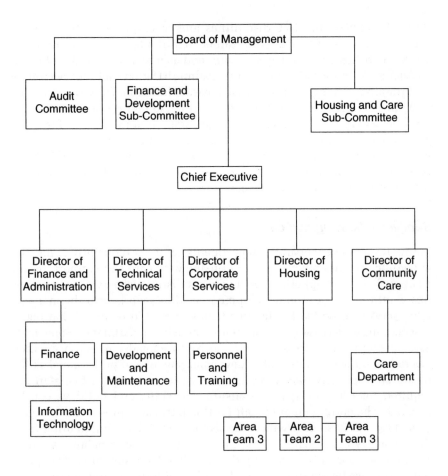

Figure 4.1   Possible staffing structure of a medium-sized RSL

housing and community care; support services such as finance, information technology, human resources and office management. Figure 4.1 illustrates a possible structure for a medium-sized association, with around 3000 homes in management and a regular programme of new development. It is also assumed that the RSL is locally based, operating in limited local authority districts.

The organisation in the example has housing management, finance and administration, technical and community care departments. As in many RSLs housing management services are provided through local area teams with offices based near to the stock in management, thus being more accessible to tenants. In this example maintenance is provided through the technical services department; however, it is common practice for maintenance teams to be integrated within area housing teams to improve the link between the two disciplines and to emphasise the customer service elements of the function rather than the technical nature of the work. There are disadvantages to both models which are explored further in Chapter 7. In the illustration given, administration includes personnel and training and is not shown as a separate function. However, in practice, most larger RSLs can support a full personnel section which may report to a corporate services director separate from the finance function. The human resources function is a vital area and one that has been the subject of several handbooks and guides published by the National Houisng Federation and others to assist associations to become more modern and progressive employers.

Supported housing and care

Many RSLs have separate departments with responsibility for the development and management of housing with care and support. In our example, whilst suppported housing is not distinguished and such activities would be part of the development section's work with the management service provided by the area teams, it should be noted that many associations do have separate supported housing departments. Some have also developed a response to community care needs, an activity which has required the development of new management and professional skills. It is a staff-intensive activity; in some cases as many as five staff are required for each bedspace to ensure that shifts and holidays can be covered. The employment of staff for this purpose represents the largest area of growth in staffing within the sector. The skills required differ from those usually found within most traditional housing associations. Since 1990 those associations entering the care field have sought to strengthen their expertise by employing people with health (including nursing) and social work qualifications. The personnel requirements are greater in this area where large numbers of staff are working (often at some distance from a local manager) with vulnerable people in a situation where stress can be great. The training and support of these workers in relation to their own health and safety, in addition to that of the residents, is paramount. Some of these issues are explored further in Chapters 8 and 9.

Decentralisation

Some larger associations have adopted a regional and generic structure and enhanced their accountability by establishing local or regional committees to which the regional or area teams report. Regional directors may have generic responsibility for, say, maintenance, housing management and development functions. Finance and administration, along with a policy unit, may remain a centralised function. The London and Quadrant

Housing Trust, a large RSL operating across many London boroughs and parts of the South-East, has adopted this structure, as have a variety of larger, pan-regional or national RSLs in order to provide greater local knowledge and a more integrated approach to the delivery of services. It is expected, for example, that the links between housing management and development will be improved so that the standard, design and types of dwelling provided better meet the requirements of tenants and those who have to manage them.

The trend towards decentralisation of services has been under way for several years. Associations have responded to growth by devolving functions on a regional or area basis. Decentralisation is seen as a means of improving knowledge of local issues and accessibility of services. National associations have adopted this path to improve their record on accountability. Decentralisation has not been heavily promoted in contrast with the local authority sector but has been the natural result of growth as associations attempt to develop closer links with tenants and their communities.

Human resources issues

The *Personnel Handbook* (NFHA 1986) offers advice and guidance on job descriptions, recruitment and selection, conditions of service, training, salaries and staff appraisal. It also considers grievance procedures and health and safety at work. Throughout, it emphasises the importance of equal opportunity and positive action in the field of employment. A further publication, *Race and Housing: Employment and Training Guide* (NFHA 1989) assists RSLs to meet their obligations under the Race Relations Act 1976. In the preface to the Guide, the Director of the then NFHA notes: 'access to housing association employment is one of the most important means of demonstrating our accessibility as housing organisations to local communities. This is an important demonstration of housing association accountability.'

In Chapter 2 reference was made to the increase in representation among housing association staff of people from the black and minority ethnic communities. A number of initiatives have assisted this trend. In particular, Positive Action for Training in Housing (PATH) has encouraged associations to take on black and minority ethnic trainees with a view to their eventually obtaining permanent employment in housing. A further initiative that is also sponsored by the Housing Corporation is 'Potential for the Top', which combines on-the-job training with management courses based at local colleges with a view to developing black and minority ethnic middle managers for senior management positions. Despite this there were, at the time of writing, only two black or minority ethnic directors of larger, mainstream housing associations. In 1997 the

Housing Corporation endorsed a report which considered the record of the sector in recruiting black people to managerial positions.[27] The report highlights the fact that black people remain under-represented as managers within the sector.

The position of women is slightly better. Women accounted for 25 per cent of the directors of all smaller housing associations in 1993. In 1997, however, only seven women were chief executives of larger associations managing over 5000 homes. There were at that time 40 such associations. There is still much to be achieved in the field of equality of opportunity at work. To this end the National Housing Federation published *Equality in Housing, A code of practice* in 1998 to enable this sector to more effectively tackle discrimination in all areas of operation, not just the recruitment and selection of staff.

Human resources issues have come to the fore as organisations have grown and have entered a period of rapid and almost continual change. Some are moving away from traditional links with local government pay awards and conditions and are embracing local pay bargaining schemes. The attraction of this stems from the greater control that the RSL enjoys over salary costs which account for over 80 per cent of operational costs in most cases. The need to steer a course through this change, which has included embracing the commercial ethos brought on by the need to raise private finance and the emphasis on performance and increased competition, has led the more progressive organisations to reconsider their staffing structures and human resources strategies to manage the process of change.

Training expenditure has increased since 1990 and many RSLs have active career development policies. Management training is also more common as performance review and effective supervision and appraisal skills are developed in organisations that were not so long ago less professional in their approach to such issues. A reflection of this is the number of RSLs now actively embarking on programmes to achieve the 'Investors in People' status awarded by local Training and Enterprise Councils.

4.10   Improving performance

Since 1989 the Housing Corporation, the Audit Commission and the RSLs themselves have taken a much closer interest in standards of performance in the sector. Best practice and performance issues are considered throughout this book and, in particular, comparative housing management reports and best value are reviewed in Chapter 7. It is useful at this stage to consider the nature and development of performance indicators as they are now key tools in improving the management and accountability of housing associations and other RSLs.

Performance indicators

The Housing Corporation has always collected statistical information relating to housing associations through the annual returns. These statistics on size and stock profile have been developed in recent years to include aspects of performance. Prior to 1991 there had been little experience within the sector of using performance indicators in comparison with the local authority sector, and there was some resistance to their introduction too. Performance indicators are becoming increasingly important as a means of comparing the performance of RSLs and for comparisons with other sectors, particularly local authorities. Performance indicators are defined by the NHF as 'facts which help us to assess whether we are achieving our targets and thereby our objectives'.[28] They may be 'can-openers' which highlight particular issues or meters which measure activities. They are tools which enable organisations to measure and improve performance but also a means of improving accountability by enabling reports to be made to funders, the regulator, local authorities, communities and to tenants on performance for any given period.

The introduction of performance indicators has caused some controversy as they can easily be misread. They should always be analysed in the context that the team or organisation is working in and it has taken several years for a system of published indicators to evolve which is both meaningful and less open to perverse interpretation and, importantly, that is agreed and owned by those whose performance is to be measured.

Since 1991 associations with more than 250 units and those developing new homes have had to provide performance information on access to their housing, equal opportunities, rent collected, vacancy rates and target times for day-to-day or responsive repairs. Since October 1991 all tenants have had the right to be given performance information on rent charges, speed of repairs, rent collection, empty properties and speed of reletting. By 1995 the Housing Corporation was in a position to publish the first report on housing associations which included some measures of comparative performance. Its second report, published in 1996, divides associations into three groups: those with over 5000 homes in management, those with below 5000 (listed by region) and those which are concerned almost exclusively with the housing needs of older people. The use of these groups followed extensive consultation and debate regarding the development of peer groups for comparative purposes. Research by the University of Wales, College of Cardiff, for the Housing Corporation had tried and failed to develop a system that was considered both robust and plausible for placing housing associations into peer groups for this purpose.[29] The groupings highlighted above and the publication of the information on computer disk now enable RSLs and other interested parties to analyse the information provided and create their own self selected peer groups.

In collecting performance information the Corporation's objectives are twofold: to improve the accountability of the sector by informing interested parties as to their performance and to provide information which will assist management boards and staff to manage their businesses more effectively. In addition to factual context statistics, in 1998 the published indicators included:

(a)   rent levels charged
(b)   rent collected as a percentage of rent due;
(c)   per cent of dwellings vacant and available for letting at the year end;
(d)   speed of reletting;
(e)   lettings granted to various groups;
(f)   management costs per dwelling*;
(g)   maintenance costs per dwelling*;
(h)   rent arrears as a percentage of gross rental income;
(i)   target times for responsive repairs;
(j)   tenant satisfaction;[30]

(* Audit Commission indicators).

Future indicators will be devised for development activities and supported housing, but no consensus had been reached for effectively measuring these at the time of writing. Moreover, financial indicators were only just available as they were felt to be too commercially sensitive for widespread publication.

Performance indicators are clearly here to stay and are an essential tool in monitoring the performance and accountability of the sector. The Audit Commission is undertaking a range of work for the Housing Corporation, including comparing the costs of associations with those of local authorities. It has also undertaken an analysis of housing association development costs. The Housing Act 1996 sections 34 and 35 placed new duties upon the Housing Corporation as regulator of all registered social landlords to set standards after consultation and to collect information on the performance of all registered social landlords. It also has a statutory duty to publish details of landlords' performance to force landlords to disclose and provide information. RSLs have been in some cases a little reticent about publishing performance information but, in the operational environment of the future which will be even more competitive, it will be demonstrable performance standards as opposed to statements of good intentions that will be the key to a successful future.

Best value

The system will also enable the sector to be brought into the 'best value' regime which, at the time of writing, was being introduced to local authorities. Best value will operate at a number of different levels.

Performance indicators will be set for national purposes by a central body and by the organisation itself, and local indicators will involve the local authority. At a national level some dozen indicators are expected, including:

rent levels and increases
rent collection
repair performance
empty property
stock condition and investment
estate management
complaints
tenant participation
tenant satisfaction
housing plus activities

Performance indicators will be collected in order to assist in benchmarking. This will allow RSLs to be compared with other similar organisations and with local authorities. Benchmarking highlights the strengths and weaknesses of the organisation in comparison with its peer group. Performance indicators also enable RSLs to give proper feedback to their customers which itself is an important aspect of the best value regime. RSLs will be expected to work with tenants through focus groups and other means to establish priorities and targets for the improvement of services. The best value regime is discussed further in Chapter 7.

Quality management

A commitment to quality services and a customer focus are therefore becoming driving forces for many RSLs. Customer expectations have risen and, from central government down, there is a clear stance which places quality management and customer needs at the centre of RSL activity. This has demanded a fairly significant shift in priorities for many RSLs and the need to change the organisational culture, internal structures and activities to reflect this and to achieve the desired outcomes. While performance indicators assist this process, many organisations are exploring quality systems and management approaches to try to ensure that service standards are improved. There have been two distinct approaches so far: Total Quality Management (TQM), and quality assurance which may lead to achievement of the International Standard 9002 for quality assured services. Each is examined briefly in turn. The TQM philosophy is 'that it is better to prevent failures from ever occuring in the first place. As time and effort are invested in training to increase prevention activities so the high cost of failure is reduced without any increase in appraisal costs.'[31]

Thus TQM is about getting things right the first time and developing a culture, systems and approaches to the delivery of services in which the needs of the customer are paramount. It involves all staff working in teams which develop well structured management systems. Performance is regularly assessed in an objective manner by the organisation itself and the desire for improvement is continuous.

British Standard 5750 (EN ISO 9000) is a nationally accepted standard for quality systems. Its application to housing associations is set out in a National Housing Federation guide.[32] Systems (for example, for the allocation of housing) are recorded and organised in a manner that allows adherence to them (or otherwise) to be tested and regularly assessed by qualified assessors. The standard is externally set and recognised and is therefore considered by some to be of greater value than TQM, especially in areas where services may be provided on a commercial, competitive basis. It is a management standard which does not regulate the product; therefore critics have said that quality assurance could in theory lead to the provision of quality-assured 'rubbish'! Others, however, believe that it is a valuable method of ensuring that levels of service consistently meet agreed performance standards. The system is assessed by a British Standards assessor and a certificate awarded for a three-year period. It is subject to interim visits, by the assessor, to ensure that standards are maintained. A provider of quality-assured services may use the famous 'kite mark' in promoting that service. This end result can help to concentrate effort to ensure that the systems are effectively developed and maintained.

Any RSL embarking on this path needs to engage and involve the whole staff in the process. As stated, this approach may involve a substantial culture change. As a result, many RSLs have established customer sevices reviews which aim to enhance services to customers and to improve performance at an operational level. Such reviews may involve quality circles, as outlined above, or lead to the pursuit of a quality assurance certification for the whole organisation or a particular service. Quality management and customer service reviews may take a number of forms. A commitment is required from the whole organisation, and ideally this commitment should emanate from the board and be driven by the senior team. Improving quality and customer service is an important topic but the detail is beyond the scope of this book; however, those readers who wish to pursue this in greater depth are referred to a Chartered Institute of Housing publication which examines the processes, techniques and approaches adopted in some detail.[33]

Governance and accountability, performance and quality services are all issues that we shall return to again and again throughout this book. This is the last of the four introductory chapters which provide the context for a more detailed examination of the financial and operational processes, and it is to the financial framework that we now turn.

References

1 *Model Rules 1997* (National Housing Federation).
2 A. Kearns, *Going by the Board – the Unknown Facts about Housing Association Membership and Management Committees in England* (Centre for Housing Research and Urban Studies, Glasgow University and as reported in *Inside Housing*, 21 October 1994).
3 Ibid.
4 *Performance Standards* (The Housing Corporation December 1997) p. 22.
5 *Payments and Benefits: Guidance on Schedule 1 of the Housing Act 1996* (The Housing Corporation 1996).
6 J. Tickell, *Boardroom Business* (Voluntary Housing Jubilee Issue, NFHA 1995).
7 Ibid.
8 *Competence and Accountability: The Report of the Inquiry into Housing Association Governance* (NFHA 1995).
9 Ibid.
10 R. Klein and P. Day, *Building on Success: Improving Housing Association Governance* (University of Bath 1995).
11 Op. cit., 8, p. 6.
12 Ibid, p. 10.
13 *Competence and Accountability: NFHA Code of Governance* (NFHA 1995)
14 Op. cit., 8.
15 Op. cit., 10.
16 J. Ashby, P. Duncan and S. Underwood, *Action for Accountability: A Guide for Independent Social Landlords* (NHF 1997).
17 Issues and Questions: Local Public Spending Bodies, The Committee on Standards in Public Life (HMSO 1995).
18 *The Committee on Standards in Public Life: Local Spending Bodies Memorandum submitted by the Housing Corporation* (Housing Corporation 1995).
19 *Local Public Spending Bodies, Second Report of the Committee on Standards in Public Life, Vol. 1. Report* (Cmnd 3270–1) (HMSO 1996).
20 P. Catterick, *Business Planning for Housing* (Chartered Institute of Housing 1995).
21 J. Ashby, *Risk Management for Committee Members* (NFHA 1992)
22 *Risk Management for Registered Social Landlords* (Housing Corporation 1997).
23 Op. cit., 22, p. 1.
24 J. Ashby and D. Joseph, *Internal Control: A Guide for Voluntary Board Members* (NFHA 1995).

25 Internal Control in Housing Associations (CIPFA/NFHA 1994).
26 *Internal Financial Control and Financial Reporting*, Circular R2-18/96 (The Housing Corporation 1996).
27 E. Bowes and G. Lemos, *Reaching the Top. What do Black People have to do to be Senior Managers in Housing Associations?* (Lemos and Crane 1997)
28 C. Legg, *Using Performance Indicators* (NFHA 1991).
29 *A Standard Classification of Housing Associations: The Housing Corporation's Response to the Report by the University of Wales College of Cardiff* (The Housing Corporation 1994).
30 *Registered Social Landlords in 1997 – Performance Indicators* (The Housing Corporation 1998).
31 P. Catterick, *Total Quality: An Introduction to Quality Management in Social Housing* (Chartered Institute of Housing 1992), p. 4.
32 *BS 5750 A Tool for Improvement* (NFHA 1993).
33 J. Passmore and S. Fergusson, *Customer Service in a Competitive Environment* (Chartered Institute of Housing 1994).

5

The Financial Framework

This chapter is concerned with grants, subsidies and sources of finance. It examines the capital and revenue regimes and considers sources and types of private finance, treasury management and the impact of private finance on the sector in relation to rent levels and financial viability. Accounting requirements are outlined and the chapter ends with a summary of the main features of the financial management of RSLs.

The basic principle of all housing finance regimes and accounting conventions is the separation of 'revenue' and 'capital' transactions. This classification divides the operational or annual running costs (revenue) from the costs of acquiring, developing and funding assets with a long-term value (capital). This convention applies equally to RSLs. Table 5.1 identifies the principal sources of capital and revenue income and the main heads of capital and revenue expenditure. This simple breakdown forms the basis of the annual accounts of an RSL to which we return later in this chapter.

Table 5.1   Capital and revenue: simplified main heads of income and expenditure

Revenue income	Capital income
Rent and service charges	Loans
Government grants and subsidies	Capital grants
Other	Gifts
	Share capital (minimal as members may only hold a £1 share each)
Revenue expenditure	**Capital expenditure**
Salaries and overheads	Development costs
Maintenance expenditure	Purchase of other fixed assets
Loan repayments	
Service costs	
Insurance costs	

In order to appreciate the current operating environment of the sector it is necessary to briefly review the traditional financial regime which operated until 1988.

5.1   The capital funding regime

Housing Association Grant prior to 1989

Traditional or residual Housing Association Grant (HAG) was introduced in 1974. The principles of its operation remained virtually unaltered until the passage of the Housing Act 1988. HAG was (and remained until 1996) payable *only* to registered housing associations, and then only in respect of eligible expenditure on qualifying projects. Since 1 April 1997, however, all registered social landlords, including housing associations, have been eligible for capital grant which is now called Social Housing Grant (SHG); this was one of the key changes introduced by the Housing Act 1996.

Pre-1989, residual HAG was payable on qualifying costs which included:

(a)   acquisition of land;
(b)   site development works;
(c)   new building works;
(d)   works of improvement/conversion and major repairs;
(e)   professional fees;
(f)   development administration allowances;
(g)   capitalised interest on loans raised during the development period.

HAG was a single capital grant paid on the completion of a project once the final outturn costs were known. On completion, the claim was submitted to the Housing Corporation or local authority for approval and payment.

The rents used in the calculation of HAG were 'fair rents' set by an independent Rent Officer. The income from the project was determined by using annual rental income net of service charges, less a voids and bad debt allowance of 4 per cent, and net of management and maintenance allowances. Allowances (which remain current for certain purposes) are notional sums fixed annually by the Housing Corporation which sets the maximum allowable expenditure on management and maintenance. An annuity factor was applied to the net rental income to calculate the loan it would service at a fixed interest rate over a period of 60 years for new build, and 30 years for rehabilitation (the expected project life). This was known as a residual loan. The amount of HAG paid was the difference between the qualifying capital costs and the residual capitalised loan. An example is given in Table 5.2.

Table 5.2   A worked example of a residual HAG calculation for a
rehabilitation project (single-family dwelling)

	£	£
Total capital cost (qualifying costs including capitalised interest)		60 000
Rental income per annum	1 560	
less 4% voids and bad debts allowance	62	
Net rent	1 498	
less management and maintenance allowances	670	
Rent available to service loan	828	
At current interest rates for 30 years this will service a loan of		7 910
HAG available (total cost less serviceable loan) under pre-1988 system		52 090

The residual system was generous, with HAG payments averaging over 85 per cent per scheme. In the case of some supported housing schemes costs could exceed rental income (due largely to staffing requirements), leaving no income to service a loan. Indeed, in addition to 100 per cent HAG, revenue assistance and 'topping-up' funding was also required (see Chapter 8).

Prior to the advent of mixed funding all development finance and long-term loans were made available by either the Housing Corporation or local authorities. This added substantially to the Public Sector Borrowing Requirement, and the Government began to view HAG as an over gener-ous and inefficient use of public resources. Although this residual approach led to high HAG levels, scheme costs were carefully controlled through cost limits. The generosity of the system was on the whole coun-terbalanced by excessive systems of scheme scrutiny and tight cost limits. Research undertaken by the NHF at the time the regime was under review suggested that it is only with grant levels of such a high order that rents could be maintained at a level affordable to housing association tenants. As we have seen, affordability became the crucial issue in the tripartite negotiations between the Housing Corporation, the Department of the Environment and the NHF concerning the detail of the post-1988 Act financial framework.

The old regime posed minimal risks other than those normally associ-ated with the development process. Each scheme required approval at every stage, including tender acceptance, by the funding agency (the Housing Corporation or the local authority). There was therefore a great deal of certainty in the process, and minimal emphasis on cost control other than that imposed through the system. The system was not designed to produce cost savings.

5.2   The capital funding regime, 1 April 1989–31 March 1997

In 1987 the DoE published its consultation paper, *Finance for Housing Associations: The Government's Proposals.*

The principal objectives of the proposed regime were, first, to increase the volume of housing that could be provided for a given amount of public money by mixing public and private finance. The principle of mixing public grant with private loans is termed 'mixed' funding. This principle still applies today. In fact, much of the post-1988 Act regime remains intact following the passage of the Housing Act 1996; therefore these principles are outlined first followed by a consideration of the main changes introduced by the Housing Act 1996. Since 1989, in the case of mixed funded schemes only the grant has counted as public expenditure, whereas when public sector loans were used the total scheme costs scored against expenditure limits.

The second objective of the 1989 regime was to increase value for money in the funding of housing association development by requiring associations to take on a greater proportion of the risk, which would in turn act as an incentive to greater efficiency. The consultation paper stated: 'the injection of market disciplines will itself lead to greater efficiency and make housing associations more independent and more responsible for the quality and effectiveness of their investment decisions and the competence of their management'. As we have seen in earlier chapters, this has proved to be the case.

The third objective was to target grant accurately whilst still taking into account scheme costs and, although the overall result would clearly be to push up rent levels, 'to ensure that rents are in the means of the normal range of those tenants who are in employment and not reliant on benefits to assist with their housing costs'. The Government was seeking to widen the role of (and therefore the clients assisted by) housing associations. In fact, as discussed in Chapter 1, benefit dependency amongst housing association tenants has increased dramatically since 1989, and grant rates have never been sufficient to enable rents to be truly affordable.

Finally, as associations were to carry an increased share of the risk, procedures and administrative requirements would be simplified. Private finance was to become the normal method of long-term funding and in order to achieve this the Housing Act 1988 introduced assured tenancies, free from rent control, and the right to buy, leaving associations to set their own rents (whilst retaining the fair rent system for existing secure tenants who derive their rights from the Housing Act 1985). The secure tenancy regime still applies to these long-standing tenants.

The capital funding regime is based upon what have become known as the 'Ryrie Rules'. These were principles established by Sir William Ryrie who, in 1981 chaired an National Economic Development Council working party on investment in the nationalised industries. The principles were, firstly, if private sector investment was to be introduced into public sector industries then the investors should not have a greater degree of security than would be available on private sector projects. Secondly, such investment should lead to improved efficiency as a result of the additional investment. Thus, under this regime, which remains current, there is no major repair funding on projects that have received grant and, after 1 April 1989, there was no Revenue Deficit Grant to protect the investor against risk, and capital cost overruns are not covered. Risk was transferred to the associations from the Government. The withdrawal of major repairs funding has led to rent increases as associations set up provisions for future repairs. This approach also reflected the policy of the last decade to shift subsidies from 'bricks and mortar' exemplified by reduced grant rates, to person or income-related subsidies. By 1996, it was clear that housing benefit could no longer take the strain as the cost to the nation rocketed. Thus, as noted in Chapter 1, the Housing Act 1996 introduced some rent constraints on housing associations and throughout the mid-1990s housing benefit underwent successive reductions and was withdrawn from a number of groups (see Chapter 7).

The result of the framework introduced in April 1989 was to create a more commercial operating climate, with associations having to ensure value for money at every stage in the development process and in their operations in general. As we shall see later, the ability to accumulate reserves to ensure viability and to meet the requirements of private lenders became a major concern of many associations after 1989.

5.3   The capital funding regime since 1 April 1997

The Housing Act 1996 introduced a number of changes to the way in which registered social landlords (RSLs) are funded. Section 28 of the Housing Act 1996 provides that that no further payments of Housing Association Grant (HAG) will be made after the commencement of the Act. The revised financial regime which applied from 1 April 1997 to all registered social landlords is set out in part I chapter III of the 1996 Act. The Act introduces the concept of Social Housing Grant (SHG), which differs from HAG in two important respects. Firstly, all registered social landlords are eligible to bid for it, not just traditional housing associations. Secondly, tenants of homes developed with SHG will, subject to certain criteria, have the right to acquire that home. Thus the right to buy, which has applied to council housing since 1980, now in effect, extends to RSL homes developed after 1997 (see Chapter 10). Part III also introduces purchase grants for this purpose and renews or changes many of the provisions of part II of the Housing Associations Act 1985 and Housing Act 1988. Social Housing Grant is payable under section 18 of the Housing Act 1996. It empowers the Housing Corporation to pay SHG to RSLs for eligible capital and revenue activities. The Corporation has issued a number of general determinations setting out eligibility for SHG and the conditions that apply to it. These are as follows.

Social Housing Grant (Capital) General Determination 1997

This determination outlines the principles for the calculation and payment of SHG for eligible capital projects. The procedures to be followed are set out in the *Capital Funding System Procedure Guide* (1997), which is referred to throughout this book. The General Determination also sets out activities that are eligible for SHG, which include:

(a)   acquiring, providing, constructing, repairing, improving, adapting or creating by the conversion of buildings dwellings to be kept available for letting;

(b)   providing land, amenities or services, or providing, constructing, repairing, converting or improving buildings, for the benefit of an RSL's residents, either exclusively or together with other persons;

(c)   acquiring, repairing and improving, or creating by the conversion of buildings, dwellings to be disposed of by sale, by lease, on a shared ownership lease, or on such other terms as may be specified by the Corporation;

(d)   acquiring, providing, constructing, repairing, improving or managing dwellings for occupation by members of the RSL where the rules of the RSL restrict membership to persons entitled (or prospectively entitled as tenants or otherwise) to occupy a dwelling provided or managed by the RSL (this refers to primary co-operative housing associations);

(e)   construction of dwellings to be disposed of on shared ownership leases;

(f)   making payments to tenants as an incentive to vacate an RSL's dwelling (Tenants' Incentive scheme (TIS))

Section 18(4) of the Housing Act 1996 also permits the Housing Corporation to appoint a local authority to act for it as its agent in the assessment and payment of SHG.

Recovery of grants

The 1988 Housing Act section 52, widened the Corporation's powers to recover payments of HAG. The Corporation was given powers to reduce, suspend or reclaim grants where 'relevant events' occurred. Examples of relevant events would be disposal of a property or a breach of a grant condition. These powers applied to all payments of HAG made since its introduction in 1974. Furthermore, if a relevant event occurred and the Corporation demanded repayment of the whole or part of the grant it was able to charge interest.

Experience of operating this system and the recognition of the need for greater flexibility in order that landlords could more effectively invest in existing stock and manage their assets better, led to one of the most important changes introduced by the 1996 Act: HAG-recycling.

Recycling of capital grants

Under section 27 of the Housing Act 1996 the Housing Corporation is empowered to issue a determination to enable an RSL to retain either HAG or SHG when it disposes of a property and to reinvest it. The general determinations on the recovery of HAG which introduced capital grant recycling were issued by the Housing Corporation in 1997.[1] RSLs may now retain recoverable grant to re-use or recycle it adding its own finance to create more homes. Circulars F2 21/97 and F2 16/98 set out the rules governing this process. The monies derived in this way are placed into a Capital Grant Recycling Fund (CGRF) and must be invested within the following three years. Properties may be provided of an equivalent size, in the area in which the original home was sold. In addition, the fund may be used to make payments under the Tenants' Incentive Scheme (see Chapter 10), and to finance major repair work to the stock, provided that the Rent Surplus Fund of the organisation stands below £500 000. The RSL's auditors are required to sign off an annual return on the Capital Grant Recycling Fund for Housing Corporation purposes.

Purchase grants

By virtue of section 20 of the Housing Act 1996 the Housing Corporation can make a grant to an RSL where tenants have exercised their right to acquire their home under section 16 of the Act. The grant is equivalent to any discount to which the tenant is entitled. These grants are not cash limited and could therefore have a significant impact on the size of the rented programme funded through future Corporation ADPs, depending on the take-up of purchase grants. Purchase grants may also be made to cover the equivalent value of discounts where a tenant has chosen to buy other than their own home, usually at the landlord's request. Voluntary Purchase Grant (VPG) may also be payable through these powers.[2]

Disposal proceeds

Sections 24 and 25 of the Housing Act 1996 direct that RSLs should establish 'disposal proceeds funds' to separately account for the net proceeds or income, from sales. These must be spent as the Housing Corporation directs, mainly for reinvestment in social housing and placed in an accountable 'Disposal Proceeds Fund'.[3] The fund receives all proceeds of disposal apart from those costs of provision that have not been provided by public grant or subsidy. Reasonable expenses may also be deducted. Interest is to be added to the Disposal Proceeds Fund. The fund may be applied for the acquisition of additional dwellings, acquisition of land on which dwellings are to be built and for the repair of vacant dwellings. The Fund should be spent in the local authority area in which the sale occurred as far as possible. Funds may be appropriated by the Housing Corporation if they have not been applied within three years or if the RSL is removed from the Register of the Housing Corporation.

RSLs now therefore enjoy a more favourable treatment than local authorities in being enabled to recycle grant and disposal receipts. Local authorities have, on the other hand, been subjected to a rigorous system for the control of spending of capital receipts.

5.4   Grant and cost control

There are two key components of the current system which together determine the level of capital subsidy: total cost indicators, or TCIs, and fixed grant rates.

Total cost indicators

Total Cost Indicators (TCIs) secure value for money by setting a unit cost limit. They are used to calculate the maximum level of grant or other public subsidy payable and are also used to evaluate cost-effectiveness in comparing scheme types. The huge increase in competition between developing housing associations for grant that has occurred since 1989 means that TCIs are less relevant than they were when first established. Associations have actively sought to reduce the procurement costs of the homes they provide and and will bid using actual costs rather than the prevailing cost indicator. TCIs cover self-contained housing, shared accommodation for general needs, sheltered housing, frail elderly schemes and wheelchair needs. They represent the *total* cost of a unit of a given size, type and for each particular area. The TCI for any unit is fixed by reference to the floor area (m^2) of each unit in the case of self-contained accommodation, or per person to be housed in the case of shared accommodation. The TCI increases according to the size of the unit. The TCI also varies in relation to geographical area. There are five such areas, A to E. A covers the most expensive areas (inner London boroughs), E the cheaper provincial areas.

TCIs include acquisition costs, works and VAT, and additional or 'on-costs'.

On-costs

On-costs include professional and legal fees, the RSL's own development administration costs and capitalised interest accrued on loans raised during the development period. A percentage of acquisition and works totals is applied to assess the on-cost allowance. For example, if acquisition and works costs total £100 000 and the on-cost percentage addition for that type of scheme is 20 per cent, then the RSL must contain those costs within £20 000. On-costs are therefore a notional figure. Grant is paid on notional on-costs; thus, if savings can be made, say on consultant fees, these can be used to reduce capital costs and consequently the rents charged, as the loan required after SHG has been paid will be smaller. The system therefore encourages RSLs to negotiate such items as surveyors' fees to achieve savings. As on-costs also include capitalised interest accrued during the development period, the RSL must also attempt to speed up the development process and reduce capitalised interest by whatever means it can.

The TCI represents an estimate of the final cost of the scheme as at practical completion, (i.e., the costs include a figure for future inflation). This is a critical feature and RSLs need to be able to forecast accurately final outturn costs several months, or even years, in advance of completion.

Multipliers

In addition to the basic costs per dwelling, TCIs are adjusted by a series of multipliers. Firstly, key multipliers are applied to the base TCI to differentiate between categories of development (for example new build or rehabilitation schemes). Supplementary multipliers are then applied to adjust the TCI to take account of the greater costs of buildings with lifts, sheltered housing schemes, or for special needs for example. Thus the basic TCI is increased (or decreased) to reflect the nature of the dwelling. TCIs are reviewed by the Department of the Environment, Transport and the Regions annually, but once a TCI is fixed at grant confirmation stage (exchange of contracts for purchase), any uplifts that occur during the development process do not apply. At times of rapid inflation the value of the TCI will therefore be quickly eroded, possibly leaving the organisation with development cost deficits. Prior to approving grant, the Corporation may agree Special Percentage Adjustments (SPAs), additions or deductions to the TCI of between 80 and 120 per cent to reflect abnormally high or low costs within localised districts of a single TCI area. Finally, schemes will only be approved up to an absolute maximum of 130 per cent.

Fixed grant rates

The system is characterised by predetermined fixed grant rates. There is a particularly close relationship between TCIs and grant rates under this system. Together they form the two determinants of capital subsidy.

Grant rates establish the maximum percentage of grant input to schemes dependent, like TCI, upon the type of dwelling and the TCI area in which it is to be developed. If other public subsidy is available (see below) then grant will be reduced pound for pound. Rates are intended to reflect the likely income from 'affordable' rents and differences in management and maintenance costs arising from different scheme types. The grant rates take into account these cost factors so that rent levels for similar accommodation are not unduly affected by the *inherent* cost of providing the type of housing required. Grant rates also take into account evidence in relation to RSLs' running costs and the incomes of households being allocated tenancies. Thus, in 1998/99 a sheltered housing scheme in TCI area A received a norm, or standard grant, of 84 per cent, and in TCI area E, 71.9 per cent. General family new build schemes in TCI area A attracted 57.7 per cent and in TCI area E a norm of 31.6 per cent, and so on. A grant matrix is provided to simplify calculations.

The grant rate is set at the outset of the scheme; it cannot be increased later to take account of actual outturn costs. Grant will be paid on the lower of the rates bid for by the RSL (see Chapter 6) or according to the amount produced by the above calculation. As with scheme costs, competition between RSLs has dramatically reduced the call on grant. In an attempt to outbid each other, associations since 1989 have consistently bid at below published rates, fuelling the Ministerial view that rates could be reduced. This action, facilitated by large reserves in some associations and/or the ability to pool rent in others, has made it more difficult for the National Housing Federation to argue for increases in the grant rates that would produce affordable rents in their own right. In 1998/99 the national average grant rate, which is set by the Minister was set at 56 per cent in comparison with 75 per cent in 1989/90.[4]

Grant is paid in tranches at three stages: exchange of contracts, start on site and practical completion. The amount or tranche of grant advanced varies according to scheme type (e.g., new-build or rehabilitation). For example, tranches for acquisition and works new build are 40:40:20 and, for rehabilitation, 50:30:20.

The tranches vary to account for the different proportions of expenditure at stages in a project according to the scheme type. The system of tranches reflects the Treasury position of ensuring that the risk is shared throughout the process. It would be far simpler (if not cheaper) to advance grant in one lump at the start of the scheme, the system adopted for the pilot programmes until 1989. The current system is cumbersome and means that RSLs may have to borrow development finance to cover costs not covered by grant far earlier in the development process which, of course, adds to development costs and subsequently rents.

Total public subsidy
A further essential feature of the current funding regime is the cap on total public subsidy. The subsidy level on any scheme cannot exceed the grant rate established for it. Thus, if an RSL receives grants or subsidy on a scheme from any other public body, it must deduct the value of such contributions from the grant receivable. Furthermore, the Local Government Act 1988 requires local authorities to obtain the special consent of the Secretary of State to dispose of land at less than full market value and, if such a disposal would afford a benefit to the purchaser, such benefits must be valued and deducted from the SHG. Thus if an RSL is attempting to make a scheme 'work' at the lower grant rates and has persuaded the local authority to make a contribution through cheap land, perhaps in return for nomination rights, then the value must be deducted from the SHG to ensure that the subsidy cap is not exceeded. Furthermore, if local authorities consider making revenue contributions instead, these must be capitalised and their net present value deducted from grant. However, private sector grants, revenue contributions to cover *non-housing* costs, and grants for historic buildings do not need to be deducted. The concept of total public subsidy closed many 'creative' routes that associations and local authorities had developed to assist in the production of affordable homes.

5.5   Supported housing

A new regime was introduced with effect from April 1991 and both risk and competition, along with value for money considerations, are now features of the supported housing funding regime. The framework was adapted to take into account additional factors relevant to the development and future management of such schemes. The system of 100 per cent capital funding remained available although rarely approved, and Hostel Deficit Grant was replaced by a flat rate 'special needs management allowance' (SNMA), known as Supported Housing Management Grant (SHMG), to meet the costs of providing additional management

support to tenants. SHMG has to be bid for as part of the annual allocation process.

In 1993 the system was reviewed again and measures introduced to
enable associations to bid for varying levels of both capital grant and
SHMG, leading to greater competition for capital and revenue resources
and to greater uncertainty in the whole special needs funding framework.
An RSL's eligibility for SHMG across the whole of its supported housing
stock is now reviewed every three years by the Housing Corporation and
can be withdrawn if it can be shown that a scheme fails to meet certain
criteria. Owing to its complexity and the particular nature of this funding
regime, special needs funding is considered separately, in Chapter 8.
Readers should note that in 1999 yet another framework was also under
review for implementation in 2003.

5.6   The procedural framework

The capital funding regime is operated through a detailed procedural
framework. The framework is based on one of two options: either scheme-
by-scheme approval, or a programme arrangement covering a number of
schemes. Programme arrangements have always been the preferred route
for landlords with large development programmes who are financially
strong.

'Funding agreements' with 'Programme' or 'Scheme Contract' routes
were introduced with effect from April 1995. The details of the Funding
Agreement procedural arrangements are examined in Chapter 6 but it is
necessary at this stage to note the key features.

Funding conditions and investment contracts

From 1 April 1995 all procedures for the Approved Development
Programme (ADP) funded rent and sale programmes were consolidated
into a uniform framework applicable to all developing RSLs. These have
to be negotiated year on year, giving less certainty to the landlord and
ability to procure savings but greater control over savings to the Housing
Corporation. Any RSL receiving an allocation from the Corporation must
enter into an Investment Contract with the Regional Office of the
Corporation. A fresh agreement is drawn up each year. As noted, the programme management arrangements are known as either 'programme contracts' or 'scheme contracts'. The only difference between the two routes
is the treatment of savings and any cost increases incurred on the development of each scheme. Grant rates for each scheme within the annual
funding agreement are fixed at the outset of each scheme as outlined
above at what is known as the grant confirmation stage. Costs over TCI

can be approved subject to scrutiny and up to the maxima highlighted above. Savings on individual schemes are transferred into a 'grant pot'. Organisations with programme contracts may recycle any savings on particular allocations according to set parameters. Savings arising through the scheme contract route must be returned to the Corporation and they will decide which scheme or RSL will be allocated the savings. Local authority funded schemes are excluded from the funding agreement unless the scheme is jointly funded with the Housing Corporation. Other non-ADP funded schemes such the Rough Sleepers' Initiative, are also excluded from funding agreements. The procedures apply to all programme headings and as stated, are considered further in Chapter 6.

Cash planning targets

Once allocations are agreed, the RSL will also settle quarterly targets for cash take-up and spend by association. The targets ensure that the Corporation meets its own cash spend target for the year and neither over- nor under-spends itself.

Each RSL must also raise loans to meet those costs not covered by grant. Since 1989 over £14 billion has been raised by housing associations from private funders. This finance has covered a variety of activities including new development. Loans raised have to be repaid through rents thus, before considering private finance and its implications for the sector (in terms of their ability to develop, their viability and financial management), it is to the revenue regime that we now turn.

5.7 The revenue regime: rent-setting

Fair rents

The prime source of income of each RSL is the rent it charges for the occupancy of its dwellings. There are two main systems of rent-fixing currently in operation which are dependent upon the nature of the tenancy. All tenancies entered into prior to 15 January 1989 are 'secure' tenancies as defined by the Housing Act 1980, with the provisions consolidated by the Housing Act 1985. Rents for secure tenancies are known as 'fair rents' and are set by an independent Rent Officer. Tenancies entered into after 15 January 1989 are known as assured tenancies and RSLs are able to fix their own rents in this case, subject to guidance laid down by the Housing Corporation. Secure and assured tenancies are considered further in Chapter 7.

The 'Fair Rent' system was introduced by the Rent Act 1965 for the private rented sector and extended to housing associations by the Housing Finance Act 1972. The provisions were consolidated in the Rent Act 1977 and subsequently amended by the Housing Act 1980. This Act was in turn consolidated in 1985 and further amendments were passed by the Housing Act 1988. There is no statutory definition of a fair rent, but guiding principles were set down in the Rent Act 1977. This states that the Rent Officer is required to take into account all relevant circumstances and in particular the age, character, state of repair and location of the dwelling. The Rent Officer must, however, disregard the personal circumstances of both the landlord and tenant and disregard scarcity. Thus the rent for a property cannot be higher due to the fact that there may be a shortage of such accommodation in the area. The Rent Officer must assume an adequate supply.

Rent officers are independent agents of central government who bring together landlord and tenant to agree the rent for the dwelling. Once agreed the rent becomes a 'registered rent', is entered on to a public register and remains fixed for a two-year period. It is illegal for a landlord to charge more than the registered rent. Applications to have the rent fixed may be made by the landlord or the tenant or jointly. Both parties have a right to consultation and if dissatisfied with the Rent Officer's decision, may appeal within 28 days to the Rent Assessment Committee.

If either the landlord or the tenant is dissatisfied with the determination of the Rent Assessment Committee then an appeal can be made on a point of law (not over the rent level alone), to the County Court, the High Court and eventually to the House of Lords. It should be noted, however, that associations have discouraged their tenants from appealing to the Rent Assessment Committee if they think the rent set by the Rent Officer is too high as invariably the Committee has determined that the rent should be even higher than that proposed initially by the Rent Officer. If this does occur,then associations are permitted to charge the original rent set by the Rent Officer.

The registered rent is reviewed every two years and, following the abolition of rent phasing by the Housing Act 1988, tenants must pay the full increase following the 28-day statutory notice period. In assessing rent levels, the Rent Officer is free to determine the rent, subject to the guidance mentioned, in any manner he or she likes. In practice, however, a system of comparables is usually adopted, although in recent years there is evidence that many officers have linked fair rents to capital values. This has led to a rapid increase in the level of fair rents since the mid-1980s.

A fair rent may consist of two elements, the occupancy element and the service charge. The service charge will be shown separately from the occupancy element of the rent if it amounts to more than 5 per cent of the rent. The service charge covers items such as caretaking and cleaning services and may also include depreciation on items such as communal furniture, lifts and boilers. If a service charge amounts to less than 5 per cent of the rent it is known as a negligible service charge and is not separately recorded by the Rent Officer. Landlords must account for service income and expenditure separately and must be able to justify to both the Rent Officer and to the tenant the level to be charged. Schedule 19 of the Housing Act 1980 (consolidated by the provisions of the Landlord and Tenant Act 1985 sections 18–30) set out the information that must be provided. Tenants are entitled to a written summary of service costs for the previous 12 months.

Service charges may be fixed or variable. In the latter case, if a variable charge is set by the Rent Officer the charge may be varied within the two-year period. This is often the practice where the charge includes an amount for heating or hot water and the landlord has no control over price increases.

The provisions of the Housing Act 1988 section 35 amend existing legislation so that the fair rents, secure tenancies and the package of rights known as the 'tenants' charter' do not apply to tenancies granted after 15 January 1989. However, in the case of any tenancy granted before this date, the rights remain. Thus, if either the landlord changes, as may occur if one registered social landlord swaps property with another or, as is more likely, the tenant is transferred to another property or requests a transfer, the tenant retains secure tenancy status including the right to a fair rent. This has financial implications for the organisation. The fair rent is likely to be lower than a rent resulting from development under the current capital finance regime. This will result in an income deficit if a tenant moving into the property can only be charged the fair rent equivalent. The problem has been circumvented, however, by regulations that permit the RSL to offset such losses against its liability for Rent Surplus Fund (or RSF: see below).

From time to time there have been calls to end the dual regime through scrapping fair rents for housing association secure tenants. This would afford associations greater flexibility in rent-setting and pooling and greater control over their prime source of income given the increased risks they now face. To date this has been resisted, and research has shown that there is an increasing convergence between fair rents and the assured rents charged on new properties and relets. This issue is discussed further later.

Assured tenancy rents

Every new tenancy granted after 15 January 1989 is an assured tenancy, regardless of whether it is for an existing property which is being relet or a newly developed property being let for the first time. This is subject to the exceptions outlined above. The Housing Act 1988 states that rents for assured tenancies should be market rents agreed between the landlord and tenant. Rent Officers have no remit to determine rents under this regime.

They will, however, if requested by a local authority for housing benefit purposes, give their view as to whether the assured tenancy rent is within market rent levels. In addition, from 2 January 1996 the Rent Officer will also give guidance on the prevailing level of market rent for that size of property in the area to be known as the 'local reference rent'. Housing benefit on a new tenancy may not be paid in full if the rent exceeds the local reference rent level. The tenancy agreement or contract may specify the mechanism for rent review and rents will be reviewed annually. The tenant may either agree the increase or refer it to the Rent Assessment Committee for the determination of a market rent. This appeal mechanism is clearly of little benefit to housing association tenants, or indeed anyone on low income who will have great difficulty in affording market rent levels.

5.8   Rents and affordability

Since 1988 associations have had to devise and adopt rent-setting policies and mechanisms. This has proved to be no easy task. In setting rents RSLs must consider not only the affordability of their rents and their accessibility to those in low-paid employment, but they also need to consider the revenue requirements of the organisation.

In Circular 05/93, *Rents*, the Corporation stated: 'associations are expected to take into account the need to cover costs (after subsidy) of loan charges, and of management and maintenance, including the requirement to make prudent provision for future repairs and in setting the rent for each dwelling should take into account its size, amenities, location and condition'.

Rent-pooling is also a common mechanism. Increased rents on older, debt-free properties can be used to subsidise costs on new schemes developed under the fixed grant regime. The extent to which this policy has assisted associations to keep rents affordable is questionable. In any event, as rents rise an RSL will literally 'run out' of low-rented property and the ability to fund schemes internally in this way.

In determining the rent for each unit, having set the annual revenue requirement, it should take into account the difference in size, type and quality of its stock. For example, having worked out an average rent for each size of property an adjustment can then be made for additional facilities such as parking space, gardens, energy efficiency or for negative factors such as poor condition and lack of central heating, weighting the rent to reflect the quality of the property.

Rent influencing

Since the passage of the Housing Act 1996, as outlined in Chapter 1, the Housing Corporation has influenced rent and service charge levels charged by RSLs on general needs accommodation through both the annual bidding process for new dwellings and the Performance Standards for older stock. Known as 'rent influencing' rather than rent control as there is an element of discretion in the process, the principles were set out in a Housing Corporation Discussion Paper published in 1996.[5]

Rent-influencing excludes smaller RSLs which are subject to the Regulatory Arrangements for Smaller Associations (RASA) regime. Rent-influencing was introduced to attempt to stem the tide of rising rents. Between 1992 and 1996 RSL rents on new homes rose by some 30 per cent and on relettings by 40 per cent. The housing benefit bill for rent allowances had increased from £1.3 billion in 1989 to £5.7 billion in 1996/97. This is clearly unsustainable. Ministers made it clear that rises were to be limited to Retail Price Index plus + 1 per cent, in 1997/98 and that RSLs may expect further reductions in future years. Each RSL must set a rent 'envelope' whereby the total rent increases for the year for all dwellings do not exceed RPI plus 1 per cent, although there may be variations on individual rents within this.

In the case of homes developed with Social Housing Grant after 1 April 1997, the rent levels are contractual and bid for through the capital programmme. The agreed rents are set at the outset and must be adhered to on completion and letting. For the remainder of the general needs stock, rent increases may not exceed the envelope of RPI + 1 per cent.

The 1997 Performance Standards detail the expectations of RSLs.[6] Rents and service charges are to be set to meet sub-market rent levels whilst taking into account their legal and financial commitments. Rents should be within the reach of those in low-paid employment, and rent policies made public.

In developing the rent-influencing policy, the Housing Corporation was persuaded to take into account the position of housing associations that had received transfer of public sector stock. Often the business plan of the Large Scale Voluntary Transfer Association is based upon rent rises above RPI plus 1 per cent, and these rises were agreed with the tenants at the time of the ballot for the transfer. Such income is required to meet loan repayments and often to undertake works of improvement and repair. Where this is the case, the Housing Corporation will negotiate the rent envelope with the individual RSL. Furthermore, representations were made to the Housing Corporation regarding the impact of rent-influencing upon stock reinvestment programmes. Again, an RSL may discuss its individual position with the Housing Corporation.

Given that RSLs are apparently committed to the concept of affordable rents, however, and given the desire to alleviate the poverty trap exacerbated by high rents, it is essential that rent envelope targets are met. Indeed, work by the National Housing Federation and the Housing Corporation undertaken in 1998 suggested that this was in fact the case.

RSLs must also be aware that the rent regime is more generous than that imposed on local authorities, although it is accepted that one outcome of this policy has been the neglect of much local authority stock, owing to lack of funds to maintain it. As stated above, the Labour Government wishes to see RSL rents fall, and it is likely that the rent envelope will be set at an even more challenging level in years to come. RSLs must therefore prepare for this, seeking ever greater cost-efficiencies.

In developing a rent setting policy therefore, each organisation has had to consider the guidelines set by the National Housing Federation the Housing Corporation and its own revenue position including its requirements for investment in long-term maintenance and other liabilities.

The affordability debate

It is the financial regime and decisions taken by each landlord in setting their rents which determines the affordability of the rents to those they house (in addition to the personal economic circumstances of each household). Affordability remains a core principle driving RSL development and guiding decisions on rent policy for existing tenants. Achieving an agreed definition has proved virtually impossible, however.

The 1987 consultation paper stated: 'In general the Government would expect associations to set their rents for newly provided dwellings significantly below the free market level.'[7] On relets it stated: 'rents for these dwellings should be put on a basis broadly comparable with that which will apply to new provision'.[8] In addition, the paper had already stated that grant for new developments should be sufficient to ensure that 'rents on these schemes are within the normal range of those tenants who are in employment'. The concept of affordability emanated from this latter statement. During consultation over the Housing Bill 1988, the then Minister for Housing, William Waldegrave, stated that rent should be within the reach of those in *low-paid* employment. This has been the benchmark for affordability since. The National Federation determined that a definition of affordability should be 20 per cent of the median net income of new tenant households in work. This figure was originally used as it compared reasonably with interest, not capital, payments by first-time buyers. In December 1993 the National Housing Federation adopted a new affordability policy which stated that rents are affordable if the majority of working households taking up new tenancies are not caught in the poverty trap (because of dependency upon housing benefit) or paying more than 25 per cent of their net income on rent. Each year, the National Housing Federation produces a matrix of rents based upon the TCI areas, dwelling size and occupancy levels, taking into account housing benefit entitlements to produce a series of rent levels (known as indicator rents) which provide a general guide to affordable rent levels. The figures for 1997/98 are reproduced in Table 5.3.

Table 5.3   Indicator rents at October 1998 (£ per week)

Floor area (sq.m. exceeding/not exceeding:	Occupancy (persons)	A	B	TCI group C	D	E
Up to 25	1	41.30	41.80	36.90	34.10	32.50
25/30	1	42.70	43.20	38.10	35.20	33.60
30/35	1&2	44.10	44.60	39.40	36.40	34.80
35/40	1&2	45.60	46.10	40.70	37.60	35.90
40/45	2	47.10	47.70	42.10	38.90	37.10
45/50	2	48.70	49.30	43.50	40.20	38.40
50/55	2&3	50.30	50.90	45.00	41.50	39.70
55/60	2&3	52.00	52.60	46.50	42.90	41.00
60/65	3&4	53.70	54.40	48.00	44.30	42.40
65/70	3&4	55.30	56.20	49.70	45.80	43.80
70/75	3 4&5	57.40	58.10	51.30	47.40	45.20
75/80	3 4&5	59.30	60.00	53.00	49.00	46.80
80/85	4 5&6	61.30	62.10	58.40	50.60	48.30
85/90	4 5&6	63.40	64.10	56.60	52.30	49.90
90/95	5&6	65.50	66.30	58.50	54.00	51.60
95/100	5&6	67.70	68.50	60.50	55.90	53.30
100/105	6&7	70.00	70.80	62.50	57.70	55.10
105/110	6&7	72.30	73.20	64.60	59.70	57.00
110/115	6 7&8	74.70	75.60	66.80	61.70	58.90
115/120	6 7&8	77.20	78.20	69.00	63.70	60.90

Source: NHF.

The regime has failed to ensure affordable rents across the sector. The grant rates themselves are too low and, in addition to servicing loans, the rents must also cover long-term maintenance requirements resulting from the phased withdrawal of major repairs capital funding. Single people fare the worst as the grant percentages produce rents of over 35 per cent of net income in some cases.

Since 1989 housing association rents have been closely monitored by the National Housing Federation and affordability has been the subject of a number of research reports which are discussed below.

The Housing Corporation had consistently refused to define affordability, stating that associations must decide what rent levels to charge and that rent determination was outside its remit. In 1992, however, it published a research report on the affordability of housing association rents which signalled a shift in its position.[9] The Corporation now monitors rents and affordability and uses these to inform decisions on grant rates. Having included rents in the bidding process for the 1997/98 allocation round as discussed above, this necessitated the publication of benchmark rents for new developments. Rents in bidding is discussed in greater detail in Chapter 6 but it should be noted here that its inclusion in the bids process as a means of assessing value for money in bids made for grant represented a new departure in that the cost to the public purse not only of capital subsidy, but revenue subsidy too, is now taken into consideration. This cost being the future housing benefit requirement implied by the rent.

Affordability is important not only as a concept, but because of the very real impact rent levels have on peoples lives and their ability to take advantage of employment opportunities. The misery of the poverty trap caused by the exorbitant marginal rates of taxation that affect those on benefits whose support is withdrawn as income rises, cannot be over-stated. Tenants on full housing benefit suffer a marginal taxation rate of 96 per cent for every pound earned as it tapers down, and must obtain huge wage increases before they are actually better off.

A further major study of investment in housing associations and rent levels was published by the Joseph Rowntree Foundation in 1995.[10] Known as the Cambridge Study, the aim of the project was to monitor the effects of the mixed funding regime on housing associations, six years on. In particular, it examined whether the regime enabled associations to achieve financial viability in terms required by lenders, while still meeting their social objectives. It also considered the factors which determine the financial strengths and weaknesses of associations, and importantly it examined trends in rental levels.

The study found that, despite cuts in grant rates and the need to raise large amounts of private finance, most developing associations remained strong with healthy cash flows and a reasonable asset base. However, more than 40 per cent of associations surveyed had no stock left uncharged and would need to restructure their loans if they were to retain a capacity to develop. Greater emphasis was now placed on financial viability and the need to achieve surpluses to satisfy the expectations of lenders than scale of provision or affordability of rents. The report found a lack of expert financial management in the associations studied, with many lacking a treasury management function and indeed proper cash flow forecasts. Rents had been rising faster than private sector rents by some 3 per cent per annum, and the report expressed concern that association and market rents could converge by the year 2000.

Indeed, the the report highlighted parts of the country (particularly in the North-East) where a variety of factors had already led to this convergence on a limited scale, in some areas and on some particular property types, notably one-bedroomed flats. Rent rises had varied from 4 per cent a year in larger associations to 12 per cent in small associations with post-1989 stock. This difference is not surprising as smaller associations, especially those with newer stock, do not have the ability to pool their rents and internally fund the new, high-rent homes with rent surpluses generated by older, debt-free stock.

Affordability was, nevertheless, the most frequently stated factor in rent setting with 84 per cent of associations taking it into account in fixing rent rises. Few considered market rents in their area: a point for concern, as once market rents are reached associations will encounter difficulty in letting their properties and experience increasing arrears as housing benefit is withdrawn. In addition, the rationale for subsidising social housing disappears, raising questions surrounding the very existence of housing associations and other RSLs. The National Housing Federation however, while welcoming the findings of the survey, has stressed that the majority of RSL rents in most areas of the country are still well below market rent levels. Their own survey, undertaken to complement the Joseph Rowntree report,[11] shows that some 18 per cent of new let rents were higher than market equivalents as determined by the Rent Officer. It also confirms that some 60 per cent of associations now pool their rents, as compared with 39 per cent in 1991.

Rent influencing, as discussed earlier, will in the coming years impact upon the rent policies of RSLs and over time reduce the overall call on housing benefit. The policy, however, does not address the key issue of affordability. In effect, it freezes a number of anomalies caused by the existence of differing rent regimes. Research commissioned by the National Housing Federation and the Local Government Association, published in 1998,[12] and a further study undertaken by the Housing Corporation published in 1999,[13] shows that there is little coherence of rent regimes within the sector, or between the social housing sectors. Thus tenants will experience very different rent levels, purely as a result of who their landlord is, rather than flowing from differences in the property or the area themselves. The National Housing Federation was, at the time of writing, arguing for a coherent, sustainable and viable rent regime which will take into account the issues of affordability and which will address the criticisms of the blanket approach produced by the policy of RPI plus 1 per cent outlined earlier.

5.9   Rent Surplus Fund

Under the pre-1988 residual grant regime, rents often increased at a greater rate than the actual cost of management and maintenance. Traditional or residual HAG was paid on the basis of conventional loans (at fixed interest rates) and notional allowances which could be deducted from rental income for management and maintenance costs. In a period of rental inflation, if actual management and maintenance costs were below these notional allowance levels, a scheme could soon come into surplus. Not all surpluses can be retained by RSLs, however.

Grant Redemption Fund (GRF)

GRF was the forerunner of the RSF which replaced it with effect from 1 April 1989. GRF was introduced by the Housing Act 1980 as a kind of 'tax' on rental surpluses. Through GRF the Government was able to recoup those surpluses; in 1987/88 the return to the Government of such surpluses amounted to some £14.7 million. GRF was recycled through the Housing Corporation's Approved Development Programme so that such surpluses were not entirely lost to the sector.

Rent Surplus Fund

The Rent Surplus Fund (RSF), replaced GRF. It was introduced by the Housing Act 1988 section 55, and applied to all accounting periods after 31 March 1989. It applies only to properties developed under the pre-1988 regime. The National Housing Federation lobbied hard for the abolition of what was viewed as taxation on rent surpluses given the risks inherent in the (then) new financial regime, but originally it lost the case. RSF was, however, more generous than GRF in that associations retained 15 per cent of rental surpluses to supplement reserves, and a further 70 per cent in order to build up provisions for future major repair requirements. The final tranche of 15 per cent was paid over to government.

In 1992 a further concession was introduced. RSLs could retain all rental surpluses but 80 per cent had to be set aside to build up major repair provisions for recently completed rented stock, leaving 20 per cent which could be used freely to supplement general reserves. Since December 1997, however, the Housing Corporation has ceased directing the use of RSF altogether. An RSL may now utilise its accumulated RSF to invest in any property requiring works which would qualify for Social Housing Grant under the category of Works to Existing Stock, including aids and adaptions work. The accumulated fund is now known as the RSF Reinvestment Fund.

It should be noted, however, that new schemes developed under the capital regime since 1 April 1989 and let on assured tenancies are excluded from RSF calculations. Other exclusions include almshouse charities, co-ownership societies and associations providing solely hostel accommodation. RSF only applies where traditional HAG has been received. However, even then, some accommodation is outside the scope of RSF. This includes properties where the only HAG input has been for major repair or miscellaneous works (see Chapter 6). Schemes provided under the 1987/88 and 1988/89 pilot mixed funded programmes are also excluded. Almshouse accommodation, hostel and co-ownership accommodation, short-life (temporary housing) and leasehold schemes for the elderly are also beyond the scope of RSF. Thus deficits incurred on hostels and short-life accommodation cannot be offset against surpluses arising on other types of accommodation.

The Housing Corporation is responsible for the administration of RSF and a detailed return is required, certified by the association's auditors and showing that the RSF calculations follow approved principles and that they are accurate. The calculation is technically complex and readers are referred to the relevant circulars and guide for further detail.[14]

5.10   Major repair funding

The phasing-out of major repair funding which covers the cost of replacing worn-out or obsolete elements of a building during its life has been referred to frequently. The calculation to set up Major Repairs Provisions (MRP) from the Rent Surplus Fund is complex. RSLs must build up MRP on stock funded under the old financial regime, as well as under the new regime. These will be funded through rent surpluses, as we have seen. The annual contributions to the Major Repairs Provisions should amount to 0.8 per cent of construction costs and fees for new build schemes and 1 per cent of reconstruction costs and fees for rehabilitation schemes based on current insurance values. Over the years a provision will be built up, scheme by scheme. Major repair funding is available from the Housing Corporation but is subject to a means test. This takes the form of a test on the organisation's reserves. If an RSL has more than £500 000 of Rental Surpluses according to the test then it is no longer eligible for major repair funding. Major repair grants will eventually cease and have been declining each year as part of the Housing Corporation's Approved Development Programme.

This concludes our review of the major components of the capital and revenue funding regimes. Readers will by now have established that the financial regime is a moving target! It is subject to constant change in detail although the principles involved have remained fairly constant since 1989.

5.11   The use of private finance

The use of private finance has become the norm since 1988. This has been made possible partly as a result of the introduction of assured tenancies, which are excluded from the right to buy and were not subject to rent control. The financial framework has allowed the transfer of risk to the associations and they are free to set their own rents within certain restrictions as discussed. The use of private funding by associations represented a significant departure from their traditional methods of operation. They have had to learn new skills, indeed a whole new language; the financial markets, like many specialist fields, have developed a jargon all their own. It was essential that each association became familiar with the language and expectations of this financial world if it was to be able to compete for and attract, funds on the scale required.

Initially, not all institutions were willing to lend to housing associations. It was a new market and the lenders were nervous and needed time to familiarise themselves with the social housing landlord as all lenders look for a secure return on their investment and will not take risks with their investors' funds. The sector has, however, been successful in attracting the funds it needed.

This success story has been represented as the first and most effective private finance initiative. Several types of lender have been attracted into the market offering varying forms of finance. A joint survey by the NHF and the Housing Corporation,[15] found that by June 1995 £8.5 billion had been committed to the sector, over £2.8 billion for large scale voluntary transfers and the balance for associations' mixed funded programmmes. This had increased by March 1997 to £11.4 billion. By 1999 it had reached £14 billion. The main sources were the UK banks, building societies and institutions. Banks had provided 36.3 per cent of committed funds, building societies and institutions 37.9 per cent and 21.8 per cent respectively. No fewer than 32 banks and 16 building societies had committed more than £10 billion to the sector. The most active banks are NatWest, the Bank of Scotland and Barclays. The most active building societies are the Nationwide, Halifax and the Bradford & Bingley. Around £1.8 billion has also been raised by the direct lending of four institutions combined with five special purpose vehicles. The institutions include the Housing Finance Corporation (THFC), the Prudential and Eagle Star. Special purpose vehicles involve a number of associations combining together to go to the markets via a specially created vehicle. HACO and Funding For Homes are examples of this. A handful of RSLs, including Home, the Peabody Trust, Sanctuary and Northern Counties, had own-name issues. Over 70 per cent of the borrowing was long term with maturity in over 15 years' time. Most of the funding was at variable interest rates.

RSLs must take a long-term view of their borrowing requirements and weigh up the advantages and disadvantages of the various loan types and conditions. To protect their investment, institutions will attach various terms to the loan, such as penalties for early or immediate redemption. Each RSL must therefore develop a borrowing and treasury strategy which matches loan finance with its needs but which also balances the risks attendant upon the different types of loan. New skills, such as financial appraisal and treasury management, have also had to be developed. Large loan portfolios, often exceeding several tens of millions, are very sensitive to changes in interest rates, given that some loans at least will be on a variable basis. Thus each RSL must ensure that it has the powers under its rules to raise the necessary finance. The rules or governing instrument of the RSL (discussed in Chapter 4) will impose borrowing limits on the organisation. The interest rates at which the RSL is permitted to borrow under its rules and its ability to use derivatives (for example, interest rate caps to protect against the risk of rising interest rates) may also be restricted. Once the appropriate rules have been adopted, an RSL will need to consider the types of private finance which are most appropriate to its needs and develop a portfolio of loans of different types to balance the risks of each. The costs of raising finance can be high and this must also be taken into account. An RSL may also require short-term finance to cover costs arising during the development period and longer-term loans to meet the costs which are not ultimately funded through grant. In this scenario the importance of effective cash flow management cannot be overemphasised.

Funding new developments

In addition to examining the overall financial strength and financial management of each potential borrower, funders will only take as security for a loan those assets (schemes) which meet their criteria. It is the development staff of the organisation, in conjunction with finance officers, who must ensure during the development process that these requirements are taken into account. If an RSL is at any time unable to repay its loans it is to these assets that funders have recourse. In particular funders seek an unblemished and unencumbered title to the land or property. Factors that might affect the choice of site include valuation, certificates of title, vacant possession, tenancies, covenants and compliance with them, nomination agreements with local authorities. Planning agreements and permission, compliance with environmental law, and performance bonds from the house-builder are all essential too. All may impact upon the eventual loan term.

Sources of finance

Funders will always take a first charge on the scheme or property. A charge is a legal charge over the RSL's assets imposed by a lender. If the RSL is unable to repay the loan the lender can force it to sell a charged asset to recover any outstanding balance. A charge can be floating or fixed. A fixed charge is a charge made on specific properties and can be secured on the scheme itself provided that the value of the scheme net of the loan is sufficient. A floating charge is a charge which, if called on, is met by selling a group of previously agreed assets rather than a specified property. This could cover all or part of the landlord's stock, in particular its vacant properties. Fixed charges are preferred, especially by small associations which may have insufficient assets which could be used to support a floating charge.

Building societies may only lend long term on completed schemes; thus it may be necessary to arrange short-term development finance too. The main advantage of building society loans is that they are fairly simple to arrange, and that societies are also willing to lend relatively small amounts. The interest rate may be higher, however, and the building society will also charge an administration and valuation fee.

Banks offer a variety of loan finance to the sector. Clearing banks will lend development period finance and offer long-term loans on a conventional or deferred interest basis. Merchant banks will offer short and medium term finance at a fixed percentage over LIBOR (London Inter-Bank Offered Rate), the rate of interest at which banks will offer to borrow and lend to each other. The percentage over LIBOR is used as a means of comparing loan terms.

An RSL may also approach the markets directly, as a handful have done to date, if they require large amounts, (usually exceeding £20 million). For smaller amounts a consortium approach is needed and is made through a broker. The Housing Finance Corporation will perform this role. Stock is issued in units of £100 at a given rate of interest and can be traded in any amount. If an RSL makes such an issue it must ensure that a sinking fund is set up, supported through the rents, to repay the principal. If the RSL has issued more stock than it requires immediately it will invest it to ensure that the interest can be met.

Funding large-scale voluntary transfers

By June 1997 over £2.8 billion of private finance had been raised to fund the transfer of over 200 000 homes from 40 local authorities under the voluntary transfer programme discussed in Chapter 2. The stock to be transferred is valued at tenanted market value. The basic principle of stock transfers to LSVT associations is that the purchaser gains income from the rents and receipts from the sale of property under the preserved right to buy. Outgoings to be offset against this include maintenance and management costs, catch-up repair costs and major repairs. The annual difference between income and expenditure is the surplus that is expected to accrue, and the greater the surplus the greater the tenanted market value of the stock. These landlords face the same, financial constraints already highlighted in this chapter: for example, the stock is valued on the basis of an ongoing contractual commitment to social renting; they will be committed to affordable rents; they must fulfil repairing obligations made to tenants on transfer; nomination rights and the whole aim of the organisation means that the ability to sell property is limited. A discounted cash flow model is used to derive the transfer price. This sets out the income and expenditure flows, usually over a 30 year period, and reduces these to a single net present value payment made to the transferor authority. Clearly the assumptions made are critical. These will include the costs of repairs, rental inflation for new and existing tenants, relet rates and right to buy sales; voids and bad debts will also be taken into account. The discount rate is set by the Treasury.

The acquiring landlord is responsible for raising the finance to fund the purchase, and details of the proposed funding package must be submitted to the Secretary of State before consent to transfer can be granted. As outlined in Chapter 2, a 30-year business plan is essential. Long-term 20–25 year finance is usually sought. Voluntary transfer associations are particularly affected by the blanket rent policy of RPI plus 1 per cent (as highlighted earlier) as some business plans are predicated upon rises that exceed this.

5.12   Treasury management

Given this high exposure to loan debt, RSLs have had to develop more sophisticated treasury management policies. Indeed, it is now a requirement of the Housing Corporation that such policies are established.[16] The treasury management function will vary according to the risks faced by each organisation. Only those that are actively developing and have larger loan portfolios will require the more extensive and sophisticated approach. It is the responsibility of the board to ensure that such policies are in place and that the risks are monitored regularly. The risks associated with treasury management include exposure to the movement in interest rates and inflation. Cash flow is also vital. The RSL must of course maintain sufficient liquidity to meet its obligations, not only to lenders but for capital payments and other expenditure. As stated, private lenders insist on a range of covenants regarding interest cover (the relationship between interest payable and surpluses) and asset cover (the value of the property available to cover loans should the need to redeem the loan arise). Failure of systems and operational risk (i.e., the failure of the board or officers to understand the detail of such transactions) all add to the need for effective treasury management.

The policy will cover such issues as methods and sources of finance: which institutions will be used, for example, and where cash will be deposited. Delegated authority will be set out, as will the policy on interest rate exposure. Cash management procedures and reporting arrangements will need to be defined. The debt maturity profile needs to be monitored. The Housing Corporation has approved the limited use of derivatives by RSLs. These can be used to minimise the risk of adverse interest movements. Derivatives may only be used to protect the organisation and not for speculative purposes; in reality they are only of interest to the few larger RSLs, and detailed regulations are set out in circular 11/95.[17]

Treasury managers (often the Finance Director), will also have responsibility for the fixed asset register of the landlord. This records the details of each property including its latest value and whether it is encumbered (i.e., being used as security for a loan facility). Security for private finance is now a vital issue for the sector, which has undertaken large-scale development since 1989. Many loan facilities have been made available with high levels of security (as much as 125 per cent).Thus if an RSL wishes to raise £100 000 it must make available properties with a value of £125 000 to secure the loan. Those with large loan portfolios, especially in low-value areas, may have limited capacity for the future. Unsecured loans will be more expensive and so affect outturn rents but may be needed in the longer term on a wider scale if RSLs are to continue to develop. 'Securitisation of rental streams' as this is known, using future rental flows (rent income) from specific units in the RSL's portfolio instead of property assets has already been pioneered by some landlords, with the Japanese bank Nomura working with the THFC. Further cuts in grant rates will only exacerbate the problem as RSLs have to find even more security to support a greater proportion of development costs through loan finance. This issue was forcibly put by representatives of private lenders to the Environment Select Committee in 1993 (see Chapter 1), when fears were expressed that some lenders could withdraw from the market if grant rates fell below 50 per cent. Clearly, the availability of funds in the future and the ability to secure them against assets is one of the fundamental issues facing the sector. Indeed, asset management, making the best use of properties by investing in them or selling some, is also now an important element of the business strategy of RSLs.

Financial viability

The Housing Corporation is very concerned to ensure that RSLs are not overexposed to development risk and that they are able to sustain the development funding that they bid for, especially in relation to the scale of their reserves and their ability to cover the cost of loans raised. Each developing landlord must prove its financial viability to the Housing Corporation.

Quarterly returns

The Housing Corporation now monitors the financial position of active registered social landlords closely. This is in recognition of the complex financial operating environment and in acknowledgement of the need to protect and be accountable for major public investment. In addition to the annual accounts (see below) and the annual return (Form RSR: see Chapter 3), those organisations which are developing or which have received stock transfers or been active in the Business Expansion Scheme must submit quarterly financial returns to the Corporation.[18] They are submitted in a standard format, including cash flows, and must be returned to the Corporation within six weeks of the quarter end. In addition, end of year, accounts must also be reconciled with the last quarter return and be submitted within six months of the year end with the annual accounts.[19] Furthermore, since July 1995, those organisations that submit quarterly returns must also submit three-year financial plans projecting their medium-term financial position in line with their business plans. The intention is that the Corporation be forewarned of any impending financial difficulty in order to avert a major disaster.[20] Such an event would have an adverse effect on the sector as a whole in relation to confidence in it, notwithstanding the impact upon the tenants of a landlord which finds itself in such difficulties. The Corporation analyses the financial strength of each RSL by reference to various accounting ratios and since 1997 it has also published information on the financial performance of RSLs.[21]

5.13   Annual accounts

Registered social landlords must prepare their annual accounts in the form that is required by the *Accounting Requirements for Registered Social Landlords General Determination 1997*. This consolidates previous accounting orders and extends section 24 of the Housing Associations Act 1985, which empowered the Secretary of State to lay down accounting requirements for registered housing associations. The requirements are detailed as the Housing Corporation issues extensive advice and guidance on accounting principles and practice.

Until 1992 the Housing Corporation also prescribed the recommended form that accounts should take. Since 1994, however, RSLs are required to follow the Statement of Recommended Practice (or SORP) which was issued June 1994 by the National Housing Federation and revised again in 1998.[22] An RSL's auditor must ensure that the accounts comply with the requirements of both the General Determination and the SORP. In addition, any RSL with subsidiary organisations must also submit consolidated accounts as parent for the Group. A landlord registered under the Industrial and Provident Societies Act 1968 is required to submit an annual return to the Registrar of Friendly Societies which incorporates details of board membership, the stock and information from the body's audited accounts. No special return is required by the Charity

Commissioners. Under the Companies Act 1985 (sections 363, 364) RSLs so registered must also make specific returns. Annual accounts must be submitted to the Housing Corporation within six months of the end of the period to which the accounts relate.

Statement of recommended practice

Since the publication of the statement of recommended practice or SORP and its adoption by the Housing Corporation, the annual accounts of RSLs have been presented in Companies Act or PLC style format. It was argued by financial commentators that the pre-1994 recommended form of accounts was incomprehensible to the financial world and that the housing association sector should be more easily compared with commercial businesses, given the need to raise large amounts of private finance. The Accounting Order sets out the financial statements required. These are:

(a) balance sheet;
(b) income and expenditure account;
(c) statement of total recognised surpluses and deficits;
(d) cash flow.

Certain notes are also required which relate to turnover and operating costs, details of lettings, comparison of costs against allowances and analysis of items shown on the balance sheet. A statement of board (or directors') responsibilities and emoluments, and the Auditors Report (as discussed in Chapter 4), are also included. Since 1997, RSLs have also had to include a statement in the annual accounts as to the status of internal financial controls (also detailed in Chapter 4).

The balance sheet

The purpose of the balance sheet is to give a 'snapshot' of the association's financial position on a particular day, the last day of the accounting period, usually 31 December or 31 March. A model balance sheet is given in Table 5.4. It is divided into two parts showing the assets and liabilities of the organisation and sets out the RSLs reserves. The assets show what is owned by and owed to, the RSL. Fixed assets represent the cost of the properties owned. Capital grant, contributions from the landlord's own reserves to fund them and loans repaid are then deducted to show the net investment in land and buildings.

Fixed assets such as office premises are also added along with any other long-term investment. These represent the total fixed assets. Current assets represent the cash or liquid assets of the RSL such as debtors, which include rent arrears, grants due, cash in hand and at the bank and stocks or work in progress. This last item relates to fees due to in-house contracting teams or materials bought for works on site, but not yet used.

Table 5.4   The Balance Sheet

	1998 £000	1997 £000
Tangible fixed assets		
Housing properties	372 699	337 853
Housing Association and other Grants	(286 124)	(272 922)
	86 575	64 931
Other fixed assets	6 569	3 821
Investment in group company	224	99
	93 368	68 851
Current assets		
Stock	1 960	36
Debtors	4 483	4 493
Cash at bank and in hand	7 459	7 228
	13 902	11 757
Creditors: amounts falling due within one year	(11 550)	(12 917)
Net current assets/(liabilities)	2 352	(1 160)
Total assets less current liabilities	95 720	67 691
Creditors: amounts falling due after more than one year	81 372	54 345
Provisions for liabilities and charges	583	620
Capital and reserves		
Share capital	–	–
Reserves	13 765	12 726
	95 720	67 691

Current liabilities which represent monies owed by the landlord are then deducted from current assets. These include outstanding invoices (creditors), any bank overdraft, and short-term loans on offices, for example. The ratio between current assets and liabilities is referred to as the liquidity ratio, and assets should at least cover liabilities. The balance sheet then shows the relationship between total assets less liabilities, sometimes referred to as the 'net worth' of the organisation. The means of paying for these assets are detailed in the lower part of the balance sheet which shows loans outstanding, reserves (including members' share capital) and the Disposal Proceeds Fund.

The SORP recommends that RSLs, unlike other companies, show land and buildings at value. The SORP recommends Open Market Value for the Existing Use for Registered Social Landlords (OMVEU-RSL). This recognises that the properties are tenanted and relates the value to the income stream that the properties will produce over time. This will depress the value of fixed assets on many RSL balance sheets and has caused some concern. The balance sheet reflects the financial strength (or otherwise) of the RSL, in particular the scale of accumulated surpluses and reserves that may provide a margin of security when assessing future risk.

In recent years the scale of surpluses amassed by the sector as a whole has been the subject of some controversy. The National Housing Federation now produces the *Global Accounts* for the sector which is based upon figures held by the Housing Corporation. For the year ended March 1997 some £6.5 billion reserves were reported by the sector.[23] These seemingly excessive figures have been used to fuel arguments that rents should be lower and that grant rates could be further cut. In general, however, this would be a misrepresentation of the financial position of most RSLs. Their reserves are not liquid; that is, they are not readily convertible into cash. Most merely represent the borrowing capacity or equity held in the stock. To release this, properties would have to be sold which are in reality tenanted. The reserves are also required to deal with the mounting costs of stock reinvestment now that capital grants for this are very scarce. In addition, loan covenants set by private funders, referred to earlier, require that substantial surpluses are generated each year to give comfort that interest payments can be covered. In fact, the average surplus per home after transfer into designated reserves stood at just £120, having fallen from £347 in 1993/94.[24]

The Income and Expenditure Account

The Income and Expenditure Account (Table 5.5) summarises all the revenue transactions for the year arising from both housing and non-housing activities. Turnover includes income from all operations exclud-

Table 5.5   *The Income and Expenditure Account*

	1998 £000	1997 £000
Turnover	21 909	21 520
Operating costs	(16 766)	(16 326)
Operating surplus	5 143	5 194
(Deficit)/Surplus on property for sale	(29)	625
Interest receivable and similar income	457	571
Interest payable and similar charges	(4 532)	(4 026)
Surplus on ordinary activities	1 039	2 364
Transfer from/(to) designated reserves	559	(1 750)
Unallocated surplus	1 598	614
Revenue reserve brought forward	7 518	6 904
Revenue reserve carried forward	9 116	7 518

ing interest. Thus turnover includes rental income but also the proceeds of sales and revenue grants. Operating costs represent all expenditure, again excluding interest. Interest receivable and payable is detailed separately. The surplus is then shown for the year and adjusted to show any Corporation Tax liability (non-charitable housing associations only) and then any grant to meet this taxation requirement (see section 5.14). Surpluses are then transferred to the balance sheet net of transfers to designated reserves (for major repairs, for example). The surpluses shown are the result of accounting transactions and records and are not necessarily cash backed; therefore cash movement is now also an essential part of the annual accounts.

The cash flow statement

The cash flow statement shows the movement of cash during the year. It records how money coming into the organisation was generated and what the cash out was spent on. The management of weekly and monthly cash flows in addition to projections over a minimum of three years are therefore also vital tools for financial management. An RSL may be generating accounting surpluses while still not generating sufficient cash income to meet its cash outgoings each year. Where this is the case, the shortfall in cash will be met by borrowing. This cannot be sustained for long however; eventually the ability to borrow will run out. This is especially the case where borrowing is to fund reinvestment in the stock rather than an income-producing asset. This 'cash gap', resulting from large-scale spending on stock investment, is an issue that several larger RSLs are now beginning to address by attempting to generate efficiency gains through cutting costs or increasing the income generated. Given the restraint on rents (the main source of cash income), new business is one way the gap can be closed. A certain amount of expansion may therefore be necessary in future if RSLs are to be able to generate the income required to meet stock reinvestment needs.

The financial statements also provide a comparison between the RSL's actual management and maintenance costs and the norms established by the allowance system touched upon earlier. The significant figure is, of course, the difference between the two. If an RSL is underspending against allowances this may not necessarily give cause for concern, although underspending against maintenance allowances may mean lack of investment in the upkeep of the properties. This may not be the case though, if all the properties are newly developed, as maintenance expenditure should be low in the early years of a scheme. If an organisation is overspending against allowances then this will raise questions of efficiency and value for money.

This brief outline of the annual accounts is sufficient for our purposes but for further information readers are referred in particular to the *Manual of Housing Association Finance*,[25] and to the 1998 SORP itself.

5.14   Relief from Income and Corporation Tax

It was noted in Chapter 2 that RSLs are subject to a wide range of taxation measures. All RSLs which have charitable status are able to claim full exemption from Income and Corporation tax by virtue of section 48 of the Income and Corporation Taxes Act 1988. RSLs without charitable status (excluding co-ownership and self-build associations) could until 1996, claim some tax relief on Corporation Tax and tax imposed on investment income through section 62 of the Housing Associations Act 1985 as amended by section 54 of the Housing Act 1988. Relief only covered tax on income derived from letting activities and was not available if an RSL was approved for tax exemptions under section 48. Fully mutual co-operative housing associations may also be eligible to claim relief under the Income and Corporation Taxes Act but have opted for relief under section 54 instead as this gave wider relief. Co-ownership societies and unregistered fully mutual co-operatives are treated like owner-occupiers in that each individual member or the association as a whole may opt for tax relief under the MIRAS scheme (Mortgage Interest Relief at Source).

Section 54 tax relief was set for abolition following a budget announcement in the autumn of 1995. Abolition was to be included in the 1996 Housing Act but was removed at the last moment following a vigorous lobbying campaign. Many large, non-charitable associations benefit from it but in particular the relief was built into the business plans of the LSVT associations and its immediate abolition would have led to rent rises and the need to restructure loans. The Treasury could no longer allow an uncapped liability of over £50 million per annum to continue unchecked, however, and section 54 relief is now being withdrawn on a phased basis, to be totally withdrawn by 2000/01. The impact of paying Corporation Tax is quite significant for some RSLs some of which have now opted for charitable status as a means of avoidance.

5.15   Alternative sources of finance

Since 1988 the sector has expanded to include involvement in the production and management of homes procured without Social Housing Grant. Some schemes involve the provision of housing at market rents, or for students and key workers, while others involve the creative use of funding regimes and opportunities, including involvement in the Private Finance Initiative. The possibilities are explored in a report published by the NHF in 1996.[26]

Business Expansion Schemes

One of the earliest examples of this diversification was involvement in the Business Expansion Scheme (BES). Now ended, the BES involved housing associations in forming limited companies, to undertake schemes that were not permissible for either charitable or non-charitable associations. Introduced in 1983, BES offered tax relief at marginal rates to investors investing £500 to £40 000. Shares had to be retained for five years and the investor paid no capital gains tax on their sale. Thus if an investor paid tax at 40 per cent, shares worth £1 000 actually cost only £600. The Finance Act 1988 extended BES to companies providing housing to rent on assured tenancies. The conditions included a maximum investment of £5 million and the company had to operate commercially with a view to making profits. The properties could not exceed a value of £125000 in London and £85 000 elsewhere. BES schemes aimed to provide housing for rent for professional and business people who could afford the higher rents that were charged. The Conservative Government hoped that the BES scheme would provide a further supply of rented accommodation and attract new investment into the rented housing sector.

Although the Finance Act 1988 specifically barred registered housing associations from direct involvement in BES they became involved by either setting up separate companies, or by providing development and management services to BES companies. The Housing Corporation, took a cautious line warning associations of the possible conflict of interest arising if staff or committee members were involved in the company. Rehousing by an association of tenants who would not normally qualify for rehousing, in order that vacant possession could be achieved after five years, was not allowed. This issue regarding the so-called 'exit route' deterred many associations from becoming involved in the scheme. The scheme raised some £320 million and provided around 7 000 homes. The BES scheme was replaced by Housing Investment Trusts, but at the time of writing few had been established.

5.16 Rents, Resources and Risks – The New Balancing Act

This is the title of a working party report published by the National Housing Federation in 1997.[27] The report highlights a number issues that have been raised throughout this chapter. RSLs are now working in a risky and complex environment and have to cope with increased competition and the changing demands made on them from partners and tenants alike. The business strategy of each RSL must balance the need to maintain rents at an affordable level within the prescribed rent envelope, with the need to meet the financial requirements of their lenders and to ensure that they are able to invest adequately in older stock. Rents, which are in effect the pricing policy of the RSL, must also be competitive and well below local market rents and the costs of owner occupation. This is becoming more difficult to achieve in some parts of the country, where the costs of owner-occupation are relatively low. New development activity and other new business ventures present additional risk. The financial impact of diversification and the internal cost of new development must be modelled into the business plan of the organisation. Some RSLs still appear to be expanding in size and area of operation apparently without due regard for the the longer-term financial risks to which some initiatives expose them. The scale of the new capital programme and the standards of development and rents to be charged need to be balanced against the need to reinvest or improve services to tenants. The desire to contribute to the alleviation of poverty and social exclusion through housing plus and other community initiatives also requires financial modelling. This may seem unduly commercial, but without sound finances the RSL (and, importantly, the tenants) cannot look forward to a secure future.

New skills have had to be learnt including cash flow and treasury management. Business strategies must allow for sustainable growth whilst ensuring that financial targets are met, including any necessary cost savings. Improvements in internal control have had to be made as a means of attempting to manage risk generally and to manage risks arising from diversification. These and other issues are touched upon throughout this book but at this point we conclude our review of the financial framework and it is to the investment, development and regeneration activities of registered social landlords that we now turn.

References

1 *The Recovery of Housing Association Grant General Determination 1996,* as amended by the *The Social Housing Grant (Recovery of Capital Grant) General Determination 1997 and Recovery of Housing Association Grant (Extension of Powers) General Determination 1997* (The Housing Corporation 1997).
2 *The Statutory Purchase Grant and Voluntary Purchase Grant General Determinations* (The Housing Corporation 1997).
3 *The Disposal Proceeds Fund General Determination 1997* (The Housing Corporation 1997).
4 *Total Cost Indicators and Grant Rates for 1998/9*, Circular F2 26/97 (The Housing Corporation).

5 *Influencing Rents – A Discussion Paper on the Social Housing Standard for Rents and Service Charges (General Needs)* (The Housing Corporation 1996).
6 *Performance Standards* (The Housing Corporation 1997), Section D.
7 *Finance for Housing Associations: The Government's Proposals* (DoE 1987), para. 14.
8 Ibid.
9 *The Affordability of Housing Association Rents* (The Housing Corporation October 1992).
10 Christine Whitehead *et al.*, *Rents and Risks – Investing in Housing Associations* (Joseph Rowntree Foundation 1995).
11 *Association Rents and Rent Policies 1991–94* (NFHA 1995).
12 *Rents in Local Authority and Registered Social Landlord Sectors* (NHF/Local Government Association 1998).
13 *Social Landlord Rents in 1998* (The Housing Corporation 1999).
14 *Rent Surplus Fund Determination* 1992 (The Housing Corporation) Circular HC 18/92; and *Revised Uses of the Rent Surplus Fund*, Circular F4 02/98.
15 *Private Finance Survey 1995* (The Housing Corporation/NFHA 1996).
16 *Treasury Management – Regulatory Policy* (The Housing Corporation) Circular HC 11/95.
17 Ibid.
18 *Submission of Quarterly Returns* (The Housing Corporation), Circular R2 16/95.
19 *Reconciliation of Statutory Accounts and Fourth Quarter Financial Returns* (The Housing Corporation), Circular R2 14/95.
20 *Three Year Financial Plans* (The Housing Corporation), Circular R2 22/95.
21 R. Lusig, *Financial Performance – How do you measure up?* (The Housing Corporation 1997).
22 *Statement of Recommended Practice* (NHF 1998).
23 *The 1997 Global Accounts of Registered Social Landlords* (NHF 1998).
24 Ibid.
25 *Manual of Housing Association Finance* (CIPFA 1998).
26 D. Joseph and Rachel Terry, *Financing the Future* (NHF 1996).
27 *Rents, Resources and Risks – The New Balancing Act* (NHF 1997).

6

Investment, Development and Regeneration

'Associations which lack the right mix of skills for this new and demanding world must either stop developing or pool their strengths and resources with others.' This was the unambiguous message given in 1989 by Lord Caithness, the then Minister for Housing, to those attending the twenty-fifth anniversary reception of the Housing Corporation. Some ten years on, his comments remain as relevant as ever.

The radical changes to the systems of capital and revenue finance introduced by the Housing Act 1988 and amended in 1996 were discussed in the previous chapter, but it is important to note the evolution of development activity during this period. From 1989 until 1994 housing association development programmes expanded rapidly. Associations responded to the opportunities presented rationally, often by developing larger schemes, and the period was characterised by a 'rush for growth'. Many associations grew rapidly and some expanded into new geographical areas which in turn led to increasing criticism of associations: for example, that they were no longer accountable to their local communities.

This chapter examines the system of capital allocations to housing associations (and other registered social landlords) and explores the development process, including the procedural framework. Long-term and day-to-day maintenance are also examined. The chapter explores some programme areas including Urban Regeneration and reviews how standards have changed since the introduction of private finance. Approaches to managing the development activity, including risk appraisal and partnership, are also considered. Issues relating to value for money in development and quality and competition are also explored. First, however, we examine the scale of housing need and demand.

6.1 Housing need

Throughout the Conservative administration of 1992–97 there were a number of assessments of the demand for social housing. One of the first, commissioned by the Housing Corporation in 1992 from the London

School of Economics (LSE),[1] examined the various methodologies for assessing need. The variety of assessment methods used up to that point had led to an increasingly varied level of estimates of need, making it more difficult to argue for a particular level of resources.

The LSE study critically analysed the various methodologies but also asserted a need for 102 500 units of social housing to be provided per annum. It made clear, however, that this figure was dependent upon a range of other assumptions, including: the propensity for owner-occupation, growth in the private rented sector, replacement of unsatisfactory housing, the rate of household formation and definitions of concealed households. The study noted that not all needs should or could be met through new building, but what was clear was that levels of investment, both public and private, were insufficient to meet demand and aspirations. The work led to a call for the then Conservative Government to assess need, which it had consistently failed to do, although it was clearly in the best position to measure such requirements. This call was echoed by the the Environment Select Committee on the Housing Corporation in its 1992–3 report.[2] In 1995, the Department of the Environment was pressed to publish its assessment of needs and it concluded that some 4.4 million homes would be required between 1991 and 2016.[3] The figures were considered controversial and several commentators, including the National Housing Federation, argued that the DoE had substantially understated the the level of need by ignoring shortfalls that already existed by 1991 and the level of repossessions (running, on average, at 30 000 per annum). The DoE figures also failed to allow for community care needs to be taken into account following the closure of long-stay hospitals. Analysis of the DoE figures undertaken by Steve Wilcox of the University of Wales for the National Housing Federation suggested that the DoE figures did not take into account the changes in employment patterns, and the impact of a low inflation economy on the propensity for owner-occupation.

In 1995 the Joseph Rowntree Foundation published a report by Alan Holmans,[4] who had previously been a housing economist at the Department of the Environment. This report forecasted a need for 240 000 homes per annum for the two decades 1991–2001 and 2001–11 to meet both the demand for owner-occupation and subsidised renting. Social rented housing needs were forecast at 90 000 a year for 1991–2001 and 100 000 a year for 2001–11. These figures compared with the DoE estimates of 60 000 to 100 000 for 1991–2001. The report highlighted the fact that the provision of social housing (largely through housing associations) had only been running at an average of about 60 000 homes a year in the period 1991/92 to 1994/95, further increasing the pressure for higher output to meet projected demand. During this period the Conservative administration set a target of 60 000 homes per annum to be provided

•

through the Approved Development Programme of housing associations. This target was achieved by counting all lettings, not just new homes created through the Housing Corporation's ADP and despite cuts to the Corporation's programme every year since 1993 (as detailed in Table 6.1). The targets were consistently met by housing associations constantly producing more homes than planned by bidding for ever lower levels of grant per unit produced. This made it difficult to argue that the level of the the programme and grant rates should be increased, or indeed maintained at prevailing levels. It was easier for the Conservative Government to ignore long-term estimates and point to the delivery of the programme as evidence that increased production was possible through a reduced programme and despite cuts to grant rates. Clearly, as highlighted in the previous chapter, this position cannot be sustained indefinitely but, in the meantime, intense competition between associations and enhanced performance undermined arguments for increased resources.

In 1995, the Environment Select Committee's *Inquiry into the Need for Provision of Social Housing in England 1991–2001* was established. Its findings were published in February 1996 with the report unanimously supported by the all-party committee. The report confirmed that investment levels in social housing were too low and would not meet need. The Committee confirmed that investment levels nearer to 100 000 per annum should be achieved. It expressed concern that published estimates did not include provision for current unmet need, and neither did they take account of the need for supported housing or community care in assessing requirements. In addition, empty properties and homes requiring demolition had also been underestimated. The Select Committee's findings appear to have impacted on the level of investment in housing provision by the current Labour Government given the release of capital receipts announced in 1997 and the more recent pronouncements by the Minister for Local Government and Housing.

6.2   The Approved Development Programme in England

The capital spending limit of the Corporation is known as the Approved Development Programme ADP. In effect it is an approval by Government of a programme of expenditure by the Housing Corporation on schemes developed in England by Registered Social Landlords, which in turn are eligible for Social Housing Grant. Full details of this can be found in the Housing Corporation's *Guide to the Allocation Process (1997)*. It should be noted that the ADP is now declining in importance as a source of funding. Local authorities are growing providers and Health and Social Services authorities are now vital funders of RSLs too. The Housing Corporation recognizes this in its consultation paper entitled

Developing Our Investment Strategy (1999). The paper notes that the Government has set a new agenda for social housing with the establishment of the Urban Task Force and the New Deal for Communities. At the time of writing therefore both the formulation of the ADP and the use of the HNI (see below) were under review. Future investment will be based upon Regional Housing Statements drawn up with Government Offices.

Quality of investment rather than volume will be the future ethos. The consultation paper is based upon four key themes set out in the Housing Corporation's strategy document entitled *Building a Better Future: revitalising neighbourhoods* (1998). The themes are:

 i)   tackling the problems of social exclusion;
 ii) improving the quality of investment strategies;
 iii) improving the delivery of services to consumers;
 iv) promoting effective public/private partnerships.

A regional perspective will replace the current top down national approach to resource allocation. If the proposed approach is adopted, transition to it will commence in 2000/01.

The Government has recently also announced its intention to move away from annuality in the public expenditure round to three-year programmes but, at the time of writing, the time-scale was as follows. In March each year the Public Expenditure Survey (PES) process starts and the Corporation prepares for the Department of the Environment a series of programme options which could be achieved over the next three years within indicative cash limits for years two and three. The discussions with the Minister also cover the Corporation's Corporate Plan. Priorities are determined and the Corporation's cash limit is announced in the Budget Statement. Once the cash limit is known the Corporation's board will submit its ADP proposals outlining the shape and size of the programme and regional distribution. The Corporation must determine the feasible level of new approvals over a three-year period, based on cost projections, grant rates and registered social landlords [RSLs'] ability to deliver. Current commitments are also taken into account. The process has been aligned with the Minister's consideration of Housing Investment Programme bids by local authorities in order that the output of both programmmes can be considered in aggregate.

The ADP is broken down into the following categories:

Capital funding

(a) mixed funding for rent;
(b) temporary social housing;
(c) works to RSL stock:
     i.   miscellaneous works including major repairs;

    ii.   works only rehabilitation;

    iii. re-improvements.

Home ownership

(d)   Tenants' Incentive scheme (to be replaced by a Homebuy scheme from 1999);

(e)   Voluntary Purchase Grant and Statutory Purchase Grant;

(f)   mixed funding for sale;

(g)   DIYSO (to be replaced by a Homebuy scheme from 1999).

Revenue funding

Requirements for Supported Housing Management Grant (SHMG) are also bid for at this stage, as highlighted in Chapter 8.

Funding for rent refers to the provision of additional homes through new building or acquisition of existing homes which may or may not require additional works of refurbishment. Existing properties which require extensive works of over £10 000 are known as rehabilitation projects. Where the existing properties are in a more satisfactory condition, there is a programme known as Purchase and Repair, introduced in 1997 to enable these homes to be acquired and refurbished for speedy letting. New build schemes may be developed on green field or brown field sites or may involve works on local authority estates in conjunction with the Single Regeneration Budget. By 1998 some 65 per cent of the programme was undertaken on redeveloped (brown field) sites.

Temporary Social Housing and Temporary Market Rent schemes (formerly known as short-life and HAMA plus programmes) bring into use otherwise vacant dwellings which require some works but which will only be available for letting on a temporary basis. In general, Temporary Social Housing schemes make use of vacant local authority or private sector stock let at affordable or social rent levels, while Temporary Market Rent Housing schemes such as HAMA plus involve the RSLs as managing agents of private sector stock, usually let at market rents. From 1999/2000 the two Temporary Housing programmes will be merged into one. Work on RSL stock brings together the three programmes listed under one single heading. This was implemented for the first time in 1996/97. Allocations to the regions were also based, in that year, on an index of RSL stock condition rather than the Housing Needs Index. The intention was to remove artificial divisions between programmes that inhibited value for money in works to homes in RSL ownership. Priority is given to bids which are part of a strategic programme of stock reinvestment based on a thorough survey of stock condition; this issue is explored further in a later section.

The home ownership categories include the Tenants' Incentive Scheme, which provides portable discounts for tenants to be used in the purchase of a private sector home. Voluntary Purchase Grant and Statutory Purchase Grant relates to the provisions of the Housing Act 1996 which, from 1 April 1997, enables some tenants to purchase their existing home in certain circumstances. Mixed funding for sale refers to the new build shared ownership programme and the DIYSO programme, whereby individuals may purchase a home on a shared ownership basis on the private market. Home ownership programmes are examined further in Chapter 10.

Rural housing

It should be noted that the Housing Corporation programme has attempted to take into account government priorities for meeting the housing needs of rural areas, although the programme has diminished. These areas suffer particular localised problems. For example, in many areas the shortage of affordable housing is exacerbated by the market for second homes which inflates the price of housing beyond the reach of the local population. Increasing rural unemployment has added to the stress, particularly as tied accommodation is sold off.

In 1998/99 the Housing Corporation National Policy Statement re-stated its commitment to the Rural Programme which provides housing in villages under 3000 in population. At least 60 per cent of the programme must be spent in settlements smaller than 1000 people. Some 750 homes will be provided in 1998/99, a fall of 40 per cent from previous years. High costs are also supported through a rural enhancement to Total Cost Indicators (see Chapter 5). This is intended to compensate for the higher cost of smaller schemes in villages and to encourage local authorities to prioritise such schemes for funding. Low-cost home-ownership initiatives are particularly encouraged. There are a number of difficulties attendant upon development in rural areas. Land with residential planning permission is in short supply and any attempt to infringe the green belts or areas of outstanding natural beauty will understandably be subject to lengthy planning inquiries and may involve local protests.

Allocation timetable

In order to establish the ADP for the coming year the Corporation reviews the previous year's programme and in July submits grant rate and Total Cost Indicator (TCI) proposals to the Department of the Environment, Transport and the Regions. The National Housing Federation will also submit its views on the ADP and grant rates for the coming year to the Corporation for consideration. During August, each Corporation Region issues a Regional Policy Statement following consultation with local authorities and associations operating in that area. In August, grant rates and TCIs are published although these are often delayed through internal Cabinet negotiations.

In November, each RSL submits its bid for capital funding and for revenue support through Supported Housing Management Grant (see Chapter 8). Indicative allocation targets for the regions are published in December and draft allocations agreed with RSLs. Formal allocations and draft cash planning targets for the following financial year are confirmed in February, although in reality there is often some slippage in this programme. Local authorities are also advised of the allocation for their areas in the coming year. Funding for non-ADP programmmes, such as City Challenge, and the Rough Sleepers' Initiative to assist the street homeless are announced separately. See Table 6.1 for the planned ADP for 1996 to 2000.

The distribution of the ADP

There are two main phases to the allocation of the ADP: first, the distribution of the national 'cake' to each region, and second, from the region to the individual RSLs and local authority areas. The regional and local authority distribution is achieved through the Housing Needs Indicators (HNIs) described next and distribution to RSLs through the competitive bidding process.

Table 6.1   The Housing Corporation's new ADP expenditure, 1996–2000 (£ million)

	1996/97 forecast outturn	1997/98	1998/99	1999/00
Mixed funded rent	650.2	433.9	391.5	355.5
Temporary social housing	28.0	21.9	20.6	19.7
Works to RSL stock	115.9	49.4	40.2	36.6
Total rent	*794.1*	*505.2*	*452.4*	*411.9*
TIS/VPG	86.7	60.6	65.4	67.0
DIYSO	62.1	35.7	37.6	37.1
Mixed funded sale	83.9	60.5	50.1	45.8
Total home ownership	*232.7*	*156.8*	*153.0*	*150.0*
Other expenditure	26.0	18.0	19.0	19.0
Total gross expenditure	*1052.8*	*679.9*	*624.4*	*580.8*
Receipts	30.0	29.0	30.0	30.0
Net ADP	*1022.8*	*650.9*	*594.4*	*550.8*

Source: Housing Corporation *ADP Bulletin* (1997/98).

6.3 Housing Needs Indicator

Through the Housing Needs Indicator the Corporation seeks to target investment accurately. For 1996/97 the formulation of the HNI was fundamentally reviewed and aligned with the General Needs Index used, in part, to distribute capital spending limits to local authorities. The principle on which the distribution is based is to target resources to those areas with the greatest needs, whilst ensuring that where possible housing need elsewhere is still considered. The HNI gives a relative measure of the needs of each local authority area and is regularly revised.

Cost compensation

Cost compensation is applied to HNI shares. Unit costs in London and the South-East are double those in the North, and additional cash needs to be made available to ensure that the volume of output reflected by the HNI scores can be maintained. The effects of cost compensation are also dampened to ensure that no area loses too great a proportion of its allocation as a result.

Each local authority area can expect Housing Corporation investment to reach 80 per cent of the level implied by HNI scores over a three-year period. There is no upper limit however, provided that 300 per cent is not exceeded over a three-year period. The remaining 20 per cent is discretionary and will take into account three factors: first, the local authority's housing strategy, especially the extent to which housing need has been comprehensively assessed to make best use of ADP funds. Renewal and regeneration strategies are also taken into account. Second, the Corporation is concerned that dwellings are used effectively including the development of empty property strategies and efficient nomination arrangements. Cost-effectiveness of the RSLs' bids is also considered in relation to the authorities enabling powers: for example, the use of planning powers and discounted land values. Third, the Corporation will take into account the effective use of RSL dwellings.

Any revision to the HNI always causes heated debate. Indicators which favour one area of the country, such as London and/or the South-East, may adversely affect northern regions. In addition, resource distribution in relation to urban versus rural areas and regeneration versus new development remain issues of concern. For example, although the Corporation has concentrated its resources in urban areas it retains a commitment to rural housing needs. As stated there are some particularly acute shortages developing in some of these areas as a result of the increase in second homes and consequent price rises. Investment in housing by local authorities in rural areas has tended to be lower than that of urban councils, and much of the stock is unfit. There is a high proportion of elderly people requiring specialist accommodation and younger people are finding it difficult to compete in the market place. Affordability issues are similar to those in urban areas. Although the Corporation does not have a specific funding allocation for rural housing, it does set targets for homes to be provided in settlements of less than 1000 people.

The post-1988 grant regime originally favoured new building as the risks attendant upon new build are lower and prices easier to negotiate and control. Until 1986 new build and rehabilitation activities had been equally funded at 50 per cent each of the programme. By 1989 the rehabilitation programme had diminished to only 26 per cent of the ADP and by 1992 it had fallen further, giving cause for concern. By the mid-1990s rehabilitation activities had begun to increase again, however, as critical reports of ever larger housing association developments on green field sites led to calls for associations to return to smaller-scale activity and to refurbishment. Many associations have also become actively involved in estate action programmes, assisting local authorities to regenerate older estates. Since the introduction of the Single Regeneration Budget in 1994 (see section 6.10), much RSL activity and the greater proportion of the Corporation's programme is once again aimed at the regeneration of older areas. This will only increase as a result of the New Deal for Communities announced in 1998.

6.4   The competitive bidding process

In August each year, the Corporation's regional offices issue Regional Policy Statements which include a standard National Policy Statement and set out priorities for investment in new schemes. All RSLs (including housing associations) are invited to submit bids for funding under the various programme heads. The allocation of resources within regions and between each local authority is determined by the HNI, as set out above. Each Regional Policy Statement will take into account, national policies and priorities.

National Policy Statements

The 1997/98 National Policy Statement reflected the impact of the Housing Act 1996. In particular bidding was extended to all Registered Social Landlords. Housing Association became Social Housing Grant, and any RSL receiving SHG would have to comply with the Social Housing Standard. In addition, tenants of homes built with SHG would have the statutory right to acquire their home with a discount. Other key changes included an increased emphasis on comparing bidders' prospective rents and an affirmation by the Housing Corporation as to the priority use of any surpluses (see below). ADP investment strategy was to be based on the following objective:

'to secure the effective and efficient delivery of new social communities and which promote regeneration'.[5]

The emphasis was squarely placed on providing for future housing needs through a clear assessment of a local authority's future requirements coupled with better use of existing stock; the revised Temporary Social Housing Initiative and new Purchase and Repair schemes were examples of this. ADP investment would be aimed at filling the highest priority gaps highlighted through discussions with the local authority. New investment would meet priorities such as community care, regeneration and reducing empty properties, and each decision to invest would take into account additional factors such as higher scheme development standards or housing plus activities. In addition, mixed tenure was promoted, as were schemes which addressed the imbalance in areas, for example, in dwelling size to impact on overcrowding or underoccupation. The Corporation's investment strategy also encouraged bids which contributed to wider social objectives, which had an element of 'housing plus' (see Chapter 7), and which would contribute to economic and urban regeneration, through linkage with the Single Regeneration Budget (see below). The emphasis remained on private sector renewal, however, rather than local authority estates. The Estates Renewal Challenge Fund (see Chapter 2) was targeted to meet this need. The 1999/2000 policy statement places area regeneration and social inclusion at the heart of the Housing Corporation's investment strategy.

In the case of rent and sale programmes, regional allocations are expected to reflect national priorities in relation to special needs and rural housing. Tenant participation strategies are also considered in the investment decisions. The Corporation's strategies for older persons' housing, and black and minority ethnic housing needs, must also be taken into account.

The Housing Corporation expects all RSLs to approach the bidding competition in a responsible way. Social Housing Grant is a means of subsidising rents charged by RSLs. Internal subsidy to reduce the amount of SHG required is welcomed; however, it is made quite clear that this should only be proposed after the RSL has retained sufficient financial strength to protect its long-term interests and that of its tenants, and has made adequate provision for current and long-term maintenance needs. This latter requirement follows from the expectation that most RSLs are expected to fund works to existing stock themselves through reserves or borrowing, rather than through the ADP. Finally, each RSL must ensure that existing rents will not rise as a result of subsidising their bids. These requirements led to a reduction in overbidding by RSLs for 1997/98, but bids still exceeded available resources by four times.

In selecting bids, value for money (i.e., costs and rent and service charge levels) is an important factor but not the key determinant.

All the factors highlighted above plus any additional wider community benefits, higher standards, the future life of the housing bought in addition to deliverability, will be taken into account. All bids are appraised on the same basis using standard forms. In allocating between RSLs the Housing Corporation will take into account the Performance Assessment and Investment Summary (PAIS) of each organisation, which considers its performance in delivering the programme each year, and its compliance with Performance and Scheme Audit standards. Its financial viability (ability to sustain a new development programme in terms of financial strength) as outlined in the preceding chapter, is also taken into account.

In assessing each bid for rented housing the Regional Office will consider local strategy, value for money, affordability, the ability to provide effective long-term management and maintenance services to tenants and the need to generate sustainable communities. This latter issue has generated major debate in the sector and we return to this issue later in this chapter. All bids must also comply with the Corporation's Scheme Development Standards (see below).

Joint commissioning

As outlined in Chapter 3, the Housing Corporation is also investigating a process of jointly commissioning schemes with local authorities. At the time of writing, a pilot was under way and had been extended to cover some 80 areas. Joint commissioning may lead to formal agreement between the council and the regional office of the Corporation in commissioning schemes, rather than the Corporation just taking their views into account. There are concerns, however, to ensure that the rules governing joint commissioning are both transparent and fair. Joint commissioning is likely to build upon the process of 'preferred partner' status which already exists in some areas. A few local authorities have undertaken a competitive review of RSLs working in their area and now work with only a limited number. This has led to fears that some associations may lose their traditional area of development activity, squeezed out perhaps by larger bodies with more to offer (especially in financial terms). Maintaining the diversity and plurality of housing association provision remains a priority, and it is to be hoped that a balance is maintained, perhaps through partnership arrangements. Joint commissioning may also open up links with the Regional Development Agencies which will inevitably have some role in the future in allocating the ADP alongside the Corporation and local authorities.

Rents in bidding

Average rent levels and housing benefit eligible service charge levels have been incorporated in the bidding process for general needs for rent and sale since 1996; supported housing remained excluded at the time of writing. The Corporation's approach to this was set out in its paper *Competing for Grant: Rents, Subsidies, Standards and Efficiency*, published in July 1995. RSLs are invited to bid against benchmark rents calculated from TCI and grant rate modelling. The benchmark rents are based on a number of archetypal units, for new building, rehabilitation, shared ownership and so on. Forecast or 'prospective' rents detail rent levels at practical completion when the scheme is built. The aim is to enable the Corporation to make comparisons between RSLs. Those RSLs charging lower rents than their competitors will gain an advantage. The Corporation produces a cost ranking, taking rents and service charges into account. At the time of writing the process was fairly new and as such it is difficult to assess what impact it will have on value for money, or indeed in restraining rent increases. The penalties incurred by those RSLs that are eventually unable to achieve the rent levels offered in their bid is also unclear. It does, however, when combined with the Scheme Development Standards offer a more rigorous assessment of value for money as lower rents cannot be achieved by lowering standards or, indeed, rents increased to pay for inefficiencies in procurement. Some commentators would argue that this framework should have been introduced in 1989 when it would have more effectively restrained housing association rent levels and suppressed the tendency to bid at unrealistic grant rates; a more 'level playing field' between different associations may also have been created.

Supported housing
In addition to the new capital programme, RSLs also bid for special needs revenue funding through Supported Housing Management Grant. Each Region receives an annual cash limited allocation of SHMG which cannot be exceeded. Strategies for investment in special needs are considered with each local authority, especially social services departments and health authorities, although to date such consultation has been more fragmented than for the general needs programme. The Corporation's investment strategy in relation to supported housing is considered further in Chapter 8. This funding framework is also under review following the publication of a DSS consultation paper in 1999 entitled *Supporting People*.

Volume bids
In addition to bids for individual schemes, associations (until recently) have also bid on a volume basis. This covered the purchase of several schemes from one or more developers, often in partnership with several other associations in order to use combined purchasing power to procure economies of scale. A standardised approach was used for components or designs often repeated on a number of sites to reduce costs. Volume bids were usually made over a three-year period to attempt to fix costs for a

longer period. Examples include the South London Partnership which comprises Wandle, Threshold and Hexagon Housing Associations with the developer Countryside PLC. Interest in volume bids reached its height in 1993 when the ADP was at its maximum. Concern regarding standards achieved and value for money, combined with reductions in the ADP has since led to their virtual demise.

6.5   Cash planning

The scale of the total regional programme is controlled by the Regional Cash Limit and Forward Commitment Limits. In order to assist RSLs in forward planning the Corporation is able to firmly commit 70 per cent and 40 per cent of the indicative cash limits for the two subsequent years following that for which allocations are being made. In addition to these pre-allocations, provisional commitments can be made for each of the two years of 10 and 20 per cent. In practice, in recent years, as the ADP has fallen Regional Offices have been less inclined to make pre-allocations. Better value for money could be achieved by committing for one year only in a climate where construction costs were falling. In addition to allocations, each RSL will be notified by March each year of its Cash Planning Target (CPT). This is literally the amount of cash that it can claim from the Housing Corporation against approved allocations for that financial year. The CPTs enable the Corporation to meet its own regional cash limit and the Corporation its target for the year as a whole. RSLs have to ensure that they are able to fund any development costs that cannot be met by cash from the Corporation throughout the development period. Once an RSL is in receipt of its allocations and Cash Planning Target for the coming year it will embark on the development process to deliver those schemes. In reality much work will already have been undertaken to inform the bidding process. The allocations form a programme of delivery from the Housing Corporation's point of view through a mechanism known as a 'funding agreement'.

Investment contracts and funding conditions

As outlined in Chapter 5, from 1 April 1995 all cash programme and non-programmed procedures for Approved Development Programme funded rent and sale developments were consolidated into a uniform framework applicable to all developing RSLs. These contracts have to be negotiated year on year, giving less certainty to the landlord and less ability to procure savings, but in turn this gives greater control over savings to the Housing Corporation. For schemes approved prior to April 1997, funding agreements applied. Each year an RSL receives a Statement of Funding

Conditions (replacing the funding agreement from 1997) which sets out the conditions for receipt of allocations. Schemes approved after 1 April 1997 (excluding works to existing stock) are also subject to an investment contract. Compliance with the investment contract is a condition of grant, and the investment contract sets out the 'agreed rent' and housing benefit eligible service charge at the point of letting. A clear relationship between this rent and the 'prospective rent' included at bid stage is expected. The funding conditions and investment contract do give an RSL some flexibility in managing and delivering its programme in that virement between allocation headings is permissible up to 5 per cent.

Funding conditions

Each year the Housing Corporation will issue a standard Statement of Funding Conditions which contains the principles to be followed and forms the basis of the capital funding system. In summary, the conditions confirm that all funding is subject to the provisions of the Housing Act 1996 and that funding is conditional upon satisfactory performance. Clearly, all grant must be used for the provision of housing which in turn meets required standards. Management and maintenance services must also meet regulatory requirements and all RSLs must take part in the Continuous Recording of Lettings CORE system. All housing developed with Social Housing Grant will be subject to the right to acquire. Rents and service charges charged at first letting should accord with those agreed at grant confirmation stage and should not be increased by more than the rent influencing formula set by the Housing Corporation (see Chapter 5). The funding conditions also set out certain procedural expectations. Each RSL must manage its Cash Planning Target CPT in accordance with the requirements set out in the Housing Corporation's *Capital Funding Procedure Guide (1997)*. Quarterly targets for cash spend must be met and the Corporation can suspend funding if an RSL is failing to comply with such conditions. Once an RSL has received an allocation it will agree its programme management arrangements. These will follow either a 'programme contract' or a 'scheme contract' route. The only difference between the two routes is the treatment of savings on each scheme. Grant rates for each scheme are fixed at the outset of each scheme at the grant confirmation stage. Costs over TCI can be approved subject to scrutiny and up to the maximum of 130 per cent. Savings on individual schemes are transferred into a 'grant pot'. RSLs with programme contracts may recycle any savings on particular allocations according to set parameters.

Programme and scheme contract routes

If an RSL accrues a positive savings 'pot' it may undertake additional units or schemes. These additional schemes must meet identified priority needs, be supported in writing by the local authority and be in an area where an RSL already operates. In addition the 'pot' can be used to support schemes where allocation costs have increased, or there are eligible cost overruns. Savings can be rolled over from one financial year to another.

Savings arising through the scheme contract route must be returned to the Corporation and they will decide which scheme or RSL will be allocated the savings. Local authority funded schemes are excluded from the contract unless the scheme is jointly funded with the Housing Corporation. Other non-ADP funded schemes, such as City Challenge or the Rough Sleepers' Initiative, are also excluded. The programme or scheme contract applies to all programme headings. All schemes that exceed TCI are subject to scrutiny, as set out in this chapter. The Corporation reviews the progress of an RSL's programme on a quarterly basis (or more often if appropriate). At the review the Corporation will consider performance against quarterly targets for scheme submission and cash draw-down as established by the Funding Conditions. They will also consider any changes to grant requirements, Cash Planning Targets and changes in in programme targets. A progress report is issued which incorporates information regarding allocation take-up, units achieved and movements in and out of the RSL's grant pot. An annual review will also take place to consider overall past and future performance. Scheme audit, as discussed in Chapter 3, also informs the development performance review process.

6.6   Managing the development process

Partners in the development process

The essence of successful development lies in the RSL taking a strong client or employer role. It will employ a variety of consultants to work on development projects usually from a panel approved by the board. In addition, an approved list of contractors is also maintained from which firms may be selected to tender for works. Larger RSLs will have a technical department which will usually contain the necessary expertise. There are six key areas of work with which staff are concerned:

(a)   the identification of sites and properties;
(b)   the specification of standards and design requirements;
(c)   scheme administration to satisfy the funding authorities (scheme-work);
(d)   procurement (tendering or negotiation);
(e)   contract supervision (project management);
(f)   evaluation of the process and the parties to it.

In order to exercise a strong client role the RSL must be in control of each task or process and maintain adequate systems to monitor development performance and costs. There must be a clear system of reporting for internal officer and board use. Established and developing RSLs may also produce standard documentation which sets out design requirements, specifies standards to be met and materials to be used. These are examined in more detail later. It is important to note that, in order to minimise risk arising from the regime introduced in 1988, many developments are now procured through a design and build route which is examined further later. These contracts offer a more limited role for consultant architects or quantity surveyors, and therefore what follows is an examination of the traditional role of each party but readers should bear in mind that this is now less likely to apply.

Architect/building surveyor

An RSL may employ an architect or building surveyor to act as the technical advisor. In the case of rehabilitation, building surveyors rather than architects may be used. The consultant is appointed from a panel approved by the board of management. To become an approved consultant the firm should supply references from previous employers, bank references, and hold adequate professional indemnity insurance. The consultant should also be able to demonstrate a commitment to the nature of the work of the RSL and a willingness to be subject to their systems of evaluation. Over the years, established RSLs will develop an expert panel of consultants who will become familiar with the employer's standards and design requirements. The architect or surveyor prepares the drawings and specifications (based upon standard documentation, if available) for the project. He or she will also obtain the necessary planning and building regulation approvals. In conjunction with the association the consultant assists in the tender process, and once the scheme is on site the architect or surveyor (as employer's agent or supervising officer) is responsible for contract supervision. The architect or surveyor certifies monthly payments to the contractor, issues variation orders, certifies practical completion of the project and, at the end of the contract, supervises the defects liability period and certifies the final account.

The appointment of consultants is made through a formal written instruction. This is usually done once a scheme either has a firm allocation or has received grant confirmation. Appointments are made according to the terms and conditions of engagement laid down by the various professional institutions, notably the Royal Institute of British Architects (RIBA) and the Royal Institution of Chartered Surveyors (RICS). These institutions have an agreed basis for scale fees to be paid at various stages of the contract. In the case of design and build contracts, architects are often only employed up to design stage; thereafter an employer's agent will manage the contract process. An RSL must be clear as to the terms and conditions of appointment. As stated, it is essential that each organisation monitors the performance of architects and surveyors who play such a key role in the development process. Any monitoring system must take into account the following factors:

(a)   the quality of design;
(b)   adherence to any standard requirements;
(c)   the speed with which the consultant responded to requests for information;
(d)   whether the timetable was adhered to;
(e)   tight cost control to prevent cost overruns;
(f)   accuracy of specification in terms of cost against tenders received, with few unforeseen items;
(g)   quality of contract supervision including dealing with defects and settling the final account;
(h)   quality of liaison with staff (and tenants in some cases) and statutory authorities.

In the case of design and build contracts, cost control presents less of a risk as these contracts are fixed price and overruns are at the contractor's risk.

The panel of consultants should be reviewed regularly in the light of such information and consultants informed of any area with which the employer is dissatisfied. Obviously, if performance does not improve the consultant will be removed from the panel.

Quantity surveyor

Quantity surveyors are usually only appointed for new build schemes or very large and complex conversion works. Although quantity surveyors have no supervisory role under the building contract, they advise the architect on quantitative and financial aspects of the contract.

The quantity surveyor prepares the 'Bill of Quantities' (on such schemes where a specification is insufficient) which is subsequently priced by the contractor. He or she will also advise on cost estimates at earlier stages of complex schemes. Once the scheme is on site the quantity surveyor advises on the value of work undertaken which then forms the basis for certification by the architect for payment. Quantity surveyors are subject to a similar process of approval before they are appointed by the RSL; however, it is usual to employ quantity surveyors with whom the architects have worked before as a close working relationship between them is vital.

In recent years many quantity surveying firms have developed their response to design and build contracts by offering project management services, taking the role of employer's agent on site.

Other consultants

On occasion, an RSL will need to appoint specialist consultants such as structural engineers or heating and ventilation specialists. The fees for all consultants must be met within the on-costs for the project. Structural engineers may be appointed when complex structural solutions are required on difficult sites, or in the case of rehabilitation when structural defects such as subsidence are apparent and require further diagnosis regarding the nature and extent of the problem.

In-house design teams

It should be noted that a few RSLs still have their own in-house staff of architects and surveyors. In recent years, however, the nature of the development funding regime has led to the disbanding of many such teams as many felt unable to cope with the ongoing overheads of such a section. The shift away from rehabilitation in the early 1990s also contributed to this. Only a handful still retain this function in-house.

Clerks of works and site inspectors

Clerks of works act as the 'eyes and ears' of the RSL through regular site inspection. However, they may only issue instructions to the contractor under the direction of the architect. Clerks of works are essential on larger new build and rehabilitation works to ensure that both quality control and high standards of workmanship are maintained. In the case of design and build contracts 'site supervisors' are used, often employed on an in-house basis. They have a very limited role in this context but are important in the attempt to ensure quality through this procurement route.

Contractors

As stated, an RSL will maintain an approved list of contractors and developers with whom it will work. In order to be included on the list the contractor must supply several references, and the association may visit examples of projects they have constructed. Details of the company's financial status and its organisation and capacity (i.e., the number and size of contracts it can cope with at one time) are also required. All contractors should be monitored and reviewed annually by the board. The RSL, as client, will be particularly concerned with the speed and quality of workmanship and the contractor's adherence to the original contract sum. Attitude to staff and tenants is also important. Although it will become familiar with its more competent contractors, in the interests of accountability it must always keep them at arm's length, ensuring that the tendering process is properly conducted. Furthermore, once the scheme is on site the RSL as employer has no right under the contract to instruct the contractor except through the surveyor or architect. Even site inspections should be pre-arranged through the consultant. On the majority of projects sub-contractors are employed to carry out specialist works, such as heating or electrical works. Sub-contractors look to the main contractor for instruction and payment. An RSL may nominate (choose) sub-contractors whose work and performance it has experience of. This can, however, lead to problems if the sub-contractor does not perform adequately by giving the main contractor a possible route through which responsibility can be disclaimed for any failure. Many RSLs now work closely in partnership with developers rather than traditional contractors, as the development climate has changed; some aspects of this relationship are explored later in this chapter.

Other officers

In addition to co-ordinating the work of the various consultants and monitoring the contractor, development staff must liaise regularly with the officers of the funding authority and with the statutory authorities. The officers of the Housing Corporation and local authorities who deal with schemework have great influence, particularly in the case of the approval of problematic schemes. Schemework scrutiny has been reduced in recent years but the importance of such liaison remains paramount.

Development staff must also liaise regularly with the planning department of the local authority to ensure that the necessary permissions are forthcoming. Liaison with building control officers is also essential in order to obtain building regulations approval.

A further office of importance until more recently was the District Valuer's Department of the Inland Revenue. At a very early stage in the development process a valuation of the site or property to be acquired will be needed. Links with the District Valuer help to speed the process up, which is important especially if the RSL is in competition with other possible purchasers. Under the current system an RSL is free to use any independent valuer, which may remove some of the delay. An independent valuation of property to be purchased is part of the process which ensures value for money and financial and public accountability.

Stages of the development process

There are seven key stages of the development process, most of which are not unique to housing association development, although all RSLs receiving Social Housing Grant have to obtain what is known as grant confirmation and satisfy various requirements of the Housing Corporation. The stages are:

(a) feasibility;
(b) grant confirmation;
(c) acquisition;

(d) design;
(e) tender;
(f) construction period;
(g) post-completion.

Where design and build contracts are used clearly, the design and tender stages are collapsed and the contractor will both design and construct the scheme according to the employer's requirements. In the case of many local authority funded projects, especially larger ones involving estate regeneration, quite lengthy 'beauty contests' or competitions are held to decide which organisation will win the project. Development teams have had to develop the ability to assemble effective bids quickly and to present their case professionally. Often the RSLs will bid in partnership with a private developer so that a negotiated contract rather than a tendered project will ensue. What follows is a brief examination of the traditional development route for the smaller project but in reality the process may be less clearly defined in its stages.

Feasibility

The first stage of the process is the identification of sites or properties suitable for development. Established RSLs will explore potential opportunities throughout the year in order to bid for capital funding in the autumn of each year. Close links must be maintained with local authorities which are, through their land disposal programmes, potentially the most important source of sites for new development; as planning authorities, they may also insist on the inclusion of social housing on larger sites. This power is examined further later. The closure of large institutions and hospitals through the Care in the Community initiative led to a substantial health authority disposal programme with the potential redevelopment of hospital sites for residential purposes. Additionally, redundant schools and church buildings are possible redevelopment sites. In recent years, several organisations also been developing closer links with private developers and they have become an increasingly important source of land and potential partnership schemes. Once a site has been identified, the RSL will carry out a feasibility study. Development risk demands that feasibilities be rigorous. In particular, emphasis must be placed upon the financial viability of the scheme. It is necessary to consider the ability of the organisation to raise private finance and the mortgageability of the project and to establish the likely outturn rent levels. In order to progress the scheme it may informally appoint an architect to work entirely at risk at this stage on the understanding that the firm will be formally instructed if the scheme progresses.

The consultant will produce outline plans showing a possible layout according to the brief given. A simple cost breakdown may also be provided. At this stage informal discussions regarding planning position may take place and possibly a site survey or site investigation if abnormal conditions are suspected. The valuer that the association has elected to use will also be approached to give an indication of the market value of the site as this is the figure that is eligible for subsidy, not the asking price. During the feasibility stage the RSL will undertake an option appraisal. This involves an examination of the various mixes, densities and layouts possible on the site until a scheme is found that meets both design and financial criteria.

The RSL will usually have a capital allocation to progress the scheme, but if it is over and above the annual allocation it will need to approach the funding authority for additional funding to take up, as often happens later in the year, any 'slippage' in the programme resulting from the failure of other RSLs to commit their allocation. The feasibility stage culminates in a financial model which indicates outturn rent levels based upon costs, interest rates and the likely length of the development period. A comparison will also be made against TCI. At this early stage the organisation must take a view, given the outturn rent levels, on whether it wishes to progress a scheme. High costs and rents will make the project uncompetitive. It should have its own internal targets which set out the acceptable parameters of risk regarding rent levels, costs and return on investment. A scheme may require support through internal funding from the RSL's own resources if the board has agreed such a policy; in which case, at feasibility stage, these requirements must be identified. If a scheme is viable and funding is available then the RSL will progress it for grant confirmation from the Housing Corporation. Following feasibility, outline planning permission will be sought from the local planning authority and negotiations will commence in earnest with the vendor.

Grant confirmation

The schemework procedures relating to the funding regime since August 1995 are laid down in the Housing Corporation's *Capital Funding Procedure Guide (1997)*, and have been simplified in many respects. The system provides for a single stage approval at the outset. The submission includes a standard form detailing all costs, sources of capital funding, a comparison against TCI and a revenue budget. The agreed rents will also be set at grant confirmation stage. The RSL must also gain consent to dispose of an interest in the land by way of mortgage to the institution providing the long-term finance (see Chapter 3). If the scheme costs exceed TCI limits, layout drawings should also be included. A statement must be forwarded which highlights and makes a case for any divergence of the proposals from the original allocation criteria, and especially divergence from expected rent levels.

As we have seen, the Corporation makes allocations according to certain priorities which reflect the nature of the need to be met; an explanation must be given in order to prevent funds being diverted from those priorities which have been identified by the regional strategy. The procedures also require the RSL to make detailed certifications. On receipt of the submission the Corporation will check various aspects of the application ensuring (in particular), that the RSL is operating within its capital adequacy ratios. If satisfied, the Corporation will confirm the TCI for the scheme net of any Special Percentage Adjustment, the scheme costs that will qualify for grant (acquisition, works costs and on-costs), the maximum cost over run figure that can be approved subject to scrutiny at final cost stage, the grant percentage applicable and the amount of grant available, including the value of each tranche to be disbursed at each stage (exchange of contracts, start on site and practical completion). Grant confirmation is critical. It is at this point that the agreed rents, TCI and subsidy levels and standard on-cost percentages are fixed. At grant confirmation the forecast estimates provided by the consultant of final outturn costs must be accurate. Undue delay in progressing the scheme to tender, adverse site conditions, changes in interest rates and high levels of building cost inflation can all produce cost overruns. If at this stage the scheme is already at 130 per cent of TCI there is no scope for funding of overruns through the subsidy system. Cost estimates must allow for the risks highlighted above.

Acquisition

Once grant confirmation is received the RSL will acquire the land or property. At this stage they may formally appoint consultants to the scheme. It should be noted that where allocations have been given for a specific site, a formal appointment may actually be made much earlier. At exchange of contracts the RSL will claim the tranche of grant due at this stage. If the HAG is insufficient to cover purchase costs short-term development finance must be raised.

Design stage

Following purchase completion the consultants will proceed to prepare detailed drawings and to make the application on behalf of the RSL for detailed planning permission. Appraisal of the scheme at this stage is vital. Appraisal may be undertaken by the board of management, but housing management and maintenance staff must also be consulted on the plans at this stage. In particular, the RSL will need to check that the proposals conform with the brief and any standard design requirements (see below). All aspects of the scheme should come under scrutiny.

At this stage the necessary detailed surveys and site investigations must be carried out. Tax on site waste introduced by the 1996 Landfill Tax must be minimised. The options available to the RSL to make any fundamental changes are of course limited given that the grant and cost limits are already set. To obviate this difficulty, many now work schemes up at risk to a much more advanced stage of design. Site layout, the most advantageous mix and density should all be decided as early as possible.

Tender stage

It should be noted that several forms of procurement are open to RSLs, and that the regime encourages use of methods other than the traditional competitive tender based upon the lump sum contract, in order to transfer risk from the RSL. Design and build is one method, and the issue of procurement is discussed separately later. RSLs are free to vary their procurement methods, although they should follow the guidance laid down in the Corporation's Scheme Development Standards. They will be audited to ensure that the methods they adopt are appropriate and fair. It is particularly important in the selection of contractors and in administering the tendering process to ensure propriety, and indeed to prevent possible impropriety, given the often very large value of the contracts at stake. If the lowest tender is too high and does not compare well with forecast estimates then the RSL will, through the consultant, negotiate savings. Making cuts at this stage is never easy and is certainly not desirable. It is important to involve housing management staff at this point as they will have the responsibility of letting and managing the finished product. They are also likely to produce very realistic suggestions for areas of possible savings. The second tranche of grant will be claimed as the scheme starts on site.

The construction period

Once the tender has been accepted the scheme will start on site. Before this, however, the RSL must enter into a formal contract as employer, with the contractor/developer. RSLs are expected to use the standard forms of contract issued by the Joint Contracts Tribunal (JCT). The supervision and administration of the contract is the responsibility of the consultant. The legally binding contract sets out clearly the rights and responsibilities of each party and it is essential that the RSL respects this and does not interfere with the running of it. Nevertheless, in order to maintain a strong client function the RSL will wish to remain involved and to monitor progress itself. There are a variety of methods of achieving this, including attendance at site meetings, reports from the clerk of works or site supervisor and site visits.

CONDAM

Since the 1 April 1995 RSLs have also had to comply with the health and safety rules for development and maintenance incorporated in the Construction (Design and Management) Regulations 1994 (CONDAM). These regulations have been introduced to improve safety and reduce the incidence of accidents in the industry. RSLs share responsibility with contractors for site safety, and arrangements must be established to manage and supervise site safety throughout the contract. An RSL must appoint a planning supervisor or achieve the function (including the maintenance of a health and safety plan and file) through the contractor or a team approach. Whatever approach is taken, as client, the RSL remains responsible.

Throughout the contract the architect will issue cost information as each certificate is authorised for payment. The cost information assists the RSL to maintain close control over scheme costs. Cost control is vital as the regime allows very little scope for additions.

Eventually the scheme reaches practical completion. Under building contract law it should be noted that practical completion does not mean that the property is available for letting but that the contractor has fulfilled the contract in completing the works in accordance with the contract documents. The consultant issues a Certificate of Practical Completion at which point the RSL claims the final tranche of grant, based upon the estimated outturn final costs. Prior to practical completion, however, the RSL will usually inspect the properties with the consultant to check for any faults or omissions. This inspection is known as 'snagging'. The property is then formally 'handed over' with the keys being passed to the landlord. The property may finally be let. Housing management staff should be involved in both the snagging and the handover of the property as they are the clients of the development section and need to be sure that they are satisfied with the standards of finish. They should also have access to a complete set of 'as-built' drawings for future reference.

Post-completion

After handover the RSL will maintain a 'retention' against the contract. This is monies held back against each certificate, until the Final Certificate is issued. This is intended to ensure that all defects are remedied. The defects liability period lasts for six months (12 for heating and service installations) from the date of practical completion. During this period, defects (which are not day-to-day maintenance items) must be attended to by the contractor through instructions from the consultant. This is a cumbersome and long-winded approach as defects are first reported by the tenant to housing management, but there is unfortunately no simpler route. After six months, provided that the defects have been attended to, the consultant will issue a Certificate of Making Good Defects, and within three months of this should agree the final account with the contractor. The Final Certificate is then issued and the retention released. The process is finally complete, and all that remains is for the RSL to evaluate performance of those involved and to obtain feedback from housing management.

6.7 Long-term maintenance

As highlighted in the previous chapter, ensuring that resources are available to fund the long-term maintenance of existing stock is a key issue for all RSLs, especially those housing associations with older stock developed at a time when standards were compromised (as discussed below). Although other maintenance services are often the responsibility of housing management and as such are discussed in the next chapter, capital works to older properties are usually undertaken by the development or technical teams. Older stock may require re-improvement to current standards, major repairs or a number of miscellaneous works undertaken to them. Major repair funding through the Housing Corporation has been sustained at *circa* £70 million per annum but is forecast to fall sharply in the period to 2000, which is a major concern to many RSLs. The prevailing view is that associations have substantial balance sheet reserves and therefore should plan to meet these needs themselves. Through the test outlined in Chapter 5, eligibility for major repair funding is assessed by the Housing Corporation and some RSLs are no longer eligible for assistance. For those that are, ADP funds are insufficient to meet requirements, and strategies to ensure that stock condition is maintained through reinvestment are required so that associations do not become the slum landlords of the future.

In 1991 the National Housing Federation published the results of a survey of stock condition undertaken by housing associations to assess the backlog of major repairs, and also commissioned research into the funding of major repairs and re-improvements. They found that in addition to immediate problems, long-term maintenance issues were being stored up for the future. Based upon estimates arising from the results of the survey, the national backlog of major repairs was assessed at *circa* £300 million. Of this, up to two-thirds related to stock funded by local authorities. The survey added weight to the debate with the Housing Corporation regarding the major repairs and re-improvement allocation process, and (as discussed) this in turn led to a new indicator of need, the housing association stock condition indicator and to a single Housing Corporation funding programme category 'works to existing RSL stock'.

Long-term maintenance plans form part of the asset management strategy of the RSL. Such strategies ensure that the value of the stock is maintained over time, thus protecting investment in it and providing further reassurance to private funders. The asset management strategy may include a programme of limited sale of unmanageable or undesirable stock, combined with policies to re-shape stock (reconverting some flats back into houses, for example). The strategy may also incorporate the re-shaping of specialist schemes such as sheltered housing for older people which has become difficult to let, as discussed in Chapter 9.

The Housing Corporation now expects all RSLs to undertake regular stock condition surveys and to plan a programme of stock reinvestment based on those findings. Indeed, under the Housing Act 1996 it has powers of entry to RSL dwellings to check on the adequacy of maintenance. Rent-setting policy and development strategies generally must take into account long-term maintenance needs. Those needs are usually well in excess of that which will be funded through the programmes detailed below or through the RSL's own Rent Surplus Fund provisions, so the Business Plan itself must incorporate the funding requirements for stock investment.

The Housing Corporation Performance Standards incorporate a number of requirements regarding long-term maintenance, including the expectation that tenants will be consulted about and kept informed of such plans.

Works to RSL existing stock (major repairs and miscellaneous works programmes)

All the provisions of the funding conditions and and programme management requirements described above are applicable to these programmes. RSLs may undertake programmes of major repairs and miscellaneous works (MRMW) to their existing stock which still attract up to 100 per cent grant aid and programmes to bring empty properties back into use. A Programme Agreement can be established for the receipt of grant or, alternatively, 'one-off' scheme-by-scheme approvals can be given. Bids for funding for these programmes are made in accordance with the time-scale described above. Only those properties not covered by the Rent Surplus Fund (see Chapter 5) are eligible for grant. Schemes developed after 1 April 1989 are also excluded, as are all low-cost home-ownership projects.

In addition to re-improvement schemes, works to RSLs' existing stock include MRMW schemes such as:

(a) works to property to achieve full occupation;
(b) major repairs to occupied property;
(c) miscellaneous works;
(d) adaptations to dwellings for people with physical disabilities.

This last programme receives priority support from the Housing Corporation and, as the sums of money involved are usually small, it is also subject to a streamlined set of procedures with minimum scheme-work being required. There is a threshold of a minimum of £500; below this the cost must be met by the RSL itself. Close liaison with social services is required. Grant claims are made at practical completion, as with all miscellaneous works programmes. Adaptation works may include the following: the provision of a ramped access; widening of paths and entrance doors; and the modification of circulation areas. Garages may be provided, as may stairlifts and hoists. Alterations to kitchen and bathroom units and layouts are also eligible for funding to make the dwelling as convenient as possible for the person with disabilities.

In addition to the above categories are included works of an emergency nature; non-emergency repairs to the main structural elements and non-emergency repairs to:

(a)   secondary elements of structural envelopes;
(b)   replacement or substantial reconstruction of siteworks;
(c)   renewal or substantial work to service installations;
(d)   remedial work for existing electrically heated dwellings (DEN3) works;
(e)   insulation/energy conservation works.

The procedures for each programme are laid down in the *Capital Funding System Procedure Guide 1997*. As stated, since 1993 two routes have been available for the funding of miscellaneous work and major repairs: the 'programme agreement' or the or 'one-off' scheme-by-scheme approval. Under the arrangements, grant is paid at 100 per cent of eligible costs. If the programmed route is followed, cost overruns will not be funded. Under the non-programmed agreements arrangements, cost over-runs will be funded up to 120 per cent. Grant is paid in two tranches: 80 per cent at start on site and 20 per cent at completion. In the case of aids and adaptations works the grant is paid in one tranche at the completion of the project. In order to enter into a programme agreement for funding for repairs to more than one property, an RSL must have undertaken a stock condition survey demonstrating the extent and type of remedial works required and estimating the costs involved. The RSL will identify funding priorities with the Housing Corporation and agree the scale of the programme over a three-year period. Performance against programme targets is reviewed annually and quarterly by the Corporation. Major repair works can now be combined with other programmes, including the re-improvement of an RSL's stock to bring it up to current standards. Re-improvement has separate eligibility criteria, and both approaches are vital in maintaining stock condition. Until 1995 the Corporation would only fund major repairs and miscellaneous works to properties it had originally financed. It became clear that this was a real obstacle to maintaining stock condition. While local authorities should still continue to accept responsibility for allocating resources to repair the stock they funded, those homes may now be eligible for Corporation funding through the ADP.

6.8   Day-to-day maintenance services

An RSL's management performance will be judged, in particular by its tenants, on the standard of its stock and its maintenance service, especially in terms of the speed and quality of day-to-day repairs undertaken. Maintenance has often been viewed as the 'cinderella' of the housing service yet, as RSL stock grows older, it has started to gain in prominence. Many landlords have enjoyed the benefits of a relatively youthful housing stock, but by the late 1980s analysis of the stock indicated a growing problem of disrepair as discussed in the previous section in the context of long-term maintenance requirements.

Those landlords that have completed stock surveys are in a position to begin to develop strategies to modernise older stock over time and to deal with any backlog of repairs. Re-investment strategies are now quite common amongst RSLs, and the majority are internally funded by the RSL itself using reserves and surplus income streams. In addition, as RSLs grow and acquire more assets, the condition of the stock becomes a crucial element of any asset management strategy. Each RSL needs to decide which properties to reinvest in, and which to sell if difficult to let or in very poor condition, in order to make the most of its asset base. Asset management strategies were considered briefly in Chapter 5.

Repairing obligations

Maintenance and the law is a complex area and space permits only a consideration of the key legal obligations which are set out below. For further detail readers are referred to a National Housing Federation guide to *Maintenance and the Law*.[6] In addition to duties under the Public Health Acts regarding fitness for human habitation and duties to ensure that properties are free from nuisance, all RSLs have an obligation under section 11 of the Landlord and Tenant Act 1985 to ensure that where properties are let for a term of less than seven years:

(a)   the structure and exterior of the dwelling is kept in a state of repair;
(b)   services including gas, electricity, water supplies and sanitation, including fittings and space and water heating, are kept in repair and proper working order.

Section 11(6) also gives the association power to gain access to the property to undertake repairs. In addition, under section 116 of the Housing Act 1988 landlords have a responsibility to maintain the common parts of a property such as the communal hallways, boilers and lifts in blocks of flats. These must also be serviced unless expressly the responsibility of leaseholders.

Under the Defective Premises Act 1972 the landlord also has a responsibility that the dwelling is fit for human habitation when any works carried out are completed, and to ensure that work done is performed in a proper manner with correct materials. It also has a duty to ensure that persons are reasonably safe from personal injury or damage caused by a defect in its property. This Act may also be used to pursue a landlord if it fails to carry out repairs.

All building regulations must be complied with, as must other relevant regulations including those emanating from the European Community, Construction, Design and Management (CONDAM: see above), health and safety and fire regulations. The Gas Safety (Installations and Use) Regulations 1994 must also be met. This involves using only persons approved by the Health and Safety Executive to undertake work to gas fittings and annual inspections, and to keep records of these checks.

All secure tenants are entitled to information regarding the provisions of section 11 of the Landlord and Tenant Act 1985 by virtue of section 104 of the Housing Act 1985.

RSLs should attempt to ensure that their contractors comply with the code of conduct in relation to staff and tenants, and that they comply with the Race Relations Act 1976 and the Sex Discrimination Act 1975.

The right to repair and the right to compensation for improvements

In 1994, new rights were extended to housing association tenants which gave them similar statutory rights as those granted to secure local authority tenants under the Leasehold Reform, Housing and Urban Development Act 1993. Under the right to repair RSLs have to establish a procedure and timescale for undertaking repairs.

A maximum cost is also set for qualification under the scheme (usually £250, which is the statutory limit). Targets are set for emergency, urgent and routine repairs. A repair notice is issued to inform the tenants of when and by whom the repair is to be carried out. If repairs are not done a second notice is issued. Once the procedure has been exhausted, and if the repair has still not been done, the tenant is entitled to cash compensation. Compensation is limited to £50 maximum.

Pursuant to the right to compensation for improvement RSLs should draw up a list of improvements that they are willing to allow tenants to carry out. Procedures are then established to enable the tenants to carry out the works subject to the landlord's consent which should not be unreasonably withheld. They are compensated for the costs on the basis of the depreciated value of the work when the tenancy ceases.

The repairing obligations of the landlord and the responsibilities of the tenant regarding access for repairs, reporting disrepair and internal decorations will be set out in the tenancy agreement. It is an expectation that each RSL will publicise the duties and standards of performance that it strives to achieve in a handbook or statement of policy.

In organising and managing the repair service the landlord will provide a responsive or day-to-day service which reacts to reports from tenants; a cyclical maintenance service which includes external redecoration and associated repairs which should be undertaken every four to five years; programmed maintenance which will include some annual contracts such as servicing gas appliances and lift installations; and planned maintenance, which involves the planned replacement of components such as roofs and windows.

Under the 1990 Environmental Protection Act action may be taken by the local authority or tenant against any landlord which fails to undertake their repairing obligations to the extent that a nuisance is created.

Principles
An effective and efficient responsive maintenance service operates on the following principles:

(a) a balance between the landlord and tenant's responsibilities;
(b) a service which is customer-centred;
(c) value for money achieved through quality control and monitoring both the contractor's and the landlord's performance;
(d) consistent operation of policies and procedures throughout the organisation (this is particularly relevant in the larger RSL; tenants should expect and receive the same standard of service regardless of the area or region in which their home is situated);
(e) sound systems of budgetary control and analysis of expenditure in terms of amount and type;
(f) equal opportunities in the operation of policies and practices and in the employment of contractors.

As with the development process, in managing the maintenance function the RSL should exercise a strong client role to ensure that the service meets their objectives. The maintenance service seeks to maximise the life of the RSL's assets and to provide a quick response to tenants' requests for repairs. It therefore follows that all repairs should be categorised in terms of priority and all aspects of the process monitored for response times and quality of workmanship. The technical aspects of the maintenance service and the management of the process deserve a depth of study that is not possible in this book, however.

The service should be operated according to the principles of customer care, which include effective communications, equal access to the service, tenant involvement in setting standards and monitoring performance, and seeking out and listening to customers' views and responding to them. Many RSLs have attempted to develop effective customer care strategies in this area and some have achieved quality assurance standards following the type of programme considered in Chapter 4.

The board or governing body should regularly monitor repair expenditure against budget and tenant satisfaction (or otherwise) with the service. Maintenance also contributes to void control in that delays in lettings may occur if a property is awaiting repair. This should also be monitored by officers and the Board.

Structure and organisation of the maintenance service

There are several distinct organisational structures for the administration of maintenance in RSLs. It may be integrated into the housing management team forming part of the housing director's responsibility, or separated into a distinct functional division with maintenance staff reporting to a separate head of department. It may be part of a development or technical department. In some organisations the function may be split with capital, long-term maintenance programmes dealt with by development or technical departments and the day-to-day service to tenants remaining with housing management.

Some professionals view maintenance as a housing management service rather than a technical function operating independently, as it is on this service that housing management services themselves are judged by the tenants. It can be argued therefore that housing managers should be able to exercise not only a client function, but also some control over the quality of this service and have some say in the spending priorities. There are, of course, strengths and weaknesses in each of the models, although the integrated model is favoured by the Audit Commission. If the integrated approach is adopted then the housing manager can exert full control over the nature and quality of the maintenance service, rather than being a client of it. However, in a larger RSL where maintenance staff may be based in each region or area team, it becomes more difficult with this model to ensure a consistency of standard and performance across the whole organisation. Conversely, the presence of a specialist maintenance department or section permits the development of greater consistency and possibly increased co-ordination and technical expertise. This structure also facilitates the development of planned maintenance services and direct labour organisations (DLOs). Few RSLs have sizeable direct labour organisations, although many employ individual caretakers for small or urgent repairs. *Managing Social Housing* (DOE 1993) found that 32 per cent of housing associations used DLOs in comparison with 91 per cent of local authorities. In general RSLs rely extensively upon outside contractors.

Repairs performance

The 1997 Performance Standards set out the expectations of repairs performance by registered social landlords. All RSLs are expected to provide a responsive service with access to emergency services providing 24-hour cover.

Studies of the sector's performance in this area have shown favourable results. The 1989 Glasgow Study found that local landlords were the best repair providers and that tenants generally (including those of national and regional RSLs) regarded their repair services more highly than did council tenants, and that they provided a better, although more expensive, service than local authorities. This is due largely to the financial and organisational differences between local authorities and RSLs. Housing associations, the report concluded, had a 'strategic repair service orientation, with high levels of regular stock inspection, planned maintenance and relatively high rates of customer monitoring'. It did not advocate complacency, however, stating that: 'in neither tenure were systems of repair monitoring or repair targets well developed, again suggesting that a more efficient approach could be developed.'

In 1993 the report *Managing Social Housing* confirmed that, despite the improvements in local authority performance since 1989 in housing management in general, the repair service remained less well perceived than that of housing association tenants. The report concluded that there was not any significant variation in performance between local authorities and housing associations. The 1994 report, *Homing in on Performance*, confirmed that local authorities spent on average £616 per dwelling per annum whilst RSLs spent on average £491 per dwelling per annum on repairs. Comparisons are difficult to make however, owing to the differences in stock types, age, and funding regimes.

The report found that there was a spread of performance in terms of meeting target response times; local authorities were less successful in completing urgent repairs within the target time than RSLs. The 1997 Performance Indicators show that response rates remained satisfactory with emergency repairs targets met in 92 per cent of cases, urgent repair targets in 88.7 per cent and routine targets met in 90.2 per cent of cases dealt with by those RSLs with over 5000 homes. The figures for those with less than 5000 homes were even better, although there are regional variations.[7]

6.9   Empty property programmes

In recent years a new emphasis has been placed on the utilisation of empty homes. The establishment of the Empty Homes Agency added momentum to this policy. The revisions to the HNI set out earlier in this chapter are based on the best use of existing stock to offset the need to invest further in new social housing. In 1997, a new framework was introduced to build on former initiatives: first, Temporary Social Housing (TSH), formerly the short-life programme; and second, Temporary Market Rent Housing (TMRH) which built upon the Housing Associations as Managing Agents Plus (HAMA Plus) schemes. Social Housing Over Shops (SHOS) is a further initiative, and all are sub-programmes of the ADP with a development component to assist in the provision of temporary accommodation which utilises empty properties. These initiatives may, in particular, assist local authorities to meet their obligations to homeless households and thereby avoid the more expensive use of bed and breakfast accommodation.

Temporary Social Housing

Temporary Social Housing (TSH) is the term used to describe the programme whereby the Corporation funds the capital costs of bringing vacant properties back into temporary use. Temporary means a life of not less than two and not more than 29 years. Short-life funding has been available since 1976 and was pursued by many co-operatives and housing associations to provide emergency accommodation in order to relieve homelessness on a temporary basis. It cannot provide a solution to homelessness, but does make vital use of properties that would otherwise remain vacant. The temporary use of properties may prevent further deterioration of an area often blighted prior to demolition. Vandalism and squatting are also reduced. Such properties are leased to the RSL and usually let on a licence rather than a tenancy so that they can be easily handed back when required for development, although the case of *Family HA* v. *Jones* (1989) cast doubt on the validity of this practice. The framework for short-life housing was completely reviewed in 1996, and following consultation a revised framework introduced. In particular the Housing Corporation was keen to extend the value for money framework to temporary housing too, and to encourage the use of private finance for these initiatives with reduced grant rates. In the event the Corporation decided to retain funding up to 100 per cent grant if required for 1997/98, but there is no doubt that schemes utilising lower grant rates will be favoured in future years. The procedures are set out in the *Capital Funding System Procedure Guide 1997* and will largely follow the procedures for rent as set out above. Grant is paid according to the levels produced by TCIs with special adjustments. Grant is paid at up to 100 per cent of cost and paid in two tranches, 80 per cent at start on site and 20 per cent at completion. The standards achieved in Temporary Social Housing cannot, of course, match those of permanent provision. Completed units must comply with minimum standards, however, as set out in *The Funding Framework for Temporary Social Housing 1997/98* (Housing Corporation 1996).

Temporary Market Rent Housing

Temporary Market Rent Housing was introduced in 1997 and built upon HAMA Plus. This in turn was introduced in 1994 and involved RSLs managing homes owned by private sector landlords where some capital works are required before the property can be let. The procedures were as for traditional rent programmes, but grant requirements were expected to be significantly lower than for rent or Temporary Social Housing schemes, although still funded at 100 per cent.

Tenancies are usually on an assured shorthold basis. The key difference between the two initiatives is that TSH programmes are intended to bring back into use public or private sector dwellings at social rents but for a limited period prior to demolition. TMRH brought back into use (at market rents) private sector properties which had been empty for at least six months. The management aspects of such schemes are explored further in Chapter 7, together with other management initiatives. In 1998, however, the Housing Corporation announced that this initiative was to be abandoned on the basis that value for money was not being achieved.

Living over shops

One further programme to consider is the initiative which brings back into use the empty space, often derelict, situated over shops. Originally devised by the Living Over The Shop (LOTS) project based at the University of York, a small pilot programme was supported by the Housing Corporation in 1990/91. Now known as Social Housing Over Shops (SHOS), the programme is part of the main ADP. In 1991 the Department of the Environment announced its own initiative, Flats Over Shops (FLOTS). This enabled local authorities to make available (through increased Supplementary Credit Approvals) local authority grant to enable housing associations to take leases on flats over shops and bring them back into use. Around £25 million was made available over three years for this initiative. Associations are unable to obtain funding for any works to the commercial premises, however. Both programmes have enabled underutilised resources to be brought back into use and have contributed to urban regeneration. A handbook written by the key architect of this initiative sets out how to make these projects work and includes a number of case studies.[8] The Corporation's scheme was evaluated by the Sheffield Hallam University in 1994[9] and it showed that the initiative offered good value for money.

6.10   Development standards

When undertaking any form of development activity, including the programmes outlined above, an area of prime concern to the RSL is the maintenance of high development standards. There are several aspects to this concept. These include, firstly, design criteria concerned with space, amenity, energy efficiency and internal and external layout of the property. Secondly, the quality of materials, fixtures, fittings and finishes must comply with agreed standards. Third, supervision must also be of a level that ensures a high quality of workmanship. Such standards may be set by the RSL itself but there are also requirements laid down by the Housing Corporation's Scheme Development Standards (1995) and Performance Standards. In addition, there are a number of external standards that will be imposed by the various parties to the development process. The planning authorities will have their own perceptions of development standards on the complete range of issues from car parking provision and the density of development to the species of trees to be planted or the colour and type of brick to be specified. There are building regulations to meet which cover every aspect of design and construction.

Standards are dynamic and subject to continual change as expectations alter and (usually) increase. The heating and insulation standards of the 1960s are considered inadequate today. Tenants have increasing aspirations: they expect more space and improved layout. In kitchen design, for example, allowance must be made for electrical appliances and space for freezers, washing machines and so on. Development standards must also take into account future maintenance needs. A balance needs to be struck between the initial costs of capital outlay and 'costs in use', or future maintenance expenditure. At times of financial stringency there is an obvious temptation to reduce initial standards of provision, but this will only store up a legacy of future maintenance problems.

All housing association development is subject to cost control. A balance must be struck between costs, standards and rent levels. In the preceding chapter the current system of Total Cost Indicators was outlined. These limits set value for money parameters and ensure that 'higher standards' are not paid for from the public purse. TCI bands are based on size, and there has been a real temptation to squeeze space standards to take the unit into a lower size band so that it requires less grant and appears more competitive. In reality the unit may look as if it will house four people, but lettings policies may restrict it to three to allow for the smaller size. That at least has at times been the intention. In reality some local authorities monitor mix and space standards very closely and RSLs have been unable to underlet owing to pressure from the local authorities, particularly those with intense homelessness requirements. The result has been intensive occupation of smaller homes, which in turn has led to problems of management. There is, then, an inevitable tension between competition and value for money and the desire for high development standards.

RSLs have to bear in mind that on average tenants move house once in 20 years. Owner-occupiers move on average every eight years. The limited mobility of the renting population means that it is almost impossible for them to improve their standard of housing; thus it could be argued that rented housing must be developed to a higher standard than housing for sale from the outset. In addition lettings criteria, often imposed externally, may result in high occupation rates, increasing wear and tear on the dwelling.

The development team is therefore faced with a range of constraints and has a difficult task to attempt to meet all requirements. This has probably never been more important. The cuts in grant rates since 1989 have led to inevitable pressure on standards. In 1991 the NFHA found that mixed funded schemes had already compromised on space to make up for reduced levels of capital grant. Two major studies on housing association development, by David Page[10] and Valerie Karn,[11] led to important debates about the changing nature of housing association development standards following the Housing Act 1988. Both are considered in greater detail below, as are the current design and construction requirements. The development of design standards is considered first, however, as some understanding of the evolution of design and construction standards aids comprehension of the current debate regarding the quality of housing association development, and highlights some of the causes of disrepair in stock not even fifteen years old.

Parker Morris

In 1961 the Parker Morris Report, *Homes for Today and Tomorrow*, was published. This set the design criteria for dwellings and their environment and in 1967 became the mandatory minimum standard for all public sector housing development, although these were officially abandoned in 1989. The Report was radical in the standards it set. Space standards were particularly generous and led to the provision of floor areas of a greater size than those found in the private sector. Parker Morris standards also became a maximum standard for general family accommodation; provision of items over and above the standard ranked as non-qualifying costs for Housing Association Grant. In addition to space requirements, guidance on storage, such as inclusion of linen cupboards and pram stores, was included for the first time. Guidance was given on the provision of the number of WCs, and on kitchen fittings and layouts. Standards of space heating were laid down, as were the number of electric socket outlets for each part of the home. Parker Morris standards were adopted by the Housing Corporation and remained the minimum until 1989, although some associations have attempted to maintain some parity with these standards since their official abandonment.

Specially designed housing

In 1969 the Ministry of Housing and Local Government introduced design guidance for housing for the elderly in Circular 82/69.[12] This set out the special features to be included in housing for the elderly. The details of this circular are discussed further in Chapter 9 but relate to location, the provision of communal facilities and space standards.

Throughout the 1970s the Department of the Environment published numerous design bulletins regarding car parking provision, safety in the home and space standards, amongst others, which related to requirements stemming from Parker Morris. In 1975, DoE circular 92/75[13] set out new cost allowances for dwellings specifically designed to meet the needs of wheelchair users and those people with mobility requirements. These were based upon occasional papers published by Selwyn Goldsmith,[14] setting out standards of design and equipment for people with such requirements. More recently, the concept of 'lifetime homes' has been developed. These are flexibly designed homes designed to cope with the changing needs of occupants over their lives. The design aspects of these schemes are explored further in Chapter 8.

As each circular was published, so the Housing Corporation adopted those criteria for approved housing association developments. Their *Design and Contract Criteria (1988)* set out the expected standards for new build and rehabilitation for rent with regard to most aspects of design. However, despite the setting of standards, tighter cost controls combined with cash limits led to many standards being lowered throughout the late 1970s and early 1980s. Associations were forced to make cuts to items such as window and roof replacements, repairing them instead. The extent of the requirement for future major repairs that this has caused is only now becoming clear and, as a result, many associations are now carrying out extensive works to properties refurbished only fifteen years ago or less.

The Design and Contract Criteria Guide was regularly updated as standards and expectations altered and was completely replaced by a much more limited document in April 1989. Reduced scrutiny and less bureaucracy were the carrot for the new system which now placed the development risk squarely upon the association. It was argued that associations should be free to develop according to their own standards. This was a double-edged sword. This freedom was welcomed by developing associations but concern was also be expressed over whether standards would be maintained, given the financial pressures that associations would face under the post-1988 Act regime. Both the Corporation and the National Housing Federation have monitored schemes to ascertain the effect of a less rigid approach to design standards.

In addition to pressure on design standards arising from the less generous financial regime, associations started to adopt new approaches to procurement to transfer development risk (as outlined below). In addition, by joining forces with local authorities using their enabling powers and in consortia with other associations in partnership with private developers, several associations developed large schemes of several hundred homes. The rapid growth in the ADP in the early 1990s with very large allocations available to the most active developing associations facilitated this process.

For a period large-scale new build developments were perceived as offering greater value for money. This led to criticism of some association developments.

Building for Communities

In April 1993, the Page Report, *Building for Communities*,[15] heightened awareness of the trend towards larger developments with standardised design which was replacing smaller developments and rehabilitation in the search for value for money. This was always disputed by the Housing Corporation, which confirmed at the time that the average housing association development still stood at only 13 units. Nevertheless it was recognised that a number of larger developments had been completed or were under way, and that further developments were planned. As discussed in Chapter 1, the number of housing association tenants dependent on benefits had grown from *circa* 60 per cent to 75 per cent in just ten years. Incomes had also declined in relation to the national average. This in turn raised questions as to the wisdom of concentrating people in such economic circumstances in larger estates that would effectively become 'ghettos' of poverty and deprivation. This would make them less attractive and possibly difficult to let in the longer term. The report also noted the high level of child densities on these estates which could contribute further to management problems. Child densities were running at six times the recommended Department of the Environment and Home Office levels.

The Page Report recommended that association developments should not exceed 40 units in order to achieve better integration into the wider community. Others argued, however, that scale is not really the issue, but poverty. Many private sector estates consist of several hundred homes and do not display some of the problems associated with larger social housing estates. It could be argued that smaller social housing developments merely hide the symptoms of poverty, low income and unemployment by spreading them out rather than resolving them in any way. This was a major flaw of the report, in that it described the circumstances of new tenants but did not acknowledge that many of the problems highlighted were the result of structural poverty and social exclusion, owing to wider economic trends and not just as a result of the design of the schemes and letting policies of the associations. Until the poverty trap (caused by a perverse blend of rent levels, housing benefit and marginal rates of taxation) is more effectively tackled, many association tenants will continue to be among the most socially excluded members of society.

Page highlighted four elements that can affect the success or failure of an estate:

(a)   the choice of site location;
(b)   design;
(c)   tenant selection and allocation policies
(d)   estate management.

The two latter points relate to the recommendation that larger estates should attempt to create 'balanced' and stable communities also comprising families in work and those on higher incomes. It suggested reducing child densities. It recognised the importance of involving housing managers at scheme feasibility stage to ensure that management issues are planned from the outset. These will impact upon the design, layout and mix of the scheme and include the consideration of other issues, such as the requirement for open spaces and play areas or community facilities.

The choice of site location is vital. The report found that too many estates were in isolated positions some distance from local facilities and transport. This deepened the effect of 'ghettoisation', contributing to social exclusion on these estates. In relation to design, it highlighted the need to build in security and space standards at the outset and to consider the need for community facilities and other amenities. The report, whilst not without its critics, was timely and taken seriously by the sector. Many of the initiatives relating to 'housing plus', community involvement and attempts to develop mixed tenure schemes flowed from the Page Report.

In 1994 Page published a further study, *Developing Communities*,[16] which sets out possible strategies (supported by a series of action sheets with references and contacts) to assist associations to plan for sustainable development and stable communities from the outset. The report has three major themes which could enable associations to get the structure right for the 'community to develop and cohere'. These include the need to plan from the outset to reduce social imbalance, the need for social infrastructure and the need to get people involved. These are not new themes but lessons that should have been learnt from earlier programmes, such as the local authority Priority Estates Projects (PEP) programmes that have been running since the late 1970s. Nevertheless these issues need to be reinforced in the context of housing association development. Social infrastructure refers to the need to ensure that schools, health facilities, shops and bus routes are in place before the development commences. The need to foster communities through the provision of community facilities is also stressed. The report emphasises the importance of a plan that will commence prior to the handover of a scheme to ensure that tenants are assisted during the period of moving in and that tenant or community associations are established to assist the community to develop. Clearly RSLs must work in partnership with others to achieve these aims. These findings are further supported by the work of Cole *et al.* (1996) which examined how residents of housing associations viewed their estates.[17]

Two earlier but important reports were concerned with the impact of the post-1988 Act regime on housing association development standards. In September 1993 a Government study, *Housing Association Standards for General Needs and New Build Dwellings* by consultants Davis, Langdon and Everest found that housing associations led private developers on design and construction standards in many respects, particularly access and mobility, thermal insulation and reduced long-term maintenance costs. Whilst the report found that their homes were not built to better standards than private sector homes, this report stated that the housing that was provided offered better mobility and fuel economy, and would be cheaper to maintain than homes in the owner-occupied sector. The report concluded that the two sectors provide different types of dwellings for different users, in different locations. It recognised the small, constrained, difficult re-development sites that associations have to work on, often in secondary locations. The report noted that this makes comparability of standards and costs difficult to estimate. However, it did confirm other research, namely that both housing associations and private developers were building to less than Parker Morris standards.

More recently, a report by Karn and Sheridan, *New Homes in the 1990s: A Study of Design, Space and Amenities in Housing Association and Private Sector Housing*,[18] clearly concluded that there had been a diminution in space standards. The report found that competition, combined with a reduction in grant levels, had led the sampled associations to reduce standards so that the number of homes below Parker Morris had risen from 53 per cent in 1989/90 to 68 per cent by 1992. Furthermore, they claimed that circulation and storage space was being diminished and that one-third of homes had insufficient room for occupants to sit down and eat together. They concluded that these homes offered poor long-term value for money. The report, however, was not without its critics given that only a small sample was surveyed and regional coverage was variable. No more than 136 properties were involved in 134 schemes submitted by 83 associations. Nevertheless, concern that the financial regime (combined with the rush to build) was leading to poor value for money in some schemes reached its height at this time. Despite the fact that most associations had worked tirelessly to attempt to maintain standards it was considered important to set new quality standards.

In 1995 quality standards defined by the National Housing Federation
and developed in conjunction the National Audit Office were adopted by
the Housing Corporation. These standards involve the layout of furniture;
thus, although not prescriptive on size, they ensure that the homes are fit
for their intended use in terms of design and layout, and imply space
standards too.

Scheme Development Standards

After the period of growth and growing criticism, the introduction of new
Scheme Development Standards by the Housing Corporation in 1995
marked an important step in defining what was to become known as the
Social Housing Standard. Tougher standards introduced in the revised
document set the parameters for comparing schemes in terms of quality.
They compliment the rents in bidding regime discussed earlier, in establishing a 'level playing field' in terms of assessing the value for money of
schemes. The Standards were introduced in 1995 and cover the quality of
housing, the probity of procurement and compliance and certification. All
schemes must comply with these standards. The section on quality of
housing sets the requirements and recommendations in relation to the
internal and external environment of the dwelling. A room-by-room
approach sets out the space required to allow movement around furniture
and is split between essential and recommended items.

Accessibility, safety and security, energy efficiency and building practice and maintenance are also covered. Issues surrounding probity
include procurement policy, the selection of contractors and consultants,
and procurement practice.

Social Housing Standard and Construction Task Force

The Social Housing Standard for general needs housing incorporates the
Scheme Development Standards outlined above and applies to all perma-
nent housing developed with Social Housing Grant after 1 April 1997.
Further work is, however, being undertaken by the National Housing
Federation on a 'housing quality index' and jointly with the Joseph
Rowntree Foundation on 'standards and quality'. Higher standards,
known as 'Scheme Development Standards Plus' are also being pursued
by some RSLs on some schemes. Thus Scheme Development Standards
will continue to be revised and incorporated into the Social Housing
Standard to apply to homes developed in 1998/99 and onwards. In 1999,
the Construction Task Force reported on standards and stated that capital
costs, construction time and defects should be reduced by 10 per cent.
Some 60 per cent of schemes should comply with these standards by 2003.

6.11   Some approaches to managing the development process

A development strategy

In order to bid effectively and to ensure that sufficient funds will be available to finance the development programme in both the short and the long term, RSLs need to plan ahead. Finance and development cannot be be viewed in isolation. Any strategy must be built on a clear knowledge of local housing needs, the organisation's market position, ability to raise the required finance whilst retaining sufficient reserves to meet reinvestment needs and funders' requirements. Any strategy should also be based upon agreed criteria regarding outturn rent levels and the ability of the organisation to absorb the risks arising from development activity. Ideally, the development strategy should form part of a corporate plan for the organisation which will outline the aims and objectives of the organisation over, say, a five-year period and which examines performance and sets operational targets for all activities including development. The development strategy must accord with the objectives and priorities of the RSL and will determine what is developed, where and to meet which needs.

The strategy is the domain of the board of management. In larger associations, once the strategy is set, the task of procuring new homes is delegated to staff. The board will monitor progress, standards and value for money through a system of regular reporting. In smaller RSLs the board may be much more involved in the development process, especially if specialist staff are not directly employed. In this case development may be undertaken by an agent, often a larger body. Where this does occur, the small RSL will have a development agreement with the agency and the board will need to monitor the performance of the agency, and indeed may comment on the scheme at every stage. Whatever the degree of involvement by the board in the development process they must determine the strategy in accordance with their aims and objectives and as a result of researching local needs. Several factors will influence the nature of the strategy, not least the priorities of the local authority(ies) in whose area the RSL operates.

Each local authority will have a housing strategy which forms part of its annual Housing Investment Programme (HIP) bid to the Department of the Environment, Transport and the Regions. The degree of sophistication of these strategies varies but they will set out the priorities of the authority in terms of housing provision. The relationship between associations and local authorities was explored in Chapter 3 and will change in the coming years as the policy of the Labour Government is implemented further. Associations' development strategies will need to take these political factors into account.

The Housing Corporation, as we have seen, also produces an annual stategy statement on a national and regional basis, and allocations will be made in accordance with those priorities. Each year the individual bids by RSLs for funding will be discussed by the Corporation with the local authority; and although the Corporation reserves the right to independence in making its allocations, it does take into account the priorities of the authority. And, as we have seen, joint commissioning will also alter the landscape. In effect, if an RSL is to attract funding, it must ensure that its schemes match the requirements of the areas in which it operates. The development strategy is eventually submitted to the Housing Corporation with the bid for funding, and its success will in part depend upon the degree to which it meets local needs.

Standard documentation

The use of standard documentation can assist an RSL to maintain the quality of its development and to ensure that its strategy, particularly with regard to standards, is met. The most common are a standard specification or technical brief for rehabilitation works, and a new build design and technical brief. Some also have procedure manuals setting out their own expectations in terms of scheme administration, liaison with other internal departments and tenants. These documents will also set out the organisation's policy regarding equal opportunities. The standard documents assist in the process of providing housing which represents value for money initially, but which will be economical to maintain in the longer term. Nothing in such briefs limits the professional responsibility of consultants, and it is important that any conflicts between the brief and the professional judgement of the consultant are aired early on in the development process. Most consultants value the standard brief as a document that will assist them in meeting their clients' requirements rather than limiting their function in any way.

Whether or not an RSL has developed standard documentation it must, as mentioned above, provide its architect or surveyor with a brief. The brief may include the following:

(a) site details, including any known adverse site conditions or unusual features;
(b) proposed accommodation including dwelling mix, the number and types of dwellings, their size (i.e., numbers of bedrooms/persons to be housed);
(c) car parking and landscaping requirements including clothes-drying and play facilities;
(d) any planning requirements or other constraints, such as easements, rights of way;

(e)   an indication of cost constraints and the likely procurement methods;

(f)   standards of construction, services, fixtures, fittings and finishes.

In addition to the brief, it is important to ensure that the consultant is familiar with the Corporation's requirements regarding design and standards and, indeed, that he or she understands the constraints within which the RSL operates, particularly with regard to funding.

Scheme appraisal and managing development risk

As we have seen, there has been a shift in design standards attributed to the system of capital funding introduced in 1989. Scheme appraisal has also been affected. The private finance regime had three objectives: to increase value for money in the production of housing association homes; to increase the number of homes provided through (initially) a real increase in the Corporation's programme combined with the ability of associations to raise private finance; and a transfer of risk to the associations, making them more responsible for managing the development process as a quid pro quo for reduced scrutiny. Associations had to become concerned with risk management not only in finance, but in development too. Each scheme now needs to be appraised against carefully chosen parameters. These will relate to costs, investment returns, requirements for internal funding and break-even periods based on different interest rate assumptions. In addition, risk will have to be managed throughout the process which, as we have seen, is lengthy and relatively complex. The risks have always been inherent in the process, but what was new was the consequence of any variations in costs. Since 1989 increased costs were no longer fully funded through subsidy. Cost overruns arise either through unforeseen items occurring during the development process or due to inadequate site and property surveys and poor estimating. Delays in decanting programmes in the case of refurbishment or redevelopment, or in first lettings will create additional costs to the organisation. Rises in long- or short-term interest rates can have a devastating impact upon outturn rents. At feasibility stage, when the financial model is drawn up, several assumptions are made in relation to the timescale for development, future interest rates, likely build costs and so on. If these assumptions are inaccurate additional costs will arise. Increases in costs must be borne wholly or in part by the RSL. These must either be paid for out of increased rents or the association's own resources. The development period risk can be minimised by stringent cost control. Developing associations were (and remain) faced with a new challenge: how to reduce costs and control them while still maintaining development standards.

Minimising risk

Associations have had, and must continue, to adopt several approaches if project risks are to be minimised. In particular they need to develop crisp systems of project management with strict internal controls. If an organisation lacks expertise it should use an experienced development agent. The performance of contractors and consultants must be monitored and closer working relationships developed with them without compromising accountability. Consultants must estimate accurately and maintain tight control over the building contract. Only contractors or developers which can maintain programme deadlines and produce a high quality of construction with few cost overruns should be employed. Delays must be minimised and the development programme managed in a way that maximises the use of grant advanced. Contract periods should be as short as possible without adversely affecting the price. RSLs should ensure that they are adequately insured, and many use bonds and also insure against latent defects. Shortly after the passage of the Housing Act 1988 a number came together to form the Housing Associations Property Mutual (HAPM) which offers a technical audit service examining plans and specifications and which offers insurance against any later major repair requirements arising from the failure of building components. Given that no major repair funding is available for post-1988 stock, HAPM is employed by some RSLs to assist in offsetting this long-term risk.

Managing the programme as a whole

In addition, organisations with larger programmes need to be able to manage the programme as a whole. The combined impact upon the association's cash flow, for example, needs to be carefully monitored. Private finance requirements need to be in place in time to meet large payments, and the impact of delayed handovers on income and expenditure need to be accounted for, as must any changes in interest rates or internal funding requirements. Claims for grant must be timely. The interface between the development staff undertaking project management and development finance and treasury management staff becomes vital where large programmes are being delivered.

Procurement methods

Since 1989 associations have changed the methods they use to procure new homes. Many previous restrictions were lifted and associations became freer to negotiate prices with contractors and developers that they know and trust. The competitive edge must not be lost, however, and greater use can be made of two-stage tendering procedures, especially for rolling programmes of re-improvement and rehabilitation. In this case competitive tenders are sought initially and prices then negotiated with the lowest tenderer. Traditional forms of contract have been replaced by 'design and build'. Many RSLs have turned to this form of contract in an attempt to fix their costs.

Design and build contracts minimise the risk to the organisation by passing it on to the developer. The developer/contractor contracts to both design and build the scheme for a fixed, inclusive price on the basis of a brief or performance specification provided by the RSL. Developers may be selected on a competitive basis or by negotiation. Design and build contracts may be undertaken on the RSL's land or land owned by the developer. In the latter case the contract is known as a package deal. The developer will make a written offer to the RSL detailing land costs, works costs and design fees.

The contractor is responsible for design, construction and supervision of the works and must take responsibility for all unforeseen items. It is this transfer of risk that makes design and build so attractive. The consultant's role is more limited. Pre-contract services include assisting the RSL with the formulation of their requirements and assessing the 'contractor's response'. They may also negotiate modifications to the developer's standard house types. Post-contract services include acting as the 'employer's agent' through periodic inspection of the scheme, agreeing periodic payments to the contractor, advising on completion of the works and agreeing the final account. The negative aspect of such contracts is, of course, that quality may be compromised. Some associations have overcome this disadvantage by producing their own standard house types which are then adopted by the developer. They act as a blueprint which can then be reproduced on different sites. One of the largest RSLs, Home Housing Association, has led the sector in this respect.

Off-the-shelf schemes

The regime has also encouraged the purchase of off-the-shelf schemes. Quite simply, the RSL approaches a developer and purchases a ready-made completed number of units. This allows for a rapid take-up of the RSL's allocation, which is especially helpful at the year end if spend is low. Space standards in particular tend to be lower and standards of construction poorer; design and build schemes are considered more acceptable.

Partnerships

The demands of the regime have also been met through very positive and productive partnerships between private developers and local authorities. There are numerous examples of RSLs working in partnership with private developers in addition to partnership with local authorities and other agencies such as health authorities and development corporations.

Planning gain and the use of section 106 agreements

Partnerships with developers often involve two particular concepts, planning gain and cross-subsidy. The planning system is important as a means for ensuring that sites are developed for social housing. Planning Policy Guidance Note 3 (PPG3)[19] enables local authorities to negotiate with developers to provide affordable housing on their sites provided that the local plan has identified such a need. This has enabled mixed tenure schemes to be developed whereby some sale receipts are used to cross-subsidise the rented housing, thus making it deliverable (and more affordable). Landowners and developers become aware that chances of gaining planning permission are enhanced by the provision of some social housing. The mechanism used is a section 106 agreement, drawn up under section 106 of the Town and Country Planning Act 1990. Through a planning agreement the local authority may insist that, in return for the permission, some contribution be made on site through the provision of community facilities or social housing, or off site to another scheme, often in the form of a cash sum to a housing association developing elsewhere. Such gains can be used to finance and subsidise developments. Such partnerships are of immense value in attracting more resources into the sector. Many local authorities have successfully used these powers to enable the provision of affordable housing in their area since 1991. This is explored in full by Dunmore (1992).[20] It must be remembered, however, that developers are not philanthropists. There must therefore be a balance struck between commercial gain and community benefit. Nevertheless, many developers established partnership and social housing divisions to respond to the lean years for house-building generally, but in many cases these have created real and lasting benefits for local communities.

In August 1996 the Department of the Environment issued Circular 13/96 on *Planning and Affordable Housing*. The circular emphasises the provision of homes in a way that is consistent with sustainable development, utilising sites in urban areas and minimising the need for travel. Affordable housing assessments should form part of the local plan with indicative targets for specific sites. This is less definite than the previous quota system which led many planning authorities to seek 25 per cent affordable homes on development sites. In London the policy only applies to sites of 25 or more dwellings and elsewhere to sites of 40 or more dwellings. This circular is therefore not likely to greatly assist the development of affordable housing on development sites.

Cross-subsidy

Cross-subsidy usually involves a mixed development of housing for rent by the RSL and for sale by the developer, with some sales profits being ploughed back into the rented scheme. Furthermore, if part of the sales are for shared ownership, with the RSL guaranteeing the marketing of the finished units, then a further subsidy may be attracted by way of a reduced contract price for the development. The developer may reduce the profit element to account for the surety of sales. Whilst cross-subsidy through partnership is valuable, some RSLs are also able to cross-subsidise their own developments. If the RSL is non-charitable or has a non-charitable subsidiary, then the proceeds of outright sales or shared ownership sales can be used to subsidise the rented element of the development.

Discounted land

Since 1989 many local authorities have enabled the development of social housing in their area through the provision of land at a nominal value (£1) or at a discounted price. Although this subsidy is taken into account in assessing the total public subsidy requirement of a scheme it has enabled many projects to proceed within the constraints of the regime. Department of the Environment consent is required to dispose of land at less than market value, and the local authority will also expect additional nomination rights to the scheme. Nominations will usually be 100 per cent in these cases for first lettings, and some authorities have attempted to achieve 100 per cent in perpetuity. This can lead to blemished title to the land, however, rendering it worthless as security for private finance.

Consortia

The consortium approach (which has both advantages and disadvantages), whilst popular in the early 1990s, now finds less favour as the preference for smaller sites prevails. The main advantage is the pooling of resources, including capital allocations and expertise. Organisations lacking development experience or unused to developing larger sites will benefit from the lead usually taken by one of the bigger or more established developing associations. A further advantage is the ability to tackle larger sites. Throughout the mid-1990s the Housing Corporation was more willing to allocate several million pounds to a single site if it met a range of needs and the allocation was spread across a number of associations which served a range of client groups. A health authority or local authority was also able to maximise capital receipts through such sizeable land disposals. Consortia were also seen to have more 'clout' with the funding agencies, the local authority and the private funders, as the risk of supporting a large development is spread over a number of agencies. Larger sites can bring economies of scale, and thus it is possible to produce more housing of a high standard of design and amenity at affordable rents. The consortium approach also offers the opportunity to undertake projects of a scale that can revitalise whole areas. The disadvantage of the consortium approach is that it may compromise the independence of the organisation; action cannot be taken unless agreed by the other members of the consortium. The planning stage of the scheme may also be longer than would be the case if there was a single developer. The consortium has presented a useful route for small and emerging RSLs (alluded to in the quotation given at the outset of this chapter). When working with powerful and experienced developers they need to ensure that they are permitted to make a full contribution and have their requirements taken into account. If they do not 'fight their corner', the larger agencies which are taking the lead may overlook their special requirements in their determination to make the scheme 'work'. In some ways RSLs may also be more vulnerable in a consortium. The collapse of one partner or their inability to raise funds may affect the whole consortium's viability. Furthermore, complex agreements are required to ensure that the action of one organisation cannot jeopardise the others

Importantly, as we have seen, there are long-term housing management considerations if there are to be several landlords present on one site. The management issues posed by multi-landlord estates are considered in Chapter 7. Such large-scale projects have been subject to criticism and the Housing Corporation, in the late 1990s, is much less willing to fund consortia schemes unless part of an urban regeneration scheme.

6.12   Urban regeneration

The regime introduced by the Housing Act 1988 did not favour inner-city rehabilitation and as we have seen, led to a major reduction in this activity. Rehabilitation was viewed as too costly and risky to undertake on any scale given the nature of the funding regime. In addition, the framework also favoured larger-scale, new developments, often on outer city or suburban sites, and development on brown land was limited. Funders were keener to support new build. The increases in the Corporation's programme and the need to deliver a huge increase in homes quickly contributed to this process. By 1993 rehabilitation had declined from 60 per cent to les than 20 per cent of the programme. The TCIs and grant rates had also made rehabilitation virtually unworkable. Cuts in local authority funding meant that spending on improvement and renewal areas was limited. Properties for acquisition were also less available during the boom years for the owner-occupied market.

Some associations did manage to keep a small programme of rehabilitation going with an element of internal cross-subsidy, but pressure eventually mounted for a regime that would allow rehabilitation to work again, particularly in inner-city areas. This activity had been the key objective of many associations, and indeed was often the driving force behind their foundation. Most remained concerned that they were being driven from this work, usually unwillingly, by an unfavourable financial framework.

The climate began to change with the introduction of City Challenge funding in 1992. This funding made available (through competition) up to £37.5 million for each of the 20 successful areas. City Challenge represented a new direction in the Government's urban policy, and aimed to revitalise run down urban or inner-city areas. Most City Challenge areas have a major housing component, with the active participation of housing associations. City Challenge was soon followed by the Single Regeneration Budget. Both programmes require RSLs to work in partnership with a range of public, private and voluntary bodies.

Single Regeneration Budget

In 1993 Sir George Young, the then Minister for Housing, made the following statement to the Conservative Party Conference: 'I know of anxieties that housing associations will build estates that repeat the mistakes of local authorities. So I am taking steps to redirect their energy back to their roots – regenerating run-down parts of the country, improving older buildings.' After this speech, urban regeneration was put back on the agenda and reshaped through the Single Regeneration Budget. The SRB brought together, under the aegis of the Secretary of State for the Environment and a ministerial committee, the combined budgets of five government departments and 20 different programmes. These budgets included City Challenge, the Urban Programme and Estate Action budgets. Estate Action, which was introduced in 1986, had enabled run-down council estates to be refurbished, often in partnership with housing associations which would provide some new build accommodation on the estates. In the same year a new agency, English Partnerships, was established to facilitate the redevelopment of brown land through grants for cleaning up the sites and to undertake infrastructure work. This included housing on vacant or derelict land. The switch in emphasis towards regeneration since 1994 under the 1992–7 Conservative administration was funded largely through existing programmes. There was little new money. Local authority programmes and the ADP had taken the brunt of the cuts.

By 1995, especially in London, there had been a shift back to rehabilitation. This often involved existing local authority stock rather than the acquisition and refurbishment of properties from the private sector. The process was aided by local authorities also discounting the prices of properties, as they had done with land. The return to rehabilitation was also assisted by a major report sponsored by London-based housing associations,[21] which highlighted the importance of rehabilitation and detailed the cost of it. The report showed that rehabilitation was a vital activity needed to improve the quality of life in inner-city areas.

The SRB represented an area of activity for housing associations additional to that undertaken through the ADP. Some SRB programmes, however, do rely on Corporation contributions and part of the ADP is allocated for this purpose as it has been for City Challenge. By 1995–96 the SRB programme as a whole amounted to some £1.3 billion. It is administered through the new Government Regional Offices (see Chapter 3) and is distributed through competitive bidding. SRB bids are usually, but not always, led by a local authority and will involve a range of partners, particularly local Training Enterprise Councils. Successful bids will lead to the regeneration of an area through:

(a)   enhanced employment prospects
(b)   sustainable economic development
(c)   improved housing condition, better choice and management
(d)   promoting initiatives to benefit ethnic minorities
(e)   improving the environment and promoting good design
(f)   enhancing the quality of life for local people.

Leverage from the private sector through private investment is also expected, and value for money criteria are important. Each bid must clearly state its expected outputs in terms of jobs, training, housing and so on. SRB bids are submitted in September each year with an announcement in January of successful bids. Implementation commences in April each year and bids may be made for one year with up to a seven-year programme. Each year must be bid for separately.

In many ways involvement in the SRB takes some RSLs back to their roots with involvement in community partnership and regeneration. They can provide useful community contacts and expertise for the local authority and have become key partners in some areas. The contribution of such housing plus initiatives to urban regeneration is explored in a Housing Corporation report produced by the Liverpool John Moores University.[22] Six case studies were undertaken and the views of the recipient residents examined. As might be expected, this research found that there was a greater sense of community on those estates were investment in housing plus had occurred. The initiatives which tackled local community needs for childcare, shops and transport had had the most impact, as had those which encouraged residents to be at the heart of the regeneration process. There is no doubt that housing plus programmes are an essential component of any programme of regeneration and can make a useful contribution to tackling the social exclusion agenda too.

Funding has also been specifically earmarked to refurbish run down local authority estates, through the stock transfer programme, as discussed in Chapter 2. The Estate Renewal Challenge Fund (ERCF) programme was running at £142 million in 1997/98 and was targeted at those estates where transfer of ownership will follow from a ballot of the tenants. Housing plus features large in these programmes too. In Tower

Hamlets, for example, the Poplar Housing and Regeneration Community Association (HARCA) has tenants on its board and a programme of community development built into its business plan. Models such as this must mark the way for inner-city regeneration of the future: delivered through the local housing company model which has more flexible powers and a wider range of permissible activities than most traditional housing associations.

New deal for communities

Following the Comprehensive Spending Review, in 1998 the Labour Government announced a release of £3600 million of capital receipts for local authorities, of which £800 million would be set aside to bring about a 'New Deal for Communities'. The initiative followed a report from the Social Exclusion Unit which considered a range of measures for dealing with the most deprived communities.[23] Seventeen pathfinder areas were identified, and 18 teams of experts covering varying policy areas were established, each with a 'champion' Minister, to report in 1999 create a National Strategy for Neighbourhood Renewal which would 'send shock waves through Whitehall'.[24] The work of the teams covered five broad areas:

(a) getting people to work;
(b) getting the place to work;
(c) building a future for young people;
(d) access to services;
(e) making the Government work better.

The whole programme is co-ordinated by the Social Exclusion Unit and is overseen by the Minister for Local Government and Housing, Hilary Armstrong. From the outset, it became clear that RSLs would have a major role to play; programmes need not be led by a local authority. The key principle of the New Deal for Communities is an emphasis on investment in people and skills, improved health and education, lower crime and unemployment levels and not just investment in buildings. Resident involvement is also crucial. The aim of the ambitious programme is to reduce social exclusion in these areas and narrow the gap between the wealthy and poor communities. The Social Exclusion Unit's report identified a number of causes for the failure of some neighbourhoods. These included the absence of effective national policies to deal with the structural causes of decline such as unemployment in these areas; a tendency to parachute solutions in from outside rather than involving the community, and too much emphasis on physical renewal rather than opportunities for local people. The programme incorporates not just the new programmes, but also the Single Regeneration Budget and Education and Health Action Zones. The detailed proposals[25] emphasise that the

New Deal for Communities is to be flexible and very local. Housing associations are specifically mentioned as lead partners, leading an holistic approach to tackling a local area with the local community and others, covering the full range of social and economic regeneration issues: crime, education, health, jobs, enterprise, housing, family policy, access to services, and information and community building. Thus the process offers a mainstream and integrated role for RSLs in the field of regeneration well beyond their traditional housing activities. As a result it is likely that those RSLs engaged in this process will evolve into local regeneration agencies, taking on a much broader role than they have had to date. Regeneration is the new social housing agenda and in future, few schemes will be approved that do not contribute to this.

6.13   Some issues for the future

In coming to terms with an increasingly commercial and competitive development climate, RSLs must not lose sight of the need for accountability in the development process. This goes beyond procurement methods and the quality of the dwelling produced, but is about best practice. Development staff are responsible for millions of pounds of public expenditure. Accountability in the development process is essential. The proper conduct of procurement is one aspect, but there are others.

As providers of housing, and important employers in the construction industry, it is vital that RSLs use their strength to work towards equal opportunities. There is a range of initiatives that they can employ: these include creating employment opportunities and engaging in the Welfare to Work programme. They should also encourage the use of small or emerging firms led by or employing black people, or women, by assisting them to get on to their approved lists, and train new development workers by participating in their regional PATH (Positive Action for Training in Housing) training scheme. RSLs should work towards employing only those contractors and consultants who are equal opportunity employers themselves, and ensure that all standard documentation clearly sets out the organisation's stance on the action that will be taken by them against a consultant or contractor who is sexually or racially discriminating. Such initiatives are necessary if equal opportunities policies are to be meaningful rather than mere pieces of paper.

They should be accountable to the community and to the tenants for the built environment that they create. Throughout the development process there should be consultation if possible, with prospective tenants in order that their requirements can be taken into account. Liaison with housing management and regular feedback from them, tenants and the maintenance function to the development process is vital if RSLs are to continue to provide accommodation that people want and find pleasant and convenient to live in. Best practice has probably never been more important. If an RSL has raised private finance it will have a huge financial commitment in terms of the repayment of loans. The houses must be lettable, and the consumer and housing management must be satisfied. Despite housing shortage the rule of the market place now applies, and the provision of the right product, at the right price, in the right place, is paramount.

Competition and quality

Given the provisions of the Housing Act 1996, housing associations will find themselves competing with local housing companies, other RSLs and possibly local authorities themselves if they expand their development activities under the Labour Government. They must be in a position to respond and demonstrate the real economic, managerial and wider social advantages of continued large-scale investment in housing associations, building on their track record to date. There is no doubt that since 1988 in addition to securing more than £6 billion of private finance (and thus stretching every pound of public money to buy on average £1.60 worth of housing) and embracing risk, associations have also embraced competition. Competition did not come about through the Housing Act 1988 itself but, since 1990, grant has been put up for auction to the lowest bidder.

Throughout the rush to build following the 1988 Act and the increases in the Corporation's ADP, associations constantly overbid for Corporation resources by three or four times each year despite cuts in grant rates. They have been enormously successful in increasing output and in ensuring that local authority and Housing Corporation priorities are met. They have, however, weakened the argument for increased grant rates in their eagerness to compete and have inherited a range of problems as a result. For all but the largest and strongest players, development at current grant levels will eventually become unsustainable unless standards or rents take the strain. Even then, many associations will have to come to terms with the fact that they cannot provide adequate security cover for future private loans, as highlighted in the previous chapter.

Although reduced since 1994, the development programme has constantly outperformed ministerial expectations. The average public subsidy per unit since 1990 has been reduced from £50 000 to £37 000. Most associations have gone to great lengths to market their services and find their unique selling points, to convince authority partners and the Corporation that their total operation, not just development but housing management and other services too, represent the best value in terms of a potential partner.

There is no doubt that competition has many advantages including potential for the reduction in costs, often with commensurate increases in output. Associations have sharpened up their act in relation to allocation policies and housing management practice, attempting to be ever more innovative and proficient.

The collection of performance indicators is making them more open to scrutiny and to comparison, both welcome aspects of competition. The benefits for associations in reducing costs are clear. The lower their costs, the higher their ability to compete with each other and with other organisations. Just as important, the lower their costs the more they can stretch public subsidy to produce more homes for those who need them.

Furthermore, the lower the costs, the less that has to be passed on in rent to people who are already on low incomes and often trapped in benefit dependency. Uncontrolled or unbridled competition, however, has its dangers particularly in the field of social housing. Firstly, the role of competition within a market economy assumes that the best price and the best quality will be achieved because the consumer can make an informed choice. This is not the case in relation to the 'market' for social housing. There is little real choice available to prospective tenants, and tenants are not often in a position to influence the quality of their homes in terms of standards of construction, space or amenity. Indeed, as a nation, we tend to understand little about the most important purchase of our lives. We appear to be more enticed by the quality of 'white goods' on offer when buying a new home than by questions of maintenance-free components or energy efficiency. Secondly, unbridled competition can also result in greater costs to the public purse. In boom times, the price of land may be bid up and associations competing against each other to purchase sites will add to this effect. Finally, competition alone will neither ensure quality or value for money.

The impact of competition on quality

Since 1993, as we have seen, there have been at least four reports that have questioned the quality of product that competition between associations for falling rates of public subsidy has produced. Whatever the relevant merits of the various reports, it is clear that a constant redefinition of value for money is required and a better balance achieved between competition and quality. The current definition of value for money embraces cost in terms of grant per unit or per person. In bidding for funding since 1996/97, this has been extended to include the revised Scheme Development Standards and rents in the bidding process.

Some would argue that standards are still not high enough. Bidding against a minimum set of standards set for space, construction and amenity (with regard to maintenance, cost and longevity), perhaps against a pattern book of standard designs as suggested by Karn which would be suitable for the larger families and high child densities prevalent in the social housing sector rather than the unadulterated standard house types from the private sector, could be used to ensure that quality is maintained within a competitive framework. The Social Housing Standard attempts to define these standards and, in the long term will be further developed to incorporate these issues.

The work being undertaken by the National Housing Federation and the Joseph Rowntree Foundation on 'standards and quality' mentioned earlier will contribute to this. Enormous benefits would flow from this approach for the economy and for society as a whole. It would ensure that the housing that is built would provide value for money in the long term and prevent the creation of homes that are either difficult to let in ten or twenty years time, or indeed which they find it necessary to demolish and re-develop, repeating the disasters of the 1960s and 1970s.

Long-term maintenance costs must be taken into account, also now a feature of the Social Housing Standard. The degeneration of the housing stock and the devaluing of the nation's asset is one of the major issues facing all sectors. The drive to improve house conditions made in the 1970s is now in reverse. Housing maintenance and the regeneration of old stock is one of the biggest issues facing RSLs and other property owners in the coming years.

In addition to standards of space and amenity, energy efficiency must also be brought to the top of the agenda, not only because of the environmental impact but because of the reduction in running costs that energy-efficient homes produce. The consequent reduction in the requirement for fuel benefits surely means that it is a false economy for any government to ignore the impact of energy efficiency standards.

Value for money in development
Two studies undertaken by the Audit Commission for the Housing Corporation, examine value for money in housing association development. The first, *Within Site*, considers the new build programme.[26] The report found that value for money was improving but that greater benefits could be achieved. Inexplicable variations were found in a number of cost areas, and the report calls for greater internal scrutiny by RSLs of their outturn costs against initial projections, and for more economies that can be achieved through the use of standard house types. The second report concentrates on rehabilitation.[27] The report notes how the nature of rehabilitation has changed. In addition to the traditional activity of acquiring terraced housing for improvement, it now embraces the refurbishment of local authority estates and the purchase of existing satisfactory dwellings. The report found that rehabilitation costs on average, represented 83 per cent of new build cost, which suggests that this programme on pure cost

terms may offer better value for money. There is a caveat, however, concerning long-term maintenance costs of those properties. In addition, it is often impossible to achieve the same standards of sound insulation on older properties, which can lead to intractable management problems. The cost of renovation can substantially exceed the market value of the property, leading to questions over the merits of such investment. Costs vary significantly, and in some cases demolition and new build may be the cheaper option. As we have seen, however, refurbishment rather than renewal can often add to the regeneration of an area, especially when undertaken in conjunction with other programmes aimed at economic and social rejuvenation.

What all the reports on standards and value for money indicate is the need to move away from the blinkered view of who can do it cheapest, the housing association, the private developer or other competing organisation, to what can be achieved in terms of a social housing policy as a whole for the nation. In 1994, the Department of the Environment produced a discussion document entitled 'Quality in Town and Country'. John Gummer, the then Secretary of State, stated in the preface:

> quality pays, good quality is good economics, the building that gleams in the sun of its first summer but is decayed and stained before its fifth, is a challenge to the judgement of its owner and designer. The wise investor considers the costs of maintenance, the availability of replacement materials, adaptability and longevity.

It is to be hoped that the combination of Construction Task Force Standards, the development of the ADP and the proposals set out in the 1999 Housing Green Paper will begin to resolve these issues.

References

1 C. Whitehead and M. Kleinman, *A Review of Housing Needs Assessment* (The Housing Corporation 1992).
2 Environment Committee Second Report Vol. 1, '*The Housing Corporation*' (session 1992–93) (HMSO).
3 *Projections of Households in England to 2016* (DoE 1995).
4 Alan Holmans, *Housing Demand and Need in England 1991 to 2011* (Joseph Rowntree Foundation 1995).
5 *The Housing Corporation London Policy Statement 1997/8* (The Housing Corporation 1996), p. 4.
6 A. Gibson, *Maintenance and the Law – A Basic Guide for Housing Associations* (NHF 1996).
7 *Registered Social Landlords in 1997* (The Housing Corporation 1998), p. 191.

8   A. Petherick and R. Fraser, *Living Over the Shop: A Handbook for Practitioners* (University of York 1992).

9   O. Chamberlain and B. Goodchild, *Social Housing Over Shops Evaluated* (Housing Corporation 1995).

10 D. Page, *Building for Communities: A Study of New Housing Association Estates* (Joseph Rowntree Foundation 1994).

11 V. Karn and L. Sheridan, *New Homes in the 1990s: A Study of Design, Space and Amenities in Housing Association and Private Sector Housing* (Joseph Rowntree Foundation 1994).

12 *Housing Standards and Costs: Accommodation Specially Designed for Old People*, MHLOG Circular 82/69 (HMSO).

13 *Wheelchair and Mobility Housing Standards and Costs*, DoE Circular 92/ 75 (HMSO).

14 Selwyn Goldsmith, *Wheelchair Housing* Housing, Development Directorate Occasional paper 2/75 (DoE).

15 Op. cit., 10

16 D. Page, *Developing Communities* (Sutton Hastoe Housing Association 1994).

17 Ian Cole *et al.*, *Creating Communities or Welfare Housing?* (Chartered Institute of Housing/Joseph Rowntree Foundation 1996).

18 Op. cit., 11.

19 *Planning Policy Guidance Note: PPG 3 (Revised)* (DoE 1992).

20 K. Dunmore, *Planning for Affordable Housing* (Institute of Housing/Housebuilders Federation 1992).

21 *Rehab works for London* (NFHA 1994).

22 *Housing Plus and Urban Regeneration: What works, How, Why, Where?* (The European Institute for Urban Affairs, John Moores University/The Housing Corporation 1998).

23 Social Exclusion Unit, *Bringing Britain Together: A National Strategy for Neighbourhood Renewal*, Cmnd 4045 (HMSO 1998).

24 Hilary Armstrong speaking at the National Housing Federation Annual Conference in September 1998.

25 *New Deal for Communities phase 1 proposals* (DETR 1998).

26 *Within Site – Assessing Value for Money in Housing Associations' New Build Programmes* (The Housing Corporation/Audit Commission 1996).

27 *To Build or not to Build – Assessing Value for Money in Housing Association Rehabilitation Programmes* (Housing Corporation/Audit Commission 1998 – DETR 1998).

7

Housing Allocations, Management and Housing Plus

Good housing is essential for the quality of life. It not only affords shelter, security and privacy but is closely linked to emotional and physical well-being. Decent housing for those on low incomes is a scarce resource; therefore, although some aspects of housing allocation are prescribed by the Housing Act 1996, it remains the first task of housing management to ensure that the homes are normally allocated to those in the greatest need. As we shall see, in recent times the need to create balanced or sustainable communities may in certain circumstances override need-based decisions. Access to housing and the selection and allocation process must be fair, open and free from discrimination. As registered social landlords have become predominant providers of new social housing, an even greater responsibility has been placed upon housing managers as 'gatekeepers' of housing opportunities. Furthermore, they must maximise the life of these limited and expensive assets through careful management and effective maintenance (as discussed in Chapter 6). Housing management and related services are the core business of RSLs and as landlords they must demonstrate to tenants and to local communities the quality and effectiveness of these services. It is essential therefore that the organisation in turn supports its housing management staff, ensuring that they are central to corporate decision-making. In future, it will be on these services that the sector will ultimately be judged, in comparison with other types of social landlord. Until 1988 RSLs had been relatively free to determine the nature and quality of their housing management function. Guided by legislation and best practice, the majority enjoyed a good reputation stemming partly from their long tradition of intensive and generic housing management, partly through the adoption by many of a code of conduct for housing management and, later, a fair housing policy (both developed by the National Housing Federation). The Housing Act 1988, however, imposed a duty upon the Housing Corporation to issue guidance to housing associations on the management of their stock which has since been extended to all registered social landlords through section 36 of the Housing Act 1996. The Tenants' Charters and the Performance Standards which incorporate the Social Housing Standard (as described in Chapter 3), set out the Housing Corporation's guidance for, and requirements of the housing management service and the basis upon which the activity is regulated. In addition, as RSLs have assumed the role of major providers of new social housing, so inevitably their services (especially housing management) have been subjected to greater scrutiny in terms of their quality, accountability and efficiency.

Many RSLs now also contract to provide housing management and related services for other landlords; Private Sector Leasing (PSL), Housing Associations as Managing Agents (HAMA) and local authority housing management contracts, won through voluntary or Compulsory Competitive Tendering (CCT), and Best Value regimes are examples of these initiatives. The emphasis is now on cost-effectiveness in tandem with improved services. How to achieve both while keeping rents affordable, at a time when tenants are becoming poorer and more vulnerable, remains one of the biggest challenges facing the sector at the present time. Recognising that housing alone cannot break this cycle of deprivation has led some landlords to provide services such as community development, or to provide employment and training opportunities; activities collectively known as 'housing plus' initiatives.

Housing management and the law of landlord and tenant represent vast areas of study, the detail of which are beyond the scope of this book. This chapter, therefore, considers only those aspects which are particularly relevant to housing associations, and concentrates on mainstream housing management and related housing plus activities. The management of special needs schemes, especially shared housing, is considered in Chapter 8, and some aspects of the management of housing for older people in Chapter 9; although, with the advent of community care and changes in the demography of RSL tenants, these divisions are becoming more artificial and increasingly less relevant.

As stated, the housing management performance of RSLs has been subjected to much closer scrutiny in recent years. The chapter draws on a number of studies which compare the sector with other social landlords, especially local authorities. These include the 1989 study on the *Nature and Effectiveness of Housing Management in England,* known as the Glasgow Study; the 1993 DoE report, *Managing Social Housing,* the Housing Corporation/Audit Commission 1995 joint report, *Homing in on Performance,* and the Housing Corporation's published Performance Indicators (1997). In terms of best practice, readers are referred to the Chartered Institute of Housing's *Housing Management Standards Manual,* which gives examples of good practice and is viewed by the Housing Corporation as a standard to which all RSLs should aspire, if not comply.

7.1   The nature of housing management

The birth of housing management as a profession is usually attributed to Octavia Hill (1838–1912). As a housing reformer she argued that the key to successful housing management was the relationship between landlord and tenant, and that a good relationship was mutually advantageous. She was, however, rather paternalistic in her approach, and not all commentators have universally admired her work. The 'Octavia Hill method' has evolved into the generic approach to housing management. In this case each housing officer has a 'patch' of properties and is the first point of contact for the tenants on all matters. The officers work in teams covering a particular area and the team provides the full range of management and maintenance services. One alternative approach is specialist in nature or divided by function. Lettings, for example, and maintenance services are undertaken by different departments and may be separated from other aspects of housing management. Many landlords have adopted a generic and comprehensive approach to housing management. This is partly the result of tradition; many older societies and trusts developed their style following the Octavia Hill model. Small associations are forced to be generic in that they do not have sufficient staff to undertake each different function. The relatively generous funding system that was in place until 1989 encouraged associations to adopt this approach which is intensive, customer-centred, and usually includes additional welfare support for more vulnerable tenants. More recently, however (as discussed later in this chapter), landlords are finding it harder to support vulnerable tenants effectively in their general needs stock, owing in part to lack of funding for this work.

The housing management structure adopted by an RSL will depend upon the size, type and geographical spread of its stock. A small association with 200–300 homes in management will employ one (or possibly two) generic housing officers, whereas a larger landlord may have several area teams operating on a generic basis but possibly with centralised lettings or rent accounting function. Organisations with larger new build estates or older trusts with tenement or mansion blocks often employ estate-based staff who work and may live on the estates. In recent years, the Housing Corporation and local authorities have become more concerned with the local base and accessibility of housing management services to tenants, increasing the number of local offices; however, pressure on costs mean that it is likely that such a proliferation of sub-offices cannot be maintained. Whatever the style or structure adopted, the functions remain fairly standard. These include lettings, which in turn encompass the selection of tenants and allocation of housing; transfers and exchanges; managing the tenancies and estates; tenant welfare and support; rent collection and accounting; rent arrears and void control; the provision of communal services such as gardening, cleaning and the management of ancillary caretaking and cleaning staff; and development-related activities. Day-to-day maintenance may also be part of this service, although more often now it is provided by the technical services department.

The housing management service is also responsible for developing and encouraging tenant involvement in both policy formulation and the provision and management of services.

The advent of call centres and customer care

Furthermore, several landlords have begun to examine other, more efficient methods of delivering responsive housing management services but at reduced cost in order that savings can be directed to long-term maintenance needs or lower rents. For example, Riverside Housing Association in Merseyside launched a new customer call-centre in 1997 that will provide a 'one stop' telephone response to tenants' queries, similar to services offered through telephone banking arrangements. This service will free housing officers for home visits for tenants who require more intensive or complex support. As more landlords adopt the call centre model, perhaps offering services to tenants of other landlords too, it is possible that the nature of the housing management service could be radically altered in the years ahead. Whatever the model adopted, all RSLs are now more concerned with customer care than in previous periods, spurred on to some extent both by changing customer expectations but also the desire to succeed in a more competitive market place.

Definitions of housing management

There is no clear definition of what constitutes housing management. Practices have changed over time and the debate continues as to whether housing managers should concentrate on the bricks and mortar function or provide more or less social welfare support. Clearly, where the housing provided is for people with greater support needs, the dilemma is less pronounced. As discussed in the next chapter, the funding regime, whilst fragmented and complex, does enable additional care and support to be provided in homes expressly provided for that purpose. There is also some funding through the Supported Housing Management Grant system to provide what is known as 'floating support' for tenants with additional support needs but occupying general needs accommodation. Housing benefit also covers some additional support costs through meeting eligible service charge costs (although, at the time of writing, this remained subject to a governmental inter-departmental review and was unlikely to continue in its present form). In the case of the management of general needs housing, most landlords offer far more than the 'core' services of lettings, rent collection, and estate and tenancy management. The work of the housing manger is varied, as this chapter will demonstrate. It may also encompass resettlement and social welfare functions, working with tenants to secure greater tenant involvement, working with the wider community through 'housing plus' and other related community and economic development activities and providing management services on a contractual basis to other landlords.

Towards equality of opportunity

Throughout the early 1980s the National Housing Federation through several publications which offered advice on best practice exhorted its members to adopt procedures to ensure that their allocation policies and other services were fair and non-discriminatory, and in the fields of both development and management to pay due regard to the needs of people from black and minority ethnic communities.

An emphasis was also placed on the need for systems for ethnic monitoring of both staff and tenants during this period. Associations began to recognise their role as employers of people from black and ethnic minority communities. This is particularly relevant in the field of housing management as tenants may feel that services are more accessible and sensitive if they can contact an officer from their own ethnic background. The use of translation and interpreters to ensure that applicants and tenants have access to the information published by the landlord in their own first language has also developed.

In 1985 The Housing Corporation, in consultation with the Commission for Racial Equality (CRE), took action to support a fair housing policy by issuing a circular (now withdrawn),[1] which confirmed that the regulatory review process would examine the extent to which associations had implemented equal opportunities action plans. This process was assisted by the Corporation's new duty to promote racial equality, introduced by the Housing Act 1988 and outlined in circular 2/90.[2] Since then, as discussed in Chapter 2, the Corporation has also actively encouraged the formation and registration of new black and minority ethnic housing associations, and has issued firmer guidance on equality of opportunity in both housing and employment as part of the Social Housing Standard element of the Performance Standards. A further area for concern is the response of the sector to the increasing racial harassment of tenants and, in some cases, staff. In 1987 the Commission for Racial Equality CRE reported on racial violence and harassment in housing. The report 'Living in Terror' confirmed the often unspoken reality that racial harassment is common and on the increase. It accepted that there are no easy solutions, but suggested policies that all agencies (including housing associations) could adopt to support the victims and deal with the perpetrators. It recommended that the Corporation should actively monitor the response of associations in this area. In 1989, the National Housing Federation produced a guide which illustrates best practice and procedures.[3] Many landlords now incorporate a clause in their tenancy agreement which prohibits racial harassment of staff or other tenants, and there are one or two cases where landlords have successfully pursued eviction proceedings through the courts on the grounds of racial harassment.

The CRE has published a code of practice[4] which assembles guidance on the range of best practice. The Corporation expects associations to conform with this and it now publishes some indicators of performance in this area. Despite developments over the last decade, many representatives of the black and minority ethnic communities remain unconvinced of the sector's commitment to equality of opportunity. Confidence was further reduced as a result of the publication of the Housing Corporation's Black and Minority Ethnic Strategy in 1996, which was viewed by some commentators as a dilution of its previous commitment to this area. The revised strategy published in 1998 (and outlined in Chapter 2) also did little to restore confidence.

7.2   Access and lettings

The Housing Corporation's Social Housing Standard and circular R3 49/96, *Lettings of Registered Social Landlord Homes,* sets out the basic expectations in relation to access to housing, including nominations and allocations. The 1997 Performance Standards, which includes the Social Housing Standard, states that:

> RSLs should normally let their homes to people in greatest housing need. Their lettings policies and practices should be independent, fair, accountable and make the best use of available stock; and they should aim to let tenancies which are sustainable in the long term and contribute to stable communities. (p.35)

The main legal requirements relating to tenant selection and allocation are set out in the Housing Act 1985 and the Housing Act 1996. Section 106 of the 1985 Act requires each association to publicise its allocations policy, including the rules which determine priority between applicants. These should be available to the public and presented in a simple and understandable format. They should also indicate the size and type of accommodation allocated to various household types. Section 106 also requires RSLs to circulate a copy of their allocations policy to the Housing Corporation and to local authorities in whose area they operate. The

Housing Corporation expects RSLs to consult with local authorities regarding their allocation policies.

Applicants should also be given access to the information they have supplied in connection with their application which is held by the landlord.

The procedures adopted must also conform to the Sex Discrimination Act 1975 which makes it unlawful to discriminate against any person on the grounds of his or her sex by treating them less favourably than others in terms of the accommodation offered or by refusing their application. The Race Relations Act 1976 also applies. Section 1 makes it unlawful to discriminate intentionally or unintentionally, directly or indirectly on the basis of race, colour, nationality, ethnic or national origins. In particular, reference is made in section 22 to letting properties, the terms on which they are offered and the treatment of individuals in comparison with others in need of similar accommodation. RSLs must also conform to the Disability Discrimination Act 1995 and monitor their performance in relation to equal opportunities policies as a whole.

In letting their homes RSLs must also comply with the CRE's Code of Practice in Rented Housing and the relevant Residents' Charters. Ethnic records must be kept, and all RSLs receiving Social Housing Grant are expected to participate in the continuous recording of lettings system (CORE). Circular 49/96 states that at least 50 per cent of all vacancies (on homes which have received public susidy) must go to those applicants nominated to the landlord by local authorities (see below). The pattern of referral to RSL homes has altered substantially in the last ten years, as highlighted by Table 7.1.

Table 7.1   Source of referrals to RSL homes

	1988 (%)	1997 (%)
Local authority nomination	24.4	46
Statutory agency	2.6	2
Voluntary agency	3.5	2
Direct application	41.3	29
Mobility schemes	1.4	2
From within RSL	–	15
From another RSL	–	1
Transfer	16.1	–
Exchange	5.3	–
Decant	2.8	3
Other	2.6	–
Total	*100.00*	*100.00*

Source: *NFHA Tenancy Census 1988*, Table 17; and *Housing Corporation General Report 1997*, Table 12.1.

These changes have been brought about by a number of factors. In particular, they are the direct result of the increased role of RSLs as providers of new homes for letting. Research published by MacLennan and Kay in 1994 on housing transfers within the social housing sector highlighted this effect.[5] The report noted that between 1989 and 1993 the rapid rise in housing completions, peaking at 62 500 in 1992/93, led to a 50 per cent increase in housing association lettings, which increased from 72 000 in 1988/89 to 109 000 in 1992/93.[6] By 1996/97 they had increased to 136 000. The figures in Table 7.1 show an increase in local authority nominations in particular, from 24 per cent to 46 per cent. As housing associations became the main source of new social housing, pressure to improve performance (especially in relation to housing local authority nominees and homeless households) increased.

The rehousing performance over the last ten years reflects these pressures, especially in relation to homelessness.

Assisting homeless people

The duties of RSLs to assist in the relief of homelessness changed with the passage of the Housing Act 1996. Prior to considering the current position it may be useful to trace briefly the evolution of these responsibilities. Local authorities had a duty, stemming from part III of the Housing Act 1985, to assist all unintentionally homeless people who were priority cases such those who were vulnerable, pregnant, or households with children, by providing permanent accommodation. In relation to the duties of housing associations, Section 72 of the 1985 Act stated:

> where a local authority requests a registered housing association to assist them in the discharge of their functions which relate to homelessness and threatened homelessness the housing association to whom the request is made shall co-operate in rendering such assistance in the discharge of the functions to which the request relates as is reasonable in the circumstances.

A report by the Audit Commission published in 1989[7] was the first to criticise housing associations' performance in this area. The Audit Commission called upon housing associations to do more in future to assist homeless people. It noted that in 1986/87, of the 70 000 homeless families housed in England and Wales, only 2000 were assisted by housing associations or new towns. The sector responded to this by working more closely with local authorities and rehousing more nominees from local authority homeless persons units. A study of access to housing association homes in relation to homelessness published by the National Housing Federation in 1994 showed that by 1990/91 housing associations had already improved their performance in this area, having rehoused

17 200 homeless households, and that this had increased to 37 460 by 1992/93.[8] During this period nominations generally increased from 24 000 in 1990/91 to 47 000 in 1992/93.

There were a number of reasons for enhanced nominations: first, associations were more able to respond. The new stock that had been developed since 1990 more closely matched the needs of homeless households. Since 1990 housing associations had been developing a larger proportion of family homes with two and three bedrooms. Prior to this, as highlighted in Chapter 1, housing association stock had comprised a greater proportion of smaller, flatted units. Moreover, as discussed in the previous chapter, from 1989 many local authorities used their enabling powers to make sites available for housing association development at reduced land values. This was in exchange for more generous nomination arrangements (up to 100 per cent in 80 per cent of land deals).

These developments led to further debate over allocation policy in the mid-1990s following the publication of the Page Report.[9] As highlighted in the previous chapter, Page warned that the development of large-scale estates of family accommodation with high child densities, often on green field sites, could lead to future management problems if not correctly planned. This, combined with the increasing poverty and dependency on benefits of some tenants, led to a debate concerning the need to create more 'balanced' communities on housing association estates to avoid creating dependency 'ghettos' in these areas. As this debate developed the Conservative Government published its proposals to limit access to permanent homes by homeless households which were eventually included in the Housing Act 1996 and which are detailed below. Since then the sector as a whole has been taking a number of steps to make their communities more stable and sustainable, as discussed later.

Nomination agreements with local authorities

As stated, the relief of homelessness by RSLs is achieved largely through nomination arrangements with local authorities. The process of nomination has evolved over time in response to both homelessness and the role of the RSLs virtually as sole providers of new rented homes. In London the National Housing Federation, the Association of London Authorities and the London Boroughs Association combined in 1989 to produce a guide on nomination procedures entitled 'Partners in meeting housing need'. This led to 75 per cent of family accommodation being available for local authority nominees and 50 per cent of one-bedroomed vacancies. In 1989 the National Housing Federation, the Association of Metropolitan Authorities and the Association of District Councils also published a joint statement on local authority nominations to housing associations. Aimed at those associations and authorities unfamiliar with best practice, it provided a firm framework for co-operation.

Nomination arrangements have been a continuous source of concern, not only because some RSLs find that these limit their ability to assist with internal transfers and other direct rehousing requests but more particularly because the process has on occasion introduced delays in the reletting process. More recently, concern has been expressed that inadequate details are given by the nominating authority on the background of some nominees, especially vulnerable single people. In the wake of some tragic events emanating from the failure of community care policies which have resulted in vulnerable people (often with severe mental health needs) being nominated to general needs stock there have been calls for improved information on the 'need to know' principle, and this is an issue we return to later.

Homelessness and the 1996 Housing Act
In 1994 the Government issued a consultation paper entitled, *Access to Local Authority and Housing Association Tenancies'*.[10] This set out a number of proposals which were eventually enacted in the Housing Act 1996. The proposals suggested limiting the duties of local authorities towards homeless people. The duty to provide accommodation would only start once investigations had been undertaken, and the duty would be met by securing access to *temporary* accommodation only and for a limited period. The paper also proposed that local authority lettings could only be made to people on their waiting lists, and the Government suggested regulating allocation policies through legislation. The regulations would cover nominations to housing associations too. Encouragement was given to the introduction of joint waiting lists between a local authority and the housing associations operating in its area. Although the proposals received some support from shire councils which welcomed the opportunity to house those on the waiting list, rather than homeless families, in general the proposals caused a furore and were strongly opposed by many housing lobby groups. Opposition to the proposals, voiced by over 10 000 responses including the National Housing Federation and Shelter, amongst others, focused on the fact that the proposals addressed the symptoms rather than the causes of homelessness. The shortage of accommodation was not addressed. There was a real fear of the return of the 'revolving door' syndrome of the 1960s whereby families were, at best, rehoused over and over again, with consequent ill-effects upon children's health and education, or at worst might be broken up. Such was the outcry that the then Conservative Minister for Housing, Sir George Young, made a statement to the House of Commons re-affirming the Government's commitment to the 'housing safety net' provided by part III of the Housing Act 1985.

In the event, the Housing Act 1996 imposed upon local authorities a limited a two-year duty to rehouse applicants who are unintentionally homeless and in priority need in temporary accommodation only. Permanent accommodation could not be offered to homeless people ahead of other categories of households on the waiting list. In its 1997 election manifesto, however, the Labour Party set out its intention to restore the local authority's duty to find permanent accommodation for homeless families, to take their rightful priority in the queue for social housing. On taking office it restored the duty to rehouse homeless households which should qualify for 'reasonable preference' in the allocation of permanent homes. This was achieved through regulations approved under part VI of the Housing Act 1996, just months after the introduction of the legislation. In addition, councils are only able to direct homeless families to private rented accommodation if it is available for two years. Thus the duty upon registered social landlords to assist with nominations to permanent accommodation remains in place.

Asylum seekers

The Housing Act 1996 and the Asylum and Immigration Act 1996 restricted the duty of local authorities to assist asylum seekers. They are not entitled to appear on housing registers, and neither may they be offered accommodation or nominated to registered social landlords. In addition, access to Income Support and Housing Benefit was also removed in a number of cases, leaving many people virtually destitute. Several court rulings have served to confuse the situation, however. Although the children of asylum seekers can be assisted under the Children Act 1989, and the National Assistance Act 1948 requires local authorities to provide accommodation and the basics for survival, the Housing Corporation advised of the risks inherent in housing asylum seekers. In 1997 it issued a circular 'Lettings to Certain Persons Abroad' [sic] (R3 04/97), which gives futher guidance in relation to lettings to persons from abroad and the impact of acceptance of nominations from local authorities of applicants who may be non-qualifying persons for local authority lettings under the Asylum and Immigration Act 1996. RSLs are urged to consider carefully prior to assisting any persons who would not be eligible for council housing, although their independence to make such decisions is recognised. At the time of writing the Government had published its Asylum and Immigration Bill which will enable RSLs to assist these groups in future.

Housing registers and the allocation of housing

Many landlords, especially those operating outside London, accept direct applications and therefore maintain their own waiting lists. Table 7.1 shows that 41.3 per cent of applications were received in this way in 1988 but this figure had reduced to 29 per cent by 1997. In 1996 the

Department of the Environment issued a further consultation paper on the allocation of local authority tenancies including nominations to RSLs.[11] The proposals set out the regulations which would apply in relation to the new powers for the Secretary of State to be incorporated into the Housing Act; these are discussed below. They included the power to pre-scribe entitlement to appear on a housing register or waiting list, exemptions to these provisions, and priorities and procedures to be followed in the allocation of housing; as such, they represented new and unprecedented powers for central Government and interference in an area that had always been in the domain of local government.

Part VI of the Housing Act 1996 (Allocation of housing accommodation) defines who can and cannot be rehoused permanently by a local authoity or nominated to another social landlord. All local authorities must establish a housing register (a waiting list) and only 'qualifying persons' registered on it may be allocated a local authority or other social rented home. A local authority must have a published scheme for deciding priorities, and section 167 lists likely priority categories. The secretary of state has extensive powers to regulate the allocation of housing and to issue guidance about the administration of waiting lists.

Common housing registers

Nothing in the legislation prevents the continuance or development of further common housing registers. Throughout the legislative process the National Housing Federation supported the introduction and development of common housing registers. These offer a single point of registration for applicants who will no longer have to be registered with several different social landlords. The first such register was established on the Wirral, Merseyside, in June 1996 between the Council and all the local housing associations. The operation of local housing registers is set out in a Chartered Institute of Housing publication,[12] and research published by the Housing Corporation on common housing registers[13] suggests that such registers have much to offer in providing tangible service improvements for local applicants. It suggested that common housing registers could be broadened to encompass special needs and sheltered housing too. Common housing registers have emerged as a result of partnership between the local RSLs and the local authority. They will succeed where a balance can be struck between the desire of the local authority to develop their strategic role and the requirement of the RSLs to maintain their independence.

Referral agencies

In addition to nominations from the local authority, associations are expected to work with other statutory and voluntary agencies and to assist in their housing requirements. Most RSLs work with a diverse range of such organisations including housing advice centres, groups working with refugees or specialist organisations assisting those with particular requirements (such as people with learning difficulties, battered women or young single homeless people). In attempting to assist these groups landlords should monitor the cases referred to them, to ensure that the needs of those cases comply with their own objectives and that the referral agency adopts and implements equal opportunities policies. All referrals should, like local authority nominations, be subject to ethnic monitoring. Some 4 per cent of all applicants are referrals from voluntary or statutory agencies.

7.3 Selection and allocation processes

The Housing Act 1996 has left RSLs with some independence in the allocation process although the regulations that were eventually agreed for local authorities may provide a template for Housing Corporation regulation of registered social landlords, through the Social Housing Standard. However regulation develops in this area, it is important to note current practice.

Any selection process must be fair and open and an association must be able to justify its criteria and the decisions it makes. It is essential that the process follows the publicised procedures and that no single member of staff has complete control of the allocation process. Applicants are interviewed either in their own homes or at the association's offices. It is important that staff are adequately trained in interviewing skills in order that the applicants' circumstances can be clearly understood. All enquiries should be restricted to relevant matters. Staff visiting must also be able to respond to applicants' questions about the association and its property and to discuss the applicants' requirements.

When letting accommodation RSLs are expected to give reasonable preference to the seven categories of need identified in section 167 of the Housing Act 1996, as amended by the Allocation of Housing (Reasonable and Additional Preferences) Regulations 1997. These are:

a) people occupying insanitary or overcrowded accommodation or otherwise living in unsatisfactory conditions;
b) people occupying housing accommodation which is temporary or occupied on insecure terms;
c) families with dependent children;
d) households consisting of (or including) someone who is pregnant;
e) households consisting of (or including) someone with a particular need for settled accommodation on medical or welfare grounds;
f) households whose economic or social circumstances are such that they have difficulty in securing settled accommodation;
g) persons owed a duty under the homelessness legislation.

Allocations should be made on the basis of meeting the highest need. There are exceptions to this, however, to provide some flexibility. In particular, if an RSL believes that special steps are required to deal with an estate that has become difficult to let, or in which the prevailing social conditions suggest that a specific strategy is required to help to build more balanced and stable communities, the Housing Corporation permits the adoption of a 'local lettings policy' approved by the local authority. In addition, if allocations to people other than those in the highest need would reduce under occupation or assist in moving people on from supported housing, or enable major works to proceed then the principle of meeting the highest need may be overridden.

Selection schemes

There is a variety of selection schemes that an RSL can use to assist in prioritising applicants. These include a points scheme which applies a numerical weighting to various indicators of need; those with the greatest number of points are housed first. Second, date order schemes rank applicants according to the time they have been on the list. Date order is seldom used on its own but is combined with a points or group system. Group schemes involve the classification of applicants into categories of need (say groups A to D, with those in group A commanding the highest priority). Each group is defined. Group A may include, for example, homeless families, cases of domestic violence or racial harassment. Many associations, however, use a merit system which is discretionary in that cases are judged on their merit, on an individual basis, based upon the application form and an interview. It is open to criticism as it is by definition less objective than a points system. A case may attract higher priority simply because the officer putting it forward argues particularly well in the applicant's favour. Merit schemes do have advantages in that they are flexible and can take into account criteria that are difficult to quantify, such as the ability to cope, or personal circumstances. In the past RSLs have tended to use merit schemes whereas, in the local authority sector, the points system predominates. The 1989 Glasgow Study[14] found that only 26 per cent of associations used a points scheme in comparison with 65 per cent of local authorities. Furthermore, 22 per cent of housing associations used a date order system exclusively, compared with only 8 per cent of local authorities.

More recent research for the Department of the Environment however, entitled *Managing Social Housing*,[15] found that, by 1993, 46 per cent of housing associations were using points schemes, 6 per cent date order and 48 per cent merit schemes. There is no doubt that, although points schemes can be arbitrary and mechanistic it is more difficult for a merit/discretionary scheme to be seen to be fair.

Managing the allocation and lettings process

When a property becomes vacant an offer is made to the applicant selected for it and he or she should be invited to inspect it. If possible, the prospective tenant should be accompanied by an officer of the association to answer any queries, although some applicants do prefer to visit alone. In making an offer the RSL must seek to match the size and nature of the property as closely as possible with the requirements of the applicant. There has to be a balance between maximising the use of the property whilst allowing scope for the changing needs of the tenant. Once rehoused, those living in the social housing sector are likely to remain there for many years and it is therefore important to provide accommodation that will meet longer-term requirements. It is at the point of allocation that discrimination in any form is most likely to occur. It is therefore an essential feature of the ethnic monitoring process in particular that the quality and location of property offered is recorded. Too often research has shown that whilst black applicants may receive offers of rehousing, those offers are concentrated in the worst stock or in the least popular areas.

The allocation process must be accountable. There should be a regular audit of allocations with clear guidelines. Applicants should also have the right of appeal if their application is refused.

Lettings statistics, including the analysis of ethnic monitoring returns, are the key to managing and monitoring the allocation process. The RSL should set itself objectives and targets to ensure that the needs it intends to meet are indeed being met and that no discrimination is entering the allocation process. The reports and analysis (with recommendations for any necessary action) should be considered on a regular basis by the board of management. Landlords may have numerous objectives and any number of ambitious plans, but it is in the allocation of their housing that their central objectives will be met. Feedback from new tenants, local authorities and other outside agencies on the organisation's performance should also be sought before it can be satisfied with its performance in this area. Performance should be matched against targets regarding the speed with which applications are dealt with and the properties let, as the allocation process will affect the landlord's performance in the control of voids, producing subsequent rent losses.

Housing allocation is, in conclusion, a balancing act which attempts to meet many (often conflicting) requirements. The need to balance external requests for rehousing against internal requests for transfers, and the decanting requirements of the development or stock modernisation programme. Sensitivity in decision-making must be equated with the desire for speed. Local authority nomination rights must be met. Each group must be offered a fair range of property in terms of size and condition. Known as the 'art of allocation', although satisfying in many respects, it is certainly not an enviable task.

7.4   Housing mobility

Those in charge of the lettings and allocation process provide the key to housing mobility for people who are dependent upon the rented sector for their housing. Housing mobility is both an essential and a desirable process. It helps meet the needs of individuals and their families for more space, or a different location to be near work, children or other relatives. Lack of housing mobility can adversely affect the economy. Housing mobility is assisted by HOMES, a national agency which assists in arranging access to affordable rented housing for people who require to move to different parts of the country. The importance of mobility within the social housing sector and an analysis of RSLs performance is given in the MacLennan and Hay study referred to above and in a 1994 Housing Corporation report.[16]

Transfers

In addition to contributing to national and regional mobility schemes, each RSL has a responsibility to meet the mobility requirements and aspirations of existing tenants. One approach is through a progressive transfer policy. Under section 106 of the Housing Act 1985, all landlords who undertake transfers must publish their policy and the rules which govern priority and decision-making.

An RSL may initiate the transfer in the landlord's interest, for example if the property is underoccupied or overcrowded. Various grounds for repossession under the Housing Acts (see below) give the body legal powers to facilitate these moves. Most transfers will, however, be in the tenant's interest and each RSL should attempt to meet the needs of tenants as far as is possible without imposing unecessary restrictions. The transfer process should also take into account the need for move-on accommodation for people living in hostels or other special projects who may now require more independent or self-contained accommodation (see Chapter 8).

Mutual exchange

The mobility of existing tenants can be improved through mutual exchange. Each landlord should facilitate this process by internal mechanisms such as notice boards at local offices where tenants may advertise for an exchange partner.

The Housing Act 1985 gives secure tenants the right to exchange. The landlord's consent must be obtained but can only be withheld on one of nine grounds set out in schedule 3 of the Act.

7.5   Secure tenancies

Effective housing management seeks to develop an open and equitable landlord and tenant relationship. The framework for this relationship derives from the rights and duties imposed by statute in addition to recognised best practice. In this section we examine the statutory rights and duties conferred upon associations and their tenants. The law relating to landlord and tenant is extensive, and much of the detail is beyond the scope of this book, so readers are therefore referred to Arden[17] and Alder and Handy[18] if they require more information than is given.

Until 1989 the majority of housing association tenancies were subject either to the 'secure tenancy' regime introduced by the Housing Act 1980 (as consolidated by the Housing Act 1985 part IV) or licences, outside the scope of statutory codes relating to security of tenure. From 15 January 1989 all new tenancies are granted as 'assured periodic tenancies' under the provisions of the Housing Act 1988 part I. The secure tenancy remains the only form of public sector tenancy whereas the assured tenancy applies to the private sector too. Thus RSLs once more straddle both housing sectors. Broadly, all tenants of RSLs will be secure or assured tenants. Fully mutual housing co-operatives registered with the Housing Corporation are not subject to the secure or assured tenancy provisions although it is recommended by both the National Housing Federation and the Housing Corporation that fully mutual co-operatives adopt the package of rights enjoyed by secure and (to a lesser extent) assured tenants. In addition RSLs may grant fixed-term tenancies or assured short-hold tenancies. In certain circumstances an RSL may also grant a licence. This may be so particularly in the case of hostel accommodation. Licences may also be granted to employees such as sheltered housing wardens, or used in the case of squatters to grant temporary use of the property. The use of licences is explored further in Chapter 8. In addition an RSL may also grant long leases in connection with shared ownership schemes; these are considered in Chapter 10.

Until 15 January 1989 all tenancies granted by registered housing associations were secure tenancies. By 1996 about 30 per cent of RSL tenancies remained secure. Secure tenancies convert to assured tenancies on reletting. A secure tenancy can be periodic (i.e. weekly or monthly) and cannot be brought to an end except by the tenant or the courts.

There are three conditions for a secure tenancy: the 'dwelling condition' means that there must be a tenancy of a separate dwelling, separate' means that essential living space is not shared (essential living space includes bedrooms and living rooms but not bathroom facilities). Hence occupiers of shared housing who have their own rooms could be secure tenants. The second condition is the 'landlord condition'. The landlord must be a public sector landlord as defined by the Housing Act 1985. This includes all RSLs which are not fully mutual co-operatives. Finally the 'tenant condition' specifies that the tenant must be an individual and not an organisation, who occupies the dwelling as their only or principal residence.

Secure tenants' rights

The secure tenant has a number of rights which as a package became known as the 'Tenants' Charter'. These include the right to buy for tenants of non-charitable RSLs (see Chapter 10) and the right to succession. Under section 87 of the Housing Act 1985, upon the death of a secure tenant the tenancy may pass to the spouse, or member of the family (parent, grand-parent, child, grandchild, brother, sister, uncle, aunt, nephew, or niece, including step-children and illegitimate children) who resided with the tenant for the preceding 12 months, provided that the successor occupied the dwelling as their 'principal residence' at the time of the tenant's death and that the tenant was not a successor himself or herself.

Secure tenants also have the right to take in lodgers. They may also sub-let part of the dwelling subject to the landlord's consent which cannot be unreasonably withheld. The right to exchange is also conferred (discussed earlier). Secure tenants also have the right to repair.

Secure tenants also have the right to carry out improvements to their home and to apply for improvement grants, provided that they have the consent of the landlord. Again, consent cannot be refused without good reason and such reasons must be given in writing.

Secure tenants also have the right to information under section 104 of the Housing Act 1985. Landlords must provide secure tenants with a written statement of the terms of the tenancy and a statement which out-lines the effect of the various terms including their rights under the tenancy and the association's repairing obligations under sections 11–16 of the Landlord and Tenant Act 1985 (see below). As we have seen, the RSL must make available information regarding its allocation policies. Information should also be provided regarding arrangements for con-sultation and, under section 105, secure tenants have the right to be con-sulted on housing management matters that are likely to affect them substantially.

Fair rents

Secure tenants are, as discussed in Chapter 5, entitled to a fair rent fixed by the independent rent officer service. The rent may be reviewed every two years. If secure tenants transfer to another property in the ownership of the landlord they retain both their secure tenancy status and the rights that go with it, including the right to a fair rent.

Variation of the secure tenancy agreement

Secure tenancy terms can only be varied by the landlord initiating variation procedures. A special procedure applies. The landlord first issues a preliminary notice setting out the nature of the variation effects, and inviting tenants' comments within a reasonable specified time. The landlord then considers the comments received and serves a 'notice of variation'. The notice will specify the date from which it will take effect (a minimum of four weeks or a month for monthly tenancies), the details of the variation and its effect.

Secure tenants have security of tenure. The landlord must comply with prescribed procedures in order to terminate a secure tenancy. The association must issue a Notice of Intention to Seek Possession (NISP) prescribed form which sets out the ground(s) on which possession will be sought and specifies the date after which proceedings may be started; the minimum notice period is 28 days. Court proceedings must be initiated within 12 months of expiry of the NISP.

Grounds for possession (secure tenancies)

The grounds for possession for secure tenancies are set out in section 84 and schedule 2 of the Housing Act 1985 as amended by the Housing and Planning Act 1986 and the Housing Act 1996. The first set largely relates to misbehaviour by the tenant and will be grounds for possession provided that the court finds it reasonable. These grounds include failure to pay rent, behaving in a manner that causes nuisance to neighbours, damaging the dwelling or common parts, or refusing to leave temporary accommodation which the tenant has been 'decanted' into during improvement works to their own home. Other grounds for possession also require the court to be satisfied that suitable alternative accommodation is available. Of these grounds the following are of particular relevance to RSLs: ground 9: if the occupier is overcrowding the accommodation; ground 10: if the landlord intends to demolish or carry out works to the property and it is not reasonable for the tenant to remain in occupation.

Ground 10a (introduced by section 9 of the Housing and Planning Act 1986) extends ground 10 by empowering the Housing Corporation to give consent to the disposal of schemes to the private sector for redevelopment. The landlord can be granted possession and the tenant subsequently evicted provided that the landlord intends to dispose of the dwelling within a reasonable time as part of the redevelopment scheme. In effect this clause is more likely to be relevant to local authorities although it caused much anxiety at the time of its introduction as representing a real reduction in security of tenure. Under ground 11 landlords can be granted possession if they have charitable status and continued occupation would conflict with their objects.

It should be noted that where tenants are forced to move as a result of improvement works they are entitled under the Land Compensation Act 1973 to disturbance payments. If they move permanently, then, subject to certain conditions, they may be eligible for a home loss payment under the Act. Given that such moves are a regular occurrence when RSLs undertake rehabilitation schemes, housing staff must be sure that tenants are properly advised of payments due.

The final set of grounds for possession require the court to be satisfied as to the reasonableness of the order and that suitable alternative accommodation is available. Ground 12 relates to the cessation of employment to ensure that the RSL can relet the property to the new employee. Ground 13 allows the RSL to seek possession where the dwelling is specially designed for a physically disabled person, and there is no longer such a person living in the dwelling and the landlord requires it for another such person. Ground 14 is similar but relates to special needs accommodation. Ground 15 is also similar but relates to properties near some facility for tenants with special needs. It allows possession if the tenant no longer requires those facilities and the landlord requires the dwelling for a person who does. This would be particularly relevant to sheltered housing schemes. Suitable alternative accommodation is defined in the Housing Act 1985 schedule 2 part IV.

7.6 Assured tenancies

Pursuant to the Housing Act 1988, from 15 January 1989 all new housing association lettings (with the exception of almshouse charities, fully mutual co-operatives and some hostels) are assured tenancies. Some amendments were introduced by the Housing Act 1996 which are discussed in the next section, but the position following the 1988 Act is considered first. The assured tenancy replaced all former tenancies for RSLs and the private sector, leaving the secure tenancy for the public or council sector alone. The main exceptions to the granting of assured tenancies by RSLs (apart from student and holiday lettings) were existing secure tenancies, a secure tenancy assigned by direct exchange with another secure tenant, a secure tenancy inherited via the right of succession and tenancy taken over by an RSL from a private landlord. Other exceptions included tenancies with low rents, business premises, licensed and rural properties, crown tenancies and properties where the landlord is resident.

The assured tenancy differs from the secure tenancy in the following ways:

(a)   the right to buy does not apply (although the right to acquire extends to homes built after 1 April 1997 and let on assured tenancies);

(b)   there is no right to a fair rent. Rents are agreed between landlord and tenant and revised annually. In the case of an appeal by the tenant a market rent will be determined by the Rent Assessment Committee. RSLs fix their own rents within the parameters discussed in Chapter 5;

(c)   assured tenants have fewer rights and are less secure (but see below);

(d)   there are no 1980 Housing Act 'tenants' charter' rights of:
   i.   consultation;
   ii.   information;
   iii. succession (the 1988 Act covers spouses and common law spouses only);
   iv.   exchange;
   v.   sub-letting;
   vi.   taking in lodgers.

Assured tenancies cannot be varied except by agreement with the tenant, however.

The statutory rights that have been lost to assured tenants are expected to be replaced through a series of contractual rights set out in the tenancy agreement. Guidance on these is given by the Housing Corporation in the various Residents' and Applicants' Charters (see Chapter 3) and form part of the 1997 Performance Standards.

The definition and other provisions relating to assured tenancies are set out in the Housing Act 1988 part I, chapter 1. Assured tenancies can be periodic or fixed term. The conditions for the tenancy are the usual ones: that the dwelling must be the tenant's principal home; it must be a permanent letting, to an individual, of a separate dwelling. The Act, however, extends the regime to those sharing 'essential living space', by introducing the concept of a 'separate accommodation' under section 3. Thus, those living in shared accommodation (i.e., who have their own room but share other facilities) have assured tenancy status. This will not affect hostels where the residents are not given exclusive possession of any part of the accommodation.

Grounds for possession (assured tenancies)

Assured tenancies offer less security of tenure than secure tenancies in that the 1988 Act introduced new and mandatory grounds for possession. There are no mandatory grounds under the 1985 Act. The grounds are listed in schedule 2 of the Act (as amended by the Housing Act 1996) and in outline are as follows:

Mandatory grounds

1 An owner now wishes to occupy the property as his or her home.
2 The landlord defaults on the mortgage and the mortgagee wants vacant possession in order to sell it.
3 Holiday lets.
4 Student lettings by an educational establishment.
5 Lettings to ministers of religion.
6 Redevelopment where the landlord intends to demolish and reconstruct and cannot reasonably do so with the tenant in residence. This is only exercisable if the tenant refuses an assured tenancy of part of the dwelling or refuses access. In this case removal expenses must be paid.
7 Following the death of a tenant if the tenancy has been passed through a will or intestacy to someone other than a person with the right to succeed.
8 Rent arrears, if at the time of the hearing and at the time of serving notice eight weeks or two months' rent is owed. This was reduced from thirteen weeks or three months by the Housing Act 1996 for weekly and monthly tenancies respectively.

Discretionary grounds

9 Suitable alternative accommodation is available for the tenant. A certificate from the local authority that it will rehouse will suffice, otherwise the court will determine the suitability of the accommodation offered. Removal expenses must again be paid.
10 Rent arrears outstanding (any amount).
11 Persistent delay in paying rent even though no arrears were outstanding at the time of the court procedings.
12 Breach of any tenancy condition other than the payment of rent.
13 Acts of waste or neglect of the accommodation by the tenant or any other person living there.
14 Nuisance, or use of the premises for illegal or immoral purposes (revised ground following the Housing Act 1996).
14a Domestic violence (following Housing Act 1996).
15 Deterioration of, or damage to, furniture.
16 Tied accommodation where the tenant is no longer in employment.
17 The tenant knowingly obtained the tenancy through deception or false statement (introduced by the Housing Act 1996).

Although notices of intention to seek possession must be issued in the prescribed form the notice period for assured tenancies is shorter; only two weeks for grounds 1, 2, 5, 6, 7, 9 or 16 but two months in any other case. Grounds 1–8 are mandatory and possession might apply in future. Grounds 9–16 are discretionary where possession may be ordered if the court believes it is reasonable to do so; however, only under Ground 9 is there an obligation on the landlord to provide suitable alternative accommodation. Ground 9 allows a landlord to obtain possession if alternative accommodation is available without any justification subject only to the test of reasonableness. The definition of suitable alternative accommodation is given in the Housing Act 1988 schedule 2 part III, and differs slightly from the definition for secure tenances given in the Housing Act 1985. In the case of discretionary grounds the court has the power to postpone or suspend the date of possession as is the case with secure tenancies; there are no such powers where possession is sought under one of the mandatory grounds. The lack of security imposed by grounds 9 and 11 (possession for persistent delay in payment of rent), is offset for tenants of housing associations to some extent in that the model assured tenancy agreement devised by the National Housing Federation and endorsed by the Housing Corporation excluded ground 11. Private sector tenants enjoy no such protection.

7.7   Assured shorthold tenancies

The Housing Act 1988 section 20 introduced the Assured Shorthold Tenancy. This form of tenancy offers more limited security of tenure, as it is for a fixed rather than periodic term, and unsurprisingly it was very popular in the private sector.

Until February 1997 the minimum term was six months and the landlord had to issue a notice at the commencement of tenancy stating that the letting was an assured shorthold tenancy. The notice had to be in the prescribed form. The Housing Act 1996 abolished both the prescribed notice and the six-month term for new tenancies. All new tenancies granted after 28 February 1997 will be assured shorthold unless the landlord chooses to grant an assured periodic tenancy, as detailed below. Assured shorthold tenancies must be distinguished from fixed term assured tenancies, the latter cannot be converted to assured shorthold at the end of the fixed-term. At the end of the term an assured shorthold may be renewed or converted to a periodic assured tenancy. Although assured shorthold may be useful for short-term lettings the Housing Corporation has re-affirmed that assured shorthold tenancies should only be used in exceptional circumstances, which an association may be required to justify to the Housing Corporation. Such circumstances include time-limited social housing (e.g. temporary social housing for the homeless and tied accommodation). Similar standards of management should apply as for assured periodic tenancies.

Assured shorthold may also be used for some special needs accommodation and for general needs accommodation where a package of care is being provided. The assured periodic tenancy remains the norm, however.

Other rights

Independent Housing Ombudsman

As discussed in Chapter 3, all tenants of registered social landlords have a right to access to the Independent Housing Ombudsman, and each RSL must provide all residents with a proper complaints procedure.

Right to a rent book

Under the Landlord and Tenant Act 1985 all landlords, including housing associations which let weekly, must provide their tenants with a rent book stating the name and address of the landlord. In the case of assured tenants, it should be noted that the form for the rent book is prescribed under The Rent Book (Forms of Notice) Amendment Regulations 1988. This includes additional information for the tenant, such as the terms and conditions of the tenancy agreement. Assured shorthold tenants should also have a rent book containing the notice in the prescribed form.

7.8   The provisions of the Housing Act 1996

Assured shorthold tenancies

The Housing Act 1996 introduced a number of new provisions. These include a simplification of the assured and assured shorthold tenancy regime.

As highlighted above, from 28 February 1997, any new tenancy created is automatically an assured shorthold tenancy which reverses the position up to that date. All tenancies are assured shortholds unless landlords take certain steps to create a periodic assured tenancy by issuing a statutory notice on the prospective tenant, stating that the tenancy is or will be a periodic assured tenancy. RSLs still remain bound to provide as much security as possible and therefore will continue to use the assured periodic tenancy.

Anti-social behaviour

Anti-social behaviour by tenants is one of the most intractable problems facing housing managers and the neighbours who experience it. The 1996 Act introduced a number of measures to combat this based on the views expressed by the Association of District Councils in its report, *Winning Communities.* The changes do little, however, to address the real problems: administrative delays in the court system, and fear of neighbours preventing people acting as witnesses in court.

Introductory tenancies

Part V section 124 of the 1996 Housing Act grants local authorities only, a discretionary power to grant Introductory Tenancies which are intended to encourage people to act responsibly. This power does not extend to RSLs, although the North British Housing Association conducted a pilot programme in Manchester in 1995 using assured shorthold tenancies. Introductory or probationary tenancies will last up to twelve months, after which the tenancy becomes secure.

The eviction process is different in that there are no grounds for possession although the tenant has a right to review. There has been substantial criticism of this form of tenancy which could be seen to stigmatise council tenants and is viewed by some housing managers as unlikely to address the most serious problems (for example, drug pushing on estates).

The Housing Corporation has issued guidance on the use of introductory tenancies by registered social landlords in the Performance Standards. Their use will only be acceptable where an RSL can demonstrate that using an introductory tenancy will assist in managing an area that has become difficult to let owing to community breakdown.

Extension of nuisance or annoyance to neighbours

Other powers to tackle nuisance include two additional grounds for possession for both assured and secure tenants. These are set out in section 144 for secure tenants which introduces a new ground 2 for possession and section 148 which introduces a new ground 14 for possession in the case of assured tenants. These sections permit possession where the tenant or person visiting the house:

(a)   has been guilty of conduct which was, or is likely to have been, a nuisance or annoyance to a person residing, visiting or otherwise engaging in lawful activity in the vicinity of the dwelling house;
(b)   has been convicted of:
     i.   using the dwelling house or allowing it to be used for immoral or illegal purposes, or
     ii. an arrestable offence committed in, or in the locality of, the dwelling-house.

The grounds are significant in that they now apply to visitors as well as residents. The grounds only require the conduct to be likely to cause, rather than is or was causing nuisance and this may enable housing officers who have received reports rather than witnesses to testify in court.

Domestic violence

Section 145 (for secure tenancies) which introduces a new ground 2 and section 148 (for assured tenancies) which introduces a new ground 14a provide grounds for possession in the case of domestic violence. This ground will enable landlords to seek possession against any tenant that has used or threatened violence to drive away their partner (or their children).

Injunctions and powers of arrest

Section 152 enables a county court at the request of a local authority to grant an injunction to stop a person from being or threatening to be a nuisance or annoyance to someone lawfully occupying or visiting the local authority's properties.

A new power of arrest for anti-social behaviour was also introduced by section 153 of the Housing Act 1996. This allows the High Court to attach a power of arrest to an injunction against a breach or anticipated breach of a tenancy. This power may apply where the landlord is a local authority, a Housing Action Trust, a charitable housing trust or registered social landlord. The breach must be actual or threatened behaviour that is a nuisance or annoyance to a person residing, visiting or otherwise engaged in lawful activity in the vicinity of the dwelling. It allows for arrest by the police only and not for citizen's arrest. It only applies to subjects of injunctions who are sole or joint tenants of introductory, secure, assured periodic or assured shorthold tenancies.

7.9   Maximising rental income

It is the task of housing management to maximise income from rents charged, through effective arrears control, and to minimise losses arising from voids and bad debts. As the prime source of revenue income, rent policy (including rent-setting and affordability) was dis-cussed in Chapter 5. In practice, the responsibility for rent-setting and review of assured tenancy rents and re-registration of fair rents for secure tenants may rest with either finance or housing management staff.

Fair rents

The basis on which fair rents are increased should form part of the rent policy of the RSL. Tenants should be informed of any re-registration pro-posed and advised of their right to consultation with the Rent Officer. Applications to re-register the rent should be made one year and nine months after the effective date of the last registration and three months before the earliest allowable date for re-registration to ensure minimum delay. The new rent should be charged as soon as possible on or after the effective date, the tenant having been given four weeks' notice in writing. As stated, there is no rent phasing on rents registered after 15 January 1989 and thus the full increase in rent including any service charges should be levied immediately.

Assured rents

Assured tenancy rents are set according to the tenancy agreement, the law and the constraints imposed upon RSLs by the Housing Corporation. The guidance set out in the Performance Standards 1997 was discussed in Chapter 5 but it is worth reiterating the main points here. The rent policy of the RSL should ensure that rents are maintained within the reach of those in low-paid employment; this will usually entail setting rents at below market levels. RSLs should not discriminate between those tenants who are eligible for housing benefit and others and should attempt to minimise dependence on housing benefit for those who receive it. The landlord must take into account the income required to cover management and maintenance costs, loan charges and future repair requirements. RSLs should supply all residents and local authorities with whom they work with a copy of their rent policy and a summary of rent levels, including a comparison of the RSLs average rents against those of other RSLs working in the area.

Service charges should also be accounted for, and assured tenants such as secure tenants are entitled to information on the calculation of any variable service charges under the provisions of the Landlord and Tenant Acts of 1985 and 1987. An assured tenancy agreement may contain a specific rent review mechanism, for example by reference to movement in the Retail Price Index. If no specific review mechanism is included in the tenancy agreement the landlord may not increase the rent earlier than 12 months after the date the tenancy commenced or the date of the last increase, and the tenant must be given one month's notice of the increase set out in the prescribed form. Finally, rent policy must accord with any guidelines given by the Housing Corporation in relation to constraining increases within a formula related to the Retail Index Price. For 1998/99 the rent 'envelope' was constrained to RPI plus 1 per cent for general needs accommodation provided by traditional RSLs.

If there is no specific rent review clause in an assured tenancy agreement then the tenant must be informed of their right to refer the matter to the Rent Assessment Committee (RAC). In the case of assured rents the RAC is charged with assessing a market rent for a dwelling; hence, unless the property is in an area with a surfeit of rented housing, this form of appeal is unlikely to be of assistance to tenants who consider that the rent proposed is already too high. If the rent fixed by the RAC is higher than that proposed (which is likely) the landlord is not bound to charge that rent but must consider the financial implications of not charging it. Each RSL must maintain proper records of rents charged and will be expected to analyse assured rents in terms of affordability and to report regularly to the board on the range of rents charged.

Rent levels

Rent levels, particularly in relation to affordability, are discussed in Chapter 5 but it is interesting to note here some comparisons detailed in the Housing Corporation's 1997 published performance indicators and in the Audit Commission's comparative report, *Homing in on Performance* published in 1995.[19] The Corporation's figures show an overall average assured rent level of £49.35 per week for 1997 (excluding service charges). The two reports highlight rent increases over the period. For example, a three-bedroom assured rent increased from £51.73 in 1995 to £59.11 in 1997, for associations with over 5000 homes. The Audit Commission reporting on 1994 noted an average association rent of £37.60 against an average council rent of £33.90. Assured rents were on average 21 per cent higher than council rents, but secure rents 3 per cent less.

Rent collection

In deciding which methods of rent payment to offer, the landlord should consider the needs of the tenant in addition to matters such as security, economy and efficiency. Although landlord and tenant law places the onus of payment upon the tenant, the convenience of payment methods is paramount as research into rent arrears shows a correlation between the scale of arrears and the method of collection. The 1989 Glasgow Study found that, despite the security risks some 40 per cent of associations in the study still continued to use door-to-door rent collection. By 1993, *Managing Social Housing* found that this had reduced so that only 5 per cent of the rent debit was collected in this way. The most common methods were bank standing orders and direct debit. The study also highlighted the importance of efficient housing benefit adminstration to housing associations in that over 25 per cent of rents were paid directly through the housing benefit system. *Homing in on Performance* found that rent collection rates in both councils and associations were high, at 98.5 and 99 per cent respectively. Housing Corporation performance indicators for 1997 show that on average RSLs are fairly efficient at rent collection with collection rates of 99.36 per cent for the peer group with over 5000 homes.

In addition to offering a range of collection methods, each RSL should operate accurate and fast accounting systems. Each rent account should be reconciled according to the payment period (weekly, monthly, etc.) and regular statements supplied to each tenant showing the balance of their account.

Most larger landlords operate computerised rent accounting systems which facilitate the production of these statements and provide the information on which the system of arrears control are based.

Rent arrears

Arrears control systems should be supportive but effective. An association should have a written policy detailing the procedures to be followed in the event of arrears arising and internal reporting mechanisms which allow the scale of arrears and the action taken to be monitored. Arrears prevention is more effective than arrears recovery; it is therefore important that swift action is taken as soon as an account shows any arrears. The role of the housing officer is vital in establishing early contact with tenants who are experiencing difficulty in paying their rent to ensure that tenants are claiming all the benefits to which they are entitled and to make arrangements whereby arrears can be repaid. Arrears recovery procedures are common to all professional housing organisations and will vary only in terms of the speed and level of arrears at which they are initiated. Usual practice includes the use of mild standard warning letters issued as soon as arrears accrue followed by individual letters and visits to ascertain the cause of the arrears and to make appropriate arrangements for their repayment. It is normal for RSLs to use eviction only as the final sanction (subject to the authority of the board of management). All stages of rent arrears control should be directed towards preventing this sanction from having to be invoked.

Rent arrears performance

The increase in rent arrears in the public sector was well documented throughout the 1980s. Local authority arrears have been the subject of Audit Commission Reports[20] and DoE circulars.[21] The problem of rent arrears in housing associations has not been so closely scrutinised although the Glasgow Study, and more recently the report *Managing Social Housing*, scrutinised the sector. In 1994, the Department of the Environment published research which evaluated the effectiveness of rent arrears control and recovery in both local authorities and housing associations.[22] It found that arrears control was a high priority and that practices were similar in both their nature and effectiveness. The report found the problem of arrears to be widespread: 43 per cent of tenants of councils and 49 per cent of association tenants were in arrears. One in six housing association tenants and one in seven council tenants owed over four weeks' rent. The average owed by council tenants was £322 as compared with £304 for housing association tenants.

Housing Corporation performance indicators show that rent arrears as a percentage of of gross rental income stood on average at 5.03 per cent in 1997, for RSLs with over 5000 homes.

Causes of rent arrears

The causes of rent arrears were found to be similar to those documented as long ago as 1983 in the seminal study by Duncan and Kirby, entitled

Preventing Rent Arrears. These include age of the household head, as younger tenants are more likely to be in arrears. Living in an area of high social and economic social deprivation; change in household composition and family crises; unemployment; low income and poor financial management; these are all associated with arrears. Arrears are also often associated with problems of multiple debt, especially fuel debt. Problems associated with housing benefit were also cited in *Homing in on Performance* in 1994 and are discussed further below.

Control of empty property

The control of rent loss due to properties lying empty is a further essential indicator of performance. It is inevitable that some properties will be void at any one time due to delays in the letting process, or if they are awaiting repair or improvement. A report by the Empty Property Unit (EPU) published in 1989[23] suggested that housing association performance in this area left room for improvement. The national rate for housing association voids given by the DoE at 1 April 1988 was 2.55 per cent (compared with 2.38 per cent in the local authority sector). By 1994 the situation had improved as more associations adopted effective procedures to control voids. *Homing in on Performance* evaluated performance in relation to reletting times. This report showed a national average reletting time of 6.2 weeks for local authorities and 3.5 weeks for housing associations. However, if total void percentages are taken at a point in time, local authorities do better. By 1997, the Housing Corporation performance indicators show that the larger RSLs achieved an average reletting time of 4.5 weeks.

The 1997 performance indicators also show that RSLs with over 5000 homes had on average 3.25 per cent of their homes vacant as at 31 March 1997. The percentage vacant and available for letting increased from 1.19 per cent in 1995 to 1.67 per cent in 1997. Research published by the Housing Corporation in 1997 by Pawson, Kearns *et al.*[24] highlighted the key obstacles to improving void performance which included delays in local authority nominations, high rates of refusals of offers of tenancies, poor house condition at the end of tenancies and slow repair services. In addition, the research also outlined the increasing problem of hard-to-let properties. Some 40 000 homes (particularly in the North West) could be described as difficult to let. Physical features, such as stock condition and design, in addition to social factors, such as demand and crime levels on particular schemes, accounted for properties becoming difficult to let. Rent levels in the North-West and the West Midlands were also recognised by the participating landlords as an underlying trend leading to properties becoming more difficult to let. This research concentrated on general needs homes, but the issue of hard-to-let sheltered and supported housing schemes needs to be taken into account too.

The relative modernity of many of these difficult to-let-homes means that this will be a major strategic issue for the sector for the future.

Housing benefit

The successive cuts to housing benefit throughout the last fifteen years, combined with the changes in its calculation, in addition to the amendments to the social security system have meant increasing poverty and hardship for many tenants. RSLs must train their staff to ensure that they have sufficient knowledge of the system to advise tenants on their eligibility for benefits. Housing officers will require continuing support from their managers to deal effectively with the often demoralising task of demanding money from those in acute poverty. Housing benefit continues to be targeted by central Government given the huge escalation in cost to the public purse stemming from it; the housing benefit bill has increased from £1.3 billion in 1989 to £11 billion in 1997. Further changes were introduced with effect from January 1996 which restrict the payment of housing benefit to eligible rents that are the equivalent of local reference rents. Where a local authority uses its discretionary power to refer a rent to a Rent Officer on which housing benefit is being claimed, the Rent Officer will compare the rent with the local reference rent. This is an average decided by comparison with other private sector rents in the area. New claimants in RSL-owned general needs properties will only be affected if rents are above local reference rents; in this case housing benefit may not be payable although local authorities do have discretion to pay more. RSL accommodation which provides care and support or supervision is exempt from these regulations.

With effect from October 1996 people under the age of 25 became no longer eligible for housing benefit payments beyond the cost of the average for shared accommodation in the area, and this was extended to all single persons under pensionable age. The two exceptions to this are young people in self-contained housing association accommodation and young people receiving assistance under the Children Act until they reach the age of 22. In addition, there have been cases where the Department of Social Security has restricted income support for leaseholders in Leasehold for the Elderly schemes on the grounds that the services provided were not connected to the provision of adequate accommodation and so were ineligible. This has had a knock-on effect upon housing benefit. The Social Security Advisory Committee issued proposals in 1996 which would restrict the eligibility of certain service charge items for housing benefit purposes. The eligibility of counselling and support costs for housing benefit remained under review at the time of writing. These changes could affect the ability of up to one million people to meet some of the costs of intensive housing management through the rents and reinforces the artificial division between housing and care that has made it so difficult for associations to meet the costs of more than a bricks and mortar housing service. These problems have been recognised to some extent by the proposals put forward in the DSS paper *Supporting People* which is discussed in the next chapter.

7.10   Managing vulnerability

One result of housing associations taking on the role of main provider of new social housing has been the increasing presence of people with support needs in general needs stock. A large proportion of nominees to their stock since 1990 has been single persons with mental health and other support needs. The increasing poverty and unemployment experienced by many tenants highlighted by the Page Report and growing poverty in society at large have added to the difficulties faced by housing managers of general needs stock; combating social exclusion is now a key element of the corporate strategy of many RSLs. All these factors have impacted on the situation and have done so at a time when the cost pressures have been greater than ever as RSL housing management activities are compared with local authorities in terms of their competitiveness and cost-efficiency. The most pressing factor has been, however, the impact of the 1990 community care legislation. The legislation is dealt with in some detail in the next chapter but at this point it is important to note that since the advent of the community care reforms introduced by the National Health Service and Community Care Act 1990, more people with community care needs are being allocated ordinary housing via waiting lists, nomination arrangements, discharge functions and homelessness units than ever before.

Research by Clapham and Franklin (1994),[25] written with Compulsory Competitive Tendering (CCT) in mind, aimed to clarify the boundaries of housing management 'by examining its role in relation to social services in meeting the objectives of community care'.[26] The study emphasises the views of those engaged in provision of community care in relation to what housing management services should be provided against what exists. The research notes that if there is to be a social welfare function within housing management that is properly recognised and funded then this has implications for Housing Revenue Accounts of both RSLs and local authorities and, of course for housing benefit; yet we have seen that the funding of additional welfare support through housing benefit is already under threat.

As stated at the outset of this chapter, there are a number of lists available which attempt to define housing management. Housing management is increasingly divided between core functions and more intensive management services. The prevailing view is that RSLs, especially in urban areas, should provide even wider housing management related services, such as community development and other 'housing plus' initiatives. Personal care and support is not carried out by housing staff, and neither is any nursing function, but many RSLs have supported housing officers, negotiating and brokering with other services on behalf of the tenant, providing more regular visits, resettlement advice and advocacy in relation to benefits. The whole lettings process, including setting up utilities and getting furniture and other support, is more intense.

A useful list of what constitutes supported housing management is given in the Housing Corporation's *Special Needs Procedure Guide* (1996).

The Clapham and Franklin Study (1994) found that the job of housing manager was getting harder as residualisation of larger estates and community care needs, coupled with pressures on costs, take their toll. Underfunding of social services is also a contributing factor as housing managers are left to pick up the pieces, or if they do not do so are failing in their duty as failure to support vulnerable tenants also affects other tenants. Housing managers are willing to take on community care needs but face significant funding constraints. The research also found that social workers and housing managers still fail to fully understand each other's role. The report notes that individual needs are highlighted by social workers while a collective view of the best interests of all tenants is emphasised by housing managers.

The report concluded that housing management where additional care needs were present was more about making the best of things and muddling through. Clearly the research has important implications. It demonstrates that joint planning betweeen housing and the social services departments, to provide a 'seamless service', is still not happening. Indeed the report found that relationships at the front line were still not always positive', indeed, they could be 'covertly,if not overtly hostile'.[27]

These findings were confirmed by a further study on inter-agency working in the field of general needs housing published by the Joseph Rowwntree Foundation in 1996.[28] The case of Stephen Laudat, a tenant of an RSL who murdered a fellow attendee at a local community centre in 1995, is a tragic case which highlights the care needs of general needs tenants. The Woodley Team which inquired into the case found a breakdown in communications between the various health and social services teams responsible for Stephen's well-being. As a result of this and other cases, such as the highly publicised Jonathan Newby case, a number of recommendations have developed in relation to improving the communications between health, social services and housing support services for those with care needs.

In particular, the Laudat case highlighted the dilemma between the need to maintain confidentiality and the need to know principle. There is a real need for community care assessments for general needs tenants but social services are stretched and only the most obviously vulnerable are assisted. A significant report which acknowledges the impact on housing associations of these issues is *Managing Vulnerability*, which was published by the London Federation of Housing Associations in 1995. Based upon a survey of 84 RSLs managing 175 000 ordinary self-contained homes in London, the report estimated that 60 per cent of new tenants housed by them were vulnerable and that numbers were likely to increase. The report noted that the nomination and allocation process (discussed above) may not include an adequate assessment of care needs and may result in people being inadequately housed. Whilst RSLs themselves are sensitive to the issue, they had not in most cases documented and recorded the problem. Local authorities tend to underutilise specialist housing as a resource for nominations.

Whilst guidance on housing and community care fom the Departments of Health and Environment advocate the need for integrated support packages, little is available, and RSLs still tend to run special needs and general needs housing separately. As a result housing managers are often dealing with tenants with challenging behaviour for which they are untrained or unprepared, and more attention is being given to fewer cases, affecting services to tenants as a whole. The cost of providing these services is difficult to assess.

Several landlords have adopted a range of solutions to attempt to deal with this issue. These include the employment of specialist staff, the provision of specialist training, and a range of special initiatives. These have typically included floating support schemes, improved links with social services and a process of effectively recording and monitoring cases that are being assisted. Joint working in partnership with specialist agencies is also being pursued. A key issue is the lack of funds for this work beyond a cash limited fund provided through the Supported Housing Management Grant (SHMG) framework, which is explored in the next chapter. Some landlords are using their own reserves or charitable funds to support these activities. *Managing Vulnerability* calls for a complete needs assessment of all local authority nominees at the point of nomination. It also calls for RSLs to develop strategies to deal with existing vulnerable tenants and for a funding system that will support vulnerable people in general needs housing. This issue represents one of the most serious problems facing the sector today.

A further report by the National Housing Federation published in 1996 and entitled *The Independence Revolution*, also examines these issues and suggests that associations should survey their tenants to assess care needs in order to plan for these in advance and to avoid crisis intervention. In 1997 the National Housing Federation then published a further study[29] which sets out some practical options for registered social landlords and other social landlords on how to meet the support needs of tenants in general needs homes. It identifies the key support services and examines the management options for providing them. Funding availability and some case studies are also included to enable social landlords to meet these needs.

Funding remains the key issue and one that is the most crucial for future resolution if RSLs operating in deprived areas and with ageing tenants are going to be able to meet their obligations as social, rather than commercial, landlords. The proposals outlined in the DSS document *Supporting People* (1999) will begin to address these if adopted, however.

7.11　Housing plus activities

The concept of housing plus is not really new to the sector. Many RSLs have been involved for several years in initiatives which have aimed at adding value, or assisting the communities in which they operate through the provision of additional facilities such as community halls, playschemes and so on. Providing community care services and assistance to vulnerable tenants as discussed above is also part of 'housing plus'. Some landlords have become involved in employment-generating initiatives too. The concept is not tightly defined but may include complementary investment such as health, education or leisure facilities procured by working in partnership with others.

Interest in these activities has increased recently owing to the dramatic change in the context in which RSLs now operate. Their primary role as providers of social housing means that it is often no longer enough merely to put a roof over someone's head; RSLs must also consider how they can use their strengths to enable and empower communities. Housing plus initiatives can contribute to both community and economic regeneration of an area. Such initiatives will increasingly form part of an RSL's strategy when developing new and larger estates, not least to avoid some of the worst symptoms of concentrations of poverty and deprivation as outlined. Furthermore, community development, training and employment initiatives are now central to urban regeneration programmes such as the Single Regeneration Budget, Estate Renewal Challenge Fund and Capital Challenge. RSLs involved in these activities will be expected to offer 'added value' through housing plus projects.

Most RSLs, particularly larger ones and those who have substantial stock concentrated in any one area, can use their asset base and links with the community through staff, tenants and partners, and combine this with their financial strength, professional skills and initiative to create a range of opportunities. The turnover of an RSL approaching 5000 homes in management is likely to be around £20 million per annum. The sheer buying power this represents if directed at creating local job or training opportunities is substantial. Increasingly, local authorities and regeneration partnerships expect RSLs to employ a proportion of local labour on new housing developments. Many are also involved in the 'New Deal' contributing to the 'Welfare to Work' progamme by offering placements or taking on young people to work on environmental schemes. The Housing Corporation now expects new schemes to include an element of these added features wherever possible, and takes this into account when allocating development funding. The Housing Corporation's National Policy Statement on funding priorities for 1997/98 highlights the non-housing benefits that can be achieved through housing investment. Their Innovation and Good Practice Grant Programme also supports these initiatives.

In 1997 the Housing Corporation published a report which illustrated how the housing plus approach to management and development could contribute to the development of sustainable communities.[30] In the same year the National Housing Federation also published a guide which illustrated how RSLs could undertake a wider role through social investment when developing new housing projects.[31]

Some RSLs have responded to the increasing desire to add value through housing investment by establishing economic development teams or housing plus teams which may be situated within the housing department. Some examples were given in an earlier report by the London School of Economics[32] launched in 1997.This report found that most landlords support the idea of housing plus although they felt that the definitions remain unclear. It reaffirmed that housing plus is concerned with partnerships, linkages and and inter-agency working, and although it was seen by some as a marginal activity it is likely that in the future housing plus will become a core activity of many registered social landlords and central to the paramount function of housing management. This is an issue to which we return in the final chapter.

Foyers

An initiative that combines all the aspirations of housing plus programmes (i.e., partnership, additional benefits, leverage, and which relates especially to the young) is the development of foyers. Foyers are based on a French housing scheme model whereby young people are offered short-term accommodation combined with employment or training opportunities. The intention is to break the 'no job, no home, no job' cycle. A pilot programme was intoduced in this country in 1992 and there are now over 60 foyers in the UK, with a similar number planned or under development. There is also an active Foyer Federation which disseminates best practice and lobbies for funding. Following the announcement by the new Labour admininstration in 1997 that foyers would feature as a major employment and training initiative, the Foyer Federation launched a campaign for a foyer in every town. Some projects have been more successful than others in securing effective funding that will enable the rents to be affordable to young people on low budgets. Although the Housing Corporation and others have made capital funds available, revenue support for the training and employment activities has been more difficult to obtain. Furthermore, most foyers have ancillary accommodation attached (providing cafés or training facilities, for example), and both revenue and capital funding is scarce for these. A variety of models has emerged.

One example is Focus E15 in Stratford, east London, which was completed by the East Thames Housing Group in 1996. The project was developed with Housing Corporation, City Challenge and internal funding as a foyer for the London Borough of Newham, through a steering group which represented a range of local interests and skills working in partnership including the local Youth and Careers Counselling Services. These bodies now have offices in the ancillary accommodation which also comprises a café, training facilities and a community radio project offering skills in broadcasting engineering. The project will provide accommodation for 100 18–25 year olds and a further 100 move-on accommodation places.

An evaluation of the pilot initiative confirmed the success of the early projects but highlighted the need (as with so many initiatives) for a reliable and integrated capital and revenue funding framework.[33] This is particularly so in the case of housing projects for single young people given the restrictions in housing benefit outlined above and the need to try to avoid creating an early poverty trap through high rents in foyer schemes.

7.12   Tenant involvement

Throughout this book reference has been made to the importance of consulting tenants in the formulation of policy and encouraging tenant participation in the management of services and the decision-making process. The best value process discussed below demands the proper involvement of tenants in agreeing service requirements and setting standards and receiving information on performance.

The Housing Act 1985 section 104 requires RSLs to publish information on the terms and conditions of their tenancies and the rights afforded to secure tenants. Section 105 requires RSLs to consult tenants on matters of housing management which will affect them 'substantially' in order that they can make their views known, and these views should be considered before decisions are taken. Section 106, as discussed, requires them to publish the rules relating to the allocation of their properties. The Housing Corporation, through the 1997 Performance Standards, has stated that RSLs, as part of the expectation regarding residents' rights, should consult with tenants and obtain their feedback in effective and structured ways on the whole range of services provided, including maintenance and improvement plans, and in 1998 the Corporation also published a revised strategy for tenant participation.[34] The strategy built upon earlier commitments adopted in 1992, and in 1998 the Housing Corporation Chairman, Baroness Dean of Thornton Le Fylde, emphasised the Corporation's commitment to genuine tenant participation (not just tenants on the board) on a number of occasions.[35] By 1994 there were 3000 tenants on the boards of RSLs, with 48 per cent having tenants on the board or area committees of the organisation and 71 per cent of landlords having adopted a tenant participation policy. In 1998 a tenant board member was appointed to the Housing Corporation Board and a tenant advisory panel established.

In 1996 the Nolan Committee had emphasised the importance of tenant involvement, as tenant involvement is perhaps the most important means of improving the accountability of the landlord (also a recurring theme of this book). The importance of this issue was examined in Chapter 4 which considers issues of governance and accountability; this chapter considers some models and processes for tenant involvement in greater detail. Tenant involvement should not concern housing management alone but impact upon the work of the development department and all operational areas. Four levels of tenant involvement can be identified: information giving and seeking, consultation, active participation and tenant control.

Information

In addition to the statutory duties to provide information each RSL should strive to improve communications with tenants through the production of simple, informative publications such as a tenants' handbook and a regular newsletter. Handbooks and other information should be available in translation where an association operates in multi-lingual areas. Tenants should have access to the details of the names of members of the board of management and on the landlords performance targets and other statistical information; an annual report to tenants on performance is also required. These reports are the subject of a Housing Corporation study published in 1996.[36]

RSLs should allow individuals access to personal information held about them on their file except where it has been provided by third parties and access would result in a breach of confidentiality. RSLs are also subject to the provisions of the Data Protection Act 1984. Information should be sought as well as given. RSLs now undertake tenant opinion surveys to ascertain the views of tenants on the performance of the organisation.

Consultation and complaints

Consultation may take many forms. Public meetings (held at convenient times and locations) and discussions with established tenant organisations are common methods, as is the use of the newsletter to request tenants' views on policy issues. It is likely, given a greater emphasis on accountability, that RSLs will show a more serious intent to consult in future. Allied to the consultation process is the provision for redress. All registered social landlords are expected to have an effective complaints procedure in place. The board should monitor the nature and number of complaints received and the officers' response to them, and as a last resort should be accessible to the tenant bringing the complaint.

In the case of the transfer of public sector stock (for example, to an RSL from a local authority), there are clear expectations of the nature and extent of the consultation exercise. These were set out in Chapter 2.

Active participation

Many RSLs have encouraged the formation of tenants' associations to represent tenants' views and, where tenants are keen, to become actively involved in the running of estates. Recently, a number of landlords have developed Estate Agreements with their tenants.These offer more than consultation and can offer the tenants' association a basis on which to monitor service standards. The operation of Estate Agreements was the subject of research published by Salford University in 1995.[37]

Membership of the board or area committee is a further means whereby tenants can participate in the control of the affairs of the organisation. The Corporation, as discussed in Chapter 4, advocates broadening the membership of the board to include tenant representation through a constituency approach, and has a tenant representative on its own board. Nolan also advocated this approach, but it is not one that finds favour with some larger RSLs which would argue that board representation and shareholding membership are not pragmatic means of achieving meaningful involvement.

Where tenants do serve on the board they may require training and support to ensure that their voices are heard. Tenants' associations should be supported through staff time and through the provision of funds and facilities; larger landlords may set aside a budget earmarked for this purpose.

Tenant control

There is a range of Tenant Management Organisations (TMOs). They comprise tenant management co-operatives, where tenants have taken over some aspects of the housing management functions; estate management boards, where management is largely delegated to the board on which tenants have a majority; and par value co-operatives, where the tenants own or lease and manage the homes collectively (as outlined in Chapter 2). There is now a greater emphasis on fostering the growth of such groups, especially on larger estates. TMOs may be independent organisations registered as Industrial and Provident Societies in their own right.

TMOs offer tenants real control and power over what happens to their homes. From the landlord's point of view, if they prosper they will offer an alternative to traditional renting, providing greater choice for tenants and improved consumer satisfaction. Research into TMOs undertaken by Price Waterhouse between 1991 and 1994 found that TMOs in the form of tenant management and par value co-operatives usually outperform both councils and housing associations in providing more effective services. The most successful were on a smaller scale with a high continuing level of active resident involvement.[38]

Tenant satisfaction

Levels of tenant satisfaction with services provided by RSLs are quite high. As long ago as 1989 the Glasgow Study found that overall there was a high degree of tenant satisfaction with the services provided. Around 76 per cent of housing association tenants and 58 per cent of local authority tenants thought that their landlord was efficient, although more housing association tenants felt that they received good value for money. Approximately 80 per cent of housing association tenants and 67 per cent of local authority tenants were satisfied with the housing management services provided. These results reflect the findings of other more recent surveys. The 1994 Housing Attitudes Survey[39] found that 85 per cent of association tenants were satisfied with their homes and gave their landlords higher ratings than councils for considering their views, keeping them informed and undertaking repairs. It is to this issue of effectiveness that we turn next.

7.13   The effectiveness of housing management

Some commentators have promoted the view that housing associations are better managers than local authorities. It has always been difficult to prove or disprove this claim owing to the lack of research. Whilst there have been several studies into the effectiveness of local authorities by the Audit Commission and academic institutions, housing associations have largely been spared the limelight.

This chapter has highlighted some reports which have considered the quality of housing management in housing associations but, in the absence of definitive studies, conclusions are hard to draw.There are certainly areas of weakness but the evidence suggests that this is not through lack of guidance on best practice. Diversity will in itself create different approaches and lead to varying practices; this book concentrates on the larger non-mutual organisations and has ignored to some extent the cooperative housing associations that have many lessons to teach.

The 1989 Glasgow Study suggested that housing associations were generally effective but expensive. The report concluded that there are good housing associations in terms of housing management and good local authorities, and dispels the myths to some extent. The Study stated that associations are regarded by their tenants as better and more caring landlords; they are more effective than councils but less economic. On average councils spent 30 per cent less on each dwelling. The report included two findings of particular concern: first, that those associations which scored highest in terms of effectiveness were 10 per cent more effective but that this improved status was secured at unit costs 50 per cent greater than those associations that scored moderately high. The report then asked 'Was a 10 per cent improvement worth an additional 50 per cent spending?'[40] Second, the report noted that over half the tenants who wished to see improved services were willing to pay 5–10 per cent more on their rent to meet the costs of such services. Since then, local authorities have been subjected to the rigours of the threat of Tenants' Choice and to the Compulsory Competitive Tendering of Housing Management regimes and, as a result, those that needed to have dramatically improved their performance. This is highlighted by the fact that in-house teams have been very successful in winning contracts. RSLs have not, so far, faced these competitive pressures although they have become more concerned with cost-effectiveness. Some are costing their activities in order that they can improve service efficiency and have more information in order to tender for management contracts. The 1995 report, *Homing in on Performance*, compared local authority and association management and service costs for 1992/93.

It found that, on average, housing associations were £91 (or 20 per cent) per property more expensive than councils. London boroughs were more expensive but associations in the North-West spent as much as London associations. There are numerous reasons for this including stock condition and type, spatial distribution of stock and the range and nature of services provided. Nevertheless, association costs will be under close scrutiny at a time when the demands on housing managment have probably never been greater. The Housing Act 1996 gave the Audit Commission new powers to advise the Housing Corporation on best practice and value for money criteria against which to assess associations.

In the wake of *Homing in on Performance* the Housing Corporation published a further study on the effectiveness of housing management, maintenance and association management in 1996 in conjunction with the Audit

Commission.[41] The report was based on case studies of good practice drawn from 12 housing associations. It recommended that more needed to be done to improve managers' decision-making capacity and to review performance standards methodically using benchmarking systems. Many of the report's findings are borne out by the 1997 Performance Indicators study.

Improved services may cost more to provide and yet RSLs are attempting to limit rent increases. This highlights a growing tension between lower rent policies and intensive management services. The future will be about reconciling these two issues: how to achieve more for less?

7.14 Best value

The advent of the 'contract culture' especially in the public sector in the late 1980s, has led to greater RSL involvement in the provision of housing management (and other) services on a contractual basis. Public sector contracts arose from the opportunities created by the Compulsory Competitive Tendering of housing management regime. More may follow as a result of best value strategies.

In the private sector housing associations have assisted local authorities to meet their obligations to the statutorily homeless by managing homes on behalf of private sector landlords on a leasehold basis. Two initiatives include, Private Sector Leasing (PSL) and Housing Associations as Managing Agents (HAMA). The development of these initiatives was also in keeping with the Conservative Government's aims of creating more social housing opportunities through increased lettings in the private sector, rather than investing in new provision.

The Compulsory Competitive Tendering of housing management

CCT was of course, the flagship policy of the 1992–97 Conservative administration and, at the time of writing, it was already being relegated by some to the ranks of history in the wake of the election of a Labour government in 1997. The Labour administration had signified during the 1997 election campaign that CCT would be replaced, perhaps with a housing quality programme system which would apply to all social landlords and which was considered above. A brief review of CCT is given in order that the 'best value' regime proposed by the Labour Government can be better understood.

Competition through compulsory competitive tendering had been introduced across a range of local authority blue-collar activities by part III of the Local Government and Planning Act 1980 and was extended by the Local Government Acts of 1988 and 1992. In 1992, the Conservative Government published a consultation paper, *Competing for Quality in*

Housing, which set out its proposals to extend CCT to those housing management services covered by a local authority's Housing Revenue Account. As before, the policy initiative was predicated on the belief that competition would act as a stimulus to greater efficiency. Local authority Housing Revenue Accounts had already been 'ring-fenced' (i.e., they could no longer be subsidised by the General Fund of the council) and, as mentioned earlier, councils were already working to established benchmarks and published performance indicators. The policy was the natural development of the Conservative Government's vision of the local authority as enabler rather than provider of services. The regime did not apply to properties transferred under the Large Scale Voluntary Transfer (LSVT) regime (see Chapter 2), and although several shire districts tendered their housing services on a voluntary basis, others were encouraged to explore the transfer route to avoid the CCT regime.

A further consultation paper, *Compulsory Competitive Tendering of Housing Management*, was published in June 1993 followed by a guidance note in November which set out the functions to be covered, the framework for the competition and the time-scale for its introduction. CCT was phased in over a three-year period, commencing April 1996. Local authorities were expected to tender 95 per cent of the value of their housing management activities and were grouped into five bands. These reflected their size and readiness for CCT, each band representing the percentage of business value that was exempted from tendering in each year. The phasing enabled authorities to break down their stock into several contracts and allowed time for the market for housing management CCT to develop. Housing management activity valued over £500 000 had to be tendered and follow the 1993 Public Services Contract Regulations which give effect to the EC Directive 92/50. The regulations covered the procedures that must be followed and prescribed the form of notices for tenders and methods of evaluating them. There were also clear regulations relating to anti-competitive behaviour. CCT required local authority housing departments to restructure to create a client side which specified, tendered, awarded and monitored the contracts, in addition to continuing to provide other central strategic and enabling services and, where housing management services were provided by an in-house team, a contracting side. The regulations provided for bids by the existing in-house team, and they have been very successful in winning these contracts. By June 1996 the overwhelming majority of contracts had been awarded to in-house teams. This in turn led some private sector managers to cry 'foul' and accuse some local authorities of anti-competitive behaviour, leading in turn to a tightening of the regulations announced in 1996.

The CCT regulations enabled tenant involvement in housing management to continue through the right to consultation over the terms of the agreement and the standards of service; tenants also had a right to be involved in the process of contractor selection. Importantly, the legislation also introduced a *right to manage,* which enabled tenant management organisations to undertake much of the housing management function, subject to certain conditions. The Housing (Right to Manage) Regulations 1994 set out the details of the procedures.

Housing associations and CCT

Housing associations were expected to become the main contractors for local authority housing management contracts. In fact by January 1996 only two or three associations had succeeded in securing contracts under this regime, with a handful of other contracts having been awarded to private contractors such as CSL and Johnson Fry. More RSLs are involved in contracts tendered on a voluntary basis, however. The majority of RSLs have not wished to jeopardise their relationships with partner councils, some of which were strongly opposed to the compulsory tendering of these services. The most common policy stance was to tender only if invited to do so. Others also questioned whether their organisation had the capacity (or desire) to manage large high-density estates, especially in urban areas, and others believed that charitable funds should not be used for such purposes.

Importantly, the CCT of housing managment in the local authority sector has led many RSLs to consider their own cost-effectiveness more seriously and to analyse their costs in preparation for bidding for these and other contracts. Clearly, in the future, RSLs will be compared closely with these contractors in terms of their efficiency and service standards and with local authorities as part of the best value regime.

Best value regime

The best value regime was developed as an alternative to compulsory competitive tendering in local authorities and was piloted by the Labour Government in 37 authorities in 1997/98 to develop a framework for it. The Government issued a Green Paper on best value to encourage responses from the profession on how to achieve best value and improved services in local government.[42] This was swiftly followed by a White Paper.[43] Best value may incorporate competitive tendering of services but also embraces a number of approaches to bring about continuous improvement in service delivery. It is not a soft option, and makes use of a number of methods in comparing performance to assess standards. It is based upon twelve principles set out in the DETR consultation paper as follows.

1 The duty of best value is one that local authorities will owe to local people, both as taxpayers and the customers of local authority

services. Performance plans should support the process of local accountability to the electorate.

2 Achieving best value is not just about economy and efficiency, but also about effectiveness and the quality of local services; the setting of targets and performance against these should therefore underpin the new regime.

3 The duty will apply to a wider range of services than CCT.

4 There is no presumption that services must be privatised, and once the regime is in place there will be no compulsion for councils to put their services out to tender, but there is no reason why services should be delivered directly if other, more efficient, means are available. What matters is what works.

5 Competition will continue to be an important management tool, a test of best value and an important feature in performance plans, but it will not be the only management tool and is not in itself enough to demonstrate that best value is being achieved.

6 Central government will continue to set the basic framework for service provision, which will in some areas (as now) include national standards.

7 Detailed local targets should have regard to any national targets and specified indicators to support comparisons between authorities.

8 Both national and local targets should build on the performance information that is in any case needed by good managers.

9 Audit processes should confirm the integrity and comparability of performance information.

10 Auditors will report publicly on whether best value has been achieved, and should contribute constructively to plans for remedial action. This will include agreeing measurable targets for improvement and reporting on progress against an agreed plan.

11 There should be provision for intervention at the direction of the Secretary of State on the advice of the Audit Commission when an authority has failed to deliver best value.

12 The form of intervention should be appropriate to the nature of the failure.

Thus best value is a complex and quite sophisticated concept and process in comparison with CCT. Tenant and user participation is also an important feature. Local authorities are expected to take a corporate overview of services and set performance measures. Each service should be subjected to planned review every four to five years. The worst areas are to be tackled first. Targets should be set for these services and published in local performance plans and an independent inspection and audit of performance undertaken.

The Housing Corporation and the National Housing Federation welcomed the concept of best value. The Housing Minister and the Housing Corporation made it clear that the regime will apply to Registered Social Landlords. Thus RSLs will not only wish to consider how to respond to the local authority agenda and the opportunity to tender to provide services, but also how to prepare themselves for the best value regime. Guidance on best value was provided by the Housing Corporation in 1999[44].

RSLs and best value

The Housing Corporation expects that RSLs should, taking into account the views of residents and the local community, set their own targets and aspirations for perfomance. Each should then undertake a performance review which would challenge the purpose of a service and compare the RSL's performance with others, including the local authority where appropriate. Targets would then be set for improving efficiency. At the time of writing, the regime for RSLs was being developed, but the Housing Corporation had suggested a number of mechanisms for encouraging best value. These included public statements on the level and range of services provided and public reports on performance, building on the annual report to tenants which is already a requirement. In addition, comprehensive service reviews are to be undertaken with a reduction in costs expected and an increase in efficiency. The best value framework is not part of the regulatory regime at present, but is an expectation.

Whilst it is accepted that continuous improvement in performance is both necessary and desirable, a number of problems present themselves. Comparisons cannot always be readily made between one RSL and another; they are diverse organisations. National performance indicators do not always make sense at a local level. Costs may be reduced but savings have to be balanced against customer-driven expectations and requirements. Many RSLs have already undertaken (or are undertaking) service reviews, especially in the field of housing management. These reviews will in future have to have regard to accountability tenant involvement, proper measurement systems and closer working with local communities to tackle issues in a holistic manner.

In the local authority sector the best value regime will be monitored by a new Housing Inspectorate established in 1999 under the aegis of the Audit Commission. The Housing Corporation continues for the time being to monitor RSLs.

Some RSLs will respond more rapidly than others, and some are already undertaking radical restructuring of services. This may include the establishment of central call centres for customer queries which could release staff time for home visits and to support more vulnerable tenants.

7.15   Managing for others

Housing Associations as Managing Agents

A further initiative which involves RSLs in the management of stock on a contractual basis are the HAMA schemes. The initiative was set up in 1991 as a pilot to encourage private landlords to make property available for letting by having access to a high-quality managing agents' service provided through housing associations. From the landlord's point of view the rental income is guaranteed, as is vacant possession at the end of the period, thus overcoming two reasons why many landlords have preferred not to let their property. Many local authorities (especially in London) have been able to replace the use of bed and breakfast accommodation with the temporary accommodation provided through these initiatives, in addition to meeting the housing needs of a range of other groups such as the single homeless, key workers and young people leaving care. HAMA has become the generic term for a plethora of initiatives (and acronyms) which usually involve the management of private sector stock, sometimes with local authority guarantees and revenue support based on a fee for each nominee. Other schemes include Private Sector Leasing (PSL) whereby properties are leased for three years from the private sector (or the local authority) with local authority guarantees. However, pressure on local authority revenue accounts has led to a diversification away from the PSL to models which require less revenue support.

A further example is the Housing Association Leasing Scheme (HALS) which has largely replaced PSL, whereby leases are taken but without the backing of local authority guarantees. Schemes that run without local authority revenue support are also known as HAMA 2 schemes. By the end of 1994, of the 6000 HAMA properties in management, 18 per cent were in receipt of no revenue support. HAMA plus commenced in 1994 and introduced capital funding into the programme, to enable repairs to be undertaken to the private sector stock prior to letting in order to add to the incentive to bring empty homes back into use.

The Housing Corporation has encouraged the development of HAMA schemes by providing grants towards the set-up costs of those associations that wish to become involved in the initiative. These are allocated on a competitive basis, however. Capital funds for HAMA plus, which became known as the Temporary Market Rent Housing initiative, was also available as part of the Approved Development Programme until 1999 (as discussed in Chapter 6).

The Housing Corporation has also funded a programme of research into these initiatives. In 1994 the Housing Corporation published a report which examined HAMA from the local authority perspective. It illustrated how the programme could act as model for the provision of temporary accommodation, and also its wider applications to meet the needs of other groups.[45]

A further report published in 1995 compared housing association and private managing agents.[46] The research found that the HAMA initiative had brought considerable benefits by encouraging new landlords to let their property, thereby providing socially managed private sector housing. Associations offered rental and reinstatement guarantees whereas no private firms offered them. As a result the management fees (which varied between associations) were usually higher than those of private agents. Associations set higher property standards, but the degree of personal service to tenants was similar. The report recommended that local authorities should set guidelines in this area for both management and property standards.

The management of stock owned by other landlords was, at the time of writing, a peripheral activity for all but a handful of RSLs; it is likely, however, to represent one of the areas of growth in the coming years, and those landlords who wish to respond to these opportunities will need to further develop their contracting skills to deliver the services successfully.

7.16   Multi-landlord estates

A further challenge for the future will be ensuring the success of newly built, larger estates, often developed by a consortium of RSLs. The pressures of the development regime outlined in the previous chapter, and the Housing Corporation's desire to fund a range of diverse landlords on larger sites, has led to the emergence of multi-landlord estates. Some larger regeneration schemes will also lead to this situation, as a number of partners are involved. The presence of more than one landlord would not be problematic had the housing management implications been considered in advance. Unfortunately this has not always been the case, and a study of these estates has shown that they have often been development-driven; housing staff were not involved at the planning stage in decisions that would impact on future management.[47] Multi-landlord estates are not conducive to estate-based management which is desirable on larger schemes, and tenants experience the impact of inconsistent rent levels, policies and procedures. This is not, of course, a criticism of housing management but of the development-driven process; the challenge for effective housing managers is to find models to ensure that these estates can be effectively managed in future.

If the quality of the housing management service is the standard against which tenants and other clients and stakeholders will judge RSLs in the future, it is essential to note that, from the tenants' point of view repairs and maintenance performance as discussed in Chapter 6 are also integral to this service. Both functions are core activities and will be paramount to the future success of each RSL as it repositions itself away from development-led activities and instead tries to provide a range of services and housing solutions for local communities, based upon the priciples of best value. We return to this issue in the final chapter but have now concluded our review of key operational activities. Next we consider some specialist areas: supported housing, community care, housing for older people, and housing for sale.

References

1 *Race and Housing Circular 22/85* (The Housing Corporation 1985).
2 *Promotion of Racial Equality*, Circular R3 02/90 (The Housing Corporation).
3 C. Davis *Racial Harassment, Policies and Procedures for Housing Associations* (NFHA 1989).
4 *A Code of Practice in the Field of Rented Housing for the Elimination of Racial Discrimination and Promotion of Equal Opportunities* (CRE 1991).
5 D. MacLennan and H. Kay, *Moving On, Crossing Divides: A Report on the Policies and Procedures for Tenants Transferring in Local Authorities and Housing Associations*, DoE (HMSO 1994).
6 Ibid, p. 15.
7 The Audit Commission, *Housing the Homeless: The Local Authority Role* (HMSO 1989).
8 P. Withers and B. Randolph, *Access, Homelessness and Housing Associations*, NFHA Research Report 21 (NFHA 1994).
9 D. Page, *Building for Communities: A Study of New Housing Association Estates* (Joseph Rowntree Foundation 1994).
10 DoE, *Access to Local Authority and Housing Association Tenancies, a Consultation Paper* (HMSO 1994).
11 *Allocation of Housing Accommodation by Local Authorities, Consultation Paper linked to the Housing Bill* (DoE 1996).
12 *Common Housing Registers* (Chartered Institute of Housing 1996)
13 D. Mullins and Pat Niner, *Common Housing Registers, an Evaluation and Analysis of Current Practice* (The Housing Corporation 1996).
14 University of Glasgow, *The Nature and Effectiveness of Housing Management in England* (HMSO 1989).
15 W. Bines, P. Kemp *et al.*, *Managing Social Housing*, DoE (HMSO 1993).
16 *Homing in on Performance, Social Housing Performance in 1994 Compared* (The Housing Corporation/Audit Commission 1995).

17 A. Arden (ed.), *Encyclopedia of Housing Law and Practice* (Sweet & Maxwell).

18 J. Alder and C. Handy, *Housing Association Law* (Sweet & Maxwell 1991)

19 Op. cit., 16.

20 Audit Commission, *Bringing Council Tenants Arrears Under Control* (HMSO 1984).

21 *Rent Arrears*, Circular 18/87 (DoE 1987).

22 B. Gray *et al.*, *Rent Arrears in Local Authorities and Housing Associations in England*, DoE (HMSO 1994)

23 B. Williams and P. Mountford-Smith, *Empty Properties Owned by Housing Associations in London* (EPU 1989).

24 Hal Pawson, Ade Kearns *et al.*, 'Managing Voids and Difficult to Let Property', *Source Research* 21 (The Housing Corporation 1997).

25 D. Clapham and B. Franklin, *The Housing Management Contribution to Community Care* (University of Glasgow, Centre for Housing Research and Urban Studies 1994).

26 Ibid, p. 1.

27 Ibid, p. 59.

28 'Inter-agency working for housing, health and social care needs of people in general needs housing', Findings, *Housing Research 183* (Joseph Rowntree Foundation June 1996).

29 S. Bennett and J. Reading, *Management Options, Tenant Support in General Needs Housing* (NHF 1997).

30 *A Housing Plus Approach to Achieving Sustainable Communities* (The Housing Corporation 1997).

31 *Social Housing, Social Investment* (NHF 1997).

32 Ann Power with Liz Richardson, *Housing Plus: An Agenda for Social Landlords?* (LSE/Tenants Resource Centre 1996).

33 *'Foyers for Young People'*, Findings, *Housing Research* 142 (Joseph Rowntree Foundation April 1995).

34 *Tenant Participation – The Next Five Years* (The Housing Corporation 1998).

35 Note in particular speech to Voluntary Board Members conference, 6 February 1998.

36 *Performance Information Reports to Housing Association Tenants* (The Housing Corporation 1996).

37 A. Steele *et al.*, *Estate Agreements: A New Arrangement for Tenant Participation* (University of Salford 1995).

38 Price Waterhouse Study, *Tenants in Control: An Evaluation of Tenant-Led Housing Management Organisations*, DoE (HMSO 1995).

39 B. Hedges and S. Clemens *Housing Attitudes Survey*, DoE (HMSO 1994).

40 Op. cit., 14

41 *House Styles – Performance and Practice in Housing Management* (The Housing Corporation/The Audit Commission December 1996).
42 *Modernising Local Government – Improving Services through Best Value*, Consultation Paper DETR March 1998.
43 *Modern Local Government – In Touch with the People*, White Paper HMSO July 1998.
44 *Best Value for Registered Social Landlords* (The Housing Corporation 1999).
45 V. White, *HAMA: The Local Authority Perspective* (The Housing Corporation 1994).
46 *HAMA: Managing the Private Rented Sector: A Comparison of Housing Associations and Private Managing Agents*, Source Insight (The Housing Corporation 1995).
47 L. Hare and T. Zipfel, *Too Many Cooks ...? A Review of Policy and Practice on Multi-Landlord Estates* (NFHA 1995).

8
Supported Housing and Community Care

Housing associations have a long tradition of providing care and support for residents as well as housing. Projects in which additional care and support is integral to the scheme are often referred to as special needs schemes or special projects. A different revenue funding regime applies to this diverse range of housing projects, which may contain features over and above those found in ordinary general needs accommodation. For example, schemes for older people or those with a physical disability may require particular design considerations or fixtures and fittings which will make them more convenient to live in. The contribution of registered social landlords to this field is one of the most vibrant and innovative aspects of their work. Although it is impossible to explore every initiative in a single chapter, some attempt is made to reflect the range of the response to these needs.

This chapter starts by considering the range and scale of supported housing and care services now provided by RSLs. The funding and management of supported housing schemes are outlined and community care policy and its impact on the sector is then examined. The chapter continues with a consideration of the needs of single people, especially the single homeless and people with AIDS or HIV. It concludes with a review of housing provision for people with physical disabilities.

Older people represent the largest client group, not only of supported housing and specialist housing associations but as a proportion of all tenants of registered social landlords. The sector's contribution to meeting these needs and the provision of related support functions, such as 'staying put' projects, care and repair schemes, dispersed alarm systems and domiciliary care, are considered in the next chapter.

8.1 Scale of need

In 1992 a study for the National Housing Federation attempted to assess the future housing requirements for people with special needs.[1] The report found from the limited data available that owing to the hospital closure programme, the demand for housing for people with learning difficulties would be around 2000 to 3000 units per annum until 2002.

A similar level would be required for people with mental health problems as a result of the closure programmes. The demand for housing for older people, particularly for those over 85 who are frail, could add a further 3000 units per annum. The report therefore suggests a requirement of 10–16 000 units per annum, to which can be added the concealed needs of homeless people, the needs of people with learning disabilities living with parents and the needs of drug users living in temporary accommodation. The total unmet need is therefore around 20 to 30 000 units per annum. This figure is supported by the research of Lynn Watson, who has devised a model for assessing housing needs in relation to community care (see below). The Environment Select Committee on Housing Needs (discussed in Chapter 6) also estimated the backlog of provision to be in the region of 25 000 units.

The changing demographic profile of the population, community care policies and the changing socio-economic climate have added to the demand for housing with care and support. As discussed in the previous chapter, the support needs of people in ordinary accommodation are also growing.

8.2   The provision of supported housing

Housing associations have been providing housing with care and support to meet these needs for many years. In 1974, when the sector first expanded dramatically, the role of housing associations was to complement and supplement that of local authorities. The Housing Corporation has provided capital funding for these projects and revenue support for intensive housing management activities since that time. There is therefore a wide range of models of support and accommodation provided by housing associations which includes:

(a)   domiciliary support to people in ordinary accommodation;
(b)   floating support;
(c)   group homes with volunteer or staff support;
(d)   direct access hostels;
(e)   sheltered housing with or without warden support for older people;
(f)   registered and unregistered care homes;
(g)   nursing homes.

The projects are provided in partnership with a wide variety of agencies, including health and local authorities and the voluntary sector. Initially, special accommodation for people with support needs was provided by housing associations in the form of shared housing. This was particularly the case throughout the 1980s, reflecting the funding framework which was designed around the concept of non-self-contained accommodation.

Funding (and thinking) during that period was still affected by the institutional approach that had dominated the provision of care. Although housing associations provided hostels or group homes on a smaller scale than the institutions that they were replacing, there were still many larger shared schemes especially for single homeless people. In addition, during this period schemes were developed to house those leaving long-stay institutions, especially people with learning disabilities. By 1991, however, the funding regime had altered to provide housing associations with revenue funding for intensive support of tenants of self-contained accommodation in addition to shared housing, through the introduction of the Special Needs Management Allowance (SNMA), known as Supported Housing Management Grant (SHMG). Although this was (and remains) a cash limited fund, it was recognised that although the additional features provided in supported housing may be in the form of bricks and mortar, most schemes also incorporate additional housing management and other support services to enable the individual to live as 'normal' and independent a life as possible. These services are increasingly being provided by registered social landlords to people in ordinary housing. It is now recognised that some people who require additional support or care require services in their usual home environment, and do not wish to move in order to have access to such services; neither would it be appropriate for them to have to do so.

Since 1990 several associations have also provided care as part of the community care initiative introduced by the 1990 National Health Service and Community Care Act. The terms 'supported housing' and 'community care' are used to differentiate different legislative, procedural and funding regimes. For the purposes of this chapter the terms 'supported housing' or 'housing with care and support' have been used interchangeably to describe specialist housing or non-specialist housing where care and support services are provided. Such services include advocacy and advice, personal assistance, emotional support and assistance with the development of independent living skills. Domestic assistance with cleaning or shopping may also be provided. The level of support is based on individual needs and may range from low support, such as welfare advice or resettlement, through to high support including personal care, funded through the community care initiative.

As discussed in Chapter 1, by 1990, housing associations had taken on the role of main provider of social housing and an unforeseen and unfortunate effect of this was the reduction in the programme of supported housing. The priority for the new development programme was at that time the expansion of provision to meet general housing needs, particularly those of the homeless. Although over 600 registered social landlords are involved in the supported housing field it has often been viewed (and treated) as marginal. In 1996/97, capital allocations for supported housing that would attract SNMA produced some 3500 bedspaces, about 13.8 per cent of the programme.

Despite this relatively low level of funding a report by the National Housing Federation, *People First* (1995), surveyed the extent to which associations had become involved in providing housing with care and support.[2] It found that they provided supported housing for approximately 350 000 people (which included older people), and that they provided over 320 000 client services to the wider community in the form of practical facilities and support services. Indeed, care services have a significant impact on the business profile of the organisations involved, accounting for some 35 per cent of turnover of those engaged in these activities. Registered social landlords provide assistance to the following groups of people:

(a)   people with mental health related problems;
(b)   people with learning difficulties;
(c)   people with physical disabilities, including wheelchair users and those with sensory impairment or suffering from degenerative or debilitating illness;
(d)   older people requiring support;
(e)   ex-offenders;
(f)   young people leaving care or forced to leave the parental home prematurely;
(g)   people with an alcohol or drug related problem;
(h)   adult single homeless people;
(i)   people with AIDS or HIV;
(j)   vulnerable women with children;
(k)   women at risk of domestic violence.

This list is not, however, exhaustive and is based on definitions of special needs used by the Housing Corporation. It should also be noted that it is not synonymous with community care client groups which, as we shall see, have been more narrowly defined.

In considering the needs of such groups it is important to avoid the tendency to stereotype or to suggest that a single solution works best. Several commentators have made this point,[3] stating: 'to look at these so-called special needs groups together is not to imply homogeneity of need among the people in each group or among the different groups' and 'generalisations are dangerous'.[4] There is no panacea and, where possible, both the accommodation and the care and support packages should be tailored to the individual's requirements and protect their autonomy. Their needs and aspirations will be as heterogeneous as society itself.

Indeed, specialist housing will be appropriate only in a minority of cases. The housing services required may include advice, staying put, or care and repair (see Chapter 9) and adaptations. Some people may require general needs housing with housing management support, sheltered or very sheltered housing. Others may require supported housing or other specialist forms of accommodation. Housing and community care strategies of both local authorities and housing associations have to take into account how this range of services can be developed.

In addition to self-contained accommodation for people requiring care and support, RSLs by 1997 had provided over 91 000 bedspaces in shared housing and, although some schemes are directly managed by the landlords themselves, a large number have been provided in partnership with voluntary groups which provide management and/or care services on an agency basis. Table 8.1 illustrates the principal needs groups served by supported housing projects.

Shared housing

As stated, much of the housing provided for single people (and some families, such as women suffering from domestic violence with children) is shared. Shared housing is a collective term that refers to any scheme where the residents share basic facilities. The term is applied to cluster dwellings, group homes where the residents may share a house in a 'family' type atmosphere taking meals together, and hostel accommodation. It is now recognised that self-contained accommodation is

Table 8.1   *Supported housing accommodation by principal client groups (1997) (shared and self-contained housing)*

	%
Older people with support needs	47.0
Mental health problems	7.9
Learning difficulties	8.5
Young at risk, or leaving care	2.7
Ex-offenders	2.4
Women at risk of domestic violence	1.4
Young mothers	1.2
People with HIV/AIDS	0.4
Physical difficulties	3.7
Drug/alcohol problems	1.7
Refugees	0.9
Single homeless	10.5
Other	11.7
Total	*100.00*

Source: Derived from Housing Corporation General Report 1997, Table 14.1.

more desirable and current schemes often include a higher degree of self-containment, such as those schemes developed for frail elderly people (see Chapter 9). The degree of sharing will vary from project to project depending upon its use and the client group it serves. Sharing may mean sharing bathroom facilities only, or shared sleeping rooms (the latter being very rare). The degree of care and support offered also varies according to the purposes of the project. Shared housing schemes serve an enormous range of needs from people with severe learning disabilities and schemes for the frail elderly which will provide substantial support and care services, to hostels for the single homeless where a single project worker or warden may suffice. Some shared housing schemes, such as those for young people, are unsupported and may provide no additional support service. Some schemes are registered care homes, which are subject to regular inspection to meet standards prescribed by the local authority inspectorate, while others are unregistered.

Many projects developed by registered social landlords to meet special needs are provided in partnership with voluntary groups such as those assisting women who have suffered from domestic violence through the provision of refuges with Women's Aid groups or the provision of group homes with MIND (The National Campaign for Mental Health) or MENCAP. Some schemes provide permanent accommodation; others provide a temporary home whilst the resident is re-settled into the community prior to 'moving on' into ordinary housing.

RSLs also provide a range of accommodation offering varying degrees of support so in theory residents may move from an intensively supported hostel to less supported accommodation such as a group home or a cluster flat, prior to moving into self-contained accommodation. Most shared accommodation is provided on a fairly small scale with limited numbers of bedspaces, to create a less institutional atmosphere.

The level of provision

As stated, housing associations became actively involved in shared housing for special needs following the Housing Act 1974. Although voluntary groups had been providing specialist accommodation long before then, the boost in funding created by the Act was only available to registered housing associations. As a result, rather than register under the 1974 Act as housing associations themselves, many agencies chose to work in partnership with registered housing associations which develop the schemes that are subsequently managed by the agency. This arrangement may change over the coming years as some larger agencies may seek registered social landlord status under the Housing Act 1996 in their own right. Partnership agreements which form the basis for such arrangements are discussed further later.

In 1981 the then Minister for Housing, John Stanley, announced a 'hostels initiative' which led to an increase in the number of shared housing and hostel bedspaces approved. As a result, by 1997 there were some 91 000 shared housing bedspaces in England; 43 per cent of bedspaces are in London and the South-East.

In 1997/98 the funding of supported housing amounted to some 14 per cent of the national programme. The largest proportion of capital, 25.8 per cent, was allocated for housing for people with physical disabilities, 18.6 per cent for people with mental health problems, 18 per cent for frail elderly schemes, 14.9 per cent for people with learning difficulties and 8.4 per cent for young people at risk.

8.3   Funding supported housing

The funding of supported housing is achieved through a complex mix of capital and revenue types from a variety of different sources. The main sources of income and expenditure are set out in Table 8.2.

This chapter concentrates on funding through the Housing Corporation but, in fact, for revenue purposes, other sources (particularly social services and health authority funding) now represent a greater proportion of revenue income for many RSLs. The situation is further complicated by the artificial divisions imposed by government of what constitutes a 'housing' rather than a 'social services' (or care) activity. Each activity remains the responsibility of a separate government department with its own rules and administrative requirements. Housing schemes offering additional care and support clearly straddle both activities. Developments in community care for those coming out of large institutions led to a relaxation in these rules in that since 1977 schemes have been jointly financed by health and housing authorities (see below), but for projects to remain eligible for housing capital and revenue grants the degree of care that can be provided remains limited.

Table 8.2   Supported housing sources of income and expenditure

Income	Expenditure
Rents	Housing costs
Service charges	Service costs
SHMG (formerly T/SNMA)	Intensive housing management costs
	Care and support costs
Topping-up funding	
(grants or care contracts)	

T/SNMA = (Transitional) Special Needs Management Allowance.

The funding framework for supported housing schemes has been in a further state of transition since 1991. A number of factors have contributed to this: First, the advent of mixed funding and the Conservative Government's desire to integrate special needs schemes into the competitive framework established by the Housing Act 1988. Since 1994, the supported housing regime has had to be linked into national community care strategy and the financial framework for the provision of community care introduced by the 1990 NHS and Community Care Act. As discussed later in this chapter, in planning community care strategies local authorities are expected to incorporate housing needs. Joint strategic planning is encouraged between housing and social services departments which will also take into account the role of the Housing Corporation and registered social landlords. Many RSLs have developed close working relationships with health authorities and social services departments, both of which now contract with them for a range of services. Health authorities have provided both capital and revenue support, especially for reprovision following hospital closure. Social services departments now purchase places in residential care homes, both registered and unregistered, and in some cases have transferred the ownership and/or management of some of their own residential and nursing homes to registered social landlords.

In order to achieve greater value for money through increased competition, the Housing Corporation announced a review of special needs funding in 1994. It undertook a consultation exercise and introduced new arrangements with effect from April 1995.

The revised framework had two particular elements: first, a competitive bidding framework for both capital and revenue funding that enables RSLs to bid for any combination of capital and revenue support for each scheme; and second, a system of periodic reviews of revenue grants. Both elements are considered further below.

Eligibility criteria

In order to obtain funding, each special needs scheme must meet certain eligibility criteria. These are set out in the Housing Corporation's *Special Needs Procedure Guide* (1996). A scheme is eligible for Social Housing Grant and SHMG funding if it meets the following three criteria:

(a) the primary purpose of the scheme must be to provide housing rather than care;
(b) the aim of the scheme must not be to fulfil a statutory duty other than under housing legislation;
(c) the scheme must either provide residents wih a permanent home or the life skills and confidence to move into permanent accommodation.

Schemes that would fail these tests would include schemes that require registration under part II of the 1984 Registered Homes Act, including nursing homes. Bail hostels and schemes providing medical care as a main purpose would also be excluded, as would children's homes and shelter only projects. Additional certifications have to be made by the association when applying for funding from the Corporation. The first certification relates to eligibility, as highlighted above. The others are that:

(a) the scheme provides for tenants with special needs who require intensive housing mangement;
(b) the scheme provides tenants with specific rights;
(c) staff are available to carry out a range of the activities defined by the Corporation as consituting housing management in special needs housing;
(d) any management agency arrangements entered into conform to the Corporation's requirements;
(e) the scheme can demonstrate that ultimate control over who is housed remains with the RSL;
(f) the scheme achieves the minimum staff to tenant ratio specificed by the Corporation and maintains the staffing level stated within its application for SHMG approval;
(g) the viability of the scheme has been assessed and found to be satisfactory;
(h) the scheme either complies with or, if developed prior to 1 April 1991, will be improved to comply with the Corporation's Design Standards;
(i) the RSL will accurately report the source and purpose of all income, including community care income, received by the scheme in such formats as may be determined by the Corporation from time to time.

Capital funding

Most schemes are funded by either the Housing Corporation or, to a more limited extent, by local authorities. Until 1991 the capital costs of most supported housing schemes were completely written off by grant so that there was no outstanding loan to be serviced from charges to the residents. The capital funding regime introduced from April 1991 integrated supported housing into the grant regime introduced for general needs provision in April 1989, as outlined in Chapters 5 and 6. The regime incorporates grant rates, TCIs and multipliers that take account of the additional capital costs of developing supported housing schemes.

The system applies to both special needs self-contained and shared housing, thus ending to some extent the previous bias towards shared accommodation. The bidding process is also integrated although, as stated, a new system of competitive bidding for supported housing was introduced, effective for the first time for 1995/96, which assesses the value for money of supported housing schemes.

The assessment incorporates both the capital and the revenue aspects of the bids (i.e., bids for Social Housing Grant and bids for revenue support) through SHMG, in order that an evaluation can be made in relation to the total cost of the scheme to the public purse. Comparisons are made between competing schemes and against the Corporation's own bench-marks. Bids will be considered for *any* combination of capital and revenue grants. The tests are applied to each bid which meet a local authority's priority need in order to compare similar projects which are intended to provide a similar service to a client group, and to compare against benchmark costs for the project type for that region.

The Corporation adds the annual equivalent cost of the capital funding required to the revenue bid in order to establish the total annual subsidy required for each scheme. The detailed calculation is set out in the *Guide to the Allocation Process.*[5] The introduction of this process brought to an end the 100 per cent capital funding of most supported housing projects. The regime has encouraged some RSLs to raise a mortgage on these schemes in order to lessen grant requirements and to increase competitiveness, which in turn has placed a strain on the revenue budgets of these projects.

Despite the competition, however, the Corporation has asserted that the investment process will continue to be needs-led. Allocation decisions will be made in the light of the priorities set out in the local authority's Housing Strategy Statement and in line with national Community Care policy objectives. The Housing Corporation expects both local authority housing and social service departments to have been consulted and to have confirmed their priority support for a scheme if it is to be funded.

Revenue funding

The evolution of revenue support

Supported housing schemes have high revenue costs in terms of staffing, maintenance of the building, care and support to residents, including in some cases the provision of meals. There are, as highlighted, several sources of revenue funding. The charges to residents are usually insufficient to cover all revenue expenditure, creating deficits. Until 1991, if the deficit was attributable to 'housing' costs, the project may have been eligible for Hostel Deficit Grant (HDG).

Introduced in 1974 HDG was a discretionary grant available only to 'registered' housing associations; it was reviewed in 1989. Following the publication in 1988 of the DoE consultation paper, 'The Future Funding of Hostels and Special Needs Housing Schemes', it was suggested that HDG be replaced. This grant would be available to housing associations regard-less of whether the scheme provided shared or self-contained housing. This was welcomed as lessening the perverse bias towards shared housing.

From April 1991 a new management allowance, Special Needs Management Allowance (SNMA), was introduced to replace HDG. Revenue support for existing schemes became known as Transitional Special Needs Management Allowance, or TSNMA.

New projects received SNMA. SNMA (or TSNMA) is payable on a bed-space or unit basis on a sliding scale according to the staff to resident ratio. This ranges from a ratio of 1:5 to 1:30. In revenue terms in 1997/98 this translated into a maximum of £3455 to a minimum of £706 per bedspace.

In 1996 SNMA became known as Social Housing Managment Grant (SHMG). SHMG is a cash grant paid annually to the RSL by the Housing Corporation, calculated against the total range of special needs provision. As stated, the allowance (which applies to both shared and self-contained accommodation for special needs) marked an important step forward in integrating special needs housing with mainstream provision, and recog-nises the additional supportive management provided by such schemes. The costs of care, however, are funded by additional 'topping up' sources. SHMG was under review at the time of writing as discussed later in this chapter.

Triennial review of revenue support

On 1 April 1995 the Corporation introduced a triennial review of SNMA payable to each RSL. The objectives of the review are:

(a)   to examine the Corporation's revenue funding commitments in the light of current housing priorities and local and national strategies, including those developed following the introduction of community care;
(b)   to ensure that, in meeting priority needs, projects are performing efficiently and effectively;
(c)   to ensure that revenue support levels are commensurate with the actual funding requirements of specific schemes.

As part of the review the Housing Corporation takes into account the views of the local authority and others as to the continued relevance and effectiveness of the scheme, and it examines a range of performance infor-mation. The budget for each scheme is also very closely scrutinised. The review attempts to strike a balance between three different principles, taking into account financial, qualitative and strategic information. The review encompasses all revenue support from the Housing Corporation (both TSNMA payments which replaced the old Hostel Deficit Grant and SNMA on post-1991 schemes). In covering all schemes the review enables the Corporation to evaluate schemes approved over 20 years ago to ensure that they are relevant to current strategic requirements.

The competitive bidding process and the triennial review were not introduced without criticism. At the time of the consultation, there was concern that in relation to bidding, organisations which specialise in the provision of supported housing would be unable to continue to provide for these needs as they would be unable to compete against larger associations which could subsidise these operations with surpluses generated through other activities. Certainly the last five years have proved to be tough ones for specialist providers. More important, however, was the perceived threat to the viability of schemes and to these bodies *per se* if revenue support was suddenly withdrawn. However, it was agreed that funding would not be withdrawn without close consultation with the association, and then only over a period of phased reductions. There is also a right of appeal on factual, procedural or strategic grounds against a decision to reduce grant. A more positive aspect of the review process is the potential to change, update or remodel schemes, especially where they have become difficult to let. This is becoming particularly relevant in relation to sheltered housing schemes (see Chapter 9).

The first round of the review was undertaken in 1995/96 and led to an average reduction in revenue grant payable to the 31 associations affected of about 6 per cent. The National Housing Federation raised concerns with the Housing Corporation that the decisions appeared less than transparent and placed too great an emphasis on the artificial split between 'housing' and 'care' services. This contradicts the laudable aim of providing seamless services regardless of whether the source of funding is housing, health or social services. At the time of writing the Corporation was considering the outcome of the second round of reviews, and may yet refine its approach.

Topping-up finance

Most schemes require additional grants or topping-up finance to meet the costs of care and support for residents over and above SHMG. There are a number of sources of topping-up finance including powers available to local housing authorities, health authorities and the Home Office to make such grants. To obtain grant approval from the Corporation, topping up funding must be identified in advance and be available for at least one year. Where an RSL is also providing care, rather than contracting this out to another care provider, care contracts will replace topping-up funding.

Charges to residents

Rents for supported housing schemes are expected to be comparable with those for general needs schemes. The majority of older shared schemes have no mortgage and additional management costs are met by SHMG; therefore rents should be set at affordable levels. Similar principles apply as in the case of general needs housing.

Service charges must be clearly identified as charges for personal services such as meals, laundry or heating, and any personal care is not eligible for housing benefit. Until recently, service charges to cover the cost of a warden and some advice and support services were eligible for housing benefit. As discussed in the previous chapter, housing benefit is being reviewed in relation to service charge eligibility, which could result in changes which may adversely affect both the income of residents and the viability of some schemes, even leading to closure in some instances. If an item is not met through housing benefit it must be paid for out of the resident's own personal income (or income support if not working). The first supported housing CORE statistics published in 1997 showed that the average rent charged in a registered home is £258.93 per week, and in a non-registered home the weekly charge is £102.67. These figures suggest that housing benefit is funding more than the cost of the housing accommodation, which is an issue considered by the Inter-departmental Review of Housing Benefit.

Residents of supported housing may also be adversely affected by a number of changes in housing benefit implemented in 1996 and discussed in the previous chapter. The sources of income available to residents of supported housing schemes and those in receipt of care to pay for care and support services are both several and complex to assess.

The fragility of the revenue funding system generally was highlighted in a report on housing and community care revenue funding undertaken by Clapham Munro and Kay for the Joseph Rowntree Foundation.[6] The report called for a system that would encourage flexible and user-centred forms of provision, and which would enhance user control and choice. The report recommended the direct payment to users of funds to purchase their own care. It also recommended that SNMA should be converted to a person-centred rather than a property-based allowance.

Supporting People

This is the title of a Department of Social Security paper published in December 1998 which proposes a revised framework for funding support services. *Supporting People* proposes bringing together Housing Benefits paid for support services, SHMG (and its equivalent in Scotland and Wales) and Probation Accommodation Grant into a single supporting people grant payable to local authorities and disbursed by them directly to individuals or to landlords including RSLs. Thus the proposals would reduce the current complexities of revenue funding and co-ordinate the various heads of expenditure. Although the proposals iterate a clear commitment to the RSLs, removal of SHMG from the Housing Corporation will cause some concern. Ring fencing arrangements should prevent loss of these funds to the supported housing sector however. If adopted the new regime will be in place by 2003. A new transitional Housing Benefit Scheme will be introduced in 1999 to pave the way for Supporting People to cover support costs. The costs will relate to the needs of the person rather than the property, thus addressing some of the criticisms of the current system. This is already the case with some care payments.

Direct payments

Direct payment, was enacted in 1996 through the Community Care (Direct Payments) Act 1996, which gives local authorities the power to adopt such an approach for people with disabilities. Clearly this system will enhance choice for care recipients but it could in fact make it more difficult to plan and fund existing supported housing schemes. Some people may prefer to use the payment to fund a live-in carer rather than move into a supported housing scheme. The system will clearly pose new challenges to service providers.

8.4   Developing shared housing

Design standards

Once an RSL has received an allocation for a supported housing project, the development process is similar to that outlined in Chapter 6. However, in the case of shared housing there are special design consider-ations to be taken into account which are set out in the Housing Corporation's Scheme Development Standards (1995). The design stan-dards set out tests of compliance, essential standards and recommended items. These include separate bedrooms, bathroom-sharing restricted to 1 per 5 people, convenient location of bathroom facilities, and expects an appropriate apportionment of private and shared spaces. The Standards make reference to the provision of catering facilities, laundries on larger schemes, payphones and visitors' cloakrooms, and communal facilities such as common room and offices. Standards are less detailed and pre-scriptive than in earlier guides, however.

In designing a shared housing scheme, liaison with the voluntary agency or internal housing management is essential. They will brief the designers on space requirements and the facilities to be provided. The relationship between individual private space and communal facilities should be considered: for example, how much private space should be provided? Staff requirements must also be taken into account: will staff sleep in or live permanently in the scheme, or only require office space? Fixtures and fittings in bedrooms or bedsits also need careful consideration, as do kitchen fittings which, if in a communal kitchen, will need to be capable of sustaining substantial wear and tear. Close consultation with the managers of the project will result in a scheme that serves its purpose more effectively and should avoid the institutionalised atmosphere so often associated with hostel-type accommodation.

When a scheme is submitted to the funding authority for approval it must be accompanied by a revenue budget which sets out the revenue viability of the project. The nature of the funding arrangements outlined earlier means that revenue viability must be established before capital funding is granted. Sources of topping-up funding, where necessary, must also be confirmed.

A Special Projects Promotion Allowance meets the additional administrative costs arising from developing special needs schemes. It is intended to cover those schemes that are developed in partnership with another agency and to meet the costs of the joint venture. For the allowance to be payable, it must be clear that the RSL does not have the expertise to manage the project unaided. For a scheme to be successful there must be close consultation and liaison between the future managers of the project and the development staff.

NIMBY

Sadly, one of the most difficult aspects of developing special needs schemes, for groups other than the elderly, is obtaining planning permission. Many organisations have encountered opposition to their schemes from local residents. Vigorous lobbying and persuasion is often needed to quell opposition. A further problem is the growing concentration of special projects in particular streets. This arises partly from the location of suitable properties, but may be caused by opposition to development in other areas. This was the subject of a report on supported housing and the planning system entitled 'Not In My Back Yard' (NIMBY) and published by the National Housing Federation in 1994 as increasing opposition to schemes planned for people with learning disabilities and mental health problems was experienced. It asserts the right of these people to live independently in ordinary communities with dignity and privacy, but makes some positive recommendations which may help to avoid the syndrome. Careful planning of a scheme in advance, and in liaison with the local planning authority, combined with a concerted approach in relation to consultation with any neighbours affected can all help to overcome fears and opposition. The more that small-scale, sensitive projects are incorporated as a matter of course into general needs developments so, over time, the more likely it is that public anxiety will subside.

8.5 Managing supported housing

Partnerships

A large proportion of supported housing schemes are developed in part-nership with voluntary agencies. Where this applies it is a condition of funding that certain criteria are met. The criteria are set out in the Corporation's *Capital Funding System Procedure Guide 1997* and are also governed by the Supported Housing Performance Standards.

The agency involved must be an identifiable legal entity, a not-for-profit body and may not be a statutory authority. It must also have the manage-ment expertise appropriate to the special needs of the proposed residents. The RSL must be satisfied that the aims of the group are compatible with its own and that it has the capacity to manage the scheme effectively, and is a viable organisation. The association will enter into a legally binding partnership agreement with the agency. The issues which partnership agreements should cover are detailed in the *Procedure Guide (1997)* and cover both managerial and financial controls. The partners are in effect 'agents', for the RSL retains ownership of the building and must ensure that all duties and the division of responsibilities from repairing obligations and allocation of accommodation to responsibilities for staffing arrangements are covered by the agreement.

Each RSL must develop a close working relationship with the agencies with whom they work and will develop both management and develop-ment arrangements which will provide a legal framework for the relation-ship. Recently, the relationship between RSLs and their partners or agents has come to the fore partly as a result of a change in accounting practice in the commercial sector and partly as the sector has grown. There has been a desire to reconcile the legal, Housing Corporation, accounting and VAT frameworks. In addition, there is an increasing concern (on the part of the Housing Corporation in particular) to ensure that effective control can be achieved where schemes are managed by other than the registered social landlords. Partnership agreements vary widely and there is consid-erable confusion as to their legal status. A risk is therefore perceived in relation to public funds and to the RSLs flowing from these agreements. The National Housing Federation established a financial and legal panel (FLAP) to examine these issues and to agree options. It has since pub-lished a modular management agreement for use in these cases.[7]

The use of licences and residents' rights

A person living in shared housing will either be a tenant or a licensee. It is important to distinguish between the two as this will affect the rights of the resident and responsibilities of the association or its agent towards the occupiers. This is yet another complex area relating to the provision of supported housing. As discussed in Chapter 7 most permanent, self-contained properties owned by registered social landlords are let on either secure or assured tenancies. Shared accommodation has most commonly been let on licences. In the *Guide to the Legal Status of Residents in Shared Housing Schemes* (NFHA 1989) Stott and Wilson identified four bases upon which landlords can maintain that a licence to occupy exists rather than a tenancy. These are: 'special intention' (that is, that the reasons for making the letting are 'special' and involve more than just the provision of accommodation); that substantial board or attendance is provided; that there is a high level of domestic services; and that the accommodation is shared. The degree to which these factors apply will determine whether a tenancy or a licence exists. In the event of a dispute the courts will decide.

In 1996 the Housing Corporation issued its *Code of Practice on Tenure* which advises on the forms of tenure that should apply to special needs housing and housing which is part of the community care programme, including tenants of general needs housing with care packages. The Code of Practice gives examples of best practice and advises when assured shorthold tenancies, assured periodic tenancies or licences may be used. The residents of supported housing may also expect compliance with the Supported Housing Performance Standards.

'Residents' rights' was the title of a report published in 1988 by the National Housing Federation and CHAR, but which remains relevant today. Residents of supported housing schemes are often the most vulnerable of individuals and the report makes some 93 recommendations to ensure that their rights are respected. These include the right to privacy, access to effective complaints procedures, the right to equality of opportunity, the right to live free from fear of harassment, protection from unreasonable house rules, access to information, and consultation over the level of charges. The report also recommends that residents should be able to negotiate the package of care and support that they will receive whilst in residence. The protection of the autonomy of residents is paramount in projects which can all too easily lead to their institutionalisation. These schemes present the greatest challenge to housing staff to ensure that they are sensitively and effectively managed and that residents have the opportunity to become actively involved in both the decision-making and management processes. Tenant participation in the management of supported housing is as relevant as in general needs housing (as outlined in Chapter 7). Research still shows, however, that many organisations fail to give a high priority to this despite a high level of interest expressed by tenants in how the projects are run. Few organisations had separate budgets for this activity and few had made provision for reviewing the process.[8]

The management of both low and high care schemes also requires a commitment to the principles of care set out in *Home Life: A Code of Practice for Residential Care*.[9] This document set the original standards required in schemes providing residential care to ensure that basic rights should be accorded to all who find themselves in receipt of care. Since that time expectations have changed and developed and organisations delivering care must develop a philosophy and means of implementing it that respects the dignity, individuality and autonomy of people in receipt of care.

Home Life and was revised and updated in 1996, its successor, *A Better Home Life*,[10] is also used by local authorities as a guide when considering registration under the Registered Homes Act 1984.

Registered Homes Act 1984 and Children Act 1989

The Registered Homes Act 1984 and Children Act 1989 provide the regulatory framework for monitoring and controlling the provision of care to vulnerable adults and children. A scheme which provides housing for more than three persons may be required to register under this first Act. The rules are complex and open to interpretation, and have considerable implications for organisations providing supported housing (especially those providing high care schemes). Registered care homes must meet detailed prescribed standards set down by part I of the Act and monitored by the Local Authority Inspection Unit which regularly visits to ensure that these standards are complied with.

The current system of regulation and inspection of registered care homes has caused some difficulty for both RSLs and their partner organisations. These include a lack of consistency, including different regulation standards in different authorities and within the same authority. Standards can create an institutional setting and work against the principles of normalisation which are sought in care homes. The standards may also lead to additional revenue costs, especially to the purchasers. These concerns were highlighted in the National Housing Federation's response to a Department of Health consultation document entitled *Moving Forward*.[11] The aim of the consultation was to consider whether the system as it applies to part I should be amended. The National Housing Federation called for a single, nationwide body with responsibility for setting and regulating standards which would take into account the role of other regulators (such as the Housing Corporation), and place the rights of service users at the centre of the system.

The Burgner Report

The final report known as the Burgner Report (published in 1996), made a number of recommendations. In particular, it noted that development in care markets required a regulatory regime that would be adaptable and flexible. It noted the lack of consistency in the current arrangements and argued for a statutory regulation based on agreed basic or minimum standards. It proposed national benchmark standards covering all client groups. Statutory regulation would be extended to cover domiciliary care services, children's homes with under four children, and day care services with a genuine care element. Dual registration in the case of nursing homes, which distinguishes between nursing homes, and residential care homes was seen as an unecessary duplication; a single category of care home was proposed for the longer term. At the time of writing, however, the recommendations were still under discussion.

Children Act 1989

The Children Act 1989 attempted to provide a comprehensive code for the protection of children and it has implications for RSLs in relation to housing management. The Act was implemented in 1991 and gave social services departments new responsibilities and duties to ensure that the housing needs of homeless 16–17 year olds and those of young people leaving care are met. RSLs work with a range of agencies to assist in meeting these housing needs, providing accomodation especially for these groups and in their role as providers of general family accommodation. The Housing Corporation has published a good practice guide in respect of housing association activities in this area which examines systems for assessment and referral, the range of accommodation that can be provided and issues such as sources of support and funding options.[12]

Move-on accommodation

One of the most pressing issues facing providers of supported housing, especially of a temporary nature, is that of finding suitable move-on accommodation. Move-on accommodation enables a person to be resettled from an institution or a hostel into permanent accommodation with or without additional support. This particular issue was raised in the SHIL/NFHA report, *Move-On Housing.*

The report covered London only, but highlighted the problem of 'silt-up' in hostels whereby residents who are ready to leave are unable to owing to the shortage of ordinary accommodation. In 1995 a report for the Housing Corporation, *Move-on from Special Needs Housing* (prepared by consultants CVS Services),[13] identified a range of problems and made a number of recommendations. The report found that there is a demand for approximately 30 000 move-on units each year. RSLs have the potential to supply just 10 700 one-bedroomed/bedsit units for move-on purposes each year but currently supply far less than that. Reasons for the lack of performance include insufficient funding, lack of knowledge of the funding available for supportive move-on accommodation, pressure from local authority nominations and lack of expertise to provide support. The report notes that local authorities also have an important role to play in facilitating additional move-on accommodation by giving it greater priority in their housing strategies, assisting through their own one-bedroomed stock, supporting capital bids for move-on schemes and supporting the provision of one-bedroomed units generally in new schemes.

The report recommended that move-on housing become one of the priorities for Housing Corporation investment and that consideration of move-on needs should become a requirement of all supported housing providers. It also recommended that the Corporation review funding mechanisms to allow revenue support to be extended to low support schemes with staff to tenant ratios of up to 1:60.

In 1996/97 just 3 per cent of the Housing Corporation's ADP Approved Development Programme was allocated to build new developments to meet move-on requirements. RSLs have been encouraged to use their existing stock to enable move-on to occur from hostels and other temporary accommodation. Until recently, revenue support has been available to support this function through Supplementary Management Grants. From 1996/97 onwards, however, move-on activities have been supported through the SHMG budget (see Housing Corporation circular F4 02/96).[14]

In developing its move-on strategy to assist the permanent resettlement of residents, each organisation should take into account a number of sources of move-on accommodation including other RSLs, local authorities, mobility schemes such as that run by HOMES, as well as opportunities presented by the private sector. The strategy should also include the priority given to move-on needs for transfer within the association's general needs stock. The Housing Corporation requires RSLs to provide information on move-on needs and strategies as part of the SHMG review. This in turn enables it to assess an RSL's effectiveness in this area. The move-on strategy, in addition to assessing sources of move-on accommodation, will also include an assessment of the annual resettlement needs of tenants and residents, means of assessing move-on needs and support requirements, and arrangements to assist the tenants through the process.

Floating support

As discussed at the outset of this chapter, supported housing has been redefined to include ordinary housing with the provision of support services. The funding regime permits the use of SHMG for floating support purposes with numbers of dwellings grouped together. The Corporation defines floating support in the *Special Needs Procedure Guide* (1996), as schemes in which the SHMG is approved on the basis that it is transferable from property to property, as when a tenant ceases to need support and the tenant of another property is identified as requiring intensive housing management. Thus rather than the tenant having to move to another independent dwelling, the support 'moves on' to another tenant. SHMG can only be used for floating support, however, where the bid is for revenue only; it cannot be granted in schemes provided through the special needs capital funding regime. The details of the support offered should be included in the tenancy agreement. Floating support is an area that will develop in future as funders are able to be more flexible and make fewer artificial divisions between what constitutes care or housing services and become able to develop a system more geared to funding the support needs of *individuals* than the dwelling they are expected to occupy. It is the means by which people can be encouraged to live more independently and could be further developed to assist tenants in general needs stock who also have support needs, as highlighted in the previous chapter. This was indeed the original intention of community care policy, to which we now turn.

8.6   The development of community care

The changes to the funding regimes and approaches to the delivery of care and support services within housing associations have reflected the development of national community care strategy. Many RSLs have developed new partnerships and established teams with the skills required to provide the complete range of care services. The aim of community care is to assist older people who are becoming frail, or people who have mental health problems or learning difficulties, to stay in their own homes for as long as possible, supported by a range of health care and social services, thus avoiding the need for residential or institutional care. Although the concept has existed for nearly 30 years, more recently community care has been associated with the closure of long-stay hospitals through the 'Care in the Community' initiative.

Both the broader policy of community care and the initiative itself have given cause for mounting concern owing to the lack of housing opportunities for those leaving institutions and the shortage of community-based care and support services, especially for the younger single person. This has led to increasing pressure upon the welfare and housing management services of housing associations (outlined in the preceding chapter) as managers attempt to cope with tenants in ordinary housing who have mental health problems but who are not in receipt of the community care support from statutory services that they require.

As long ago as 1989 the report, *Housing: The Foundation of Community Care* stated that progress was slow and uneven; hospital rundown was outstripping growth of community services; social security funding fuelled institutional options; transitional funding was non-existent, local planning chaotic, staff training inadequate and joint finance ineffective. It confirmed, however, that despondency was misplaced as official reports presented positive options for the improvement of community care. The report also noted the importance of the housing element of community care, stating: 'If community care is the human body, housing is the backbone.'[15] Housing associations have played an important role since then in collaborating with health and local authorities to provide accommodation to assist those who are leaving institutions, and to maintain others in the community.

Joint schemes with health authorities

Two initial and essential elements of early community care policy were joint planning and joint finance. Introduced in 1976, joint planning involved collaboration between health authorities and local authorities to plan complementary services. A structure was established to facilitate this; Joint Consultative Committees (JCCs) were established to advise health authorities and the corresponding local authorities on the provision and planning of services. Since 1984 voluntary bodies have been represented on local JCCs. Joint finance arrangements permitted a health authority to use some of its resources to support social services spending on particular projects carried out by the local authority which are beneficial to the National Health Service (NHS). The support could also be in the form of capital or revenue expenditure. Joint finance could also be used to assist projects in the voluntary sector. Revenue funding under joint finance, however, was time limited and was usually tapered over a seven-year period (although this could be extended to thirteen). It is assumed that over time the financial responsibility for projects will be taken over by social services departments. Joint finance amounted to some £100 million per annum, about 1 per cent of the total health service expenditure. This budget has since been transferred to social services departments.

The Health and Social Services and Social Security Adjudications Act 1983 (HASSASSA) extended the powers of health authorities to make grants to fund housing schemes either from joint finance allocations or through their mainstream budget. Health authorities could fund up to 100 per cent of the capital costs of housing schemes developed by registered housing associations. The schemes had to be for the elderly, those with mental health problems or learning difficulties. They could be managed by a voluntary agency or directly by the association. However, where such capital grants were made it was a requirement of funding that first lettings be to people leaving hospital, although subsequent lettings may be to people already in the community. The schemes were usually developed as shared housing, which may provide a high degree of support and care. Schemes often took the form of group homes or frail elderly accommodation (see Chapter 9). If a high degree of care is involved in shared accommodation then the project may qualify as a registered home. Through the powers granted under the HASSASSA Act, health authorities also made revenue payments to meet the staffing and running costs of the projects. These took the form of 'dowry' payments, paid on a per capita basis, for individuals leaving long-stay hospitals. Unlike joint finance, payments from the mainstream budget are not time limited. The HASSASSA Act introduced a system of capital funding through health authorities which opened up the possibility of housing associations entering into management agreements with them. This is not permitted where schemes are funded by the Housing Corporation. Housing associations have to combine health authority funding with private finance to support further schemes.

Consortia

The use of the consortium approach for general development schemes was discussed in Chapter 6. This approach has also been adopted to co-ordinate responses to the Care in the Community initiative in local areas. The consortium is usually a registered company and charity and includes housing association and voluntary body representation. The consortium approach brings advantages. As resources are pooled there is greater access to both funding and expertise in terms of planning, developing and managing the projects. Consortia have developed throughout London and in other parts of the country. A report published by the National Housing Federation and The National Council for Voluntary Organisations explored the use of this approach further.[16] The funding system remains as complex as ever. There are several sources of capital and revenue funding with different rules and conditions for eligibility attaching to each. The level of care permissible on Corporation-funded schemes is limited. Capital funding from health authorities is only available if the scheme will assist those leaving hospital. Thus, a scheme could fall between two stools, attracting neither source of finance. The Housing Corporation has also been reluctant to fund schemes associated with hospital closure owing to pressures on its own programme, and also because it expects health authorities to support these schemes.

8.7   NHS and Community Care Act 1990

Community care has had a long and fitful history over the last 30 years, and means many things to different groups of people.

The Griffiths and Wagner Reviews

In 1988 two reports with implications for community care were published: the Griffiths Review, 'Community Care – Agenda for Action' and the Wagner Report, 'Residential Care: A Positive Choice'. Both reports recommended that people should be given the necessary support to be able to stay in their own homes for as long as possible. Griffiths in particular made radical recommendations regarding the operation and delivery of community care services. At that time no single department had overall responsibility for the delivery of care, and services were fragmented and patchy, led by traditional patterns of provision and funding rather than the needs of the individual users. Griffiths recommended that social services departments should become the lead authorities responsible for assessing needs and developing packages of care to meet the requirements of individuals. The local authority would act as enabler, purchasing rather than providing services directly. Griffiths also recommended what is known as the 'mixed economy of care' where services are provided by a plurality of bodies.

In 1989 the government published the White Paper, *Caring for People – Community Care in the Next Decade and Beyond.*[17] The Act itself received Royal Assent on 29 June 1990. Part III of the legislation enacted many of Griffiths' recommmmendations and took full effect in April 1993. Since 1993 the interpretation of what is meant by community care has changed. It is no longer concerned just with those people formally discharged into the community from hospitals and other long-stay institutions, but is intended to include all people who have some additional care and support need which, if provided, will enable them to stay in their own homes for as long as possible. Whilst the aim and philosophy is laudable and widely supported, pressure on resources and lack of co-ordination between, the departments involved (health, social services and housing) at both central and local levels has meant that in reality the provision of care services remains patchy and inconsistent on the ground.

In the policy guidance to the 1990 Act, community care is described as providing services and support which people who suffer from the problems of ageing, mental illness, mental handicap or physical or sensory disability need to be able to live as independently as possible in their own homes, or in homely settings in the community. Thus from the outset the official definition of recipients of care has always been narrower than the client groups of supported housing as listed above, which has also created some problems. The White Paper and Policy Guidance listed the objectives of community care policy as follows.

Aims of community care

To promote the development of domiciliary, day and respite services to enable people to live in their own homes wherever feasible and sensible.

To ensure that service providers make practical support for carers a high priority.

To make proper assessment of need and good care management the corner stone of high quality care.

To promote the development of a flourishing independent sector along-side good quality public services.

To clarify the responsibility of agencies and so make it easier to hold them to account for their performance.

To secure better value for money by introducing a new funding structure for social care.[18]

The intention was to enable as many people as possible to live as normal a life as possible. People were also to be given a greater say in the services they required and local authorities were to ensure that the right amount of care and support was available to achieve independent living. In addition, however, the cost of social security had been rising dramatically and the Conservative Government clearly recognised the opportunity to cut costs by enabling people to be cared for in their own homes. Indeed it is estimated that many more people are cared for by their families rather than through the formal community care provision, saving an estimated £6 billion to the Treasury.

Over a three-year period resources were transferred from the Social Security budget to local authority social services in the form of Special Transitional Grant, 85 per cent of which had to be spent in the independent sector (which amounted to government estimates of what was being spent in that sector) to ensure the development of a mixed economy of care with a clear split between purchasers and providers of care.

From 1 April 1993 local authority social services departments became responsible for planning, co-ordinating, purchasing and inspecting community care provided through a mixed economy of care. The strategic basis of the service is the community care plan. Community care is complex to plan and provide. It has involved the setting-up of new teams within social services departments to assess individual needs, and to purchase and manage care. In effect social workers became budget holders, able to purchase packages of care, including domiciliary services, for their clients to enable them to live independently. It was intended that support for carers in the form of respite care would also be a high priority.

Community care plans

Section 46 of the NHS Community Care Act 1990 requires local authorities to publish community care plans, to keep them under review and to replace them as required. The plans should include an assessment of needs of the local population and strategic objectives over the next three years.

The initial plans included details of the arrangements for the assessment of individuals, how purchasing is organised and how homecare or domiciliary services were to be expanded and improved. In addition, the plan had to set out how the social services department would co-ordinate provision with health and housing services. Arrangements for care management and details of how the independent sector would be stimulated were also included. Details of training for care staff and the arrangements for establishing inspection and registration units were set out. The Act introduced independent inspection units established under the aegis of the Director of Social Services. The units inspect care homes to ensure that they comply with the requirements of the 1984 Registered Homes Act; this whole process was subject to review at the time of writing as discussed earlier.

Current community care plans cover similar ground. Typically they will include an assessment of need, details of priority client groups and services currently available and targets for the future. Assessment processes and care management arrangements are included, as are training and staff development. Purchasing strategies and reference to housing strategies may also be included.

8.8   Housing strategies and community care

Community care policy recognises that more and more people will be cared for in their own homes and that housing especially for the largest needs groups (the elderly, and people with mental health problems and learning disablilities), which provides adequate facilities with appropriate support is crucial. The co-ordination of a national and local strategy to accurately assess needs and provide for these has been hampered through lack of a joint approach and strategy between health, housing and social services departments. This lack of joint strategic planning has been the subject of several reports, and failure to address housing issues has to some extent undermined the community care initiative as a whole. The failure to co-ordinate effectively at a local level mirrors the lack of joint working which has also typified the approach at central Government level. Differing philosophies, agendas and funding regimes have prevented the Environment and Health departments in particular from developing joint approaches to community care strategy. If central government departments have a poor record in this area it is not surprising that liaison at a local level has also been weak. The detrimental effect of this lack of co-ordination has been recognised from time to time, however, and the role of housing in particular in contributing to community care was enshrined in a joint Department of the Environment/Department of Health circular on housing and community care published in 1992 which stated, 'adequate housing has a major role to play in community care and is often the key to independent living'.[19]

The circular emphasised the importance of assessing individual housing need and the requirement for housing and social services departments to set up close working relationships between care managers and identified officers in housing departments. Referral processes were to be established in order that the housing needs of indiviuals with care requirements could be met. The role of housing associations was not fully recognised in the circular, however, and neither was there any clear assessment of needs and the resources required to meet them. The lack of both has continued to dog the implementation of community care.

In 1993 the Community Care Support Force (which had been established a year earlier to assist local authorities and health authorities to implement community care policy), published a document with local authorities, the Housing Corporation and the National Housing Federation to call for joint working relationships to tackle the housing agenda involving social services, health and housing authoritites.[20] It also called for plans which would assess need and co-ordinate planning and resource bidding cycles, building community care housing needs into the local authority strategy statements and the Housing Corporation's planning process. The paper also called for the individual assessment of need to incorporate housing input and highlighted the need for collaboration in relation to homeless people. The least institutional response was recommended, encouraging the use of schemes that would allow people to stay put in their own homes. The report encouraged a purchasing strategy that would make use of services provided by supported housing providers, including services for a range of other vulnerable groups such as drug or alcohol misusers. It called for the production of a strategy that would meet new needs using Housing Corporation and other funding, and which recognised the type of purchasing contracts that are required for the housing sector.

In 1995 and 1997 further joint guidance was published by the Departments of Health and Environment on community care, housing and homelessess which was intended to supplement Circular 10/92. Once again it advised on the establishment of joint strategies for housing and community care, and stressed the importance of joint planning and commissioning strategies.[21] Clearly there is a plethora of guidance; however, the evidence on the ground is that there is still some way to go before effective strategic planning is achieved.

Joint commissioning is defined as 'the process by which two or more agencies act together to co-ordinate their commissioning, taking joint responsibility for translating an agreed health, housing and social care strategy into action for the benefit of service users and carers'. An introduction to the process was published by the Department of Health in 1995.[22]

The Chartered Institute of Housing has also issued advice for housing departments on developing joint working with social services with the aim of establishing local strategies for housing and community care.[23] This Guide suggests that the central aims of the housing and community care strategy should be to promote and support independent living and to provide a full and flexible range of housing options. It suggests a number of policy objectives:

(a)   to assist owner-occupiers who wish to remain in their own homes;
(b)   to sustain existing tenancies where people require additional support;
(c)   to assist disabled people who wish to move from the parental home;
(d)   to facilitate moves from long stay residential care institutions;
(e)   to provide access routes from hostels into mainstream housing ;
(f)   to pre-empt moves to inappropriate forms of accommodation;
(g)   to reduce homelessness among people with support needs;
(h)   to prevent homelessness arising through family stress or crisis;
(i)   to facilitate discharge from hospital to suitable housing;
(j)   to provide housing for those leaving residential school/college.

The strategy would comprise a number of elements including the provision of new and additional housing, property related services such as alarm systems and adaptations, conversion and upgrading of property, (e.g., extending a scheme to provide extra care). Support to individuals is a further key element, as is access to housing through allocation policies, such as the organisation of waiting lists and the development of move-on strategies and transitional arrangements to cope with discharge from hospital or from care.

The Guide also highlights the importance of mapping resources (i.e., assessing the gap between community care housing needs and supply). In relation to the assessment of needs reference is made to the work undertaken by Watson (one of the authors of the Guide) with Harker which established a model for housing needs assessment for people with learning disabilities.[24] Known as Housing Pathways, the model can highlight gaps in provision, moves between different forms of provision and access routes into mainstream housing.

It also highlights pressure points and blockages in the system and the position of marginal or neglected groups. What this model attempts to overcome is the situation where the strategic planning process for community care is divorced from actual service delivery. Currently assessments appear to be driven by provision rather than needs, and unmet need is often inadequately recorded. The full details of the housing pathways pilot programme and the operation of the model are given in a joint Chartered Institute of Housing/National Housing Federation publication.[25]

8.9   Registered social landlords and community care

The requirement that 85 per cent of the newly transferred funds be spent on services provided by the independent sector to create the mixed economy of care opened up new opportunities for RSLs. Several have been able to develop their role based on their experience in the provision of supported housing and have developed new partnerships with health and social services to expand the range and nature of services that they provide including the development of domiciliary services and to build on their existing community links. Domiciliary services and other initiatives designed to enable people to stay in their own homes longer are examined in Chapter 9. As illustrated above, community care is about the provision of services to individuals, preferably in their own home. In some ways, therefore the development of supported housing projects (whereby support services are only available in specially developed accommodation) is at odds with the ethos of community care. Community care is, however, relevant to all RSLs. It may be that their involvement is limited to accessing packages of care for general needs tenants or they may provide supported housing. Some have now embraced the delivery of care as a core function and have established specialist teams, departments and subsidiaries to deliver these services. RSLs must ensure that they develop an effective dialogue with the local health and social services departments in order to contribute to planning at a strategic level but also to ensure effective collaboration in relation to tenants with care needs.

Where care has become part of the core business of the association it is important that the RSL recognises how this will reshape the organisation as a whole. This includes the skills represented on the board itself in addition to the operation of the finance, development, housing management and maintenance functions too. Personnel and training services become even more essential as the management of care is very labour intensive and, where registered care homes are provided, staffing levels are high. This may soon lead to the emergence of care staff as the largest staffing group within an RSL. These staff have particular management and training requirements and, being non-office based, require the development of new systems and communications processes. The whole ethos and culture of the care profession is new to most (although not all) housing associations. This, combined with the fact that the organisation is taking on responsibility for some of the most vulnerable members of society, sometimes with challenging problems, means that highly effective sytems of management are required. These need to be combined with an approach to the delivery of care services which values and encourages independence, treating people with dignity and respect.

Managing risk

On a more prosaic level, the delivery of care is challenging in financial and administrative terms too. In addition to personnel and training support, the financial requirements are becoming even more complex and risky. As highlighted earlier, RSLs are becoming increasingly dependent on a variety of sources of revenue support for special needs schemes, and vacancies are funded by health or social services on an increasingly fragmented basis. Where an RSL is also providing care, rather than contracting this out to another care provider, the major purchasers are now social services departments.

Under the 1990 NHS and Community Care Act bedspaces are purchased in care homes for people assessed as in need of these services. In addition, relationships with health authorities now feature more prominently. Several RSLs have extensive contracts with health authorities to provide care in schemes provided by the health authority or the Corporation. Where a purchaser buys all or the majority of the bedspaces in a care home under what is known as a 'block contract', the authority enters into an agreement with the RSL as provider of those services which sets out the extent and nature of the care and related services to be provided to each resident. Until 1995 most care contracts were funded on a block basis which, although renegotiated every one to three years, offered some degree of certainty in relation to care income. As social services take over and reprovision schemes come to an end, care purchasers are increasingly using 'spot contracts' whereby individual contracts for care are purchased. As budgetary pressure increases on care service purchasers and competition with the private sector care providers increases the risk to RSLs providing care will grow. The revenue funding is becoming less certain and they cannot always be sure that contracts will be renewed. The advent of 'spot' rather than 'block' purchasing, whereby a single place in a project is purchased puts the organisation at greater financial risk than was the case when the scheme was commissioned, perhaps only a few years earlier. Health and social services authorities may find that the prices of the bedspaces in schemes that they commissioned are now too expensive. This could leave some RSLs with revenue difficulties.

A careful balance has to be struck in the market for care between providing a quality client-centred service and charging prices that are competitive when compared with other providers. The risks need to be carefully monitored and the Housing Corporation will examine exposure to risk through the delivery of care services, particularly to non-tenants, very carefully in the coming years. Community care is also an area of opportunity for RSLs, however, and one which enables them to meet the greatest social needs. The delivery of high care, whether to the association's own tenants or to other groups, requires careful planning and monitoring in relation to the organisation's total operations.

These issues are highlighted by the report *People first*,[26] which found that out of the 600 housing associations involved in supported housing, three out of every five staff members were involved in care and support work. The majority are employed in supported housing schemes and care homes and, at the time of writing, this represented over 62 000 people. The report highlights the extent to which housing associations are now providing community care services, including peripatetic services to 32 500 people.[27] Community facilities such as alarm systems, care and repair and advocacy provided by housing associations were delivered to 290 000 people. In conclusion, the report notes: 'housing associations can choose different levels of involvement in community care but they cannot ignore it. Associations must assess the impact of community care on their work to ensure:

(a) that the needs of all their tenants are assessed and appropriate services are arranged whether provided by the association or other bodies;
(b) that there is a strategy to make best use of existing stock and to adapt and respond to changing needs where appropriate;
(c) that where involved in care and support provision, staff training and expertise within management and committee structures is suitable for a different revenue intensive and substantial business;
(d) that the implications of taking on additional care and support activities are carefully considered in order to manage the potential risks and uphold standards of service'.[28]

A further report *Contracting for Care*, published by the National Housing Federation in 1996, reiterates these points and offers guidance to RSLs wishing to develop care services. Commissioned by the London Federation of Housing Associations, it investigates the potential role of associations in the community care market in London. It highlights the complexities of the various markets for care and the pressure on costs which can impact on the quality of service offered.

It examines the extent of competitive pressure from the private sector that already exists in this area and emphasises that any move into community care is an important, corporate strategic decision. The choices available to the board are explored and advice given on winning and managing contracts.[29]

Despite the welter of advice and guidance there remains concern that housing is still the missing link in the care chain. A report by four chief executives of housing associations experienced in the provision of care stated: 'there is a widening gap between the vision and the reality of community care'. To some extent they were responding to the tragic deaths caused by people with care needs whom the system had failed (referred to in the previous chapter), but they were also concerned to open up the debate on the governance of community care which they perceived as 'having a direct negative impact on the lives of vulnerable individuals'.[30] The report argues that the vision of a seamless health and social care service can only be achieved by a new system of governance which would ensure that the collaboration that is required between departments would actually occur, and thus put in place the first prerequisite of community care. They argue that health and social services still fail to link up with each other and with housing, leading to a continuation of 'the revolving door syndrome for many of the most vulnerable users of community care services'. The report highlights gaps in provision, duplication of effort and problems that are 'shunted between agencies because the system focuses on active caseloads, filled beds and throughput, not positive or negative outcomes for service users'.[31]

The findings of this report are supported by research undertaken for the Joseph Rowntree Foundation which examined the housing preferences of people who require additional care and support.[32] It found that unless a crisis situation has arisen moves are unlikely to occur, yet those wanting self-contained housing see obtaining suitable housing as their first priority above negotiations for support services. The study concludes that this runs counter to the concept that housing needs are assessed as part of a community care package. People who had been living in a sheltered or supported environment often lack the money and other household skills for independent living, and this too may hold them back. The Joseph Rowntree Foundation has reviewed 21 projects in its community care programme. Its findings, unhappily, also reflect the criticism outlined above and highlight again the failure of implementation on the ground to live up to the claims of the policy.[33]

Clearly, community care has impacted on housing associations in a number of strategic and operational areas. The growth of these activities has implications for the future management and development of those organisations that choose to enter the field. As we have seen, however, even those RSLs that choose not to provide care services directly will have to ensure that the community care needs of tenants in ordinary accommodation are met, and that as owners and managers they are in a position to ensure that care provision by others is to appropriate standards. In 1999 The Royal Commission report into long term care emphasised the key role that housing plays in community care. If the Commission's recommendations are adopted, housing (and RSLs) will become central to community care policy.

8.10   Assisting single homeless people

This section concentrates on single people and on the single homeless in particular. Most single people do not have health problems, and the needs of single homeless people are met by housing associations through the normal sources of permanent and temporary accommodation as outlined in the previous chapter. Some people do require support, however, and

RSLs assist through the provision of supported housing and a range of other initiatives. Several RSLs are active in the provision of accommodation for single people and others have provided hostel places. In London, in particular, bodies such as the English Churches Housing Group actively work with voluntary agencies to assist people sleeping rough through the provision of direct access hostels and night shelters.

In 1993 the Department of the Environment published a survey of single homeless people in England[34] which was based on interviews with people sleeping rough, living in temporary hostels and night shelters, and in bed and breakfast accommodation, in order to ascertain the characteristics of people sleeping rough in particular and the reasons they become and remain homeless. It also examined the support needs and housing preferences of these people. The report found that the majority of single homeless peole were men and that the overwhelming majority were not in paid work and were dependent upon income support. Most mentioned either parental home or their own flat or house as their last permanent place of residence. More than 25 per cent of those people in bed and breakfast accommodation or hostels had slept rough at some point during the previous year. Most were seeking accommodation but could not afford it and had difficulty in gaining access to suitable housing. Over 80 per cent of single homeless people wanted their own flat or house. The preference was for self-contained, not shared, accommodation; unsurprising findings.

Rough Sleepers Initiative

As numbers sleeping rough on the streets increased, pressure was placed upon the Conservative Government to take action. In 1990 the Department of the Environment launched a range of initiatives which have become known as the Rough Sleepers Intiative (RSI). The first programme, RSI-1, allocated £96 million to voluntary organisations and housing associations to work together to provide a range of accommodation, both permanent and temporary, and the provision of support services such as outreach work and resettlement advice for single homeless people in London. A Clearing House was established through the Housing Services Agency to provide a mechanism to match needs identified by the voluntary agencies with the supply of places available through the housing associations. The associations work with the Clearing House to provide the accommodation which is managed by the referral agencies which work with people with a history of sleeping rough. These agencies nominate clients to ten 'gatekeeping' agencies which in turn nominate on through the Clearing House to RSLs. The support packages provided by the associations are either funded through general revenue or through 'RSI' SHMG.

The first initiative was evaluated in 1993 by Randall and Brown for the DOE.[35] It found that several thousand homeless people had been assisted through the initiative. Between 1990 and 1993 around 840 new beds were provided in temporary direct access hostels, 700 places in bedsits and flats through Private Sector Leasing, and 2200 permanent homes provided by housing associations. In addition, some 700 extra beds were funded by the DoE as cold weather shelters. In 1990 the Department of Health also launched the Homeless Mentally Ill Initiative. This was a £20 million project which funded 750 hostel places and five community psychiatric teams.

No fewer than 750 move-on places were provided through Housing Corporation funding, with care and support funded through local authority social services departments. RSI resulted in a significant reduction in the number of people sleeping rough in London, and in 1993 the initiative was extended for another three years. An additional £86 million was made available, with the majority earmarked for the provision of 1500 new permanent self-contained move-on units. The homes were produced by ten associations which had developed a track record under RSI-1. The London Federation of Housing Associations has produced a useful analysis of the RSI initiative.[36]

In 1996 RSI-3 was announced following a joint review of strategy by the inter-departmental review group led by the Department of the Environment. Around £73 million was made available, with clear targets set for monitoring performance and action plans.[37] In view of the fact that *official* estimates of the numbers sleeping rough had fallen to 270(!), and was considered a success, the initiative was to continue in London and any centre that could prove the need. The Labour Government provided a further boost to the RSI initiative by announcing in July 1998 a further £50 million to 'clear the streets' by cutting rough sleeping by two-thirds by 2002, as part of its social exclusion initiative. With effect from March 1999, the government intends to fund organisations charged with clearing the streets by creating additional hostel beds and developing mentoring schemes for single homeless people. A central unit headed by a 'Street Czar' will be responsible for implementing this policy.

Rent deposit funds and guarantees

A number of housing associations have worked with local authorities and voluntary agencies to assist single homeless people to overcome the difficulty they experience in obtaining suitable accommodation caused by landlord requirements for rent deposits. The Notting Hill Housing Trust (NHHT) in London pioneered a rent deposit fund scheme with funding through RSI-1 in 1992. An evaluation of this scheme and other schemes in which rents were guaranteed for a period (usually of up to six months) was undertaken on behalf of the Department of the Environment in 1994.[38] The research found that the the NHHT Rent Deposit Fund was successful in rehousing 450 people from its target group in the private sector. It also made a number of recommendations to improve the operation of such schemes, including limited checks of property quality and landlord management to ensure value for money. It also recommended that rent guarantee schemes rather than rent deposit funds should be favoured as they are less open to abuse.

8.11   HIV/AIDS and housing

In recent years housing associations have contributed to the provision of housing for people with HIV or AIDS. Some existing tenants may be HIV positive or have developed the illness itself. This has implications for housing management and for staff generally. Tenants who have become ill may experience harassment; they may also require special facilities in the longer term that will allow them to remain in their existing home. Tenants may also request transfers to accommodation nearer to support networks and medical facilities. Associations need to train staff to deal with the possible harassment of such tenants and develop policies relating to matters of confidentiality and protection of the tenants (or staff) affected. In 1987 the AIDS and Housing sub-group of the London based Special Needs Housing Group set up Strutton Housing Association to promote the provision of housing for people with HIV/AIDS.

Housing Corporation Circular 40/87 (now withdrawn)[39] and the *1989 Good Practice Guide* set out the design considerations for housing for people with AIDS and related illnesses. The latter states: 'there is evidence that maintaining good standards of general health can inhibit the development of AIDS in persons with HIV virus. Housing is of prime importance and should offer privacy in a stress-free environment protected from harassment and physical attack.'[40] In 1989 the National Housing Federation published *Housing and HIV Disease: Guidelines for Housing Association Action*, which advises housing associations on issues such as harassment, confidentiality, equal opportunities and the allocation of housing and other resources.

The type of housing required varies according to the personal circumstances of the individual but, in addition to being self-contained, it should be large enough for a carer to stay overnight and close to the facilities mentioned above. All units should be 'wheelchair accessible', and both bathrooms and kitchens may need to be designed for wheelchair use. Mobility standards must be incorporated throughout. Heating installations are also of prime importance. Those standards recommended for elderly persons' housing including heated circulation areas should be achieved. Security and safety measures are highlighted, including the need for door entry phones, toughened glass in ground floor units and adequate fencing to deter intruders.

A survey by the AIDS and Housing Project for the London Borough of Newham in 1994[41] confirmed the findings of several other surveys on the housing needs of people living with HIV. Problems of mobility and managing day-to-day tasks were common. Space was required to allow someone to stay during illness, and stress caused by harassment, financial problems, unwanted sharing and insecurity of tenure was prominent.

In 1996 the AIDS and Housing Project reported on the role of the HIV specialist housing sector.[42] It highlighted the crucial role played by housing support services and confirmed that early intervention by housing support agencies could prevent expensive intervention at a later date. It also demonstrated that tenants in receipt of an intensive housing management service also make fewer calls on acute and primary health services. It highlighted the importance of joint commissioning in this field too. The report made a number of recommendations in relation to the organisation and provision of services. It called for support agencies to clearly define the services provided and to have referral and selection policies that make services as accessible as possible. It recommended that housing and social services departments should develop joint assessment criteria. Social services departments should have the strategic planning and purchasing function for care, and the needs of people with HIV/AIDS should be built into the the community care plans (as discussed above). The report argues that joint assessment, monitoring and purchasing of support could reduce duplication of effort by providers. The report also notes the need to fund projects on a more sustainable basis than spot contracts in order to achieve long-term financial stability.

8.12   Assisting people with physical disabilities

According to the 1991 OPCS survey there are some 6 million people in Britain with some form of disability. There is no easy definition of disability: it covers a range of conditions including chronic illness, blindness, deafness, inability to walk and mental disability including severe mental illness.[43] Physical disability in the housing context has been defined as 'any physical condition causing a handicap which may be exacerbated by unsatisfactory housing conditions or alleviated by suitable ones'.[44] The degree of disability suffered will vary considerably. A person may be literally confined to bed. He or she may be chairbound (i.e., completely confined to a wheelchair). In Britain this applies to some 200 000 people. There are a further 200 000 people who possess wheelchairs but are semi-ambulant and are able to walk to a limited extent, perhaps with assistance.

Disability in general terms is often considered to be a problem of age; 85 per cent of people with disabilities are over the age of 50 and 70 per cent over the age of 65. However, as some 60 per cent of wheelchair users are under the age of 65 it is important that the needs of elderly people and wheelchair users are distinguished. The Chronically Sick and Disabled Persons Act 1970 requires local authorities to have regard for the housing needs of disabled people. Since its enactment housing solutions have included the provision of mobility housing, wheelchair or specially designed housing, and adaptations to existing dwellings. More recently there has been increasing pressure for the development of 'lifetime' homes that are accessible and adaptable to people's changing circumstances.

Mobility housing

Mobility housing is defined as ordinary housing which does not incorporate special features but owing to certain aspects of its design, it is convenient for people with disabilities to live in. It is also accessible to visitors with disabilities. Some 25 years ago, the Housing Development Directorate Occasional Paper 2/74, *Mobility Housing*,[45] set out the main features.

Mobility housing is considered suitable for people with disabilities who do not use a wheelchair and for wheelchair users who can manage in the home largely without one. It is not considered suitable for people who are chairbound or use their chair in the kitchen or bathroom. Mobility housing has four essential features:

(a) a ramped or level entrance and flush threshold;
(b) main entrance, and internal door sets not less than 775 mm wide and corridors at least 900 mm wide;
(c) WC at entrance level;
(d) in two-storey dwellings staircases capable of taking a stair lift or space provided capable of taking a chair lift from the ground floor to a bedroom.

Thus the main difference between ordinary housing and mobility housing is ease of access and more circulation space to allow easy manoeuvring of a wheelchair.

Wheelchair housing

Wheelchair housing has a greater number of special features. In addition to those listed for mobility housing these may include: access to the property from a covered carport or garage, preferably at the same ground level; door handles, window fastenings, lighting sockets and switches at waist height, about 600–1200 mm, for convenience of reach from a wheelchair; specially designed kitchens with knee spaces under cooker hob, sink and work surfaces for ease of preparation of food; bathrooms with knee access to basin, baths with grabrails and platforms at one end to allow greater convenience of transfer from the wheelchair, and space around the WC for the wheelchair to facilitate transfer; extra space in bedrooms to allow room for the wheelchair; and the construction of ceilings capable of taking hoists, especially in bedrooms and the bathroom. Turning space throughout the dwelling is essential, and should allow around 1500 mm diameter minimum. The location of the accommodation is also a prime consideration. It should be conveniently situated and close to all amenities.

The Housing Corporation design standards for both general accessibility and wheelchair housing are set out in the 1995 Scheme Development Standards.

Adaptation of existing housing

As discussed in Chapter 6, grants are available to housing associations through the aids and adaptations programme to convert existing housing to mobility or wheelchair standard. Adaptation includes building a ramped access, and installing special kitchen and bathroom facilities (perhaps in ground floor extensions where possible). The widening of doorways and corridors and the raising of electric points and switches may also be necessary. Stair lifts and chair lifts can be installed in two-storey houses to enable the tenant to use the upper floor.

Accessible homes

Several RSLs, such as Habinteg and John Grooms specialise in the provision of housing for people with physical disability. Others include some wheelchair units in their general needs schemes. The Housing Corporation figures show that by 1997 some 16 000 self-contained wheelchair units had been provided by RSLs in England.[46]

The numbers of accessible homes developed, both wheelchair and mobility, has declined since 1979, however, reflecting the reduction in public sector house building programmmes. Since the 1970s there has been growing awareness of the needs of people with disabilities and the importance of access to the built environment as a means of improving integration to achieve greater equality of opportunity. There has been growing support for incorporating improved access into all housing, whether public or private sector, to enable the integration of elderly and disabled people.

In 1992 the Access Committee for England (ACE), which was established in 1984 as a focal point for issues of access for all people with disabilities, published a document entitled *Building Homes for Successive Generations: Criteria for Accessible General Housing*. Whether called accessible housing, barrier free, or adaptable housing the common feature is that it 'can be easily adapted to suit the physical needs of most people, including those who are disabled, without major structural alteration, and that can, without adaptation, be visited by wheelchair users'.[47] The common features are similar to mobility housing; level access, adequate door widths and circulation space and an entrance level toilet.

ACE called for amendments to part M of the Building Regulations (which have enforced the development of access standards to public buildings since 1985), to be extended to housing. In 1995 the Department of the Environment issued a draft building regulation for consultation which has now been implemented. Part M ensures that minimum accessiblity is built into all new housing developments.

Lifetime homes

A range of bodies (including some RSLs, ACE and the National Housing Federation) have joined with the Joseph Rowntree Foundation to promote the concept of accessible and adaptable homes under the banner 'Lifetime Homes'. Lifetime Homes are designed to:

> meet the needs of their occupiers throughout their lifetime. The design features help parents with young children as much as grandparents who come to stay. The homes can cope with life events such as a teenager breaking a leg and being in a wheelchair for a few weeks. They can be visited by anyone, young or old, able-bodied or disabled. The homes are easy to adapt if a member of the household becomes disabled or frailer in old age.[48]

The Joseph Rowntree Foundation Lifetime Homes Group has published a range of criteria which consitute the essential features of a lifetime home. In addition to accessibility, the requirements of the ACE document are incorporated. At least one commentator has shown that if an association meets the Housing Corporation's mobility criteria and has adequate space standards, and if adaptations for a carport and a hoist (for which funding is available) are added later, the total increase in cost for a two-bedroomed house in 1995 was £1000 and for a three-, four- and five-bedroomed house, as little as £337.[49] While these minimal costs can only be achieved by planning for lifetime criteria from the inception of a scheme, Lifetime Homes standards can also be incorporated into the modernisation programmes undertaken by housing associations. Research for the Joseph Rowntree Foundation found that up to three-quarters of the standards could be readily achieved as part of a refurbishment programme at little or no extra cost.[50] With the pressure on scheme development costs as outlined in Chapter 6, the temptation is to ignore calls for these standards which go beyond Housing Corporation criteria. However, as demonstrated, the costs are not onerous if they result in the provision of homes which will genuinely cater for the changes in family circumstances, and the changing demographic needs of society as a whole, well into the future.

8.13   The future of supported housing

Housing with care and support is a complex area which is undergoing immense change as a result of developing demographic and social trends, which in turn have influenced community care policy. This chapter has only been able to touch the surface of such issues. In 1996 the Housing Corporation published a discussion paper for supported housing which set out the aims and objectives of the Corporation's supported housing strategy and considered options for assessing need, investment frameworks and the regulation of supported housing. It was expected that, following consultation, a clear strategy for supported housing would emerge. At the time of writing, however, factors such as a change of government and the Inter-departmental Review of Housing Benefit have led to the document being viewed merely as a position statement.

This chapter has noted several issues for resolution in any future strategy, in particular that the funding regime will have to alter over time to reflect current thinking and needs on the ground. Funding must take a more holistic approach, with support going to the individual that needs the care rather than a 'bricks and mortar' subsidy to the dwelling. If introduced, this approach in turn will have an impact upon the viability of existing projects. The revenue funding system also needs to address issues such as move-on accommodation and the funding of floating support. In addition, there is a need to ensure that there is effective inter-departmental communication with joint planning and commissioning of schemes and services. Needs should be effectively assessed to ensure that requirements are properly built into local strategies.

Investment strategies are needed to ensure that the best use is made of existing stock and that any new schemes that are developed are flexible in use. A system of regulating and measuring performance needs to be devised to ensure consistent standards nationwide. In this context the National Housing Federation has developed a voluntary Housing Care and Support Code, and the Audit Commission was at the time of writing examining the housing aspects of community care.

References

1 Office For Public Management, *Assessment of the Housing Requirements of People with Special Needs over the Next Decade* (NFHA 1992).
2 L. Potter and T. Roose, *People First – Housing Associations Caring in the Community* (NFHA 1995).
3 A. Purkis and P. Hodson, *Housing and Community Care* (Bedford Square Press/NCVO 1982), p. 1.
4 M. Smith, *A Guide to Housing*, 3rd edn (The Housing Centre Trust 1989), p.351.
5 *Guide to the Allocation Process* (The Housing Corporation 1997).
6 D. Clapham, M. Munro and Helen Kay, *A Wider Choice – Revenue Funding Mechanisms for Housing and Community Care* (Joseph Rowntree Foundation October 1994).

7 *Financial and legal arrangements between housing associations and other bodies managing supported housing (FLAP), NHF Update in Housing Today*, 3 July 1997.

8 *Tenant Participation in Supported Housing*, Joseph Rowntree Foundation Findings, Housing Research 177 (April 1996).

9 *Home Life: A Code of Practice for Residential Care* (Centre for Policy on Ageing 1984).

10 *A Better Home Life: A Code of Good Practice for Residential and Nursing Home Care* (Centre for Policy on Ageing 1996).

11 *Moving Forward – A Consultation Document on the Regulation and Inspection of Social Services* (Department of Health September 1995) and *Moving Forward – A Consultation Document on the Regulation and Inspection of Social Services*, NFHA Response (Housing Federation February 1996) unpublished.

12 Helen Kay *Housing Associations and the Children Act* (The Housing Corporation 1996).

13 *Move-on from special needs housing*, Source Insight 8 (The Housing Corporation 1995).

14 *Supplementary Management Grants and Higher Management Allowances*, The Housing Corporation Circular F4 02/96.

15 A. Wertheimer, *Housing: The Foundation of Community Care* (NFHA/MIND 1989), p. 3.

16 A. Wertheimer, *Housing Consortia for Community Care* (NFHA/NCVO 1988)

17 *Caring for People – Community Care in the Next Decade and Beyond*, Department of Health, Cmnd 849 (HMSO 1989).

18 *Community Care in the Next Decade and Beyond: Policy Guidance*, Department of Health (HMSO 1990).

19 *Housing and Community Care* Circular 10/92 (DoE/Department of Health).

20 *Integrating the Housing Agenda into Community Care* Community Care Support Force (Department of Health 1993).

21 *Community Care Housing and Homelessness* Draft Guidance DOE/Department of Health (1995); and see, for example, Lund and Foord, *Towards Independent Living? Housing Strategies and Community Care* (The Policy Press 1997) and *Housing and Community Care, Establishing a Strategic Framework* (Departments of Health and Environment 1997).

22 *An Introduction to Joint Commissioning* (Department of Health 1995).

23 L. Watson and T. Conway, *Homes for Independent Living: Housing and Community Care Strategies* (Chartered Institute of Housing 1995).

24 L. Watson and M. Harker, *Community Care Planning: A Model for Housing Need Assessment with Reference to People with Learning Difficulties* (Institute of Housing/NFHA 1993).

25 L. Watson, *Housing Needs and Community Care: The Housing Pathways Pilot Programme* NFHA/Chartered Institute of Housing 1996).
26 Op. cit., 2.
27 Ibid, p. 14.
28 Ibid, pp. 35–6.
29 S. Goss, *Contracting for Care: A Guide for Housing Associations* (NFHA 1996)
30 M. Harker *et al.*, *Making Connections: Policy and Governance for Community Care* (Special Needs Housing Association Group (NFHA) 1996).
31 Ibid, p. 7.
32 *Housing Choices and Community Care* Findings No.168 (Joseph Rowntree Foundation 1996) by the University of Southampton based on a study by Hudson, Watson and Graham.
33 L. Watson, *High Hopes: Making Housing and Community Care Work* (Joseph Rowntree Foundation 1997).
34 I. Anderson, P. Kemp and D. Quilgars, *Single Homeless People*, DoE (HMSO 1993).
35 G. Randall and S. Brown, *The Rough Sleepers Initiative*, DoE (HMSO 1993).
36 A. Drury, *Street Homelessness – A Way Out, The Housing Association Contribution to the Rough Sleepers Initiative.* (NFHA 1995).
37 *Rough Sleepers Initiative – The Next Challenge* (DoE 1996).
38 G. Randall and S. Brown, *Private Renting for Single Homeless People: An Evaluation of a Pilot Rent Deposit Fund*, DoE (HMSO 1994).
39 *Housing for People with AIDS* Circular 40/87 (The Housing Corporation 1987).
40 *Schemework Procedure Guide 1989* (The Housing Corporation), p. 17.
41 L. Firth, *HIV/AIDS & Housing Services in Newham* (Newham Council and AIDS and Housing Project 1994).
42 S. Bennett, P. Molyneux and C. Yates, *Adding Value – The Role of the HIV Specialist Housing Sector* (AIDS and Housing Project 1996).
43 P. Spicker, *Social Housing and the Social Services* (Longman/ Institute of Housing 1989).
44 Op. cit., 4, p. 373.
45 S. Goldsmith, *Mobility Housing*, HDD Paper 2/74 (HMSO 1974).
46 *General Report 1997* (The Housing Corporation).
47 *Building Homes for Successive Generations* (ACE 1992), p. 4.
48 *Lifetime Homes* (Joseph Rowntree Foundation Lifetime Homes Group, Undated).
49 Clare Wright, *Raising Standards Won't Break the Bank*, Inside Housing, 21 April 1995.
50 *Incorporating Lifetime Homes Standards into Modernisation Programmes*, Findings Housing Research 174 (Joseph Rowntree Foundation April 1996).

9

Meeting the Needs of Older People

Registered Social Landlords have a long tradition of meeting the housing requirements of older people. This chapter examines the scale of the need and the range and nature of the response to it. Three particular aspects of provision are highlighted: the development of specially designed housing, the provision of extra care and the development of home care and home improvement initiatives. The chapter also explores how housing policy in relation to the elderly is changing to reflect demographic trends, people's aspirations and community care legislation.

9.1 The ageing population

Owing to longevity brought about by improved health care, diet and environment, the proportion of people over official retirement age in England and Wales grew from 6 per cent in 1901 to 18.4 per cent in 1991, or nearly one in five of the population. By 2031 this is projected to have reached 26 per cent.[1] In addition, the numbers of older retired people (those over 75 and 85) are also increasing. In 1991 those over 75 accounted for 7.1 per cent of the population; by 2031 they are projected to reach 11 per cent. Those over 85 will also rise reaching 13.5 per cent by 2031.[2] Whilst many people in the under-75 age group largely continue to enjoy good health and mobility, some over 75, although not requiring hospitalisation or full residential care, may need greater support to enable them to remain in independent accommodation, and this has policy implications for housing providers.

Of the older population nearly two-thirds are women and some 3 per cent are from black and minority ethnic communities. The 1991 census also suggests a large increase in the number of black and ethnic minority older people over the next 20 years.

The 1991 ensus found that there were 6.9 million households containing at least one person over retirement age. Of these a growing proportion were living alone. Since 1951, as a percentage of all pensioners, those living alone increased from 14.4 per cent to 45 per cent in 1991. The implication of these trends for both housing and care policies is also substantial. Housing associations and other registered social landlords will not only need to respond to these needs but consider the effect of these demographic changes in relation to the needs of their existing tenants who will also be ageing and may therefore require additional care and support, preferably in their own homes.

Income and affordability

Low income is also common amongst elderly people. Most have to cope on a fixed income, and recent changes to the social security system and housing benefit have hit many pensioners hard. Although the average income has increased as private income has supplemented state retirement pensions, the pattern of growth has been uneven owing to different life opportunities. The average income in 1992 for retired households was £175 compared with a national average of £343. However, two-thirds of retired households had incomes below this level and more than one-quarter had an income of less than £80 per week.[3]

The report *Making Ends Meet*, which examines the affordability of housing association rented housing for older people, notes that (as expected) poorer households live in social housing. About 47 per cent of older households taking up housing association lettings in 1993/94 were in the bottom 20 per cent of the national income distribution, and 90 per cent were in the bottom 40 per cent of the income distribution.[4]

The number of housing association older tenants in receipt of housing benefit increased from 79 per cent in 1989/90 to 84 per cent in 1993/94 reflecting the trend across the sector's households as a whole (as outlined in earlier chapters). In addition, the impact of rising rents on those with marginal incomes who are not in receipt of housing benefit has been particularly severe.[5]

Poor housing conditions

The 1986 English House Condition Survey published in 1988 found that elderly people were more likely to suffer poorer housing conditions than the population as a whole. Of all unfit dwellings, 79 per cent were occupied by households headed by someone of over 60. Of households lacking one or more basic amenities, such as an inside WC or hot water, 84 per cent were headed by a person over 60.

The 1991 House Condition Survey published in 1993 found that in the owner-occupied sector, older households comprised 74 per cent of the lower income band living in the worst housing. Lone older households were also overrepresented in the worst pre-1919 detached and semi-detached houses. In the private sector, 46.3 per cent of lone older households live in the worst housing, especially pre-1919 terraced houses.

In the housing association sector, 8.9 per cent of older households live in the worst housing, in comparison with 6.2 per cent in the local authority sector. Whilst decent housing is a prerequisite for the quality of life at all ages, it could be argued that good housing standards are even more important for older people who may be likely to go out less, perhaps confined through illness or disability.

Ethnic elders

Although ethnic minorities represent just 5.5 per cent of the total population, ethnic minority pensioners are the most disadvantaged group of all elderly people. Currently only 3 per cent of the ethnic minority population is over 65, but it is ageing more quickly than the rest of the population. The housing needs of ethnic elders were first examined in detail some years ago by a working party of Age Concern. In the report *Housing for Ethnic Elders,* it was argued that there was a strong case for the separate provision for ethnic elders on the basis that: 'It is clear that the present generation of ethnic elders often find it difficult to integrate because of language, cultural and other difficulties, including their experiences of prejudice and discrimination.'[6] The report also emphasised that ordinary sheltered housing often ignores the cultural, religious and dietary needs of ethnic elders. Given that housing associations have traditionally operated in the inner city where 90 per cent of ethnic elders live, and their wide experience in responding to special needs, many associations have over recent years attempted to address these needs.

Ethnic elders are, of course, no more homogeneous than the elderly population in general, perhaps even less so, and schemes are required for many different groups. The types of development that are needed encompass the full range outlined in this chapter, from ordinary self-contained flats to extra-care schemes which would cater for the special needs mentioned above. In addition to such special provision, registered social landlords must ensure that people from ethnic minorities in their area have equal access to their housing and that their allocation policies do not discriminate against such groups. These issues were discussed in Chapter 7.

9.2   The scale of provision

Some 642 000 units of subsidised specialist accommodation is provided by approximately 3000 housing providers according to a survey of older people undertaken for the Department of the Environment and published in 1994.[7] It lists four specific types of specialised housing provision for elderly people:

Category 1 accommodation – for the more active elderly, this may provide some common facilities but these are optional

Category 1.5 accommodation – is broadly similar to category 1 housing but must have an alarm system and warden support (no communal facilities are provided)

Category 2 accommodation – sheltered housing, with warden call system and communal facilities such as common room, laundry room and guest room must also be provided

Category 2.5 accommodation – (also known as 'very sheltered', 'extra or extended care', or 'frail elderly' schemes); these schemes offer greater degrees of care and support than category 2 'sheltered' schemes, including assistance with personal care, meals and so on

There are, of course, other forms of housing such as shared housing and group homes, 'granny annexes' and supportive houses, some provided by specialists such as the Abbeyfied Society, (see below). In addition, some registered social landlords have started to provide care services to older people and others with high care needs. Some are developing residential care homes; others have taken over the management of local authority owned residential care homes. In addition, a few specialists also provide nursing care as some local authorities have transferred ownership and or management of these homes to the independent and private sectors. The provision of home care services is examined further in section 9.6 but should be read in the context of community care legislation and its impact upon housing policy and housing associations, as outlined in the previous chapter.

   The DoE survey found that, of the total subsidised provision, over half is in the form of traditional sheltered housing, with just 2 per cent frail elderly accommodation. At a regional level, the North-West region had the largest numbers of subsidised specialist units and the Northern the smallest. The provision of sheltered housing across the country is not uniform either. The survey found that 73 per cent of the specialised stock was provided by local authorities, 23 per cent by housing associations, 1 per cent by Abbeyfield Societies and 3 per cent by the almshouse movement.

9.3   The providers

Some 700 housing associations provide some form of special housing for the elderly. The 1988 National Housing Federation census of housing association tenants found that 34 per cent of households were headed by people over retirement age. Since then, the number of older people housed by housing associations has increased by 18 per cent, although CORE returns show that new letting declined from 30 per cent to about 19 per cent. By 1997 some 165 000 units of self-contained sheltered units were provided by registered social landlords with a further 13 300 shared bed-spaces.[8] There are, however, three groups with particular experience of this work. The first comprises the large specialist, traditional housing associations such as Anchor, Hanover and Housing 21 (formerly the Royal British Legion Housing Association), which have had long experience in providing housing almost exclusively for the elderly and between them account for nearly half the sheltered housing stock.

The almshouse movement

The second group is the almshouse movement, which pioneered housing for the elderly. Although almshouses are legally and administratively distinct from housing associations, they do form an essential part of the voluntary housing movement. Since 986 AD the almshouse movement has grown, and it now comprises over 1700 members owning over 2300 groups of almshouses, accounting for approximately 21 000 dwellings. Most almshouse developments consist of 12–24 dwellings with a courtyard layout, and many have resident wardens. Since 1981, over 18 000 new dwellings have been provided and over 3000 properties rehabilitated. Much of the funding for this work has come through loans and grants from the Housing Corporation as several almshouses originally registered in their own right as housing associations. Other members used the development services of other housing associations. Today, however, several almshouse charities are considering taking advantage of the opportunity to de-register with the Housing Corporation and so ease the administrative and regulatory burden upon themselves.

Abbeyfield

The third distinct group is the Abbeyfield Society. Founded in 1956 in Bermondsey, the Abbeyfield Society now comprises a federation of some 600 local societies providing 1000 houses which by 1995 accommodated 8000 residents. Abbeyfield Societies house seven to nine people in separate bedsitting rooms in family-sized houses. Residents have their own furniture and lead their own lives, but have two meals per day provided by a resident housekeeper. The Society aims to provide: 'a balance of privacy and companionship and of security and independence for elderly people who would otherwise be alone and at risk'. Abbeyfield pioneered the development of extra-care schemes for frail elderly people.

Older people in general may have some housing problems in common. The house may become too large as the family grows up and moves away. The property is often old, in poor repair, difficult to heat and expensive to maintain. Staircases are sometimes a problem. Demand for alternatives increases as the population ages. Despite, however, the apparent similarity of need amongst elderly people, it is essential that a range and variety of alternative housing solutions are offered. Butler, Oldman and Greve put it thus over fifteen years ago: 'Old people are no more homogeneous than the rest of the population. Their characteristics, needs, demands, aspirations and circumstances are multitudinous, reflecting as they do the life experiences and social and genetic inheritances of the millions of human beings who comprise "the elderly".'[9]

This proposition conveys an important message for everyone concerned with the formulation and implementation of housing policies for older people, touching as it does the very heart of the matter: that is, no single form of provision could possibly meet the differing housing needs and demands of this section of the population. The term 'elderly' itself, applied as it is for actuarial convenience to those people over retirement age, is a label which encourages ageism, an attitude that leads to a stereotyped view of older people, suggesting that a particular policy can provide a panacea for the housing problems facing this group. Such a view is patently unacceptable, if only due to the age range concerned. There is no reason to suppose that the housing needs of a frail 90-year-old widow bear much resemblance to those of an active and healthy couple who have just retired. The housing association sector has a long and often pioneering history in providing a range of housing alternatives for older people which reflects the heterogeneity of this group.

It will be noted from the list of housing types highlighted above that housing for older people is characterised by arbitrary categorisation stemming from either the funding regime under which the accommodation was procured or physical design features of the schemes themselves. It is now acknowledged that these divisions are inappropriate and that the response to the housing needs of older people should be the provision of care and support tailored to meet individual requirements. Recent developments in housing policy for older people have concentrated on means of assisting people to stay in their own homes even though they may be becoming more frail or require additional support to do so. Home Improvement Agencies offering Staying Put and Care and Repair schemes, dispersed alarm systems and domiciliary care services are all part of this provision.

Research and lobbying by the National Housing Federation and the major housing providers for this group, particularly the Anchor Trust have led to this more user-centred approach. In 1993 the National Housing Federation published a policy statement, *Rented Housing for Older People*. The policy directions highlighted by this statement were reflected in the Department of the Environment's Survey on the housing needs of older people (1994) and by the Housing Corporation's strategy document, *Housing for Older People*, launched in 1996. In its submission to the Housing Corporation[10] the National Housing Federation emphasised a number of key issues: first, the need to reshape the existing sheltered housing stock to meet extra care needs. Furthermore, evidence has been mounting that there is overprovision in some geographical areas and that the design of a proportion of older sheltered housing is making it difficult to let. The National Housing Federation has argued for the provision of a new single framework for supported housing to replace all the existing categories, together with a portable allowance system based upon people's care needs. These changes would place provision of housing for older peole firmly within the community care framework and reflect both the demographic changes and aspirations of older people. Most people would wish to remain in their own homes, supported by appropriate packages of care. We return to these policy issues later, but first explore both 'sheltered' housing and 'extra care' schemes in a little more detail.

9.4   Specially designed housing

The evolution of scheme design

As we have seen, the most prevalent form of specialist provision is sheltered housing. There has always been some lack of clarity as to the exact definition of sheltered housing. However, the accepted elements are that it is specially designed for older people, includes an alarm system to summon assistance and is served by a resident warden. Sheltered housing dates from 1948, the nomenclature being derived from the Ministry of Health's Housing Manual (1944) which suggested that such schemes should be sited in spots that were 'sheltered from the wind'! Until the 1960s, however, very little sheltered housing was developed, although the English Churches Housing Group, (formerly Church Housing Association), did pioneer 'Churchill Houses' with housemothers or wardens in the 1950s. Then, in 1962, Peter Townsend published *The Last Refuge*,[11] which was essentially a seminal polemic against the institutionalisation of older people resulting from the quality of life in residential homes provided under part III of the National Assistance Act 1948. Standards were reconsidered in the Ministry of Housing and Local Government Circular 82/69, *Housing Standards and Costs, Accommodation Specially Designed for Old People*, which set the original scheme design standards for local authority capital approval and subsidy. It also provided design standards acceptable to the Housing Corporation and the Department of the Environment. The Circular first introduced the two distinct categories of housing for older people; Category 1 and Category 2. The latter was 'to meet the needs of less active elderly people' and consisted of grouped flats leading on to heated, enclosed corridors with the services of a warden and communal rooms to encourage sociability. In practice, this distinction has been difficult to maintain and the circular was withdrawn in England in 1980.

Two-thirds of housing association sheltered units have been completed since 1970 and, of these 60 per cent are one-person dwellings and 38 per cent two-person. Approximately 68 per cent of schemes conform to the standards suggested in Circular 82/69 in that they consist of up to 30 units; the others range from 31 to 50 units. Smaller schemes were recommended as they blend more easily into surrounding housing and avoid the segregation of elderly people from the rest of the community.

Location was and remains a vital design factor. Any scheme should be close to shops, especially post offices for the collection of pensions, and transport facilities should be readily available. The scheme should also have a lively outlook on to scenes of activity where possible. The Circular also set space standards of 33 square metres for one-person bedsits and 48 square metres for two-person, one-bedroom units. The units also incorporated a kitchen, bathroom and storage space. In recent years, however, the rather cramped bedsit, usually a living area with bed recess, has become difficult to let and it is recommended practice that no further bedsit accommodation be provided except in extra-care schemes. The communal facilities which are the hallmark of sheltered schemes were intended to make up for the smaller space within the dwellings. These may include a common sitting room or rooms, a laundry for tenants' use and a guest room for visiting friends and relatives that can be booked by the tenants when required. No less than 76 per cent of housing association schemes contain these facilities. The Housing Corporation Scheme Development Standards 1995 set out current design requirements for all housing for the elderly, including communal facilities.

A survey by the Anchor Trust (formerly Anchor Housing Association)[12] in 1986, updated in 1994, of 100 of its sheltered schemes found the use of their communal rooms to be fairly high. Common rooms, especially the communal lounge, are intended to combat loneliness and isolation by providing social activities for the tenants and to act as a focus for the community to develop. It is recognised, however, that tenants should have the right *not* to participate in social activities if they so wish.

As long ago as 1984 an Age Concern Working Party expressed some concern over the value of communal lounges, particularly given the evidence of their underuse in some schemes. Their location within the scheme, the design of the room, avoidance of an institutionalised atmosphere, and the attitude of the warden or scheme manager are all factors which affect the benefits of such a facility. As the provision of common rooms reduces the overall size of individual flats, Age Concern recommended that providers needed to consider at the outset whether a common room was truly necessary.

The report also argued that tenants must have control over the use of the room and, in particular, given the service charges payable, be consulted if such a facility is to be made available to the local community. On the subject of common rooms it concluded: 'More attention should be paid to the design of such facilities and their presupposed usage at the planning stage – smaller informal areas being preferred to a large communal lounge. As a general principle common areas should not be provided at the expense of loss of living space.'[13]

Alarm systems

A further feature of sheltered schemes is the alarm system which allows tenants to call for assistance in an emergency by alerting the warden; 80 per cent of housing association schemes provide alarms with speech facilities with three or four emergency pull cords usually sited in the bathroom, bedroom and living area. The system is also used by many wardens for routine calls to tenants for daily 'check-ups'. An early survey[14] found that although the alarm call system has always been considered an essential feature of sheltered schemes, the tenants that they interviewed expressed little interest in it and made minimal usage of the system. Indeed, in some flats the pull cord was tied up, rendering the system inoperable. The survey found that 81 per cent of tenants in the sample had not used the alarm system at all in the previous year. The findings correspond with those of the Anchor survey. Seventy-three per cent of Anchor tenants reported that they had never used the call system in an emergency. There is no doubt, however, that the alarm call system does provide an additional sense of security.

The Anchor survey found that the use of the system for daily check-ups was valued by the tenants; 88 per cent of their wardens offer this service and 96 per cent of tenants felt that this was not an intrusion but a necessary precaution. The high level of ownership of telephones was noted in both surveys: 51 per cent of Anchor tenants had telephones, which could make the installation of these expensive systems questionable. It could also be argued that alarm and intercom systems may undermine rather than enhance the independence of older people, and the temptation may be to rely on technology rather than human contact.

The role of the warden or scheme manager

The warden or scheme manager provides an essential service in sheltered housing. It is, however, only in recent years that this role and the pressures faced by staff have been properly recognised. Each organisation has a policy preference in relation to this role. This usually includes providing general support to occupiers, dealing with any emergencies that arise, the administration and care of the building and the encouragement of, though not necessarily the provision of, social activities. These functions may appear straightforward, but staff may often become overburdened. Where tenants have become frail or suffer some long-term illness, or disability, due to lack of outside support from health and social services or relatives, the carers can be drawn into housekeeping or even nursing roles, both of which are inappropriate in non-frail sheltered housing. The problem of increasing frailty of tenants becomes more intense in the long-established schemes. The training needs of wardens and managers were recognised with the launch of a national certificate for wardens by the Chartered Institute of Housing. Most registered social landlords now recognise the importance of providing adequate training and managerial support for these scheme-based staff, as they commonly become the co-ordinators of care and support packages for increasingly frail residents.

Allocation policies

Given the problems facing the warden, the success of a development will depend to a great extent upon achieving a balance in the age and fitness of the tenants. If active, younger residents are included they can assist the warden by becoming involved in supporting their less mobile neighbours. The achievement of such a balance is in turn dependent upon the allocation policy. There is an obvious dilemma: if tenants are fit they do not require sheltered housing, but if they are unfit they may be unsuitable for it. Nevertheless, it is now recognised that allocation policies should be addressed to try to ensure the balance of care needs which the scheme can support.

Tenant satisfaction

The issues raised so far pertain to the design and management of sheltered housing from the viewpoint of the manager. Of equal importance must be the response of the consumers to the accommodation and facilities provided. The early Leeds study recorded a high level of tenant satisfaction with their homes and, despite the managers' concerns with the increasing ill health and frailty of some tenants, the tenants did not find this particularly upsetting or troublesome. A comprehensive survey of housing association tenants' views is given by the Anchor Trust satisfaction reports. Although Anchor is only one of several associations developing sheltered housing, as a major provider its findings must be of interest to those who wish to know the consumers' view and to gain insight into the characteristics of tenants in these schemes. The survey found that the typical Anchor tenant is a widow in her mid to late 70s. Only 10 per cent were aged 85 or over; 80 per cent lived alone; and one-quarter had no surviving child.

A further survey of Anchor applicants found that reasons for their leaving their previous home included the property becoming too large for their needs, stairs becoming a problem or the garden and property too hard to maintain. Personal reasons included general worries over health in 21 per cent of cases, loneliness and desire for company in a further 21 per cent, and fear of burglary affected 13 per cent of applicants.[15]

A very high level of satisfaction was recorded, with 90 per cent of tenants responding that they were pleased or very pleased to have moved into an Anchor scheme. In addition to the tenants' views on the warden and on the common room, the survey revealed two other areas of importance. Nearly 80 per cent of the tenants expressed a desire for a separate bedroom, however, as opposed to the bed-sitting room. Indeed Anchor's policy changed and it has built no further bedsits. More recently, in response to letting difficulties, Anchor like many providers, has also decided to concentrate its resources on high care schemes and home care, developing no further category 2 schemes.

Despite the high degree of tenant satisfaction, the management problems of some schemes remain unresolved. In some cases tenants are becoming too frail to cope in sheltered housing, placing a burden on the warden. The response to this issue has been the development of extra care schemes for frailer older people which are examined further below. Despite the popularity of sheltered housing, much of it has become more difficult to let in recent years according to a study undertaken by Tinker Wright and Zeilig for the Age Concern Institute of Gerontology.[16]

Difficult-to-let sheltered housing

Clearly, difficult-to-let sheltered housing represents a waste of expensive subsidised resources. The research set out to define the problem, assess its scale and to find examples of good practice to deal with such schemes. In defining sheltered housing the research used the same definitions as the Department of the Environment 1994 survey detailed earlier. The survey found that there was a real and widespread problem. In addition to local authorities, 92 per cent of which reported some difficult-to-let property, 79 per cent of large housing associations also experienced difficulties in letting some sheltered housing. Category 2 accommodation was the most difficult to let for a variety of reasons. As expected, bedsits and schemes with shared bathrooms were particulary hard to let. The preferences and aspirations of older people for higher quality accommodation, despite the pressure of being in housing need, had led to their refusing offers of this type of accommodation. Location was also an issue in some cases. Poor access and external environment were items particularly disliked by the tenants of these schemes. As a result several associations were reassessing their category 2 schemes. The strategies adopted had included marketing the schemes, reviewing allocation policies, and changing the use of some schemes if possible. Some were also undertaking refurbishment schemes and considering disposal.

The report was published at a time when the Housing Corporation was consulting upon its older persons strategy, and clearly this study influenced that document. The report had confirmed the high cost of some of these schemes and highlighted limited overprovision in some areas. In addition, it raised a number of key issues for the future. For example, it recommended that the DoE and the Housing Corporation should consider further whether the different funding regimes for specialised housing remained appropriate. It emphasised the need for more small mainstream housing (from which domiciliary care services can be accessed) and very sheltered housing built to higher standards to meet high care needs. Once again the importance of housing as part of any community care strategy was emphasised. The report recommended that each provider develop a strategy to deal with the problem. In the case of future schemes it suggested that no further bedsits should be developed, and that elderly people who often express a preference for non-specialised accommodation should be fully advised as to the the options available to them. The National Housing Federation together with Housing Corporation has published an appraisal guide to assist registered social landlords in considering future options for sheltered schemes.[17]

9.5   High care schemes

Frail elderly, high care or extra-care schemes have developed as a result of a number of factors. Some housing associations became involved in this type of provision because they wished to continue to provide accommodation for tenants who had become too frail to cope with traditional sheltered housing. Some extra-care units have been developed within existing sheltered schemes as part of the process of re-shaping provision discussed above. The development of extra-care schemes also reflects the desire to assist elderly people in maintaining their independence for as long as possible by switching resources from hospitals and residential homes to housing schemes with support services as part of the community care initiative. Extra-care facilities may be provided in conventional sheltered schemes, but specially designed schemes have also been developed. This section concentrates on the latter. The provision of high care schemes by housing associations for older people (and those non-elders with support needs), together with home care services, represents a significant contribution to community care policy which was explored in the previous chapter.

As mentioned earlier, the Abbeyfield Society pioneered the development of extra-care schemes in the mid-1960s. As residents became frailer they found that they could not provide suitable care for them in their conventional supportive houses. Extra-care schemes were therefore developed to try to keep residents under the Abbeyfield umbrella, if possible until they died.

Extra care is required for an older person when, in spite of being relatively healthy and mentally stable, he or she is frail to the extent of requiring assistance with fundamental physical activities. They require help, for instance, in dressing, eating, walking, getting in and out of bed, in bathing and sometimes in going to the lavatory. Sometimes physical frailty is accompanied by incapacitation caused by incontinence, arthritis or asthma, which, although requiring care and comfort, do not necessitate the level of comprehensive medical or nursing attention normally given in a nursing home or geriatric ward.

Housing association schemes for the frail elderly also offer services of a less intimate nature, such as housekeeping and personal affairs, which might include assistance with shopping, medication, orientation, transport and laundry. Most schemes for the frail elderly managed by housing associations provide some degree of personal care which is defined in the Registered Homes Act 1984 as 'assistance with bodily functions'. High care schemes are therefore a housing provision, but with the addition of personal care. Schemes are funded through the same framework as outlined in Chapters 6 and 8, although several registered social landlords have developed schemes with health authorities and other purchasers outside the Housing Corporation funding framework. As a result, the role of the Housing Corporation as funder and regulator has become less fundamental for those RSLs concerned with meeting community care needs.

Standards

A Better Home Life, discussed in the previous chapter,[18] sets out the standards required of a provider's management of all residential and nursing home schemes. Essentially a code which sets out the principles of good practice in such schemes, it details how those principles can be put into practice. The Code is concerned with the dignity, rights and respect afforded to the residents and is also used by local authorities as a guide when considering registration under the Registered Homes Act 1984. Staffing is intensive in comparison with sheltered housing schemes; each scheme will usually have a manager and deputy, kitchen and domestic staff and care assistants, and a package of care will be agreed with the resident and the commissioning service.

The Housing Corporation Scheme Development Standards (1995) set out the design criteria for these schemes. Units may be self-contained or shared, although the latter are discouraged, and the full range of communal facilities is included. Many high care schemes are now registered care homes with the additional regulation and standards that this status implies. As the population ages, even if the number people in residential care remains static, there will be a massive need for a further residential places.

The costs of providing care for people in old age and how to meet them is one of the most important issues of social policy facing society as we move into the twenty-first century. At the time of writing some institutions were beginning to address this issue. For example, in 1996 the Joseph Rowntree Foundation called for free care in old age backed by compulsory care insurance.[19] Whatever the final shape of the funding framework, the sector will provide much of the care required, although the costs of providing high quality, low-density schemes may make it more difficult for them to compete with the private sector, as discussed in the previous chapter.

9.6   Home care

The report, *People First*, highlighted the extent to which housing associations are now providing community care services: they offer peripatetic personal services to more than 32 500 people.[20] Community care facilities such as alarm systems, care and repair and advocacy provided by registered social landlords are delivered to over 290 000 people.[21] The 1994 DoE survey[22] found that two out of three elderly households have no need for any form of subsidised, specialised housing and that, of those that do have a need, 70 per cent would prefer to remain in the house they currently occupy with the assistance of aids and adaptations and/or domiciliary care and support. The survey also found that at all levels of dependency the staying at home option for an older person is considerably cheaper than a move to specialised accommodation.[23] The picture, however, changes dramatically for high dependency needs. Although the figures are to be treated with caution, in these cases the costs of putting together care packages for people with high care needs in their own home is considered likely to be much more expensive than residential care. As a result, in the longer term, although domiciliary care is central to community care philosophy, a peverse incentive to continue to develop residential care for these groups exists.

Home improvement agencies

In order to remain coping at home many older home, owners will require a range of assistance. A further study by the Anchor Trust examines in detail the future of home ownership in an ageing society.[24] As we have seen, although many people may wish to stay put, large numbers of pensioners face poor housing conditions and this may be compounded by lack of income, or savings, to put the property right. In addition, some elderly people will require advice and assistance if they are to embark on works of improvement or repair to their homes. Two particular initiatives have been developed to assist in such cases, the most notable being the 'Staying Put' project devised by Anchor Housing Trust and 'Care and Repair' schemes originally sponsored by Shelter and the Housing Associations Charitable Trust (HACT). Both are now operated through Home Improvement Agencies (HIAs) of which there are now some 200 across the country.

Staying Put

The Anchor Trust set up a pilot project in 1978 to help elderly owners with repairs and improvements to their properties, and the resultant report published in 1980 coined the phrase 'staying put'. Since then the service has grown, with teams now operating throughout the country. There were three main components to Anchor's Staying Put scheme based upon the problems faced by elderly home owners revealed by the pilot project: first, a full counselling service which assists individuals to decide upon the solution which meets their own particular requirements; second, the scheme offers financial advice and assistance. An important feature of the project has been the involvement of building societies. Although some owners obtain financial help from local authorities through house renovation grants, many people do not have the means to finance the proportion of costs that are not grant-aided. The societies have offered interest only loans with the principal repayable on the sale or inheritance of the house. The final component is assistance with the work itself. The project worker will provide advice on what improvements, repairs or adaptations are needed, often in conjunction with other support services such as occupational therapists; help will also be given with any form-filling required for grant aid, and with planning, organising and supervising the works. Through these three elements the project attempts to overcome the major obstacles facing elderly owners who wish to remain in their current home.

Care and Repair

Also assisting older people to remain in their own homes are 'Care and Repair' schemes. The first of these projects, the Ferndale Home

Improvements Service, was set up in 1979 by Shelter and Help the Aged Housing Trust in the Rhondda Valley. The works carried out under this initiative were initially less substantial than those that typified Anchor's projects. The principal objective of the scheme is to help elderly owners who may have neither the resources nor the desire to carry out the major works often entailed by applications for house renovation grants. Eventually, Care and Repair Ltd was established in 1986 in partnership with Anchor as a national co-ordinating body for care and repair projects. It set a target of establishing an Home Improvement Agency (HIA) in every local authority area. By 1990, 76 agencies had been established and, as stated, by 1996 (as it celebrated its tenth anniversary) there were 200 HIAs, two-thirds of which receive funding from the Department of the Environment. HIAs now spend £38 million on repairs to enable people to remain in their own homes. They have been able to lever in £1 million of private finance for every £1 million of public money received. Home Improvement Agency Grants would become part of the *Supporting People* grant if the proposals outlined in chapter 7 are implemented.

Home-care services

A number of registered social landlords, as we have seen, now provide domiciliary care services for their own tenants and tender for contracts to provide home care for purchasing authorities. This is a relatively new area of operation but it is a growing market. In 1988 some 488 000 people were in receipt of home care services, including 157 per 1000 people aged 75 or over; by 1991 this had increased to 626 000, or 187 per 1000 people aged 75 or over. Provision of these services has barely kept pace with the expanding need.[25]

Although, once again, RSLs cannot compete with the private sector in terms of price for large-scale general services without major internal investment, they can provide a 'niche' response. Innovative responses include peripatetic care schemes such as the extra care team at Hyde Housing Association in London which provides additional short-term personal care to residents in sheltered schemes in a number of London boroughs.

Dispersed alarm systems

Many landlords are now taking advantage of new technology to provide dispersed alarm systems for their older tenants, and in some cases for tenants of the private sector and owner-occupiers. The nature of these systems has been well documented elsewhere but it may be useful to note here the essential elements. The main feature is a central control unit, staffed on a 24-hour basis, which can be linked to either a sheltered housing scheme or an isolated home by means of radio communication or the telephone network. The system may offer a speech or non-speech facility. In an emergency the operator may be contacted by activating a push button on the radio or dialler itself, by tugging pull-cords which are installed around the dwelling or by remote triggering devices which can take the form of wriststraps or pendants worn around the neck. Once an alarm call is received, the central control will alert relatives or emergency services or, if this facility is offered, contact a mobile warden who can attend to the call immediately.

Dispersed alarm systems are also used to link up sheltered schemes with central control to provide relief cover for the manager of sheltered housing schemes.

9.7   Policy and strategy for the future

We have seen that there has been a rapid increase in the proportion of older people within the population as a whole, and this trend will continue. Large numbers of pensioners endure inadequate and sometimes intolerable housing conditions. However, no single form of housing provision can offer the perfect solution in meeting the diverse needs of this heterogeneous group. A variety of options must be offered, which will allow older people choice in what may be their last home.

The National Housing Federation launched a policy statement in 1993 which formed the basis for its 1995 response to the Housing Corporation's consultation paper, *Housing for Older People*, published in November 1995. The National Housing Federation's strategy is based on a vision for the future achieved through a combination of three means:

(a)   accessible housing with specific features that make it particularly suitable for older people based upon clusters of homes built to lifetime homes criteria or similar standards;

(b)   Flexible housing support: a range of housing management services which would allow an older person to maximise their independence, funded through a revised revenue grant allowance that would be portable, and attach to the person not the property; it could therefore be provided to older people regardless of their accommodation;

(c)   supported housing for people who can no longer live on their own and which provides a higher level of housing management and support which would replace the current categorisations and enable the full range of support to be given, if necessary up to 24-hour care. This would be achieved through new building and adaptation of existing stock.

The National Housing Federation has also repeated calls for the Departments of Health and Environment to work together and with social services authorities to fully resource the needs of older people.

Most of these issues were incorporated into the Housing Corporation's 1995 consultation paper. The final policy document, *Housing for Older People*, was launched by the Housing Corporation in March 1996. It confirmed that each local authority housing strategy should identify the needs of older people, including those from ethnic minorities, before funding for additional schemes would be considered. Although it stopped short of abandoning the old scheme categorisations it has confirmed that strategies should cover the whole range of housing and care packages available. The Housing Corporation also expects the support of health and social service authorities before agreeing to fund any new schemes. Resources for a change of use of scheme or for improvement will also depend upon a proper local needs assessment. The Corporation's policy sets housing firmly within a community care framework and also calls for an integrated and and co-ordinated approach to meeting older people's housing and care needs. It recognises that housing, support services and care form a continuum, and that artificial divisions created by funding regimes can reduce the effectiveness of delivery on the ground. The strategy document represents an important development in housing policy for older people and has a number of implications for registered social landlords. The DSS paper *Supporting People* addresses a number of these issues too.

Demographic changes, the advent of community care and clear policy direction from the Housing Corporation mean that RSLs must review their strategies for assisting older people. This includes assessing the needs of older tenants in general needs accommodation, in addition to those in specialist schemes. Landlords may wish to take adavantage of aids and adaptation funding from the Corporation, as outlined in Chapter 6, to provide aids to independent living such as stairlifts and grabrails. The role of the warden may need to be reconsidered, especially where tenants are ageing. Some landlords will need to consider providing more intensive housing management services for older tenants, and both the organisation and the funding of such services needs to be planned.

Registered social landlords will also need to ensure that their tenants can access the care packages that they require and some may wish to provide this care directly. As we have seen, some organisations may also need to appraise existing sheltered housing schemes to assess whether they need to be refurbished or reshaped.

Allocation policies and marketing may need to be changed and the scheme upgraded or a change of use considered. The availability of (and access to) additional care and support services for all tenants will need to be evaluated, and some RSLs may wish to consider whether sheltered schemes could become centres of care for older people living in the community. If a scheme needs upgrading, or if there is overprovision then the use of a scheme can be changed: for example, a scheme can be downgraded to provide accommodation for older people with lower support needs, or provide for a different needs group. In the case of higher dependency, some additional high care units could replace some sheltered ones. The scheme could be sold or transferred to another landlord. Whatever solutions are decided upon, clearly they should be agreed with the local housing and social service authorities.

Registered social landlords are essential providers of housing for older people. Their contribution must be measured not only by the amount and quality of the housing that they provide but also in terms of the pioneering work of the sector in this field, from the original contribution of the almshouses to the high care schemes of today. Changes in society, such as increased labour mobility and more women at work, mean that many more people will face old age alone, often without the support of close relatives. We all expect to become old eventually, and the policies that are pursued now will become the realities for many of us in the future.

References

1 S. Rolfe, S. Mackintosh and P. Leather, *Age File '93* (Anchor Housing Trust 1993).
2 Ibid, p. 12.
3 Ibid, p. 56.
4 A. Marsh and M. Riseborough, *Making Ends Meet – Older People, Housing Association Costs and the Affordability of Rented Housing* (NFHA 1995).
5 Ibid, p. 41.
6 *Housing for Ethnic Elders* (Age Concern 1984).
7 P. McCafferty, *Living Independently – A Study of the Housing Needs of Elderly and Disabled People*, DoE (HMSO 1994).
8 *Registered Social Landlords in 1997 – General Report* (The Housing Corporation 1998).
9 A. Butler, C. Oldman and J. Greve, *Sheltered Housing for the Elderly: Policy, Practice and the Consumer* (Allen & Unwin 1983), p. 162.
10 *A Strategy for Housing Older People – A Policy Response* (NFHA 1995).
11 P. Townsend, *The Last Refuge* (Routledge & Kegan Paul).
12 *Tenants' Survey Report* (Anchor 1986 and 1994).
13 *Sheltered Housing for Older People* (Age Concern 1984) p. 14.
14 Op. cit., 9, p. 202.
15 P. Niner and M. Riseborough, *Who Wants Sheltered Housing? The Findings of a Survey of Applicants for Anchor Sheltered Housing* (Anchor Housing Trust 1994).
16 A. Tinker, F. Wright and H. Zeilig, *Difficult to Let Sheltered Housing*, The Age Concern Institute of Gerontology (HMSO 1995).
17 *Appraisal Guide for Sheltered Housing* (NHF/1996).

18 *A Better Home Life: A Code of Practice for Residential and Nursing Home Care* (Centre for Policy on Ageing 1996).
19 *Inquiry into Meeting the Costs of Continuing Care* (Joseph Rowntree Foundation 1996).
20 L. Potter and T. Roose, *People First – Housing Associations Caring in the Community* (NFHA 1995), p. 14.
21 Ibid.
22 Op. cit., 7.
23 Ibid, p. 76.
24 R. Forrest, P. Leather and C. Pantazis, *Home Ownership in Old Age – The Future of Owner-Occupation in an Ageing Society* (The Anchor Trust 1997)
25 Op. cit., 1, p. 49.

10
Housing for Sale

So far we have concentrated on the provision of housing for rent. Since 1980, however, housing for sale has become an important activity for some registered social landlords. Although some organisations had been under-taking sales initiatives to assist low-income first-time buyers prior to the advent of the Conservative administration in 1979, most did not become involved in these initiatives until the passage of the Housing Act 1980. That Act, which led to a radical change in the direction of housing policy, was the first vehicle through which the Conservative Government (1979–97) would pursue its ideological commitment to mass home owner-ship. The right to buy (and other low-cost home-ownership initiatives which were launched as a result) has been well documented and subjected to substantial evaluation elsewhere. This chapter is therefore confined to a review of the nature of these initiatives as they apply to housing associ-ations and to the sector's contribution to home-ownership policies.

10.1 The range of initiatives

Registered social landlords provide low-cost home-ownership through a range of initiatives:

(a) conventional shared ownership;
(b) shared ownership for the elderly;
(c) improvement for outright sale;
(d) Do It Yourself Shared Ownership (DIYSO) (to be replaced by Homebuy with effect from April 1999);
(e) Tenants' Incentive Scheme (TIS) (to be replaced by Homebuy with effect from April 1999);
(f) Voluntary Purchase Grant (VPG).

In addition, all schemes developed to rent with Social Housing Grant after April 1997, unless exempt, are also subject to the right to acquire.

Expenditure on these activities through the Housing Corporation's Approved Development Programme has expanded substantially throughout

Table 10.1   The Housing Corporation's ADP 1980–2000: low-cost home ownership (England only, excluding right to buy)

Year	£m
1980–81	30
1983–84	129
1988–89	124
1996/97	233
1997/8	157
1998/9	153
1999/00[i].	150

Source: The Housing Corporation.
i. Forecast/outturn

Table 10.2   Number of homes sold or ready for sale 1991–97 (Housing Corporation Funding, excluding wholly private funded schemes, England only)

	Improvement for sale	LSE	Shared Ownership	DIYSO	Total
1991/92	310	1 327	3 175	170	4 982
1992/93	412	1 177	4 403	198	7 976
1993/94	193	1 127	6 068	5 325	12 713
1994/95	86	968	6 159	5 877	13 090
1995/96	66	774	7 110	4 844	12 794
1996/97	92	649	5 838	2 487	9 066
Total					*60 621*

LSE = Leasehold Schemes for the Elderly
Source: The Housing Corporation.

the last two decades, peaking in 1996/97 as highlighted in Table 10.1. Table 10.2 shows that over 60 000 homes have been provided by associations in England since 1991, bringing the total of low-cost home ownership homes owned or managed to over 81 000.

The objectives of the home ownership programme

In its 1996/97 National Policy Statement the Housing Corporation set out the objectives of the home ownership programmes:

(a)   to release rented accommodation;
(b)   to help people into owner-occupation who could not otherwise afford it;

(c) to contribute to regeneration;
(d) to contribute to the creation of mixed communities.

In order to better achieve these objectives the Corporation introduced flexibility at regional level in distributing the sales programme between incentive schemes, new build and rehabilitation, shared ownership, DIYSO and improvement for outright sale. It is to be allocated in accordance with locally agreed needs and market demand rather than predetermined programme balances. This change reflected the success of the programmes in different parts of the country. Conventional shared ownership, for example, was selling well in London and the South-East, whereas demand for it in parts of northern England became limited owing to the lower costs of outright purchase. Sales initiatives clearly have an important role to play in the regeneration of urban areas. Mixed tenure schemes, which may also incorporate homes for outright sale (often built by a developer partner) can help to attract more economically active households back into an area and encourage others who might consider moving out of the area to stay if ownership is an option.

The 1998/99 Policy Statement re-emphasised the role of these initiatives in releasing, or reducing, demand for social rented housing in areas where demand for it is high. Sales are targeted at existing tenants of local authorities and housing associations. Priority is also given to households drawn from local authority or housing association waiting lists in addition to other applicants who cannot afford suitable accommodation without subsidy.

The commitment to increasing home ownership was embodied in the Housing Act 1996 which enables tenants of charitable housing associations and assured tenants to purchase their existing home. Introduced initially with effect from 1 April 1996 on a voluntary basis as Voluntary Purchase Grant, the Act introduced a mandatory scheme, the Right to Acquire, whereby tenants of schemes developed with Social Housing Grant after 1 April 1997 would have the right to purchase their home subject to certain criteria and the availability of funds to support the discount scheme. The details of Voluntary Purchase Grant and the Right to Acquire are discussed further in section 10.4.

There are a number of different housing for sale programmes and each is briefly defined below in order to illustrate the variety of initiatives in place. Most are a variant of conventional shared ownership.

Shared ownership

Shared ownership schemes may be provided through new building or rehabilitation of existing properties. Shared ownership is so-called as the landlord and the purchaser both own equity in the property. The landlord holds the freehold of the property. The purchaser buys a proportion of the equity or value of the property, usually 25, 50 or 75 per cent, 50 per cent being the most usual, on a leasehold basis and may purchase further tranches as his or her income increases. This process, known as 'staircasing', may continue until the purchaser becomes the outright owner. The landlord receives grant on the unsold equity and the purchaser pays a subsidised rent on the outstanding amount of equity, which remains in the ownership of the RSL.

It should be noted, however, that some schemes (particularly in the South-East) are progressing without any grant assistance, provided that there is some other form of subsidy, such as reduced land value. Nearly 2000 homes had been added to the stock using only private finance between 1992 and 1997.[1] Schemes which are developed in rural locations may be part of the Corporation's programme to provide affordable housing in these areas, and there may be limits on staircasing and restrictions on re-sale to ensure that the property remains available for the intended client groups. Shared ownership schemes may also be developed on a self-build basis, where the cost to the leaseholders is reduced by the value of the 'sweat equity' they provide through their own labour.

Do-It-Youself Shared Ownership

In 1992 the Housing Corporation re-launched DIYSO which enables a purchaser to choose a property on the open market to be purchased by the association on their behalf, subject to the usual approval criteria. The DIYSO purchaser then buys the proposed portion of equity and the remainder is owned by the RSL in the same way as conventional shared ownership. As stated, from April 1999 DIYSO will be replaced by Homebuy. Although a two year extension to 2001 on local authority funded DIYSO has been granted.

Shared Ownership for the Elderly

Shared Ownership for the Elderly provides sheltered housing on a long lease for older people, defined as 55 years or older. Until 1988 the purchaser acquired 70 per cent of the value of the property outright, with Housing Association Grant meeting the remaining 30 per cent; this system was known as Leasehold Schemes for the Elderly. Since 1988, however, schemes for the elderly have been provided on a shared ownership basis too. At the time of writing new models were being explored in the form of equity release schemes which will assist older home-owners whose homes are in poor condition. This initiative is explored further later in this chapter.

The aim of the Government in encouraging these initiatives was to increase the supply of low-cost homes and to reduce the entry costs to low-income buyers. Improvement for sale has the additional objective of renovating the older housing stock.

Improvement for Outright Sale

Rehabiliation for Outright Sale involves the purchase and rehabilitation and/or conversion of an older property, with the payment of grant to cover the difference between the sale value of the property and the excess costs of acquisition and works.

Shared ownership and charitable housing associations

As outlined in Chapter 2, until 1994 it was unclear whether, apart from Leasehold Schemes for the Elderly, charitable associations could undertake sale activities. Thus many charitable associations set up non-charitable subsidiaries in order to pursue them. In April 1994 the Charities Commission published their long-awaited guidance on this issue, which was of importance to those charitable associations which had been undertaking sale activities on the basis that it was a proper activity for a charitable organisation. The guidance encapsulated in Housing Corporation Circular 29/94, *Charitable Housing Associations and Shared Ownership*, sets out the circumstances in which charitable housing associations may legally provide housing through shared ownership and DIYSO. Broadly, shared ownership activities and DIYSO are permitted provided that the schemes are incidental to a rental scheme, or the majority of the lessees are proper beneficiaries owing to age, infirmity or relative poverty.

As a result RSLs were advised to define their views on what consitutes poverty and to develop guidelines on permissible applicants for shared ownership schemes and to monitor changes in personal circumstances. As a result of this advice some charitable landlords are now undertaking sale activities, and others have wound down their non-charitable subsidiaries. Many charitable associations have, however, chosen to retain their shared ownership subsidiaries rather than bring the function into the parent body as the separation of activities has worked extremely well in many cases, and in others there is a wish to retain access to the more flexible powers of a non-charitable vehicle.

10.2   The right to buy

The right to buy, introduced by the Housing Act 1980, has had a more limited impact upon housing associations than local authorities as the right is only conferred upon *secure* tenants of *non-charitable* housing associations, and then only if the property they are living in has received grant. During the debate over the Housing Bill 1980, the movement lobbied successfully (largely through the House of Lords) for the exclusion from the right to buy provisions of tenants of associations with charitable status, arguing that the sale of homes provided by them would be contrary to their objects and seriously undermine their contribution to meeting housing needs. It was also argued that voluntary and independent bodies should not be forced to sell their stock.

Several amendments have been made to the original scheme, including the extension of the right to include purpose-built and adapted homes for those with physical disability. Amendments introduced by the Housing and Building Control Act 1984 and the Housing and Planning Act 1986 made the scheme more generous in order to encourage more secure tenants to take advantage of it. The 1984 Act also introduced a scheme of 'transferable' or 'portable' discounts for tenants of charitable housing associations which was eventually replaced by the Tenants Incentive Scheme (discussed further below). The Leasehold Reform, Housing and Urban Development Act 1993 introduced further changes to the right to buy, including the abolition under section 11 of the right to a mortgage, the right to defer completion and the right to a shared ownership lease where applications to buy are made after 11 October 1993. This Act also introduced the Rent to Mortgage scheme discussed below.

The current framework of the right to buy includes eligibility for the scheme after two years' tenancy of a public sector dwelling. There is a generous system of discounts on the sale price of the dwellings, ranging from 32 per cent to 60 per cent, rising by 1 per cent per annum for each year of tenancy for houses and from 44 per cent to 70 per cent rising at 2 per cent per annum for flats. Thus tenants of flats can reach the maximum discount level within 15 rather than 30 years of tenancy. The maximum discount is currently £50 000 on both houses and flats. Secure tenants of properties that have been transferred to a registered social landlord from a local authority (see Chapter 2) also benefit from the 'preserved right to buy'. If tenants subsequently sell the property they have purchased within three years then the discount is repayable on a sliding scale, reducing from full repayment to one-third after three years. Thereafter there are no repayment provisions. In addition to generous discounts, tenants with the right to buy also enjoyed the right to a mortgage subject to income status, until this was withdrawn in 1993.

By virtue of the Housing (Service Charge Loans) Regulations 1992, however, most long leaseholders of flats purchased under the right to buy had the right to a loan for service charges in respect of repairs during the first ten years after the grant of the lease. In 1997 further Directions were issued by the Government which gave social landlords the discretion to waive or reduce leaseholders' service charges in certain circumstances. The aim of the Direction was to assist some leaseholders who had been experiencing difficulty in meeting service charge costs which had rock-eted, particularly in relation to works costs, causing both hardship and controversy, as it was argued that few leaseholders realised the future extent of their liabilities when exercising their right to buy in the boom years.

It should be noted that discounts are subject to 'cost floor' limits. Until 1988 the cost floor prevented sale of the properties developed since 31 March 1974 at discounts which reduced the price to below those costs expended by the landlord on buying, improving or building the dwelling, provided that a minimum of £5000 had been expended. The cost floor rule protects investment by the landlord and ensures that the organisation is not left with outstanding loans which cannot be repaid. The Housing Act 1988 altered the cost floor rule which now only applies to expendi-ture incurred during the eight years prior to the tenant making an applica-tion. The Act also introduced what is known as the 'preserved' right to buy. This protects the secure tenant's right to buy if he or she transfers to a development let on an assured tenancy managed by the same landlord. This has posed a financial problem for landlords if they are faced with the sale of a newly developed property as, if the tenant is entitled to a large discount, as a result of the cost floor rules landlords may find that receipts cover as little as half the value of the property.

In 1998 the cost floor rules for both the right to buy and the preserved right to buy were under consideration. The proposals would extend eligi-ble repair costs to a period of ten years and raise the value to £7500. The raising of the cost floor, if implemented, could leave some landlords in the position of having to sell a property at a loss.

Some 19 000 housing association homes were sold through the right to buy between 1980 and 1989. Sales reached their highest level in 1988/89 and have since declined. Some 2-3000 homes have been sold in the sector each year since then. These levels are minimal when compared with the sales of local authority housing, which amount to over one and a half million since 1980.

Rent to mortgage

In July 1992 the Department of the Environment issued a consultation paper on rents to mortages in order to attempt to extend the right to buy even further amongst secure tenants. The scheme was introduced by the Leasehold Reform, Housing and Urban Development Act 1993. Procedural details are given in Housing Corporation circulars 40/93 and 23/96.[2]

Under the scheme secure tenants of non-charitable housing associations of two years' standing may purchase a share of the value of their house or flat that is the equivalent of the value of a mortgage that their rent will support. The maximum proportion that can be purchased is 80 per cent. Exclusions include tenants with the preserved right to buy and tenants entitled to housing benefit in the period up to 12 months before they claim the right. The purchasers are entitled to discounts at the same percentage levels as right to buy, but the discount is based on the proportion of the value being purchased rather than the full value of the property. This sounds rather like conventional shared ownership, but it differs in that the owner does not pay rent on the unpurchased portion of their home. The association's charge on the house must be redeemed on sale or within one year of the death of the purchaser unless there is a successor. In this case, successors are encouraged to buy out the association's interest in the property with further discounts of up to 20 per cent available on the charge if redeemed within one year. The introduction of the scheme was opposed by the National Housing Federation on the basis that it could undermine lender confidence in non-charitable housing associations which would lose both assets and income streams as a result. Since its introduction, however, few tenants have exercised this right.

10.3   Homebuy and the Tenants' Incentive Scheme

In 1998 the Government announced its intention to replace both DIYSO and TIS with a programme known as Homebuy. Homebuy will only be available in areas where there is a shortage of social housing. Under Homebuy qualifying tenants would receive interest-free equity loans funded by Social Housing Grant to meet 25 per cent of the cost of the home. Eligibility criteria and cost limits will be similar to DIYSO. 75 per cent of the cost of the property must be met by a mortgage raised by the buyer. This will mean that 25 per cent and 50 per cent tranches may no longer be purchased which in turn makes Homebuy less helpful to first-time buyers than DIYSO.

The Tenants' Incentive Scheme (TIS) was introduced in 1990 and the arrangements are outlined in the Housing Corporation's Tenants' Incentive Scheme Procedure Guide and in circular F2 07/97.[3] The scheme replaced the Home Ownership scheme for Tenants Of Charitable Housing Associations (HOTCHA) and covered both tenants of charitable housing associations and assured tenants who were, of course, excluded from the right to buy. HOTCHA was introduced by the Housing and Building Control Act 1984 to enable certain tenants of charitable housing associations to take advantage of a discount scheme. In this case the discount was used to purchase a house on the open market rather than the tenant's own home.

The aim of TIS was to widen opportunities for home ownership, thus releasing housing for rent for those who need it. It was based upon similar schemes operated by some local authorities and pioneered by the London Borough of Bromley.

The equivalent schemes of portable discounts in the local authority sector are known as Cash Incentive Schemes (CIS). The TIS scheme enabled cash incentives to be paid to tenants to assist in their purchase of a property on the open market.

RSLs bid for grant from the Housing Corporation to support the scheme. If a purchaser subsequently sold their property the cash incentive had to be repaid in full in year one, reducing to one-third after three years. Eligibility was subject only to two years' tenancy, which need not be continuous. In preparing its scheme an RSL took into consideration certain target groups of tenants. It also reviewed its stock and the demands made upon it. Each landlord also consulted with the local authority when preparing bids. For 1997/98 the cash payments varied from £16 000 in TCI area A (Inner London) to £9000 in TCI area E. Until 1996 the sole objective of the scheme was to house statutorily homeless households in dwellings vacated by recipients of a TIS payment. This requirement, which was intended to ensure that homelessness was assisted by the scheme and contributed to broader objectives in relation to the allocation of social housing, was removed with effect from 1 April 1996. To improve the targeting of the scheme, purchase price limits were also imposed. For 1997/98 the limits were in two tiers: homes up to and including two bedrooms and homes with more than two bedrooms. Purchase price limits varied from £82 600 and £100 200 in TCI area A to £50 000 and £58 900 in TCI area E. The application of these limits in relation to household size and bedroom requirements was carefully scrutinised by the Housing Corporation. TIS payments have also been available since April 1996 to purchase 'Park Homes'. These are new homes which conform to certain British Standards and which enjoy a ten-year structural warranty with permanent planning permission on a 'protected site' under the Mobile Homes Act 1983. Landlords operating a scheme entered into a programme agreement with the Housing Corporation (see Chapter 6). TIS was, of course, cash limited, unlike the right to buy, and a landlord's ability to assist its tenants to become owners through the scheme was limited by the money allocated to it each year through the capital allocations process.

Evaluation of the Tenants' Incentive Scheme

Research undertaken for the Department of the Environment and published in 1995[4] found that between 1991 and 1994 no fewer than 14 150 properties were released through the scheme at a cost of £174 million and an average purchase price of £58 000. The research found that the scheme was successful in meeting the then Government's twin aims of assisting tenants to achieve owner-occupation and to release vacant properties to house homeless families. Around 80 per cent of purchasers said that they could not have managed to buy without the assistance of the TIS payment. There was a high degree of satisfaction with their new homes, with only 6 per cent of purchasers regretting their move. Both the Housing Corporation and four-fifths of those associations operating the scheme also felt that it had been successful. TIS has been most successful in London and the Home Counties with demand outstripping supply, as might be expected. In lower cost areas, the supply of TIS cash has out-stripped demand. In order to reduce the demands on TIS several associations have continued to exclude one-bedroomed properties from the scheme even though officially this rule has now been relaxed. The research found that most households had children under the age of 16 and in childless households the age profile was young with few heads of household over 60 years. One-third of TIS recipients were from the ethnic minority communities. Virtually all household heads were in employ-ment (as would be expected) and the average gross household income nationally was £18 500 per annum.

On a number of occasions the Conservative administration had failed to extend the right to buy to tenants of charitable associations and to assured tenants. TIS represented a means of extending home-ownership opportu-nities to these groups and, as we have seen, has been successfully oper-ated and valued by those associations who implemented it. From 1989 the opposition to home ownership initiatives, once so vehemently expressed by many in the sector, diminished. This was partly in recognition of the success and popularity of the sales initiatives with tenants but also in recognition of the importance of developing mixed and balanced commu-nities. Home-ownership initiatives can be used to develop mixed tenure estates (although TIS is the one initiative that works against this objec-tive). Furthermore, in recent years the Labour Party also expressed posi-tive support for the right to buy and other sale activities, and it has continued to support these initiatives since coming to power in 1997, replacing TIS and DIYSO (as stated at the outset) with Homebuy.

Voluntary Purchase Grant

Voluntary Purchase Grant enables eligible tenants of RSLs to purchase their current home or, in some circumstances, another property owned by their landlord, rather than a home on the open market. A separate consul-tation paper on Voluntary Purchase Grant was published in 1995 although it was linked to the Conservative Government's White Paper, *Our Future Homes.*[5] Voluntary Purchase Grant is based more closely on the principles of TIS than the right to buy. It is cash limited, allocated on a first come, first served basis, and there are fixed grant limits (as opposed to discounts) based upon the value of the house. While the scheme was to be introduced on a voluntary basis, the Government expressed confidence that housing associations 'will wish to participate in the Voluntary Purchase Grant Scheme: tenants buying their homes help to build balanced and strong communities'. The consultation paper confirmed that the intention was therefore to introduce a statutory or mandatory grant making it a condition of all future development grant funding that associations commit themselves to tenants being able to purchase these new houses and flats.

Voluntary Purchase Grant (VPG) was designed to complement TIS. As a result of submissions made by the National Housing Federation and individual associations, the final proposals as set out in the Housing Act 1996 were more acceptable to the sector than the original consultation proposals. A number of significant exclusions were achieved during the passage of the Act, especially in relation to rural housing, special needs accommodation, homes awaiting major refurbishment and subject to section 106 agreements. In addition, some amendments were also made to the financial and administrative requirements of the scheme.

The operation of VPG is set out in Housing Corporation Circular F2 06/96, *Voluntary Purchase Grant and Voluntary Purchase Grant Scheme Procedures (1996)*. Since 1 April 1996 (prior to the passage of the Housing Act 1996) registered housing associations have been able to offer grants to eligible tenants to assist in the purchase of the home they occupy. It is a condition of the grant that the total proceeds from the sale after the deduction of outstanding loans and sale expenses be held in a ring-fenced account to enable the association to provide replacement properties. In this respect VPG differs significantly from the right to buy where receipts were repaid to the Housing Corporation and recycled through the Approved Development Programme.

All secure and assured tenants of registered social landlords who occupy self-contained accommodation are eligible for the scheme. Two years' tenancy is required but this need not be continuous. Where demand exceeds supply a waiting list should be established with priority decided by date order.

Eligible properties

Within each local authority area where a landlord has an allocation, all properties let as a separate dwelling are eligible for the scheme. Exclusions are as for the right to buy and include:

(a) homes which are not self-contained;
(b) sheltered housing for the elderly, the physically disabled, the mentally ill and mentally disabled;
(c) homes which are particularly suitable for elderly people and are let to or lived in by a person aged 60 or more;

(d)   tied accommodation occupied because the tenant is employed by the association;
(e)   homes leased temporarily from another landlord;
(f)   homes in rural settlements of fewer than 3000 people.

In addition, the RSL may decide to exclude further properties, such as:

(a)   homes where the current value is less than the cost of provision;
(b)   homes where the landlord is undertaking major works of refurbishment within the next three years;
(c)   homes subject to restrictive covenants excluding nomination agreements which are not part of section 106 agreements (see Chapter 6);
(d)   homes built with private funds or charitable donations.

Where tenants wish to purchase a property covered by one of the exemptions or do not wish to buy the home they live in, the landlord has the discretion to offer another eligible property and claim VPG or, if it has a TIS allocation, it may enable the tenants to purchase on the open market. This option may also be offered where the exemptions do not apply but for management reasons the landlord does not wish to sell. In addition, from April 1998, landlords have the ability to target certain estates where there is low demand or where they wish to introduce tenure mix. Although each landlord has complete discretion over which properties to include, a proper published policy must be drawn up.

Purchase price

There are no value limits in relation to properties eligible for purchase under VPG, and for 1997/98 discounts ranged from £16 000 in TCI area A to £9000 in TCI area E. If the tenant sells within three years of completion, the discount will be recovered in whole or in part. The property is disposed of at open market value less the grant. All proceeds including the grant are paid into a ring-fenced account less loan debt and expenses. The proceeds of the account may be used to provide replacement homes through new build, rehabiliation, off the shelf purchases, or to carry out works to the landlord's own stock provided that empty properties are being brought back into use. In deciding on the location and type of replacement properties RSLs are expected to consult with the local authorities and the Housing Corporation. The proceeds of the account cannot be used to reduce the grant requirement for new schemes funded by the Housing Corporation or local authorities. All proceeds should be re-used within a three year time-scale. An annual return is submitted to the Housing Corporation setting out payments into the fund, discounts repaid and replacement units provided and in the pipeline.

10.4   The right to acquire

The Conservative administration finally achieved its aim of extending the right to buy their home at a discount to more tenants of registered social landlords through part I of the Housing Act 1996. With effect from April 1997, all self-contained homes to rent built with Social Housing Grant are subject to the right to acquire provisions of the Act. The scheme differs from the the right to buy in a number of respects, not least in that the proceeds of sales can be used to provide replacement properties. The proceeds must be placed in a Disposal Proceeds Fund which must be separately accounted for by the RSL. These properties will themselves be subject to the right to acquire once built. The Disposal Proceeds Fund will be reviewed by the Housing Corporation on a three-yearly basis. Only secure and assured tenants of new homes or homes transferred to an RSL from a local authority after April 1997 are eligible. Secure tenants also continue to enjoy the right to buy while assured tenants of homes developed with traditional Housing Association Grant remain excluded from these programmes, although they may have access to Homebuy and VPG. Once again, to be eligible, a minimum tenancy of two complete years is required, although this need not be continuous.

Exclusions from the right to acquire

There are a number of exclusions from these provisions. These include:

(a)   properties let in connection with employment;
(b)   properties specially designed for people with a physical disability;
(c)   properties forming one of a group for people with special needs, including those with a mental disorder;
(d)   warden-controlled properties for the elderly;
(e)   properties which have not received any public subsidy;
(f)   some rural properties in specially designated areas;
(g)   properties where the net debt is equal to or greater than its current value;
(h)   properties held on crown tenancies;
(i)   properties where the freeholder is not an RSL or a public sector landlord;
(j)   properties where the RSL has insufficient legal interest (i.e., leases on houses under 21 years and on flats under 50 years).

The levels of discount are fixed by the Secretary of State and paid as grants to the RSL after completion of the sale. Discounts are repayable in the first three years; in full in year one reducing to one-third in year three. Detailed procedures are set out in the Housing Corporation's *Capital*

Funding System Procedure Guide (1997). At the time of writing the impact of the Right to Acquire was unclear as few eligible homes had yet been completed. Given the economic status of many new tenants, however, and (of course) the ability to replace sold stock, it is not thought likely that the scheme will have anything like the impact of the original right to buy, at least initially.

10.5   The funding and procedural framework

From 1 April 1993 the funding framework for conventional shared ownership and other housing for sale initiatives was aligned with that for housing for rent; this was outlined earlier in Chapter 5. In addition, since 1 April 1995 housing for sale has followed procedural arrangements similar to those for housing for rent, as detailed in Chapter 6. Thus housing for sale schemes are incorporated into Funding Agreements and may follow the programme contract route or the scheme contract route, as detailed in Chapter 6.

As we have seen, an RSL with an allocation for housing for sale will be able to develop a range of options. These include shared ownership with an initial share of 25–75 per cent of the equity. There is also a self-build option where some of the equity is achieved through labour input during the construction period. Shared ownership for the elderly limits equity sale to between 25 and 75 per cent of the equity, and staircasing is also restricted to 75 per cent, at which stage no rent is paid on the unsold equity. Homes may also be provided for outright sale by rehabilitation or improvement.

The move to a common framework as far as possible with housing for rent had four main objectives: to ensure that housing for sale provides the full spectrum of opportunities to complement the provision of rented housing; to increase the volume of housing for sale through the greater use of private finance; to give incentives to cost control through limited grant input and the transfer of development risk to the landlord; and to simplify the process of developing housing for sale by introducing a common grant framework. This section concentrates on those criteria and procedural issues which are specific to sale initiatives. They are highlighted in the Housing Corporation's 1997 *Capital Funding System Procedure Guide.*

For a scheme to obtain approval it must be undertaken by a registered social landlord. The proposed scheme must meet both the Housing Corporation's and the local authority's priorities, and meet an identified need for the home ownership tenure proposed. The location of the scheme should take account of the Housing Corporation's Priority Investment Areas.

Priority investment areas

These are areas of rural or urban housing stress which rank for priority investment of public funds. They include areas identified as having priority by regional offices of the Housing Corporation including urban programme areas, particularly City Challenge. All areas covered by an Urban Development Corporation are included, as are those areas identified by the local authority as having priority for urban renewal or estate action. The aim of the Priority Investment Area strategy is to concentrate funds in those places where both need and demand can be clearly identified. Rehabilitation for Outright Sale schemes may only be undertaken in these areas. Schemes which are in Priority Investment Areas enjoy more generous grant levels, as illustrated in Table 10.3.

All new build schemes (which may be developed on a design and build basis or through the purchase of off-the-shelf units) must conform to the National House Builders Council (NHBC) standards and the Housing Corporation's scheme development standards. The dwellings must also be marketable and able to attract a mortgage. Wherever possible property should be acquired on a freehold basis but, if acquired as a lease, the outstanding term of the lease must be sufficient to allow underleases to be granted (see below). The qualifying costs for schemes are as for rented accommodation and include acquisition, works costs and an allowance for on-costs. The marketing costs of the dwellings are met from the on-cost percentages. The costs of the scheme are approved at grant confirmation stage as in the rented regime, and must reflect final outturn costs. Grant limits are also predetermined. At grant confirmation stage the rents and housing benefit eligible service charges are also agreed. If final levels are as agreed at grant confirmation stage, the investment contract with the Housing Corporation has been met. If they are higher then it has not. In this case the Corporation will scrutinise levels. If rents or service charges as a percentage of unsold equity have decreased or increased in the range of 0.01 to 2 per cent, the Corporation will determine whether these variations are acceptable.

Table 10.3   Low-cost home-ownership grant rates 1996/97
(factors to be applied to the appropriate rented mixed funded grant for each project 1996/97)

Sale programme	Priority Investment areas	Other areas
Shared ownership	58%	50%
Shared ownership for the elderly	68%	60%
Improvement for outright sale	33%	—

Social Housing Grant is paid on all housing for sale schemes (excepting DIYSO) as for rented schemes. The RSL receives a fixed percentage of HAG based upon rates set annually and applied to the relevant TCI for the area. Grant is paid in three tranches. There is a special multiplier to apply to base TCIs for sale schemes too. A special low-cost home-ownership factor is applied to the appropriate rented grant rate for each project. For 1996/97 the factors were as highlighted in Table 10.3.

The funding agreement between the Housing Corporation and the RSL is subject to a similar review mechanism as for rented schemes. Disposals of properties by way of a lease is also covered by the Housing Corporation's General Consent (see Chapter 3) and should be entered on the landlord's own register of disposals.

Post-completion

Once a scheme is completed the RSL must submit to the Housing Corporation a copy of both the grant apportionment and post-sales monitoring forms. The grant apportionment records the amount of grant attributable to each property for both conventional shared ownership and shared ownership for the elderly. This enables a record to be kept for the recovery or recycling of grant at the appropriate point. Since 1997 RSLs have been able to retain grant following the sale of a tranche of equity; this is placed into a Capital Grant Recycling Fund (CGRF) and used for investment in further properties. Details of grant recycling are given in Chapter 5. Progress on sales of completed schemes must also be monitored and reported to the Housing Corporation on a quarterly basis. This enables the Corporation to evaluate the RSL's own sales and marketing strategy and performance. The recovery and recycling of grant by the Housing Corporation in the event of staircasing sales is subject to detailed procedures and calculations. These are set out in the 1997 *Capital Funding System Procedure Guide*. Sales of properties are based upon open market values, with vacant possession as certified by an independent valuer.

Staircasing

Staircasing is the process whereby the lessee is able to purchase further equity shares in the property. Once the owner has notified the landlord that he or she wishes to purchase further shares the association must apply for a value to be set by an independent valuer within 14 days. Once the valuation has been established the owner has three months to decide whether to proceed with the purchase of the share. The transaction must be completed within the period stipulated in the lease. As each tranche is sold the landlord will repay the amount of loan apportioned to that share and place the grant in the CGRF. Any surpluses which remain as a result of rising values can be retained by the RSL. If the proceeds are insufficient to meet the amount of grant apportioned to that tranche of equity then the Corporation may consider grant deferment.

10.6 Additional procedural considerations

Conventional shared ownership

Conventional shared ownership (as opposed to DIYSO) offers those on low incomes the opportunity to purchase a stake in their newly developed home. The purchaser buys a proportion of the dwelling on a long lease and pays a proportion of the rent for the remainder. Housing benefit may be claimable on the rented element according to the circumstances of the owner. The minimum stake is 25 per cent of the market value of the property, but future tranches may be acquired in any proportion provided that no more than four steps are required to achieve full ownership. The client group will normally be first-time buyers with priority given to those on public sector landlord waiting lists, those vacating public sector properties, those wishing to move to another area to take up employment and others in housing need who cannot meet the costs of full ownership.

The lease

As we have seen, for a dwelling to qualify for grant it must meet certain criteria laid down by the Housing Corporation which also provides a model lease. Where the RSL owns the freehold the lease should be for 99 years. Where only a leasehold interest is held, all underleases granted by the RSL will be for the remaining period of the RSL's lease less five days. The premium paid for it must be based upon a percentage of the current full market value of the dwelling and, as stated, the initial equity stake must be no less than 25 per cent. The lease must allow the leaseholder to purchase further stakes one year after the initial purchase, if desired. The lease should clearly set out the repairing obligations of both parties. In the case of houses, repairs are usually the responsibility of the shared owner, while in the case of flats internal repairs and decorations are carried out by the leaseholder but the landlord covenants to maintain the communal and external elements of the building. The lease also specifies management and insurance responsibilities.

In the case of schemes which form part of the Corporation's rural programme, provisions may be incorporated which enable the property to be repurchased once the maximum share has been acquired and to restrict the level of equity that can be purchased to 80 per cent. These measures ensure that the homes developed to meet the needs of first-time buyers on low incomes can be kept for this purpose.

The management of all leasehold property is now subject to the guidance laid down by the Housing Corporation in The Leaseholder's Charter and the 1997 Performance Standards introduced pursuant to section 36 of the 1996 Housing Act. The guidance covers the selection of leaseholders and shared owners, terms of the lease and the principles to be adopted for rent setting and service charges. Information on service charges and leases for leaseholders and to prospective purchasers are also covered by the Standards.

Rents

In the case of shared ownership the rent review mechanism should be set out in the lease. Until 1987 shared ownership rents were fair rents fixed by the Rent Officer under the Rent Act 1977. Schedule 4 of the Housing and Planning Act 1986 (introduced by statutory instrument) amended the Rent Act 1977 in respect of shared ownership leases. From 11 December 1987 rents on shared ownership schemes were deregulated and associations were permitted to agree rent levels with the leaseholder at the time the lease was granted. The rents should cover the long-term loan, management and insurance costs and any service charges which should be itemised separately. In relation to service charges the provisions of the Landlord and Tenant Acts 1985 and 1987 (see Chapter 5) also apply. There is no ruling regarding the type of mechanism to be used for rent reviews but, in the case of publicly funded schemes for Rent Surplus Fund purposes, rents will be assumed to have risen in line with the Retail Price Index.

Following the Housing Act 1988 all shared ownership leases granted after 15 January 1989 are assured tenancies where the rent is more than two-thirds of the rateable value of the property. Where the rent is less than two-thirds it will be a housing association tenancy under the Rent Act 1977 but will not come under the jurisdiction of the Rent Officer; thus since 1989 all shared ownership leases have been subject to deregulated rents. Rents should be set with due regard to affordability and be sufficient to meet loan repayments. They are also subject to the rent influencing regime discussed in Chapter 5.

Leasehold Reform Act 1967

Shared ownership leases for houses and bungalows are subject to enfranchisement under the Leasehold Reform Act 1967, unless they comply with the regulations introduced by schedule 4 of the 1986 Act or unless there is a provision that the rent does not fall below two-thirds of the rateable value. The schedule includes a lengthy list of provisions but, in essence, if the lease is granted by a Registered Social Landlord, and is granted in accordance with the terms discussed above, then the lease will be exempt from the provisions of the 1967 Act.

Self-build shared ownership

Self-build schemes must be able to demonstrate a cost/value relationship of 80–100 per cent. The costs of the scheme must be at least 20 per cent less than the value of the completed dwellings. The scheme is developed by a self-build group which must be registered with the Registrar of Friendly Societies. The self-build group will work with a registered social landlord who will claim grant on its behalf. As stated earlier, in the case of self-build shared ownership a proportion of the equity is granted as a reward for the self-builder's labour. If this amounts to less than 25 per cent then the self-builders must purchase enough of the equity to achieve a minimum stake of 25 per cent. The lease is a lease under which the tenant will or may be entitled to a sum calculated by reference to the value of the dwelling, rather than the premium paid as a percentage of open market value.

10.7   Shared ownership for the elderly

Shared ownership for the elderly was preceded by Leasehold Schemes for the Elderly, which provides sheltered accommodation for older people who require additional support. It also assists those on low incomes who may or may not already own their own homes, as the initiative is grant-aided. Furthermore, as each purchaser moves, their previous home is released to meet general housing needs. Leasehold Schemes for the Elderly were funded through the Housing Corporation and until 1989 the total costs were reduced by Housing Association Grant of 30 per cent. This enabled the 60-year leases to be sold for 70 per cent of the cost of development. Management of the scheme is provided by the RSL and is funded through a service charge. The lease is determined on death or removal of the lessee and, prior to 1989, would revert to the association which offered a new lease at 70 per cent of current value. On the death of a lessee the appreciation in value is returned to the lessee's estate. In recent years these schemes have also been funded with private finance without public susbsidy. HAG-funded Leasehold Schemes for the Elderly did not expand to the extent that was anticipated, due to the fact that, even with the 30 per cent subsidy, the purchase price was beyond the reach of many older people. As a result the National Housing Federation called for a flexible leasehold scheme programme that would incorporate shared ownership. This would allow owners to purchase a lower percentage of the equity and extend the benefits of Leasehold Schemes for the Elderly to more elderly people. As a result, shared ownership for the elderly was introduced in 1989. It is now developed through the common grant framework discussed earlier. The new system allows buyers to purchase 25 per cent of the equity, up to a maximum of 75 per cent.

The lease

There are additional requirements for elderly persons' leases. It is a requirement of the Housing Corporation for scheme approval that the lease be granted to a person of 55 or over. The lease should state that no rent is payable once the purchaser has acquired 75 per cent of the equity. The lease must also comply with schedule 4A of the Leasehold Reform Act 1967 and Statutory Instrument 1987 No. 1940 if it is to qualify for grant and if it is to be exempt from the provisions of the 1967 Act. The main provisions include covenants to provide a warden service, restricting assignment to persons over the age of 55 except to a spouse, and an absolute covenant prohibiting the underletting by the tenant of the whole or part of the dwelling. The lease must not provide an option for the tenant to acquire the landlord's interest. This restriction ensures that the control of the property remains with the landlord and, although the leaseholder has the right to assign the lease, very often it will be to someone from the RSL's own list; thus the accommodation is retained for use by older people on low incomes as intended.

Equity release

The previous chapter highlighted the poor housing conditions faced by many older people, particularly home-owners. Following research for the Joseph Rowntree Foundation published in 1995,[6] a consortium of ten associations funded further detailed work to promote the case for assisting elderly owners to stay in their own homes by helping them to improve or adapt their home to make it more suitable through 'equity release shared ownership'. The scheme was not in operation at the time of writing but both the Housing Corporation and the Department of the Environment were viewing the proposals positively.

The details of the scheme are set out in three policy and practice papers.[7] The proposals build on assistance to elderly owners provided by care and repair schemes and the work of Home Improvement Agencies as discussed in Chapter 9. The proposals would permit the full rehabilitation and improvement of property using the shared ownership model. The scheme proposes that the owner sells the property to the RSL and reinvests as much of the proceeds as possible into the property to keep the need for grant to a minimum. The works would be undertaken by the RSL. The owner then repurchases a share in the property. The rest of the equity remains with the RSL, funded by a loan repaid through rent paid by the shared owner. Grant is paid to the same level as for Rehabilitation for Outright Sale (see below). The scheme enables an older person to stay put, to retain part of the value of their home and to have their home improved and adapted to meet their needs. The problem of deteriorating owner-occupied stock is also dealt with through this simple scheme. It clearly addresses a number of national housing policy issues and policy in relation to the needs of older people; whether the scheme will develop and prove popular with local authorities and older people themselves remains to be seen, however.

10.8   Rehabilitation for outright sale

Since 1988 outright sale schemes can be undertaken on the conversion, improvement or repair of any existing property. Properties developed for outright sale are directed at first-time buyers and people on housing association or local authority waiting lists. The property is purchased on the open market, improved and then sold on either a freehold basis or on a 99-year lease. Housing Corporation consent is required for disposal through outright sale. All schemes must be developed in Priority Investment Areas. Grant is payable at the relevant percentage of qualifying costs according to the cost area in which the property is being purchased.

10.9   Do-It-Yourself Shared Ownership

Do-It-Yourself Shared Ownership or DIYSO was reintroduced by the Housing Corporation in 1992. This scheme was a further variant on shared ownership. Rather than an RSL developing a new or improved home for sale, first-time buyers were able to seek out a property on the open market in England (new build or second hand, within set value limits) that they wished to purchase. With the assistance of an RSL which purchases the property on their behalf, an individual was able to acquire the property on a shared ownership basis. Since April 1996, however, with the exception of applicants with a disability or where a permanent family member has a disability, only tenants of local authorities and registered social landlords and those accepted as statutorily homeless were eligible to purchase through the Housing Corporation's DIYSO programme. This was to improve the targeting of the scheme and bring about increased vacancies for reletting in the social housing sector. Prior to this, 40 per cent of purchasers were from the private sector. The principles of DIYSO were similar to conventional shared ownership, although the funding and procedures differ. These are set out in the Housing Corporation's 1995 *Do-It-Yourself Shared Ownership Procedure Guide*. Properties could be purchased up to the same value as set out for the Tenants' Incentive Scheme above. Value limits were reviewed annually, however. In order to ration DIYSO to cope with the demand for it (it had been introduced in 1983 and then withdrawn as funding was not able to meet demand), RSLs bid for funding and were allocated funds through a Funding Agreement for a specific area of operation, usually a local authority district(s). Once again, shares may be purchased up to 75 per cent, although 50 per cent tends to be the norm. Grant was applied to the unsold portion of the equity at published rates. In 1996/97 these amounted to 73.3 per cent in inner London through to 59.3 per cent in TCI area E.

In 1995 the Housing Corporation published an evaluation of DIYSO undertaken by the School for Advanced Urban Studies (SAUS) in Bristol.[8] At the time of the study the monthly cost to the purchaser of a conventional shared ownership home was, on average, about 80 per cent of the costs of full ownership. The research found that DIYSO offered reasonable value for money, both for the purchasers and in subsidy terms. There was a high level of purchaser satisfaction with the scheme, although take-up was patchy.

Like most home ownership initiatives the demand for DIYSO is much higher in the south of the country than in the northern regions. The Housing Corporation has responded to this, as we have seen, by adopting flexible policy stances towards low-cost home ownership which vary from region to region. In 1998, the government announced plans to replace DIYSO with the Homebuy scheme with effect from April 1999. Unfortunately, at the time of writing, no detailed information on the scheme was available. DIYSO had however been given a two year extention to 2001 where funded by local authority SHG.

10.10   Mortgage rescue

Throughout the 1990s, in response to the increasing rate of mortgage repossessions which have run, on average, at 50 000 per annum, housing associations attempted to develop mortgage rescue schemes to assist home owners in financial difficulties. Research by the Housing Corporation[9] shows that, despite the demand for such schemes, the response has been limited. Since 1991 some 1800 households have been assisted by such initiatives, through six different models of mortgage rescue. Most involved purchase of the property by the association using their reserves, a low interest loan or a combination of loan and grant from a local authority, which allows owners to remain in their homes as assured tenants or as shared owners.

The obstacles to greater success have included legal and financial difficulties, but the most insurmountable has been the lack of subsidy for such schemes. In comparison with other subsidised schemes, mortgage rescue would not compare favourably in value-for-money terms, and as a result few schemes have been developed. The single most successful initiative, which accounts for two-thirds of those assisted, was achieved through establishing two fully mutual associations. The scheme was developed by the English Churches Housing Group working with the Circle 33 Housing Trust and a single lender, the Bradford & Bingley Building Society. Mortage rescue schemes will not increase unless there is a shift in policy to introduce measures to enable the initiative to work. At the time of writing, this appeared unlikely.

10.11   An evaluation of low-cost home-ownership initiatives

Assistance to groups on the margins of home ownership is a valuable activity *per se* but it may also bring other benefits. In particular it may release much needed rented accommodation for those households for whom even low-cost home-ownership is unattainable or that do not wish to become home owners. Home-ownership initiatives can also contribute to the regeneration of an area by creating more stable and balanced communities.

That owner-occupation is the most desirable form of tenure is a view that has long been espoused by the Conservative Party and now, it seems, by the Labour Party too. Chamberlain stated that it 'enlists all those who are affected by it on the side of law and order and enrols them in a great army of good citizens'; to the 1982 Conservative Party Conference Mrs Thatcher affirmed 'There is no prouder word in British history than freeholder.' Owner-occupation carries with it an image of worthiness, of status, that renting does not. The 1996 White Paper, *Our Future Homes*, reiterated the then Conservative Government's commitment to the growth of home ownership. This commitment is now apparently shared by the Labour Party, although perhaps with less obvious vigour.

All tenure preference surveys since 1983 have shown that owner-occupation is the preferred tenure of over 70 per cent of the population (although it is considerably lower for specific groups such as those over 65 and local authority tenants). The most recent housing attitudes survey commissioned by the Department of the Environment confirmed that there remains a strong general preference for owning rather than renting. Fifty per cent of all renters would prefer to own and one-quarter of all local authority and housing association tenants would like to buy. Cash incentive schemes were considered a better option than the right to buy.

As long ago as 1986, Booth and Crook[10] noted the problems attendant upon attempting an evaluation of low-cost home-ownership initiatives given the variety of objectives of the programme and the range of target groups that the policies were devised to assist. Surveys undertaken by the National Housing Federation have shown that the housing association programme is certainly assisting first-time buyers and those on low incomes, and therefore although the programme still has its critics it appears to be meeting these objectives at least.

An appraisal undertaken for the Department of the Environment,[11] which covered all providers of conventional shared ownership including local authorities and the private sector, found that over 80 per cent were first time buyers. Of these, 40 per cent had rented, and a similar proportion had lived in someone else's household. Thirty-seven per cent were childless couples, and 25 per cent single. Shared ownership appeals to younger people; 65 per cent of household heads were under 30 years of age compared with 13 per cent nationally. The degree of satisfaction with their home was high amongst shared owners: 96 per cent liked their home and only 19 per cent had any criticism of it at all. Staircasing had been limited, however; only 4 per cent of shared owners had gone on to purchase further shares. Shared owners viewed the tenure as a start on the housing ladder, and over 80 per cent had a positive attitude towards this residual form of tenure.

Ethnic minorities and shared ownership

A study by the published by the Moat Housing Group[12] investigated the access of people from minority ethnic communities to shared ownership housing. The report found that ethnic minorities were underrepresented in this form of housing which, at its peak, accounted for almost one-third of the new development programme of the sector. Low income alone could not account for this, and the report highlights the need for greater understanding and promotion of these schemes to these diverse communities.

Recently some black-led housing associations, notably Ujima Hosing Association, have endeavoured to develop shared ownership to meet the needs of their client groups. The stay of execution of DIYSO is in part to enable more people from these communities to take advantage of its relatively low entry costs.

Mixed tenure and stable communities

As discussed in earlier chapters, there is a growing concern in the sector to reverse the balance of estates provided by registered social landlords to attempt to ensure that more economically active households are attracted into an area to dilute concentrations of poverty and low income. Home-ownership initiatives can be combined with other approaches as a means of contributing to this and many schemes, especially those on larger sites, now incorporate an element of housing for outright sale and shared ownership. Although critics argue that mixing tenure can lead to management problems, the evidence from many RSLs is that such estates can and do work.[13] Furthermore, surpluses generated by sales schemes can be used to subsidise the cost of rented homes on larger schemes, giving both greater choice and increased affordability.

Flexible tenure

In addition to mixed tenure, some registered social landlords and other policy analysts are exploring the potential of flexible tenure. A joint report by the National Housing Federation and the Council of Mortgage Lenders[14] called for new ways to be developed for paying for housing to reflect different housing and employment patterns. Flexible tenure, if developed, would enable owners to staircase both up and down if their circumstances altered. An owner-occupier in difficulty could trade down to shared ownership, and a shared owner to renting and so on. Different tenures would sit side by side, peppered through estates rather than in separately identified blocks as is usual in mixed tenure developments. The report noted the need for a tax regime that puts ownership and renting on the same footing, in addition to a political consensus to make this work. Flexible mortgages would also be required. There are now one or two pilots in England pioneering flexible tenure, and many more in Wales. In particular, the Joseph Rowntree Foundation has experimented with this form of tenure on its New Earswick estates with some success, arguing that it can help to avoid the stigma at times associated with social housing estates.[15]

There are caveats,however. While a change of tenure can develop the confidence of individuals and communities, the diversification of tenure is not a panancea for alleviating social exclusion or indeed for regenerating areas in decline. Improved education and training, combined with increased employment opportunities, are more likely to bring about the resolution of these issues, rather than mixed or flexible tenure alone. Registered social landlords must attempt to connect with, and contribute to, all these agendas if their programmes of tenure diversification are to succeed.

References

1 *Registered Social Landlords in 1997, General Report* (The Housing Corporation 1998), p. 25.
2 *Leasehold Reform, Housing and Urban Development Act 1993*, Circular HC 40/93 (The Housing Corporation) and *Rent to Mortgage Scheme – Notification of changes to the first and second multipliers and relevant amount*, Circular F5 23/96 (The Housing Corporation).
3 *Tenants' Incentive Scheme (TIS and Do It Yourself Shared Ownership (DIYSO)* Circular F2 07/97 (The Housing Corporation).

4 H. Angle, A. Bellchambers and Dr S. Nuttall, *Cash Incentives to Housing Association Tenants: A Review of the Tenants' Incentive Scheme*, DoE, Housing Research Report (HMSO 1995).
5 *Proposals for a Purchase Grant Scheme for Housing Association Tenants* (DoE, June 1995).
6 'Equity Release Shared Ownership', *Housing Summary* 9 (Joseph Rowntree Foundation October 1995).
7 N. King, *Shared Ownership for the Elderly by Rehabilitation and Equity Release, Policy Paper, Guidance on Practice and Procedures and Funding* (Nigel King Associates 1996).
8 G. Bramley *et al.*, *Do-It-Yourself Shared Ownership: An Evaluation* (The Housing Corporation 1995).
9 *Housing association involvement in mortgage rescue, an evaluation of the initiatives*, Source Insight (The Housing Corporation 1995).
10 P. Booth and A. Crook (eds) *Low Cost Home Ownership Initiatives: An Evaluation of Housing Policy under the Conservatives* (Gower 1986).
11 Cousins *et al.*, *An Appraisal of Shared Ownership*, DoE (HMSO 1993).
12 T. Brown and J. Passmore, *Minority Ethnic Communities' Access to Shared Ownership Housing* (Moat Housing Group 1995).
13 P. Redman 'Time to Mix It Up', *Housing Today*, 14 August 1997.
14 R. Terry *Changing Housing Markets. The Case for Flexible Tenure and Flexible Mortgages* (The National Federation of Housing Associations and the Council of Mortgage Lenders 1996).
15 *Mixed and Flexible Tenure in Practice* (Joseph Rowntree Foundation 1996).

11

Future Prospects: Some Conclusions

Change is not new to housing associations. Since the nineteenth century they have adapted to different social, economic and political climates. What is certain, however, is that the registered social landlords (RSLs) of the twenty-first century will be different from the traditional housing association of the 1990s. The sector weathered the impact of the Housing Act 1988 and embraced the introduction of private finance, emerging in the 1990s perhaps a little leaner and more efficient, but largely unchanged; the housing association of 1979 is still recognisable as such, in terms of activities and ethos, in 1999. The Housing Act 1996 and the advent of a Labour Government in 1997 heralded yet another era for the sector, and the factors which have and will contribute to this further change have been discussed throughout this book. This chapter sets out some concluding thoughts on future issues and possible scenarios. It commences with a brief review of the economic, social and demographic factors which will impact upon RSLs over the next decade. This is a huge and complex policy area, beyond the scope of this book, but further references are given to assist those readers who wish to know more. We then consider the implications of the policy context for the sector as a whole and for individual RSLs.

11.1 Making connections

Housing policy and the activities of registered social landlords cannot be viewed in isolation. If housing need is to get the political attention and levels of public investment it deserves, then housing policy-makers must demonstrate the links with other economic and social policy arenas. As stated at the outset of Chapter 7, good housing is essential for the quality of life. It not only affords shelter, privacy and security but is closely linked to physical and emotional well-being. Good housing can therefore contribute to, and complement, other aspects of social policy. A number of reports have highlighted these connections.[1]

Housing and social policy

It is estimated that poor health caused by bad housing conditions costs the National Health Service (NHS) some £2.4 billion each year. The link between housing and public health was recognised in the nineteenth century (as discussed in Chapter 1). The health needs of homeless families and those who sleep rough is well documented. The link is quite concrete in the case of supported housing and housing for older people, and those with physical disablilities. Good housing is also a prerequisite for effective community care policy.

Housing is also linked to the employment and labour markets. Britain needs a flexible and mobile workforce if it is to maintain its international competitiveness. A supply of decent, affordable housing contributes to this. This will include tenure diversification too, as discussed in Chapter 10, with greater demand for flexible tenure and mortgage packages, perhaps with an increase in shared ownership and other low-cost home-ownership initiatives. Investment in housing construction can boost the economy as a whole, as has been demonstrated a number of times throughout the twentieth century.

Affordable housing can assist the unemployed to get back to work and lift families out of the poverty trap. A number of reports have also demonstrated the link between housing conditions and educational attainment: temporary or poor housing can affect children's performance in school. At a practical level well-designed housing, constructed on estates with security in mind, can help to reduce crime in urban areas. All these considerations should place the housing policy agenda at the heart of social policy.

With this in mind the National Housing Federation produced a technical briefing for the new government in 1997.[2] The document encouraged the Government, amongst other things, to review the funding of social housing and to unlock local authority finance. This was in fact achieved, to some extent, with the announcement in 1998 of the release of £3.6 billion of capital receipts. The National Housing Federation also proposed that the housing benefit system should be reviewed and that the planning system should be used to better effect, to enable the creation of more affordable housing. In 1997, the Government announced its Comprehensive Spending Review across government as a whole. Two major pieces of research were commissioned by the National Housing Federation to submit to the review as part of the consultative process. The first examined the options for funding affordable social housing,[3] and the second the links between housing benefit, affordability and work incentives.[4] A Green Paper was announced in the March 1999 Budget which will further examine these issues. It is clear that the Government intends that the £3.9 billion provided by the Comprehensive Spending Review will be property targetted. Wider reforms of Housing Benefit are expected in addition to an overhaul of the rents system.

The operating environment

For the foreseeable future the operating environment for registered social landlords will continue to be dominated by two factors, competition and choice. This is the prevailing ethos which faces all sectors and indeed reflects the international context. But, for RSLs, there will be an even greater emphasis on accountability and service to consumers. Competition between RSLs for funding, particularly as the sector grows through stock transfer, is likely to intensify, demanding greater efficiency and value for money across all activities. Housing management will become paramount as RSLs are embraced by the best value regime.

Demographic change will also influence the operating environment. Household growth forecasts are at the centre of debate in housing policy, as discussed in Chapter 6. There is a projected increase of some 4.4 million households by 2016 and the need for a further 1 million social homes by the year 2011. RSLs will undoubtedly continue to provide for these needs but in a more commercial and diverse way. In addition to household growth, as a nation, we face a backlog of disrepair across all sectors. The 1996 English House Condition Survey (the results of which were awaited at the time of writing) is likely to estimate this at £20 billion in the local authority sector and at least £1 billion in the independent sector. The future emphasis will therefore also be on stock reinvestment and regeneration of communities. As discussed in Chapter 8, the future of supported housing and the need for an appropriate funding regime, set against a backdrop of an ageing population with increasing community care needs, will also impact upon the sector. There is also evidence to suggest that there is a significant mismatch in stock owned by RSLs and future needs. This is especially the case for older persons' housing, as discussed in Chapter 9, and in some areas of the country where rent levels and the location of RSL stock are leading to problems in letting. Research published by the Housing Corporation in 1997 looks in some detail at future stock and tenure issues.[5] The report estimates that 4 per cent of housing association tenants have fewer bedrooms than they need, whilst just over one in three households has one or more surplus bedrooms. Some 43 000 homes are estimated to be unfit, (about 7 per cent of the stock).

The Government's agenda

At the time of writing, the government had embarked upon a series of constitutional changes to national, regional and local government. The impact of the new national assemblies and Regional Development Agencies (RDAs) remains to be seen. RSLs must learn to deal with these new agencies whose brief derives from this Government's concern with democracy and local accountability. At a more prosaic level, the impact of RDAs and mayoral government in London will also affect RSLs and the Housing Corporation; the shape and role of the Housing Corporation may yet change, as highlighted in Chapter 3.

Welfare reform, and welfare to work, combined with reform of the educational system are at the heart of the government's strategy to tackle social exclusion. The sector must connect with this agenda and is well placed to do so.

Tackling social exclusion

A report published in 1995 by the National Housing Federation, *The Price of Social Exclusion*, raised the issue of the emergence of an 'underclass'. It highlighted real concern for the growing divisions in society and the role that housing plays in shaping or combating social disadvantage. It suggested then that coherent strategies were required between health, employment, education, housing and other services and concluded that 'good quality, affordable and secure housing will be an important part of the solution'.

In particular, the report called for the need to:

(a)   review affordability and the poverty trap in relation to rent levels and housing benefit;
(b)   maintain levels of investment in social housing;
(c)   develop complementary investment strategies, in that it is insufficient to act on housing alone;
(d)   review tenants' rights and security.

The report also stressed that social and welfare roles must be integrated. None of these ideas is new to housing management or to the sector as a whole. It has long recognised and performed the wider management role; indeed activities such as those undertaken by the community development units of RSLs and the Foyer movement are examples of how the sector can contribute to the process of combating social exclusion.

The activities of RSLs in undertaking other housing plus initiatives and community regneration programmes also contribute to this agenda. In 1998 some 65 housing associations signed up to the recommendations of a report by Professor David Clapham,[6] which acknowledged the difficulties faced by housing management in particular owing to the greater vulnerability of housing association tenants and which examined the housing plus activities of RSLs and the contribution they can make to these needs. However, it could be argued that the work of RSLs can only make a marginal difference; as major purchasers of services and as (often large) local employers, there are initiatives that can be undertaken which will help to alleviate poverty and to improve the quality of life for tenants and their children. A strong link with other agencies, especially the statutory services, is the only way to achieve this, along with sound information on community needs and desires. The role of RSLs in tackling this agenda was also set into context in an essay commissioned in 1997 by the National Housing Federation.[7]

By 1998 a number of housing associations and other RSLs had begun to contribute to the welfare to work and New Deal initiatives of the government. Some had attempted to take the lead role in providing 'gateway' training for young people, while others were employing individuals on environmental improvement schemes. Foyers were also contributing to this process. In the future, it is likely that these activities will grow and develop in a group of RSLs committed to these areas of activity, whereas others may pursue more commercially viable activities such as providing housing through various private finance initiatives and will come to resemble property companies rather than community-based organisations.

RSLs are also well placed to contribute to the Government's regeneration strategy announced in 1998 (see Chapter 6). The New Deal for Communities places them at the heart of the renewal process, and it is likely that many urban RSLs will lead partnerships to tackle these areas. In addition, others may well reinvent themselves as regeneration agencies or add this function to their other activities in a more structured manner. There is a new agenda for housing and regeneration to which RSLs must connect. A report published by the National Housing Federation in 1998 sets out the vision and the action required.[8]

In addition, it is likely that the new Housing Inspectorate established under the aegis of the Audit Commission will examine not only housing management issues and best value, but also housing's broader role in the community.

11.2 Managing for the future

The dilemma facing RSLs is how they can continue to respond effectively to these needs through a programme of supportive housing management and community development and community care services, whilst controlling their costs and positioning themselves to compete with other providers. Purchasers of RSL services are themselves coming under budgetary pressure, which in turn impacts upon the sector.

There is ongoing concern regarding the process of residualisation of social housing as poverty and unemployment increase, especially in inner urban areas, with few economically active households being nominated by local authorities to association homes. This results in increasing benefit dependency amongst tenants and raises concerns that as rents rise, the poverty trap experienced by many new tenants (in particular) will deepen. The possibility of further cuts to the benefit system would not only exacerbate this issue but could also weaken the sector's ability to attract private finance.

Pressures on social housing investment and on grant rates will have a number of implications for the sector. In addition, there is likely to be a shift towards home ownership initiatives in the form of loss of stock through the right to acquire. Developments which utilise lower rates of public subsidy will need to be devised if the sector is to continue to grow. Pressures on the programme are likely to come at a time of rising land and building costs and interest rates, making it more difficult to maintain both standards and affordable rent levels. Furthermore, activity will shift more towards rehabilitation of older stock, including modernisation of stock owned by RSLs. Greater emphasis is being placed on urban and economic regeneration, with less new build development on green field sites.

Restructuring of the sector

The financial constraints, combined with the introduction of further competition, will lead to an inevitable restructuring of the housing association sector. This activity has been limited to date with only a few notable mergers and restructures effected. It is likely that this activity will increase in future, however. Each RSL must continue to consider its own position in the medium term as the picture develops.

Small RSLs and newer, black housing associations are particularly vulnerable in the current climate. As RSLs prepare to meet the challenges set before them there is increasing evidence that some may consider merger to be the best way of obtaining the range of skills and the asset base required to give them the necessary managerial and financial strength to meet these challenges. Sharing costs could lead to reduced overheads, and consequently lower rent levels (all imperatives for merger). The decision to merge will, of course, rest with the respective boards of the RSLs and a number of issues will have to be faced, in particular the extent to which the proposed partners complement each other and share similar objectives. There is also the question of the impact upon tenants and staff. Policies and practices would need to be altered too, to ensure consistency.

Mergers can bring particular advantages for the small association, although larger associations have perceived its advantages too. Small associations have felt especially threatened by the impact of private finance, as discussed in previous chapters. In particular, the requirement for a strong asset base positively places small associations and co-operatives at a disadvantage.

There is no doubt that the emphasis on efficiency and the criteria for success point to mergers most probably through the group structure model discussed in Chapter 2. This is the view espoused by the Housing Corporation which, while opposed to large-scale mergers for the purposes of aggrandisement, can see the advantages presented by the group structure.[9] This approach enables financial and technical strengths to be developed through mass, but also protects the autonomy of smaller organisations and may ensure that the very diversity of the sector, which has often been cited as its greatest strength, will not be lost.

Emphasis on performance

A performance culture now dominates in every area of activity, but housing management in particular will be in the spotlight as both the Audit Commission and the Housing Corporation begin to scrutinise RSL costs against those of local authorities and other providers as part of the best value regime, possibly through the new Housing Inspectorate which has been established for local authorities. At the same time, expectations of RSLs from partners and tenants will be high. RSLs have a limited ability to continue to cross-subsidise rented homes in the medium term. Their ability to provide security for future loans on current terms is also time limited.

The need to reduce and control costs and increase efficiencies is greater than ever before. While the need to generate reasonable surpluses to satisfy lenders, to support the stock modernisation programme and to enable development to continue at affordable rents continue to be overriding aims, a clear focus needs to be set and an order of priority devised to make the most effective use in the medium term of limited resources. Sound financial planning and management is the key. A proper strategy for managing the assets of each RSL in relation to available security and stock reinvestment will be a crucial element of any corporate plan, as will be the need to explore more innovative private finance arrangements. RSLs will increasingly become revenue-led organisations more concerned with the provision of high-quality services and well-maintained homes than expansion as development-led growth becomes less dominant.

All activities will continue to be subject to scrutiny in terms of delivering value for money. Tough and effective budgetary control will need to be implemented. Although much has already been achieved, a further change in culture is required. If greater demands are to be made upon staff they must be equipped to respond and must feel valued in the process. Modern human resources and training strategies are required. Some RSLs are also beginning to look further afield to Europe to find ideas to assist in meeting the challenges they face.

The European connection

Clearly, many of the issues that face RSLs as providers of social housing are common to housing organisations across the EC. These include an increase in homelessness, the need to regenerate urban areas, the ageing population, the need to cut energy consumption and to improve the environment. It is in relation to these trans-national issues that RSLs should seek to develop their European strategies, not least to attempt to obtain funding and other support.

European Community policies and objectives have impacted upon the sector in a host of ways, for some time. For example, RSLs are affected by a number of directives in relation to tendering, contracting, health and safety and employment conditions. The advent of Compulsory Competitive Tendering for housing management (in particular) has already brought companies from other parts of the EC into the UK, competing for (and winning) management contracts. Thus Europe represents both opportunities and competition.

Some RSLs have already developed substantial links with social housing providers in other parts of the EC with a view to sharing experiences to develop new organisational approaches to the management and provision of social housing. Each RSL should attempt to keep abreast of new developments in the EC for funding social housing, and other new initiatives that relate to other aspects of their work, such as community development and employment and training initiatives.

Management will be paramount

Housing management (including maintenance) will be paramount to the success of RSLs and, for many, especially those working in deprived urban environments, housing plus will *be integral to* rather than *marginal to* management activities. There are four imperatives for this, most of which have already been discussed. They are: the impact of the external operating environment; tenants' demands; financial imperatives and the resurgence of regeneration; and an holistic approach to urban renewal. Many RSLs are now embarked upon reviews of their housing management and maintenance services, and their customer services as a whole. In addition to the search for greater efficiency, many are exploring centralised call centres as a means of improving services. The use of call centres for routine matters such as rent account queries and repairs can release housing officer time and enable them to go out to estates to visit those tenants requiring a more intensive service. The housing officer based at home, working with tenants from a lap-top computer, is already a feature in some RSLs.

In the foreseeable future, while some RSLs may expand their operations by managing stock for others, some may also choose to contract out core services such as management and maintenance, if they are certain to achieve improved standards and lower costs. The achievement of this 'marriage' is surely the biggest single dilemma facing the sector for the coming decade. There is a caveat here, however: whilst contracting-out services may have its attractions, RSLs will also need to guard against losing that sense of team and belonging to an organisation, in which all involved believe and are committed, a trait that has distinguished the sector to great advantage for so long. Whatever course is followed, each landlord must carry its tenants with it, involving them in a meaningful way in the decision-making process. This aspect of accountability is one on which the sector will continue to be judged in years to come.

To summarise, the key dilemmas facing the sector include increased competition forcing RSLs to cut costs even further at a time when higher quality and standards are expected in all activities; attempting to square the circle to cope with the risk imposed by the control of rental increases whilst seeking to charge affordable rents, set in a coherent and transparent manner; loss of stock as homes are sold under through the right to acquire and Voluntary Purchase Grant with a corresponding reduction in assets and income which are unlikely to be replaced; pressure to become more commercial in terms of management costs, including overheads in both general and supported housing, whilst resisting the temptation to abandon housing plus agendas to concentrate on the basic core functions. RSLs are working in a changing environment and each must adapt to change if it intends to survive, and each must position itself for success by learning new skills and ways of working. Competence, cost-efficiency (combining cost-effectiveness with affordability and quality) and account-ability are the keynotes for the future.

In addition to these challenges, housing associations and the RSLs of the future must remain committed to building stable and inclusive com-munities. For many hundreds of years the independent housing sector has attempted to ensure that decent quality affordable housing is available for all who need it; as we enter a new millennium the need still remains great.

References

1   See, in particular, A. Jackson, *The Approved Development Programme 1998/99* (NHF 1997); *The Fifth Pillar – Towards New Housing Policies* (NHF 1997); and M. Wagstaff *The Future of Independent Social Housing* (The Housing Corporation 1997).

2   *Ten Steps for the New Government. A Technical Briefing* (NHF 1997).

3   A. Holmans and C. Whitehead, *Funding Affordable Social Housing – Capital Grants, Revenue Subsidies and Subsidies to Tenants* (NHF 1997).

4   S. Wilcox and H. Sutherland, *Housing Benefit, Affordability and Work Incentives: Options for Reform* (NHF 1997).
5   M. Wagstaff, *The Future of Independent Social Housing*, Research Paper 25 (The Housing Corporation 1997).
6   D. Clapham and A. Evans, *From Exclusion to Inclusion – Helping to Create Successful Tenancies and Communities* (Hastoe Housing Association 1998).
7   C. Murphy, *Something Must Be Done – Social Housing: Social Exclusion* (NHF 1997).
8   GLE Regeneration Strategies, *Regeneration and Communities: A New Role for Housing – Linking Competitiveness, Social Cohesion and Quality of Life* (National Housing Federation 1998).
9   See Anthony Mayer, Chief Executive of the Housing Corporation, in 'Personal Agenda', *Agenda magazine*, October 1996.

Select Bibliography

J. Alder and C. Handy, *Housing Association Law*, 2nd edn (Sweet & Maxwell, 1991).

J. Ashby, *Risk Management for Committee Members* (National Housing Federation, 1992).

J. Ashby *et al., Action for Accountability: A Guide for Independent Social Landlords* (National Housing Federation, 1997).

P. Catterick, *Business Planning for Housing* (Chartered Institute of housing, 1995).

P. Catterick, *Total Quality: An Introduction to Quality Management in Social Housing* (Chartered Institute of housing, 1992).

P. Day and R. Klein, *The Regulation of Social Housing* (NFHA, 1996).

CIPFA, *Manual of Housing Association Finance*.

K. Dunmore, *Planning for Affordable Housing* (Chartered Institute of Housing/Housebuilders Federation, 1992).

Department of the Environment, *Finance for Housing Associations* (1987); *Housing Corporation Prior Options Study* (1995)

S. Goss, *Local Housing Strategies* (National Housing Federation, 1997).

Housing Corporation, *Black and Minority Ethnic Housing Policy* (1998); *Capital Funding Procedure Guide 1997; Source/Insight Research Publications; House Styles – Performance and Practice in Housing Management* (1996); *Performance Standards and Regulatory Guidance for Registered Social Landlords*, (1997); *Registered Social Landlords in 1997 – General Report; Registered Social Landlords in 1997 – Performance Indicators.*

D. Joseph and R. Terry, *Financing the Future* (National Housing Federation, 1996).

V. Karn and L. Sheridan, *New Homes in the 1990s: A Study of Design, Space and Amenities in Housing Association and Private Sector Housing* (Joseph Rowntree Foundation, 1994).

C. Murphy, *Something Must Be Done – Social Housing Social Exclusion* (National Housing Federation, 1997).

National Housing Federation, *A Guide to the Housing Act 1996; Access, Homelessness and Housing Associations* (1994); *Appraisal Guide for Sheltered Housing* (1996); *Changing Housing Markets: The Case for Flexible Tenure and Flexible Mortgages*, (1996); *Competence and*

Accountability: The Report of the Inquiry into Housing Association Governance (1995); *Competence and Accountability: NFHA Code of Governance* (1995); *Model Rules 1997; Financial Planning: A Practical Guide* (1996); *Funding Affordable Social Housing* (1998); *Housing Management Manual for Supported Housing; Independence Revolution: Tenant Support in General Needs Housing* (1998); *Long-Term Maintenance: The Problems Facing Housing Associations 1991; Rents, Resources and Risks – The New Balancing Act* (1997); *Social Housing Social Investment* (1997); *The Price of Social Exclusion* (1995); *Too Many Cooks...? A Review of Policy and Practice and Multi-Landlord Estates* (1995).

D. Page, *Building for Communities: A Study of New Housing Association Estates* (Joseph Rowntree Foundation, 1994).

J. Passmore and S. Fergusson, *Customer Service in a Competitive Environment* (Chartered Institute of Housing, 1994).

B. Randolph (ed), *Housing Associations after the Act* (NFHA, 1992).

L. Potter and T. Roose, *People First – Housing Associations Caring in the Community* (National Housing Federation, 1995).

A. Power with Liz Richardson, *Housing Plus: An Agenda for Social Landlords?* (LSE/Tenants Resource Centre, 1996).

S. Wilcox and H. Sutherland, *Housing Benefit, Affordability and Work Incentives: Options for Reform* (National Housing Federation 1997).

J. Zitron, *Local Housing Companies: A Good Practice Guide* (Chartered Institute of Housing, 1995).

Periodicals and bulletins

Findings (Joseph Rowntree Foundation)
Housing (Chartered Institute of Housing)
Housing Today (National Housing Federation)
Inside Housing (Chartered Institute of Housing)

Index